CORRESPONDING INFLUENCE: SELECTED LETTERS OF EMILY CARR AND IRA DILWORTH

Edited by Linda M. Morra

Emily Carr (1871–1945) is an iconic figure in Canadian culture, known internationally for her painting, which depicted the extraordinary British Columbia mountain landscape along with its indigenous inhabitants and their cultural iconography. Carr's writing career came later in her life, and as it developed, she met Ira Dilworth (1894–1962), the British Columbia Regional Director for CBC Radio who came to play a significant role in her life. *Corresponding Influence* is a collection of selected letters the two shared during the life of their friendship.

Over the years, Dilworth acted variously as Carr's editor, writing agent, sounding board, professional and personal adviser, and most importantly, close friend and confidante. The letters provide a narrative for the latter part of Carr's life and illuminate the impression Dilworth made on the development of her writing. In addition to a critical introduction and annotation throughout, editor Linda Morra has included an unpublished story by Carr called 'Small's Gold.' *Corresponding Influence* will prove essential reading to anyone hoping to understand Emily Carr's extraordinary life and work.

LINDA M. MORRA recently completed a SSHRC postdoctoral fellowship at the University of British Columbia.

Corresponding Influence:

Selected Letters of Emily Carr and Ira Dilworth

EDITED BY
Linda M. Morra

UNIVERSITY OF TORONTO PRESS
Toronto Buffalo London

University of Toronto Press Incorporated 2006
Toronto Buffalo London

Reprinted in paperback 2008

ISBN 978-0-8020-3877-7 (cloth)
ISBN 978-0-8020-9575-6 (paper)

Library and Archives Canada Cataloguing in Publication

Carr, Emily, 1871–1945.
Corresponding influence : selected letters of Emily Carr and Ira Dilworth / edited by Linda M. Morra.

Includes bibliographical references and index.
ISBN 978-0-8020-3877-7 (bound) ISBN 978-0-8020-9575-6 (pbk.)

1. Carr, Emily, 1871–1945 – Correspondence. 2. Dilworth, Ira, 1894–1962 – Correspondence. 3. Painters – Canada – Correspondence. 4. Authors, Canadian (English) – 20th century – Correspondence. 5. Editors – Canada – Correspondence. I. Dilworth, Ira, 1894–1962 II. Morra, Linda M. III. Title.

ND249.C3A3 2005 759.11 C2005-903123-9

University of Toronto Press acknowledges the financial assistance to its publishing program of the Canada Council for the Arts and Ontario Arts Council.

This book has been published with the help of a grant from the Canadian Federation for the Humanities and Social Sciences, through the Aid to Scholarly Publications Programme, using funds provided by the Social Sciences and Humanities Research Council of Canada.

University of Toronto Press acknowledges the financial support for its publishing activities of the Government of Canada through the Book Publishing Industry Development Program (BPIDP).

For my parents,
who understand far better than I do what a labour of love truly involves

Contents

Preface

In the fall of 2002, I commenced a new direction in my research related to Emily Carr. Initially, while examining the major holdings at the British Columbia Archives and Records Service (BCARS), the Vancouver Art Gallery, the McMaster University Archives, and Special Collections at the University of British Columbia, I was interested in writing a book that would bring attention to Carr's life and development as a writer and to her published work. As I transcribed segments of her correspondence and that of her editor, Ira Dilworth, with this book in view, I realized there was little I wanted to omit. The correspondence itself provided an interesting narrative about Carr's life and development as a writer in the last five years of her life. During this period of my research, I interviewed Doris Shadbolt for an issue of *Books in Canada* and, when I explained how my work seemed to be moving in the direction of transcribing the extant letters for publication, she advised me, in the spirit of a generous scholar, to pursue it. My research supervisor, Professor Eva-Marie Kröller, was equally enthusiastic and supportive. In this manner, my research blossomed into the current book.

The process of transcribing the letters of Emily Carr and Ira Dilworth was complicated partly by the fact that their penmanship was not always easily legible: '*I* can't read my *own writing*,' Carr herself asserted in one letter (ca. 8 January 1942) to Dilworth, '*how can you?*' Untangling their correspondence was also rendered difficult by inconsistently dated letters. Dilworth's letters were not preserved entirely chronologically, and many of them from the last year of their correspondence seem to be missing. Carr's hazy sense of grammar and punctuation was also challenging. In one letter (12 October 1942), she confessed: 'It gives *me* awful puzzling & I simply *have to re-read* my letters over. I write quickly &

leave out words & they don't make sense or put things hind before. The English language *is* crazy. Some same words mean 20 different things & others have 20 words meaning one – Foolishness! Ach! Words!' She often wrote without punctuation or capitalization, giving her prose what Susan Crean has called 'the feel of stream-of-consciousness writing' (23). Punctuation seemed to be of little concern to Carr: she flagrantly defied grammatical structure by placing periods and commas where they were not required or omitting them altogether. In addition, she frequently misspelled words, sometimes in a variety of ways.

Although I have endeavoured to be faithful to the original letters, exceptions were made for the sake of accessibility. I have altered Carr's spelling, but, to be certain that my editorial hand is almost always visible and, simultaneously, to prevent the text from being littered with square brackets to signal where changes were made, I have provided a list of the words that have been amended, with Carr's original spellings (see Appendix A). Although added or altered punctuation has been placed in square brackets, words that have been capitalized (to correspond to altered punctuation or to signal proper nouns) have not; the inclusion of missing apostrophes to indicate the possessive has not; and the inclusion of opening or closing quotation marks (when it was clear where quotation marks should be placed) has not. To have indicated such changes with square brackets would have distracted readers. Since the alteration of punctuation may affect the meaning or construction of a phrase, however, I have in those instances employed square brackets.

The sheer volume of the letters also made it difficult to narrow down the correspondence: those that were fragmentary, that were repetitive in terms of their content, that focused on more mundane affairs such as the weather or gardening, or that did not contribute to the larger narrative of Carr's life were omitted. Even so, there were a number of letters that were delightfully engaging and that I would have liked to have included. If I could have flouted contemporary publishing standards, which do not allow for six-hundred page books, I would have done so, but I was obliged to be judicious about which letters were to be selected. Those that are representative, that exemplify the full range of their writers' preoccupations, with an emphasis on Carr's writing and painting career, are included: they reveal, among other things, Dilworth's influence upon Carr's decisions related to her writing career and manuscripts; why she began to write; and the anxiety and labour expended in the process of writing and painting. The division of letters by year makes more evident the trajectory of their friendship, from the first tentative gestures, to more intimate disclosures, and then to a slackening in intensity. A couple of Dilworth's letters that were directed to Carr's publisher, W.H. Clarke, are included to demonstrate how Dilworth negotiated on Carr's behalf in relation to her publications and, more largely, her public life. Whenever possible, letters are annotated to identify persons, places, and works of art, or to indicate a lapse in the narrative unfolding in the letters.

In the process of transcribing, selecting, editing, and annotating the letters, there were a number of people who were extraordinarily helpful and supportive and who deserve to be mentioned. To Eva-Marie Kröller, who deserves accolades in her capacity as a research supervisor, I owe a debt of gratitude. She was the paragon of kindness during the most labour-intensive parts of the project: her diplomacy and astuteness were consistently timely and invaluable. I am also indebted to Professors Fred Flahiff and David Staines, whose patience and general academic advice were of incomparable value. I deeply appreciate the editor at the University of Toronto Press, Siobhan McMenemy, for her direction about certain editorial considerations in the process of completing the manuscript: her incisive and practical remarks helped me to make sound editorial decisions. I wish to acknowledge the thorough work of Frances Mundy, the copy editor, Barbara Tessman, and the readers for the University of Toronto Press, whose responses to the manuscript were enthusiastic and thoughtful. I am also grateful to the Social Sciences and Humanities Research Council and the Aid to Scholarly Publishing which provided me with the financial means to complete this project.

I am especially grateful to the heirs of the Carr and Dilworth papers for being exceedingly accommodating and permitting me to reproduce the letters from the Inglis (MS 2181) and Parnall (MS 2763) Collections housed at the British Columbia Archives and Records Service. Without their consent, these letters would have remained unpublished. I am thankful to Kathryn Bridge, the Manager of Access Services at BCARS; to the team of archivists there, including Katy Hughes, Margaret Hutchison, Del Rosario, and especially Michael Carter and Frederike Verspoor; and to the archival technicians, including Chris Spires, Enza Pattison, Diane Wardle, and Kelly Nolin, and especially Bev Gripich, who is a wizard with dictionaries. I am grateful for the cooperation of Julie Warren, the Licensing Agent at BCARS. I also appreciated the sense of humour and many kindnesses of the security staff there. My thanks to the staff at the Vancouver Art Gallery, Special Collections, the Department of English and the Centre for Research in Women's Studies and Gender Relations at UBC, and the McMaster University Archives. I appreciate the attention, input, and good will of Doris Shadbolt, Gerta Moray, and Susan Crean. Sandra Djwa generously allowed me to peruse her research notes on Ira Dilworth.

I am grateful to those who, in one instance or another, cheered me on, gave me some direction, or provided me with information about a reference that eluded me: Susanna Egan, Manuela Costentino, Jane Flick, Anna Russell, Ray Deonandan, Tina Trigg, Paula Greenwood, Douglas Newell, Kate Ready, Neil McArthur, Gerald Lynch, Peter A. Parolin, Emiko Morita, Selma Ramovic, Francis Nowaczynski, Mark Sailor, Marco Timpano, Lisa Morawecki, Zanna Downes, Gary Kuchar, Keith Wilson, Teresa Petruzzo, Ulrich Teucher, Anna and Matsuo Higa, Grace Schieda, Nancy Wong, Melinda Collie, Cynthia Smurthwaite, Derek Young, Sally Clark, Wesley Kronick, Rosemary Daniels, Martha Perry, Barry Konkin, Iris Von Schoening, Hiroshi Hayashihara, Peter Lalani, Wendy Hatanaka, Farzad Farshi, Merhdad Farbod, Sherrill and John Grace, Patrick Alarie, Carmen and Mary Petriglia, and Laurie Aikman and her parents. I am grateful to John and Mary Pavia, and Rayleen and Peter Forrestall for their prayers. I appreciate the members of the Vancouver tango community for teaching me to play so that the book did not devour me whole. My thanks to Brian Fawcett for editing the introduction and suggesting that I go on a semi-colon diet. A special thanks to Sherrill Grace, whose support I will never forget.

I especially appreciate the following friends and family members, who, in my time of greatest need during the production of this manuscript, showed support: Aloysius Fekete, for his timely provision of *Eats, Shoots and Leaves*; Arthur Shimizu, Wendy Roy, Garth Cantrill, Lesley Horton, Monica and Gabriel Monty, and Sharon Davidson for understanding and listening; Margaret Tucker, Diane Helliker, and Colleen Franklin, for the abundance of their love and resourcefulness; Susanne Morra, for her example of strength and practicality, and Mark Morra, for his unflagging love and reassurance; and Ben and Leo, for daily reminding me of my priorities. I am especially grateful to my parents, Anthony and Jessie Morra, whose love and patience went beyond the bounds of all expectation, and who taught me, among other things, never to give up hope.

Abbreviations

BS *The Book of Small*
GP *Growing Pains: The Autobiography of Emily Carr*
HP *The Heart of a Peacock*
HS *The House of All Sorts*
HT *Hundreds and Thousands: The Journals of Emily Carr*
KW *Klee Wyck*
P *Pause*

CORRESPONDING INFLUENCE

Introduction

On Sunday, 31 August 1941, Ira Dilworth, the British Columbia regional director for CBC Radio, wrote warmly to Emily Carr about the friendship they had cultivated over the previous year and a half: 'Our friendship,' he observed, 'is one of those great, rich things in life which seem too great and wonderful to be true. I keep expecting to wake up and find that I have been dreaming.' Carr's sense of their relationship was expressed in equally affectionate terms: 'Love & *friendship* – big, big things. Yours has meant so much ... so *very* much.'[1] Dilworth was also to become extraordinarily important to her and to her artistic endeavours in several other ways: he edited her manuscripts, set up introductions with persons from whom he believed Carr's literary career would benefit, discussed the merits of poetry and of writing in general with her, was an arbiter on her behalf in negotiating publishing contracts, and acted as a support and adviser when she found herself at a loss in a world that frequently challenged her. The flurry of correspondence exchanged from its inception in early 1940 to her death in March 1945 reveals the hitherto unexplored, complex mentoring process sustained between Dilworth and Carr, and his substantial, virtually immeasurable, influence upon her writing career. It also demonstrates the unfolding of a relationship that was both professional and personal.

Carr is recognized both nationally and internationally as a productive artist, having produced an impressive number of canvases and sketches, and, to a somewhat lesser extent, as a relatively prolific author, whose writings resulted in seven major books – *Klee Wyck* (1941), *The Book of Small* (1942), *The House of All Sorts* (1944), *Growing Pains: The Autobiography of Emily Carr* (1946), *Pause: A Sketch Book* (1953), *The Heart of a Peacock* (1953), and *Hundreds and Thousands: The Journals of Emily*

Carr (1966).[2] She was also an inveterate letter-writer who possessed little patience for those who did not respond to her missives expeditiously, and who characteristically divulged or withheld information from those with whom she corresponded. With a sense of justification, she thus indicated to Dilworth that for a 'letter to be a correspondence [there] must be a spontaneous loving outpour from one to another[.] How can you "respond" if there is not a "co"?'[3] On another occasion, she asserted that 'I *will not* write *one-sided*[.] Why should one? It's like talking to yourself in a cupboard.'[4] She refused to share intimate details if she felt her privacy was not being respected. When in London, for example, she reshaped her letters when she believed she could no longer trust her correspondents: 'I wrote long letters home ... but they lent my letters round to some people I did not like and I got mad and quit writing beyond facts that were so dry, nobody was interested: don't you hate public "common to all" letters? One never writes or talks the same to all people[,] do they? With most people you exchange *doings* not *thinkings.* I *can't* write *thoughts* to anyone I don't like[,] can you?'[5]

In part, the letters exchanged between Dilworth and Carr attest to Carr's confidence in Dilworth, to her need to write almost compulsively to him, and to his relative consistency in responding. Of the more than 440 extant letters, approximately 196 were written by Dilworth and 250 by Carr. Of these, 142 were selected for this volume to represent the body of their correspondence. By the third year of their acquaintance, she was sending him between two and five letters a week, even if she did not receive an immediate response, and she spoke unreservedly about a range of subjects: these two facts also indicate that she trusted and relied upon him. Carr clearly enjoyed that they eventually became more than 'only ornamental friends' – that is, acquaintances who discussed mundane affairs – and that they were prepared to share their '*goods & bads.*'[6]

Although they both wrote frequently, Carr's letters were considerably longer and more numerous than those of Dilworth, who occasionally found it necessary to account for how the demands of his job at the CBC in addition to those of his own personal affairs (such as the deteriorating health of his mother) preoccupied him and interfered with maintaining the 'dizzy rate of correspondence'[7]: 'Here I am a most belated straggler of a writer! I have neglected you miserably but actually, Emily, my days ever since I reached the East have been feverish in the extreme. They have been filled to the brim and over it with meeting after meeting.'[8] Carr repeatedly expressed irritation with these delays or with his negligence in responding directly to her queries: 'What's the good of asking questions you don't answer???'[9] She took up the facetious practice of employing 'R.S.V.P.' to draw his attention to questions she particularly wanted answered.[10] Yet she was also sensitive to the demands she was making upon him, often apologized for her own irascibility, and worried about offending him. 'I was angry with myself for having contributed to your overburden,' she admitted in one letter, 'Be *honest* with me. I and my work have been the last straw sometimes[,] eh?'[11] Dilworth possessed an abundance of patience with these outbursts and reassured her that 'it will take more than one letter or a dozen to offend me seriously.'[12] However often she lost patience with others for their inattention to her missives, she was quite willing to overlook signs of neglect on Dilworth's part and was quick to acknowledge that 'a duplex person "Artist & writer" is extra nuisancy.'[13]

Carr kept most of Dilworth's letters, postcards, and notes. In the last year of their correspondence, he seemed to have written less frequently, but also some of his letters seem not to have been retained. Her letters to him, conversely, seemed not to have been kept with any consistency until about the middle of 1941, after which time he seems to have diligently preserved each letter. The correspondence, therefore, will seem somewhat imbalanced: Carr's letters outnumber Dilworth's in the last two years, while Dilworth's letters outnumber those by Carr in the first year, with apparently little or no response from Carr herself. In part, there were indeed fewer direct replies from her at the outset. The inception of their correspondence was mediated by Flora Burns, one of Carr's earliest editors, critics, and close friends.[14] Carr was not answering many letters at the time because she had been admitted on 6 June 1940 to St Joseph's Hospital in Victoria for an extended stay.[15] Burns wrote on Carr's behalf and sent Dilworth some literary sketches, 'a new group dealing with her memories of Victoria,' and 'a number of other reminiscences which you would find very interesting.' She went on to suggest those stories that Carr herself believed he would 'find suitable for the readings' he would make over the air for the CBC.[16] She also conveyed to him the progress of Carr's recovery, which rendered it 'impossible for her to do anything herself at the present time.' A couple of days later, Burns noted that Carr was 'better,' although the return of her health was still 'slow.'[17] Writing again on 14 June 1940, she mentioned the 'Early Victoria' series, a manuscript that Carr referred to as a 'A Little Town and Little Girl' (the title of the second part of *The Book of Small*) and that Burns was in the process of typing on her behalf.[18]

Dilworth responded directly to Carr about a week later. While he made no mention of the Early Victoria series, he indicated that those stories in his possession that formed a part of 'Woo's Life' were not appropriate for broadcasting purposes, but 'should be quite successful as a publication' after 'minor changes' were made.[19] The dynamic between the two – her appeal to his editorial eye, his readiness to assist – was already visible at this early stage. In December 1941, she wrote that 'I do value having *you* to talk my work over with for I know you understand.' No letters from Carr seem to have been retained by Dilworth, however, until around 7 February 1941. The next letter to have been preserved, months later, is dated 26 August 1941. After that point, it seems that most, if not all, of her side of the correspondence was kept by Dilworth, likely because he came to recognize how the letters significantly reflected her literary development and shed light on her life as an artist.

The correspondence reveals dimensions of Carr's life as a writer and of Dilworth's manifold influence that have been only cursorily examined in biographies on Carr: the precise nature of her relationship with Dilworth; the kind of role he played as editor, arbiter, and friend; the collaborative effort involved in the arduous process of publishing her manuscripts; the genres and styles of writing for which they both expressed admiration; and the manner in which he endeavoured to negotiate business matters on her behalf. He mediated, for example, her interaction with Graham McInnes of the National Film Board and with W.H. Clarke, her first publisher: believing he could 'speak for [her],' Dilworth responded directly to these men about matters related to her work.[20] However presumptuous his gestures may appear, Carr gave him full licence to take on this responsibility and suggested that her 'feelings should [not] be consulted *too* much' about such matters.[21] In writing her biography, she conferred with him about a number of matters, including whether or not she ought to write about the unfolding of her literary career: 'The last phase will be most difficult & is the worst remembered, partly because it is *too new*[,] partly because my brain is old. Is it necessary to include my writing? Is the Biog *me* entire or just the story of my *painting*?' Ultimately, she instructed Dilworth to '[c]hoose which you want'[22] because, as she suggested in a letter dated 12 October 1943, the 'Biog' was no longer hers: 'it's *yours* & before I alter it[, it] *must* be with *your* consent.'

Some of Carr's correspondence, including that with Nan Cheney, Humphrey Toms, John Davis Hatch, Edythe Hembroff-Schleicher, and

Ruth Humphrey, has been published,[23] yet the intriguing exchanges with Dilworth, which encompass the most significant years of her literary career, have never been made available to the public except to appear as short segments in biographies. These letters are also immensely valuable because they reveal the manner in which Dilworth strove to introduce Carr to a larger artistic circle of which he already formed a part – Duncan Campbell Scott, Robertson Davies, and W.H. Clarke are examples of distinguished Canadians mentioned in their correspondence. The letters also draw attention to the wider social, cultural, and political context out of which Carr worked and which shaped her thinking about particular historical events, including the Second World War and its effect on the West Coast. In the late 1930s, when her declining health obliged her to stay indoors and forfeit further travels to her beloved woods, she focused on her writing pursuits – and, with Dilworth's attentive assistance, her public career as a writer was inaugurated.

Carr and Dilworth were indirectly introduced prior to the commencement of their correspondence, which seems to have been initiated when Carr's literary sketches were first brought to his attention in 1939 by Professor Ruth Humphrey. Humphrey had previously done some editing on Carr's manuscripts and her enthusiasm for the sketches was immediately shared by Dilworth.[24] He arranged to have her stories read over the air on the local CBC station by Professor Garnet G. Sedgewick of the University of British Columbia, although two readings were apparently delayed, the result of war-related matters, as a letter from Dilworth indicates: 'Unfortunately the series will be interrupted next Monday & the following Monday too ... I hope your friends see [the advertisements announcing the delay] and are not disappointed by finding you replaced by a talk connected with war effort.' He hastened to add that this decision was not his own: 'Such talks are "musts" and originate in the East. You may depend upon it that the cancellation was not made here.'[25] Between 1940 and 1942, her stories continued to be broadcast, but over the national network, with Dilworth, instead of Sedgewick, reading them.

Even at that early stage, Dilworth was providing sympathy and encouragement, which Carr needed and had been seeking. In one of her initial letters to him, for example, she confessed that 'I always *think* [the stories] are going to be better than they are and when they are not, I'm sore. Words on paper show up all slovenliness & ignorance so very plainly.'[26] In a letter dated 29 February 1940, Dilworth responded in a manner that demonstrates his support and enthusiasm: 'We had a great many very interesting comments on them. A great many more, I should say, than we have had on any other talks or readings.' Carr sent another sample of her writing, 'Woo's Life,' to be read over the air. Although he did not immediately send constructive criticism, it is apparent that he wanted to provide her with a candid, attentive, and forthright response when he could afford 'a few moments to write [her] the notes' he had promised.[27] He assured her, in a letter dated 5 February 1941, that '[a]nything you do will always interest me and I shall always try to let you know frankly what I think.' With great diplomacy and sensitivity, qualities that distinguish all Dilworth's letters, he proceeded to offer Carr what she had been soliciting from other persons such as Humphrey and Sedgewick prior to meeting Dilworth – what she referred to as 'good crits' about her work. 'I want to know [about *adverse* crits],' she insisted, because '[o]ne learns so much by cuts of the whip even if they do hurt.'[28]

Dilworth was an ideal editor, in part because of his formal training and his previous occupations. Before his employment at the CBC began in 1938, he had been an instructor at Victoria High School, where he had matriculated in 1911. In 1915 he graduated from McGill University with first rank honours in French and English. He intermittently continued his education at Harvard, where he completed his master of arts in 1920 and commenced advanced research between 1924 and 1925. During this period, he also taught part-time at Victoria High before he was hired as principal of that school in 1926, at the age of thirty-two.[29] He retained this position until 1934,[30] when he secured a post as a professor of English at the University of British Columbia. After having been recruited for the CBC, he operated as the head of the BC region and manager of station CBR for the next nine years, the period during which he commenced his interaction with Carr.[31]

Undoubtedly he drew on the experience and knowledge garnered in these positions when he suggested 'minor changes' to Carr's writing. With respect to 'Woo's Life,' for example, he asserted in a letter dated 20 June 1940 that it seemed at times that 'you were perhaps too conscious that you were telling the story and that you wanted to make Woo interesting.' On 17 August 1941, he carefully observed that 'the story of Adam is very strong and real' before proposing that that story would 'make a good ending,' but only if she 'could indicate its relation to the other experiences.' Almost invariably, such criticism is counterbalanced by his sense that his remarks need not be taken too seriously: on 17

August 1941, for example, he suggested that 'perhaps [her story] is better as it stands and I am just suffering from one of my frequent blind spots.' Whether this kind of comment was a reflection of his genuine modesty or of his perspicuity in terms of how best to appeal to Carr – or both – he was patently successful: time and again she expressed gratitude for his insights. Often he allowed such criticism to be enfolded in what he conceived of as the merits and strengths of her writing: 'the impression of simplicity and lack of effort,' an impression that belied Carr's tireless perseverance and her countless reworking of her stories.[32] The fact that critics continue to find this facet of Carr's writing so arresting reveals his critical astuteness.

Dilworth's success as her editor is particularly evident when he is contrasted with those who preceded him. Humphrey, Sedgewick, Burns, and, to a much lesser extent, Margaret Clay, Nan Cheney, Lawren Harris, Frederick Brand, Fred Housser, Eric Newton, Katherine Pinkerton, Edythe Hembroff-Schleicher – these persons, among others, participated in some capacity in providing constructive comments on her writing, or in editing, typing, or circulating her manuscripts.[33] At Humphrey's promptings, for example, Carr sent drafts of twenty stories to Sedgewick, who was the head of the Department of English at UBC between 1920 and 1948 (Walker 53).[34] Sedgewick had previously critiqued a couple of her stories when Fred Brand brought them to him,[35] but, as Carr noted with pride in a letter to Humphrey, he had observed that she had since then 'improved very much in style.'[36] In 1937, Sedgewick responded more fully and with moderate praise but was sufficiently encouraging that Carr felt confident about proceeding with her stories. Even though he believed that they were not 'likely to have a large audience,' 'the select few will be appreciative.'[37] He concurred with Humphrey that the Macmillan publishing company ought to be approached. He indicated that, if they were to respond favorably, he would be willing to edit the manuscript and draft an introduction for the stories. Carr's attempt to publish with Macmillan in 1937 did not succeed: Hugh Eayrs wrote back that, however much he enjoyed the stories, he felt they would not receive sufficiently broad attention.[38]

The stories, many of which seemed to have been the early versions of those that eventually appeared in *Klee Wyck*, in addition to *The Book of Small* and *The Heart of the Peacock*, were sent to Farrar & Rinehart in 1940 in an unsuccessful attempt to have her work published in book form.[39] The associate editor of Farrar & Rinehart, J. King Gordon, rejected the stories on the grounds that they were 'more suitable for magazine than for book publication.'[40] This decision, founded on his belief that the stories did not operate or coalesce as a whole, was tempered by his perception of their individual merit: 'I have read them and find them delightful, and some of them masterpieces of their kind.'[41] They did not conform, however, in their arrangement and content to his sense of what would constitute a unified entity. As Paula Blanchard notes, Humphrey's editorial influence on Carr at this time did not tend towards demanding 'classic plot construction and a tidy dénouement,' but rather towards 'the mood and character sketches that came naturally to Emily' (259). Publishers at this time, however, were more interested in books that adhered to the former rather than the latter. *Klee Wyck* would find its first publisher with Oxford University Press a year later, only after Dilworth had begun to work more closely with Carr's manuscripts and had made further editorial suggestions. Farrar & Rinehart later agreed to publish an edition of *Klee Wyck* in the United States at the time of the release of the second printing of that book in Canada.

Flora Burns, as noted, was also involved in editing Carr's manuscripts in the early 1940s, but quickly deferred to Dilworth's editorial authority: when *Klee Wyck* was published, she sent him a letter, dated 18 November 1941, in which she thanked him for his 'untiring efforts' and 'enthusiasm' in relation to the book, and 'for what you have done in bringing to publication in such perfect form a great contribution ... to Canadian literature.' Dilworth's response to Burns indicates that he was aware of his status as one in a succession of editors and that, correctly, he alone could not accept praise for his contributions to Carr's work. His acknowledgment was his way of expressing appreciation for 'how much [she] and Miss Humphrey did for Emily in the early days of her struggle with literary form.'[42] Still, Carr elected, 'since the days of Ruth and Flora's crits,' to send her manuscripts directly to Dilworth, in part because of her '*terrific* veneration for learned ones.' She perceived him as one of '[t]hose who have toiled through years of steady application & learned the rules of the game.'[43]

Carr's partiality for Dilworth over the course of the next few years also arose from the fact that, as she observed in a letter to contemporary artist Myfanwy Pavelic,[44] she felt that he gave her the latitude to express herself, only making corrections when necessary. Dilworth would not change or 'allow to be changed one word'; he attended to matters of punctuation and grammar and addressed ambiguous passages or phrases, but, she believed, he '*never* re-writes or re-words me.' The emphasis on herself – the 'me' that he might have 'reworded' – rather than on her book reflects how she felt her person might have been controlled by editing, or how self-representations might have been adversely modified by editorial interference. Carr noted her partiality for his revisions compared to those made by previous editors because they 'liked to stick in muddling comments' and to replace her wording with their 'own dictatorial, pedantic expressions which altered all the meaning.'[45]

In another letter to him, she noted the following about a story that was subsequently published as 'Ducks and Father and Mother' in *The Heart of a Peacock* (153–4):

> Do you know that[,] 'til I grew up[,] to pass a poultryces & see dead ducks hanging up turned me deadly sick[?] That killing took place under the 'killing tree' in the cow yard. It was in the original 'Cow Yard.' Ruth cut it out as also she cut out 'Father is a Cannibal' which was also in Cow Yard. Ira, *must* people always insist on glad merry things? Life is not like that as you intimated in your last letter. It's the downs that strengthen & assist the ups. I did not put in all the awfulness I might have.[46]

Although Carr clearly valued Humphrey for her 'good help and ideas,' as she informed Hembroff-Schleicher in a letter dated November 1936, she also felt that her condensation of and changes to 'The Cow Yard' spoiled it for her.[47] Dilworth, conversely, 'made me take them all out and go back to my own way':[48] 'I was grateful in one way and angry in another when Mr Dilworth saw their corrections ... Though being a professor of English he made me *see for myself.*'[49]

Carr's own high school education was adequate but she had chafed under the curriculum, which, fortunately, had been augmented by extracurricular drawing classes.[50] Her subsequent unfamiliarity with the rules of English grammar, her desire to know 'the *rules* of the game,'[51] made her feel insecure about her writing: 'You know how ignorant I am when it comes to constructions & literary value[.] There are only two rules that I know in writing = see the thing as *clear* as you can and try to *show* it never using *big* hard words where little ones will do.'[52] Consequently, she felt ill at ease without Dilworth's approval. As she asserted in one of her letters, '[y]ou have to be my measure stick.'[53] She believed that without his assistance, *Klee Wyck* 'might never have come into being except as a still-born.'[54] One can only speculate about the veracity of Carr's belief. Yet Dilworth evidently had some understanding of their collaboration in producing her books. When *Klee Wyck* was finally published, he wrote about the 'thrill' of having '*our* book in my hands.'[55] Peter Smith's assessment of him not only as an 'enthusiastic promoter' but also as 'the midwife' of Carr's work is given credence by Dilworth's sense of his place in her artistic life, whether he overstates the case or not (84).

Perhaps part of the status he acquired as her editor in the last four years of Carr's life – certainly the role she herself conferred upon him – resulted from the fact that he was not only a respectful and attentive reader, but also an appreciative audience. Dilworth had been raised in Victoria (although he had been born in 1894 in High Bluff, Manitoba) and was familiar with Carr's neighbourhood and such locales as the Dallas Road cliffs and Beacon Hill Park. He was also familiar with Victoria's particularities, its people, including Carr (although he had never been formally introduced to her),[56] its architecture, and its plant life. He thus claimed that her 'Wildflowers' manuscript, which to date remains unpublished and focuses on the types of flowers distinct to Victoria, 'should interest me very specially: I was always devoted to the out-of-doors and particularly to wild flowers [in] ... Victoria. Indeed one of the things I miss and have always missed in Vancouver is that marvelous wealth of flowers which Victoria possesses.'[57] More generally, they shared a fondness for the West – Victoria and Vancouver – and disliked the East, that is, Toronto and beyond. In a number of his letters, written while in an airplane or in a hotel because he found himself on yet another of his many business trips to Ottawa, Toronto, or Montreal, he would declare how the 'East seems more and more of a mystery to me. I feel an alien, an outsider here and I have to get back to the West to have a sense of belonging.'[58] These sentiments appealed to Carr and were those with which she easily identified. Feeling anxious that he might take up permanent residence outside of their beloved West, she declared to Dilworth, 'Don't *you* go and let them lasso you in the East or I'll give right up & dig my grave under the big maple.'[59]

With their friendship firmly rooted, by 1941 Dilworth felt sufficiently comfortable to relinquish the more formal use of 'Miss Carr,' and, with a triumphant cry of 'There now – I've done it!,' refer to her as 'Emily.'[60] Simultaneously, Carr abandoned 'Mr. Dilworth' for 'Ira.' If the lack of formality suggests a deeper level of intimacy, the other ways in which they addressed each other reveal how their developing friendship was multifaceted. On 22 November 1942, Carr playfully introduced the nickname she was to use for Dilworth on many occasions: she referred to him as her 'Eye,' what she conceived of as an '*appropri-*

ate name' for her editor and for one who was to keep faithful watch over her paintings and manuscripts on her behalf after she died. As literary executor and co-trustee (with Lawren Harris) of her estate, Dilworth was also regarded as her 'Guardian': 'It is specially nice of you,' she asserted in one letter, 'to be good to your "paint"-wards on top of all the "write"-wards.'[61] He was also invited to take charge over 'Small,' a complex persona adopted by Carr that engaged the memory of her childhood self and that eventually became the heroine of *The Book of Small.* In 'Flower Five' of 'Small's Gold' (reproduced in Appendix B in the present volume), she recounts the manner in which she approaches Dilworth and invites him to undertake responsibility for her books, her paintings, and Small.

Apparently, after he agreed to assume this position, Carr telephoned him to announce that he had been officially made 'the legal guardian of Small.' Dilworth, replying later by letter, exclaimed, 'Bless the child's ever-young heart! Nothing could give me greater joy than to give her whatever care she needs and is within my power and ability to give.'[62] Discussions about 'Small,' her dislikes and likes, her conception of the world around her, her assessment of certain people, and so forth, form a substantial part of their ensuing correspondence. In November 1941, Carr explained, for example, how '"Small" was not built for great cities. London nearly killed her[;] Paris nearly killed her ... In those wild coast places out west there was *never* that desolation of utter loneliness crushing down upon one, like Small felt in London.' In another letter, Carr sent a photograph of herself as a child to Dilworth, who responded thus: 'The picture has not increased the reality of Small for me – that would be impossible. It has made her physical image a little more definite and that is really interesting. She looks just as she should. I can see her in the Cow Yard, by the Sunday evening table at Bible Reading, up on the Goldstream flats, wondering about the mystery of time. It is a great joy to have a tangible token of my beloved ward.'[63] Dilworth frequently assured Carr that Small was indeed his 'beloved ward,' even directly addressing letters to 'Small,' rather than to 'Emily,' and receiving responses from the former rather than the latter. In one instance, he wrote to Small to thank her for her 'confidence and [her] love,' which he considered to be of the utmost importance: 'It has been a joy to get to know you and to help you say things to other people.'[64] He then thanked her for her 'imaginative treatment' of chrysanthemums in 'Small's Gold,' which '*Emily* said I might want to *burn*' rather than preserve.[65] With a degree of exasperation, he declared: 'That manuscript will be one of my real treasures ... Will [Emily] never learn that we understand and love each other – you (Small) and I?'[66]

Dilworth asked Carr to permit Small to accompany him to special events – a supper with Harris, his vacation away from Vancouver, various readings of her work – and, upon his return from such events, apprised Carr of her behaviour. On 16 April 1943, for example, he provided details of Small's responses to those to whom Dilworth was being introduced at a reception held by Oxford University Press: 'Small was thrilled and behaved like a lamb all day except once when an effusive member of Canadian Authors Assoc'n came up to gush. Small almost shrieked in my ear, "Now's your chance, Eye – kick her in the shins!" I was afraid the authoress would hear but she didn't: she was too full of her own importance and the fact that *she* has written poems which she wishes to send to me to read.' The manner in which Small is figured by both Carr and Dilworth suggests some of the complexities of their relationship. Carr as 'Small' was nurtured by Dilworth, comforted by his paternal overtures, and supported by his gestures of emotional support and guidance – so much so that she could speak frankly to him, as she had never done before, about what is now famously referred to as 'the brutal telling,' that is, her father's manifestly uncouth approach to broaching matters relating to human sexuality.[67] Small afforded them both the opportunity and the freedom to express themselves in ways that might have been otherwise more constrained. Ulitmately Carr proclaimed that '[k]nowing you ... chased the bitterness out of Small.'[68]

Dilworth referred to *Klee Wyck* in a manner that shares affinities with their treatment of Small – as a living entity. In one instance, he recalls with fondness how they have 'watch[ed] her grow': '[s]he was such a dear, engaging thing as an infant – difficult at times, temperamental about such things as naming!'[69] In another, he sees 'Klee Wyck' as a young woman whose apparel – that is, the book cover itself – selected for her foray into the public realm renders him nostalgic: 'I know this dress is a costly one – but I much prefer her in her ordinary rich-coloured house dress, don't you? This new gown is the sort of starchy outfit people force themselves into for church, weddings, funerals and other often uncomfortable experiences. However you and I have seen her in a great variety of dresses – in fact in no dress atall and then we saw a beauty in her heart that no dress will ever be able to destroy.'[70] Aside from suggesting his aversion to pretentious external appearances, an aversion that Carr would have readily shared, this particular letter reveals the intellectual, emotional, spiritual – and even somewhat erotic – overtones to their relationship.

A personified 'Klee Wyck' never figured as large in their exchanges as did 'Small.' In particular, the adoption of the 'Small' persona provided Carr with the imaginative space necessary to resist conforming to the 'adult' world of social conventions and cultural norms. Although Dilworth credited 'Small' on several occasions with seeing the world uniquely, it was also his indirect way of praising Carr herself without occasioning embarrassment. On 14 August 1941, for example, he wrote, 'What a power that girl has to find life and sense its realities! And what a joy that Emily is kind to her and lets her speak out now as "the elders" did not always let her speak then! How she must enjoy being understood! She has lots more to say and I want to hear it all. She is my ward, you know.' Carr, similarly, argued that he would particularly enjoy some parts of her 'Biog.' – what was published posthumously as *Growing Pains: The Autobiography of Emily Carr* and what is given to Dilworth as a Christmas present in 1941 – specifically because of contributions made by his 'own ward': 'She writes those parts for me.'[71]

Even as they expressed great affection in such letters, the business component of their relationship was not neglected. On 12 July 1940, towards the beginning of their correspondence, Dilworth mentioned that he had been attempting to contact W.H. Clarke, the manager of the Canadian branch of Oxford University Press, in order that they might meet and discuss the possibility of publishing Carr's literary sketches. By March 1941 he was able to persuade Clarke of the merits of her work. Dilworth's discussions with Carr subsequently shifted towards such matters as Clarke's decisions regarding the manuscript and galley proofs, and the deliberations involved in the selection of titles that she and Dilworth had produced. On 1 June 1941, Dilworth clearly voiced his preference for 'Sketches in Cedar' as the title for what later became *Klee Wyck*: 'I think we should definitely decide on that.' A month later, however, he offered her a new list from which the final title was eventually derived:[72]

Totem Talk
Klee Wyck – Laughing One
Between Cedar and Salt Water
Ucluelet and Other West Coast Stories

By October 1941, *Klee Wyck*, Carr's first book, was published, and, only a year later, *The Book of Small* followed. The letters reveal the negotiations involved in the editing, selection of titles and dedications, cover design, and many other matters related to her manuscripts.

After Dilworth introduced Carr and her work to Clarke, he also brought her into contact with a number of esteemed literary and artistic individuals of his acquaintance. The tendency to create and foster cultural circles manifested itself in his early days as a principal and college teacher, when 'he held regular evenings of music and poetry at home': he 'not only "placed" his students academically, he educated them in the larger aesthetic sense.'[73] As Sandra Djwa notes, he 'belonged to that breed of early twentieth-century teachers who saw the teaching of intelligent young men as his mission in life' (52). To this end, he also held regular gatherings for a group, who referred to themselves as 'the Fossils,' on 'Thursday evenings to read poetry, listen to music, and discuss art and literature.'[74] He likewise sought to draw Carr into a social and cultural circle that included prominent contemporaries such as Nellie McClung, Arthur Benjamin, and Roy Daniells and that he thought would please and benefit her. McClung, for example, wrote her on 27 February 1943 upon the strength of hearing about her 'through our mutual friend, Mr. Dilworth.'[75] On discovering the prospect of a visit from Carr in Vancouver in 1941, Dilworth suggested a number of people who would enjoy seeing her or making her acquaintance: 'I know Nan [Cheney] and Lawren [Harris] will want to come in & the English singers. Arthur Benjamin, the English pianist & composer, who has now made Canada (Vancouver) his home is a great admirer of your work and would love to see you – so would Professor Gage.'[76]

He also sent copies of her work to the English-Canadian poet, and the deputy superintendent-general of the Department of Indian Affairs, Duncan Campbell Scott, who apparently had been eagerly anticipating her work and whose opinion was of importance to her. Dilworth thus recounted to Carr his visits with Scott, the latter's appreciation of the canvases he had purchased from Carr, and the many other 'delightful things [he had] to say about you and your work': 'He had heard the readings on the air and had enjoyed them very much indeed. You should see your two pictures. He has hung them to great advantage, one on each side of a large and beautiful window.'[77] Dilworth also mentioned to Carr Scott's preference for the title 'Stories in Cedar' rather than 'Klee Wyck' because he believed that 'his judgment will mean something to you.'[78] Scott himself directed at least one letter to Carr, dated December 1941, in which he commended her first book.[79] This contact – and the manner in which Scott is discussed in the letters – is of interest given recent debates about Scott's ambivalence towards First Nations cultural groups. He wrote poetry that evinces sympathy for their plight, yet he was also utterly relentless in administering policies that enforced their assimilation in Canada.[80] Carr has been both faulted and defended for her depiction of aborignals in *Klee Wyck*, her canvases, and elsewhere:[81] her association with and admiration for Scott complicates this facet of her work.

The letters make clear that, in addition to introducing her to such persons, Dilworth endeavoured to draw attention to her writing. He wrote articles for the magazine *Saturday Night* in which he advocated the merits of her writing and painting. As he indicated in a letter to Carr, this task was far from easy, given his desire to avoid being either 'too formal' in his approach or 'too personal,' especially since he recognized 'how you hate the idea of "wearing your heart on your sleeve for every daw to pick at" – to quote our fool friend Shakespeare.'[82] He ultimately decided to send to her whatever he wrote about her because 'I want it to please you.'[83] Dilworth conceived of his role as arbiter in relation to Carr with great earnestness and believed it to be of importance in national terms. Whenever she expressed concern that he (and Harris) 'were put to bother,' he reassured her that it was 'a sheer joy to me to have any part' in assisting her and furthering her interests as a Canadian artist because 'my life is definitely dedicated to the service of Canada.'[84] If, as he claimed, his life didn't 'make much difference one way or the other,' he believed that *her* life and *her* contributions to Canadian letters were of consequence.[85]

Such devotion is also manifested in the numerous instances when he wrote introductions or biographical sketches for such books as *Klee Wyck* (1941), *An Address by Emily Carr* (1955), and *Growing Pains* (1946). He believed that her best literary work would emerge in her later years, as it did: 'Remember, my dear,' he noted by way of encouragement, 'that the great Italian composer of opera, Verdi, did his most original and, in many respects, his most significant work after he was 80 years old.'[86] Since he also maintained that Carr, like all artists, often expressed 'certain wise things about art and life,' he urged her to be cautious about discarding documents that might be of significance later or 'destroying papers etc that may be of interest.'[87] With such an understanding about her role and future acclaim, especially in relation to her ability to articulate 'the spirit and heart of Canada,' he encouraged her to keep these papers, including the letters of Harris: 'we have woefully little wisdom and cannot afford to waste any or allow it to be destroyed.'[88]

It was not only scholarly concern for crucial drafts of her work, which she had suggested she was going to burn, that motivated him. The devastation being wreaked elsewhere by the Second World War made Dilworth sensitive to the general vulnerability of art. He and Carr discussed at length the effects of the war, ranging from its direct impact on their lives to their mutual sense of how it was causing havoc internationally, destroying human life and cultural artefacts, and obscuring the best that humanity had to offer. Carr, expressing deep anxiety about the war, effectively described it as parasitic, consuming everything in its path: '[i]t spreads & spreads – a badness, so *very* bad, eating up all the nations.'[89] Dilworth focused on cultural loss: 'One of the great tragedies connected with wars is that so much that represents the finest and wisest achievement of men runs the risk of being destroyed.'[90] In addition, he was anxious about how the war affected radio content and fuelled racial prejudices, specifically, misplaced hostility towards the Japanese:

> This horrid war, Emily, it is bringing such terrible things to the surface! Just now I am having to watch night & day to keep irrational, stupid horrific things off the air which would make us go head towards the Japs in this country. I know we have to be careful and I am sure there are some of them in this country who are bad eggs but so many of them are loyal & true and fine and will suffer with the rest if we unleash the furious beasts in some of our white Canadians. This sort of race habit is one of the most tragic concomitants of war.[91]

He urged Carr not to feel discouraged by the war's malignant effects, but rather to 'carry on your distinguished work' which she might consider as a way 'to re-affirm our faith' in the things for which they both stood.[92] The greatness of humanity, he asserted, would be fostered and perpetuated through art: 'We must keep it alive so that when this grim horror of war and suffering is over, it will assert itself and heal the wounded world.'[93]

Given the purpose and significance he attributed to Carr's work, he became deeply concerned about the security of her canvases. In 1943 Dilworth took precautions to have them transported to the safest venue he could locate: 'I was hopeful that we could have found a place for them in Victoria where they would not have seemed so far away from Vancouver; as a matter of fact I am still trying. I am investigating the possibility of finding some space in the Parliament B'ldgs. They should be safe and secure. An old pupil of mine is the head librarian and, if anything can be done, he will do it for me.'[94] By this time, Carr relied upon Dilworth and his decisions regarding her canvases – in this case, the initial forty-five oil paintings that formed what was called the Emily Carr Trust and that was to be left as a gift to British Columbia[95] – and all of her manuscripts. As one of her 'Beloved Trustors,' the other being Harris, Dilworth was permitted to 'do *whatever [he saw] fit* with [his] wards.'[96] Carr did not have children, but she regarded her manuscripts and canvases as the equivalent. She could be at peace knowing that her work was in capable hands: 'I am so glad & at peace that "Small" & all my M.S. are yours[.] It would have hurt to leave my children in un[-]understanding hands. I'd rather have burned them than that.'[97] Her 'Last Will and Testament,' which was addressed to Dilworth and is included in this book, underscores her faith in and deep affection for him.

Her faith was well placed. After Carr's death in 1945, Dilworth succeeded in securing the publication of another three of her books: *Growing Pains, Pause: A Sketch Book,* and *The Heart of a Peacock.* It is such involvement in the publication of Carr's manuscripts that have led critics to speculate that Dilworth was responsible for the expurgated edition of *Klee Wyck,* the 1951 edition with which most people have come to be familiar. The original edition, published in 1941 by Oxford University Press, was reprinted in 1951 by Clarke, Irwin & Company for educational purposes: that is, they were planning on distributing the book in classrooms across the country as part of their Canadian Classics series of educational texts. In anticipation of such wide circulation, as recently noted by Kathryn Bridge, one story and certain passages of others were excised, in particular those that expressed sympathy towards the plight of First Nations cultural groups, those that condemned the patronizing attitude towards them, and those that expressed contempt for missionaries who had interfered with First Nations cultural development and family life. These excisions were raised with Dilworth in the most casual manner by R.W.W. Robertson, the editor at Clarke Irwin, who suggested that they were planning to do a 'first run in the trade edition, with some very minor cuts.'[98]

Robertson's interventions demonstrate that the editorial process is not necessarily benign, reflect how much may be at stake in the rendering of a manuscript into a book, and indicate how Carr's conception of Aboriginal cultural groups was profoundly distorted by these interventions. Yet Dilworth himself endeavoured to be faithful to Carr's wishes, from the articulation of her larger political and social concerns to the more minute turn of expression. When he realized that the original manuscript had been substantially altered, he immediately wrote to Robertson to express his reservations: 'I was very much disappointed,' he wrote, 'to find that omissions and excisions had been so extensive ... If these decisions are not yet irrevocable, I should like to bring some points to your attention for consideration, since I was not consulted at all before the decisions were arrived at.'[99] The response was not what Dilworth anticipated. On 10 April 1951, Robertson wrote to Dilworth that, in light of the fact that *Klee Wyck* was to be circulated throughout the Canadian school system, the publisher was 'anxious that nothing should be allowed to prejudice that aim, and the question was raised whether some references to missionaries in one or two of the early essays in KLEE WYCK might offend any members of the teaching profession.'[100] Although Clarke Irwin was determined not to commit any 'violence either to the spirit of Miss Carr's writings or to their style,' the editorial staff decided the omissions were necessary. Dilworth's response suggests his indignation at the lack of respect for Carr's literary aims and political views:

> You say that you had a fixed determination to do no violence to the spirit or style of Miss Carr's writing and I am sure you make this statement in good faith but in my opinion you have not been successful in avoiding just that.
>
> I know Emily was inclined always to ride a horse hard but this question of the attitude of the missionaries towards Indian customs and even the Indians themselves was not a hobby-horse. It was a deep conviction and in 'Ucluelet' she spoke clearly, simply and honestly out of that conviction. I can quite see that some of the things that she said might be offensive in a school textbook but I really think you have gone too far.[101]

He concluded by noting that his uneasiness about the 'degree of expurgation to which the text is subjected' was related to those 'who know and revere the text very highly.' In other words, the text's initial critical reception demonstrated that people knew and appreciated Carr's dismay at the manner in which First Nations cultural groups were being treated, and Dilworth believed that these same persons would be appalled by how significantly it had been modified.[102] Notwithstanding Dilworth's protests, the passages under dispute were removed from *Klee Wyck* and the book was reprinted in that form for years until Douglas & McIntyre reprinted the original edition in 2003.

If Dilworth was unable to persuade the editor of Clarke Irwin of the merits of the parts that were subsequently removed, he was successful in many other aspects in relation to Carr's writing. It seems strange that Carr and Dilworth's correspondence has been neglected, especially when one considers his inestimable influence upon the trajectory of her career and her elevation in the past ten years from national icon to a figure of international importance.[103] Perhaps because a threat to the lingering belief that Carr was a struggling artist who suffered alone, Dilworth's support, even its bare bones as manifested in his sustained correspondence with her, has received little attention. Ultimately, the correspondence sheds light upon a key figure in Carr's life, a person upon whom she heavily relied, and reveals new contours of her personality.

NOTES

1 Ca. 4 January 1942.
2 I have not included Carr's posthumously published addresses as 'major books.' Carr's own assessment of her dual artistic approach indicates that she believed her writing was 'the secondary of my two occupations,' which she undertook when she became 'physically unfit to go away into the woods' (National Archives of Canada, Canadian Authors Association Fonds, MG 38 I 2, letter from Carr to Malcolm Ross [Wartime Information Board], 27 July 1943, volume 1, file 21).
3 Ca. September 1943.
4 31 October 1944.
5 30 November 1941.
6 11 May 1942.
7 28 September 1941.
8 8 December 1941.
9 24 November 1942.
10 See, for example, her letter dated 8 November 1942.
11 2 January 1944.
12 25 May 1941.
13 24 April 1942.
14 See British Columbia Archives and Records Service (BCARS), Flora Hamilton Burns Fond, MS 2786; also see Hembroff-Schleicher, *Emily Carr*, 277–8.
15 See Carr's letter to Ruth Humphrey, dated 10 July 1940, in which she claims that 'All sorts of letters [are] waiting but I can't collect my wits – hands can do it OK but not brain – it is such an effort to think clearly' (Humphrey and Blissett, 135).

16 BCARS, Flora Hamilton Burns Fond, MS 2786, letter from Flora Burns to Ira Dilworth, 12 June 1940, box 1, file 9.

17 14 June 1940.

18 See also Carr's letter to Ruth Humphrey, 25 May 1940, in which Carr mentions that Burns has only 'partly typed "A Little Town & a Little Girl"' and Dilworth's visit and the stories he takes with him for critique (Humphrey and Blissett, 133).

19 20 June 1940.

20 Graham McInnes had reviewed one of Carr's exhibitions in an article, titled 'World of Art,' which appeared in *Saturday Night.* Dilworth's letter is dated 6 November 1941.

21 29 March 1942.

22 28 December 1941.

23 Doreen Walker, ed., *Dear Nan: Letters of Emily Carr, Nan Cheney and Humphrey Toms*; 'Letters to John Davis Hatch, 1939–43,' Edythe Hembroff-Schleicher; *M.E.: A Portrayal of Emily Carr*; and Ruth Humphrey and W.F. Blissett, 'Letters from Emily Carr.'

24 According to Doreen Walker, Dr Ruth Humphrey first brought Carr's manuscripts to the attention of Dr Garnet G. Sedgewick in 1937 and then to the attention of Ira Dilworth in 1939 (101).

25 12 July 1940. According to Hembroff-Schleicher, Carr's stories had been read on CBC broadcasts on 29 January and 5 February (*Emily Carr*, 38).

26 7 February 1941.

27 12 July 1940.

28 7 December 1941.

29 Smith 83.

30 Ibid., 78–85.

31 Smith observes that '[d]uring the period, he was personally active as conductor of the Vancouver Bach Choir, and music was at the centre of his life. His cultural influence, direct and indirect, was now enormous' (84). After this period, he was 'transferred to Montreal ... to become general supervisor of the CBC's International Service' (84).

32 20 June 1940.

33 Also see Tippett's assessment of Burns and Humphrey's impact upon Carr as a writer (221).

34 As Blanchard notes, Sedgewick had seen some of her stories previously, since 'Fred Brand had shown him some stories a few years earlier' (273).

35 Fred Brand was the husband of artist Edythe Brand, one of Carr's friends and future biographers.

36 Letter to Ruth Humphrey, 10 August 1937 (Humphrey and Blissett, 111).

37 *HT*, 21 Dec. 1937, 296.

38 See Tippett 250; BCARS, Edythe Hembroff-Schleicher fond, MS 2792; and Hembroff-Schleicher in which a letter from Carr, dated October 1937, indicates that she has heard from Eayrs, who 'likes the stories but feels ... that the public would not and they don't want to risk it' (1969, 104)

39 Another attempt was made in 1938, as a letter to Lorne Pierce, editor of Ryerson Press, indicates: 'I do not know,' she wrote, 'how to write well or express myself in words but what I have earnestly tried to do is to show honestly & sincerely Indians of British Columbia coast as I have experienced them' (Queen's University Library, Lorne Pierce Papers, Carr to Pierce, n.d. [Feb. 1938], as quoted in Tippett, 250). The manuscript was lost and, when located a year later, returned to her (see letter from Carr to Ruth Humphrey, 23 May 1938, Humphrey and Blissett 131).

40 BCARS, Parnall Collection, MS 2763, letter from J. King Gordon to Emily Carr, 26 June 1940, box 3, file 10.

41 Ibid.

42 BCARS, Flora Hamilton Burns Fonds, letter from Flora Burns to Ira Dilworth, 18 November 1941, box 1, file 15, and letter from Ira Dilworth to Flora Burns, 22 November 1941, box 1, file 15.

43 6 November 1942.

44 Myfanwy Pavelic (b.1916) is a Canadian artist and was one of Carr's good friends.

45 BCARS, Myfanwy Pavelic Papers, Accession No. 94-5907, Emily Carr to Myfanwy Pavelic, 7 January 1942.

46 8 May 1942.

47 Hembroff-Schleicher 1969, 91.

48 Ibid.

49 BCARS, Myfanwy Pavelic Papers, letter from Emily Carr to Myfanwy Pavelic, 7 January 1942.

50 See Blanchard, 44–6 and Tippett, 11.

51 BCARS, Myfanwy Pavelic Papers, letter from Emily Carr to Myfanwy Pavelic, 7 January 1942.

52 18 January 1942.

53 8 November 1942. Conversely, Dilworth never felt at ease in terms of expressing his opinion about paintings. In a letter dated 1 June 1941, for example, he wrote, 'I know I am only a layman and I do not judge a picture by the accepted aesthetic rules, nor can I use the art critic's jargon in speaking of it.'

54 24 December 1941.

55 26 October 1941. Italics added.

56 Blanchard 274.

57 5 February 1941.
58 17 March 1944.
59 30 November 1941.
60 25 May 1941.
61 28 April 1942.
62 18 July 1941.
63 1 August 1941.
64 14 November 1942.
65 Ibid.
66 Ibid.
67 See letter dated 24 November 1942, included here; see also Tippett (14) and Blanchard (53, 91) for interpretations of the 'brutal telling.'
68 24 November 1942.
69 12 November 1941.
70 26 December 1941.
71 11 December 1941.
72 18 July 1941.
73 Blanchard 274; Djwa 53.
74 Tippett 195.
75 BCARS, Parnall Collection, MS 2763, file 14.
76 31 August 1941.
77 9 June 1941.
78 11 July 1941.
79 He wrote that he was 'pleased with the format & with Mr. Dilworth's introduction & I think the color prints came out well,' although he acknowledged that 'there is always something to be desired even in the very best work in this kind. [...] "Sophie" is one of the best sketches.' Carr's letters to Scott have been preserved in the National Library, Elise Aylen Fonds, LMS-0204, box 10, file 31.
80 See Brian Titley's *A Narrow Vision* and Stan Dragland's *Floating Voice*.
81 See, as examples, Marcia Crosby's 'Construction of the Imaginary Indian'; Ried Shier's interview with Lawrence Paul Yuxweluptun, titled 'Native Son'; Gerta Moray's 'Wilderness, Modernity and Aboriginality in the Paintings of Emily Carr'; and Robert Linsley's 'Landscapes in Motion: Lawren Harris, Emily Carr and the Heterogenous Modern Nation.'
82 17 August 1941.
83 Ibid.
84 25 May 1941.
85 Ibid.
86 2 October 1943.

87 Ibid.
88 22 February 1942.
89 7 December 1941.
90 22 February 1942.
91 6 January 1942.
92 20 June 1940.
93 21 December 1943.
94 Ca. July 1941.
95 The works in the Emily Carr Trust, which originally comprised forty-five of Carr's paintings, were also shown in a retrospective exhibition at the Art Gallery of Toronto. After the war, they were sent to the Vancouver Art Gallery permanently (see Blanchard 284). By 1966, the trust included approximately 170 paintings. For details regarding the development of the trust, see Hembroff-Schleicher, *Emily Carr,* 145–67.
96 22 March 1942.
97 4 January 1942.
98 McMaster University Archives, William Ready Division, Clarke, Irwin and Company Ltd. Fonds, letter from R.W.W. Robertson, editor, Clarke, Irwin and Company, to Ira Dilworth, 19 March 1951.
99 Ibid., letter from Dilworth to Robertson, 9 April 1951. As quoted in Bridge, 8–9.
100 Ibid., Robertson to Dilworth, 10 April 1951. As quoted in Bridge, 9.
101 Ibid., letter from Dilworth to Robertson, 17 April 1951. As quoted in Bridge, 9–10.
102 Ibid.
103 See, for example, Sharyn Rohlfsen Udall, *Carr, O'Keefe, Kahlo: Places of Their Own,* which was the corresponding catalogue for an international travelling exhibition.

Letters: 1940

[Typed] Vancouver, B.C.
February 29, 1940

Dear Miss Carr:
I am returning all your scripts. This I should have done as soon as the fourth talk on the air was completed. We had Dr. Sedgewick[1] leave the scripts each time after he had read them. We have to keep a copy on file at the office of all scripts which are used at the station. These copies are made by our stenographic staff and then filed away and are not open to the public. They are simply kept for reference in case any controversy should arise.

I do think your sketches should be published. We had a great many very interesting comments on them. A great many more, I should say, than we have had on any other talks or readings.

I am so glad you are getting your roots down again. Somehow I feel happier when I think of you being up in the old locality, although your little house on Beckley Street seemed very comfortable.[2] I hope you will

1 Carr sent Dr Garnet G. Sedgewick (1882–1949), head of the Department of English at the University of British Columbia (1920–48), twenty of her stories in June 1936 at Dr Ruth Humphrey's promptings (see Walker 53). The series of broadcasts of Carr's stories was referred to as 'Emily Carr's Notebook' (see British Columbia Archives and Record Service (BCARS), E.M. Hembroff-Schleicher Collection, MS 2792, letter from E.M. Watson to Emily Carr, 8 October 1941, box 2, file 1).

2 Carr had lived on 316 Beckley Avenue in Victoria between January 1936 and 25 February 1940, after which time she moved to her sister's house on St Andrew's Street (part of the original Carr family property).

be supremely happy in your new quarters, and that your work goes on without too much interuption [*sic*].

It is kind of you to remember about the sketch. I am of course thrilled. I shall let you know when I can be in Victoria and see you. As a matter of fact I am going over to speak to the Women's Canadian Club next Tuesday, but whether I shall have time to call and see you or not I do not know.

Before we conclude this little chapter of our relations (I mean the broadcasting chapter) I hope you will believe me completely sincere when I tell you how very much I have appreciated meeting you and talking things over and how deeply indebted we are to you for your ready co-operation with us.

Kindest personal regards.
Yours sincerely,
I. Dilworth, B.C. Regional Representative

ID: HH
Miss Emily Carr,
218 St. Andrews Street,
Victoria, B.C.

[Typed] Vancouver, June 20th, 1940
Miss Emily Carr,
218 St. Andrews Street,
Victoria, B.C.

Dear Miss Carr: –
I have thoroughly enjoyed reading your manuscript of Woo's Life.[3] I am not sure that except in parts it would be satisfactory for broadcasting but I feel strongly that it should be quite successful as a publication.[4] Certain minor changes, I think, should be made.

I have felt a bit the quality of which you yourself were conscious, judging from your letter, namely, a certain amount of effort which is not

3 'Woo's Life,' stories about Carr's pet monkey, form the sixth section of *The Heart of a Peacock* (572–606).

4 See Carr's letter to Dr Ruth Humphrey, 25 May 1940, in Humphrey and Blissett, 133.

characteristic of your best writing style. One of the things that endears your sketches to me most of all is the impression of simplicity and lack of effort. This, combined with your vivid preception [*sic*] and ability of describing what you perceive, is most appealing. In the story of Woo I have felt at times that you were perhaps too conscious that you were telling the story and that you wanted to make Woo interesting. When you forget this and let Woo take charge of you and your style the manuscript became interesting to an absorbing degree.

I am afraid this is not very helpful but you asked me to be frank. I think the people who move through your narrative very real. Their characters are well established and are well maintained.

I am watching the mails anxiously for more of your sketches. I am to read the first of these in a new series on July 1st at 6:30 to 6:45, our time. I was wondering whether you would send me back 'When Lizzie Was Mad Right Through' and 'The Cow Yard'?[5] As you know, I am very keen about the latter. It would have to be condensed to bring it into fifteen minutes. If you would permit, I would try to do this, not by altering any of your writing, but by trying to cut out two or three episodes. I am extremely interested to hear of your latest work 'Victoria Seen Through the Eyes of a Young Observer.'[6] This will perhaps give me material which will be as satisfactory as the two mentioned above could be and might make something in the nature of a consecutive series.

We expect to have at least four occasions for your sketches. They are going on the National network this time which means that they go right across to Halifax. Of course with the war and all its demands upon us we never know at what moment we may have cancellations.

I do agree with you that it is a ghastly business this war and you know that I agree that the world is a wonderful place if it were not for some of the people in it. My mother who perhaps has a bit of the quotation habit of your sister very aptly describes the situation when she quotes:

'Where every prospect pleases,
And only man is vile.'[7]

5 These two stories, the first titled 'How Lizzie Was Shamed Right Through,' appear in the first section of *The Book of Small* (85–93, 21–33).

6 This 'latest work' is probably an early version of what later appears in *The Book of Small*.

7 An excerpt from the hymn written by Bishop Reginald Heber (1783–1826) titled 'From Greenland's Icy Mountains.'

But one must not be discouraged. Never did we need to re-affirm our faith in the things you stand for in your art more definitely than we do today. So hurry up and get well to carry on your distinguished work.

Mr. Graham McInnes called to see me yesterday and said he expected to see you when he was in Victoria.[8] I sent my good wishes by him. He seems a bright and interesting young chap. Incidentally, he writes very well.

Kindest regards.
Yours sincerely,
I. Dilworth

Vancouver, B.C. [12 July 1940]

Dear Miss Carr:
Thank you a thousand times for your trouble in sending the pictures![9] They arrived yesterday and are charming. A number of people have seen them and all have admired them. They are finely contrasted in subject and manner of treatment too, I think. Of course I know nothing about style or manner in painting – so I just sit and enjoy each of them separately and then the pair of them together.

Did you hear 'Loyalties' & the Dr. Helmcken sketch on Monday?[10] I thought they went very well. Many people have praised them. I am very glad they are being so well received. People find it a comfort to hear something so straightforward and simply human in these tortured, twisted & bewildered days.

Unfortunately the series will be interrupted next Monday & the fol-

8 Graham McInnes, a Toronto journalist and art critic, published *A Short History of Canadian Art* (1939), *Canadian Art* (1950), and an article on Emily Carr, which appeared in a column titled 'The World of Art' for *Saturday Night* (Toronto) (see Walker 74). He later worked for the National Film Board of Canada.

9 The canvases to which he refers are probably those mentioned in the same letter, finished oil-on-paper sketches of the Gorge and Portage Inlet, where Carr had painted in September 1939.

10 Dilworth is referring to the sketches that later appear as 'Loyalty' and 'Doctor and Dentist' in *The Book of Small* (191–8; 199–203). 'Dr Helmcken' was Dr John Sebastian Helmcken, who arrived in Victoria in 1852 'as the fort's first physician . . . [and] served as the first speaker of the legislature' (Blanchard 47).

lowing Monday too. (Our next sketch will come on July 29th.) We have sent careful notice of the change to all the papers, particularly to Victoria. I hope your friends see these and are not disappointed by finding you replaced by a talk connected with war effort. Such talks are 'musts' and originate in the East. You may depend upon it that the cancellation was not made here.

I think I shall next read 'The Cow Yard' which, as you know, I admire very much.

Meanwhile I am trying to get a few moments to write you the notes I promised concerning 'Woo's Life.' My publisher friend of whom I spoke (head of the University of Oxford Press in Canada) did not come as I expected.[11] I still expect him.

And here I sit writing with the bright colours of last Autumn's beauty shining down on me from your sketch of The Gorge or Portage Inlet forest clearing. It is really a comfort.

I do hope this finds you much better.

Kindest regards.
Yours sincerely,
I. Dilworth

July 12 '40

11 Dilworth is referring to William H. Clarke, the manager of the Canadian branch of Oxford University Press and, later, president of Clarke, Irwin & Company.

Letters: 1941

Friday [7 February 1941]

Dear Mr. Dilworth,
I expected you yesterday with your friend & you did not come and here's the M.S. – another disappointment – I always *think* they are going to be better than they are and when they are not, I'm sore. Words on paper show up all slovenliness & ignorance so very plainly. Isn't there a difference in thinking & doing? I think writing is *good* because it shows you all sorts of shortcomings you did not know you had. I don't see how anyone who writes could ever feel *conceited* unless perhaps he knew *every rule of the game* & knew how to think *clear* thoughts and how to *express* them. Perhaps then he might have good reason.

Well, anyhow if wild flowers[1] is a poor thing[,] it helped me tremendously over a bad time & I am grateful to the flowers.

Don't keep me *too* long waiting for your reaction to 'wildflowers[.]' I was not born with patience nor have I acquired it.

Today has been wonderful[,] winter & spring shaking hands.

Sincerely,
Emily Carr

1 'Wild Flowers' is an unpublished collection of essays about British Columbia's wildflowers.

[Typed] Vancouver, March 17th, 1941

Miss Emily Carr,
218 St. Andrews Street,
Victoria, B.C.

Dear Miss Carr: –
At long last I am writing you again and am about to announce the great event, namely, the arrival of Mr. William Clarke of the Oxford University Press. Mr. Clarke is in Vancouver and we plan to go to Victoria Tuesday night – tomorrow. I hope we will be able to spend a good part of Wednesday discussing publication of your manuscripts with you. May I 'phone you when I get in to Victoria on Wednesday morning?

I hope you are well and that you will forgive this very small and business-like note. I returned from the East by 'plane last night and find myself snowed under with an accumulation of correspondence.

Yours sincerely,
Ira Dilworth

Vancouver, B.C.,
Sunday, May 25, 1941

Dear Emily:
There now – I've done it! I feel quite like one of your Indians except for the fact that they would have abbreviated it into Em'ly which, after all, is more beautiful still.

First of all – many thanks for your letters. I always like them and am thrilled to get them even if, at times, I do not answer at once. You should not have felt so contrite about your brief note: after all I had been silent for an impossible length of time. I am sorry you felt so badly about writing it. I think we understand each other pretty well by now and you must remember that it will take more than one letter or a dozen letters to offend me seriously.

Your second letter was absolutely marvelous. I am glad you enjoyed the readings. Those two sketches are really superb – many people have 'phoned to say how much they enjoyed them. You must not give me so much praise. Like you, I am a little afraid of praise. Quite sincerely, if I succeed in pleasing you with the readings I am more than satisfied. Mr. Clarke sent me a wire from Toronto after the first reading saying how thrilled they had been with it. As a matter of fact, I was disappointed in the first one – I really read badly. It came in the midst of a very busy afternoon. I had to tear myself away from a crowd of worries and try to get away to Greenville.[2] Whe[n] I can[not] be in the place myself it is useless for me to try to take others there. And that first afternoon I did not feel that I was really successful.

Yesterday's mail brought the first 'galley' proofs of the book[3] – perhaps you received a copy. There were eleven of them which represents about 35 pages of printed material – that is only about 1/4 of what we have sent. I am going to correct these proofs tonight and shall let you know if there are any points which need special attention.

I shall quite definitely be in Victoria either Tuesday or Thursday. I shall see you there and shall try to get the remaining sketches ready to send.

I am so thrilled that you are pleased with the plan Lawren Harris[4] and I are working out for your pictures.[5] It is a sheer joy to me to have any part in this. You know my life is definitely dedicated to the service of Canada (I hope you don't think that an egotistical thing to say – after all my life can't make much difference one way or the other) – and it is the West of Canada which, in my opinion, matters most. Its importance will increase as the colour and beauty of its life, both past and present, come to be known and appreciated. In the revelations of that beauty and significance, art, in all its forms, is of the utmost importance. The artist sees things imaginatively and so penetrates beyond the surface and the circumference. He gets into the centre of things and speaks from there – if he speaks clearly enough he brings a revelation of the meaning of life to those who hear or see his work. You remember what Shelley said, trying to describe the skylark. He said the bird was:

2 'Greenville' appears in *Klee Wyck* (64–75).

3 Dilworth is referring to the galley proofs for *Klee Wyck*.

4 Lawren Harris (1885–1970), a founding member of the Group of Seven and proponent of Canadian art, was considered by Carr to be a source of inspiration for her second phase of painting. In 1927, she visited Ottawa and met him and other group members for the first time (see 'Meeting with the Group of Seven,' *HT*, 3–19, and 'Lawren Harris,' *GP*, 340–52). Harris's letters to Carr have been housed at BCARS, Inglis Collection, MS 2181.

5 Dilworth is referring to the establishment of the Emily Carr Trust, which originally comprised forty-five of Carr's paintings.

'Like a Poet hidden
In the light of thought,
Singing hymns unbidden
'Till the world is wrought
To sympathy with joys and fears it heeded not.'[6]

There you have the secret of how art teaches – not consciously, not in a preachy way, but by a revelation of the beauty it has beheld – a revelation so memorably expressed that the world must stop in its hurry and watch for a moment. After all, daffodils and skylarks' songs were always beautiful but their beauty became current coin and passed among men more freely after Shakespeare had spoken of the daffodils dallying with the winds of March and the skylark singing at heaven's gate,[7] or after Wordsworth had seen his 'Crowd,' his 'host of golden daffodils, fluttering and dancing in the breeze,' and Shelley had saluted the lark in his beautiful phrase,

'Hail to thee, blithe spirit!
Bird thou never wert
That from heaven or near it
Poureth thy full heart
In proper strains of unpremeditated art.'[8]

How much the work of Wordsworth and Shelley have had to do with the molding of our minds and spirits no one can say.

But this is too long already. I intended only a note to say that I shall be over on Tuesday or Thursday.

Yours most gratefully,
Ira Dilworth

6 Dilworth is quoting from the poem 'To a Skylark' by Percy Bysshe Shelley (1792–1822).

7 Dilworth is referring to Shakespeare's *A Winter's Tale* (4.4.120) in which Perdita catalogues such flowers as 'daffodils / That come before the swallow dares, and take / The winds of March with beauty.' The second allusion to Shakespeare is probably Sonnet 29: 'Haply I think on thee, and then my state, / Like to the lark at break of day arising / From sullen earth, sings hymns at heaven's gate'; or is possibly a reference to *Cymbeline*: 'Hark, hark, the lark at heaven's gate sings, ... And winking Mary-buds begin to ope their golden eyes. / With every thing that pretty is' (2.3.19, 23–5).

8 Dilworth is referring, respectively, to 'Daffodils' by William Wordsworth (1770–1850) and to 'Ode to the West Wind' by Shelley.

Sunday Evening:
June 1, 1941

Dear Emily,
At long last the final pages of the mss. have gone to Mr. Clarke and the Oxford University Press. This should mean that we will have the complete galley proof within two weeks. I told Clarke that we both like the title 'Sketches in Cedar.'[9] I think we should definitely decide on that.

Thursday's visit was a grand experience for me. Indeed, all those visits have been grand. The work on your stories has brought more joy and satisfaction than I shall ever be able to express to you or anyone else. Whether the result be a great, spectacular success for the book or not is a matter of secondary importance. If, as you say, your work has received a fresh impetus from going over the writings – that is the really important thing. And I had ample evidence of that in the canvas I saw – it is really very hard to put into words, but that picture did something to me. It has great power, I think. As I said to you, it simply snatched me up. Those two totems, grim and tragic, towering up into the sky have stayed vividly in my mind ever since. The picture is tremendously alive. Of course I know I am only a layman and I do not judge a picture by the accepted aesthetic rules, nor can I use the art critic's jargon in speaking of it. I can merely say, quite simply & sincerely, that it is a great picture for me and I thank you for it.

I know I must have acted like a goof when you gave the picture to me. I was so taken by surprise that I was speechless – but *was I proud*!! That feeling of pride remains deep down inside me. The picture will mean a great deal to me not only for its own intrinsic beauty & strength but also because of the circumstances which led to your giving it to me. Thanks, Emily, a thousand times – IPOO times, to be exact.[10]

What a thrill it must be for you to go over the old Indian material and see it now from a different point of view – perhaps with more perspective. What a grand thing life is, anyway! And how incalculable and mysterious art is!

9 'Sketches in Cedar' is a preliminary title for *Klee Wyck*.

10 Dilworth is referring to Carr's story, 'Century Time,' in which she describes how First Nations people had carved what had looked to her like 'IPOO' on a series of gravestones. In fact, the 'P' was the number nine inverted, as she discovered, and the only date recorded on their gravestones because, as she explains in the story, only 'centuries' were relevant to First Nations' sense of time (*KW* 132–5).

Now, I must close this note. I shall count the days until I have a chance to see my totem poles again. Meanwhile accept my most affectionate regards. Don't work too hard.

Sincerely,
Ira D.

Monday am.
P.S. Your letter has just come and a few minutes earlier a telegram calling me East. I shall leave Tuesday afternoon. I shall make a recording of my reading for Wednesday afternoon and I shall write to you from the air. I am so happy that Lawren's arrangements are working out and also about your latest gift to me. You are really too, too good. But more of that later. I wish I could catch a glimpse of the pictures before I have to leave the East. I shall be away about ten days. I shall see Mr. Clarke. If you have some suggestions write to me airmail at the CBC, 55 York Street, Toronto.

Best wishes,
D.

Ottawa, Ont. June 9, 1941

Dear Emily:
This must be a very brief note. As you see from the address above, I am at the 'hub' of existence in Canada and, as you may imagine, I am very busy.

In my spare time I am going over very carefully the galley-proof which was sent me some weeks ago. I have come upon a point in 'Greenville,' which has always worried me and which I have always neglected to take up with you. You refer to the skunk cabbages as 'Hippocrates of loveliness.' I do not get the allusion in 'Hippocrates.'[11] Do you refer to the aromatic odour – to call it by no worse name or has there been some mistake at this point? You have possibly an idea here which does not occur to me. Can you send me a note about this airmail to CBC, 55 York

11 In 'Greenville,' the phrase to which Dilworth refers has been altered to read 'hypocrites of loveliness.'

Street, Toronto? If I can have it by Friday I can get the galley-proof completed and turned over to the Oxford Press before I leave Toronto.

I had time with Duncan Campbell Scott on Saturday afternoon.[12] He had many delightful things to say about you and your work. He had heard the readings on the air and had enjoyed them very much indeed. You should see your two pictures. He has hung them to great advantage, one on each side of a large and beautiful window. The light is excellent. What will delight you most of all is the fact that the room[,] which is a very large one[,] is almost completely given over to Canadian things. Duncan has some really lovely Indian things. His pictures, all but one, are by Canadian artists. Duncan pointed this Canadian quality out to me. He is absolutely delighted with your pictures. They really set the room off. He has had all kinds of people in to see them.

Unfortunately I am being kept down East a bit longer than I thought would be the case. I shall not get away from here until the end of this week which means that I shall not be able to get to Victoria until sometime next week. Ottawa is very lovely just now – the elm trees are a delight. But I grudge every moment that I have to spend away from my beloved West and the 'Juice of Life.'[13]
Kindest regards.

Sincerely yours,
Ira x.

June 10, morning –
Do not bother about the 'Hippocrates' business. It will be time enough when I return to the West.

12 One of the major Canadian Confederation poets, D.C. Scott (1862–1947) also wrote fiction (notably *In the Village of Viger* [1896]) and was the deputy superintendent-general of the Department of Indian Affairs. He was exposed to Carr's work much earlier, at the *Canadian West Coast, Native and Modern* exhibition at the National Gallery in Ottawa (30 November 1927 – January 1928). Marius Barbeau (1883–1969), anthropologist, ethnologist, and folklorist, invited him in his capacity as deputy minister to see her paintings. Scott, apparently, wanted to 'buy some of [her] work for his Department' (letter to Carr, 15 March 1928, E.M. Hembroff-Schleicher Collection, MS 2792, box 2, file 9 'Corres-pondence Emily Carr/Marius Barbeau').

13 *Juice of Life* was painted ca. 1930 and is part of the Art Gallery of Greater Victoria collection.

Vancouver, B.C.
July 11, 1941.

Dear Emily:
Greetings and salutations!

This note must be almost a 'hully-up paper.'[14] The first part of it will be an answer to your letters which arrived one on Tuesday when I was in Victoria and the other this morning.

The questions about the pictures have been answered by Mr. Clarke's request that they be sent East. I hope you did not worry too much about them or have too much trouble over their shipping. I was delighted to know that Willie Newcombe[15] had been in to assist you with this.

I am relieved too about the title of the book. The one they have chosen is not by any means perfect but I think from the sales point of view (which Mr. Clarke has to think about) it is a good one. There will be many people who will like the title – your friends throughout Canada will welcome it. People who heard the radio readings will recognize the connection at once. By the way Duncan Campbell Scott thought it was the best of those I told him of ('Sketches in Cedar,' 'Stories in Cedar,' [Ucluelet?], etc). I am not sure whether or not I told you that Duncan liked it. I know his judgment will mean something to you.

Now as for your coming to Vancouver – we shall be delighted. You will be welcome in our house – mother will be thrilled. Mind you we have a very plain home, almost bare perhaps and practically no grandeur but you would be comfortable in it. I do not want you to undertake the trip to save me time and trouble. I wish you would realize that it is a pleasure for me to go to Victoria and that my visits to your home and studio are a joy. The work which we have done together on your stories and our talks about your pictures have been a real stimulus and encouragement to me. They have helped me in my other work. You must remember that *I*

14 Dilworth is referring to 'The Hully-up Paper,' a sketch that appears in 'Indian and Other Stories' in *The Heart of a Peacock* (540–4) and which Carr initially wrote for a writing class in the summer session of the Provincial Normal School in 1934 (see Hembroff-Schleicher 1978, 278).

15 William A. Newcombe (1870–1955), son of Victoria ethnographer C.F. Newcombe, was noted for his knowledge of First Nations cultures and was a collector of First Nations material. He was appointed to the Emily Carr Trust by Carr herself in 1942. The Newcombe Family Papers have been preserved at BCARS, MS 1077. The pictures being shipped were needed for reproduction in *Klee Wyck*.

have had very few friends in my life – lots of acquaintances but they did not *get inside* me as you do. You must therefore decide to come to Vancouver if it will give you pleasure and if it will be safe for you to take the boat trip.

I can quite understand your desire to get away to the woods & the country for a while. The Japanese gardens sound wonderful to me. Now that the title is decided and the pictures sent[,] you may feel free to go.

I am glad you are enjoying the poets again – especially Browning. He said some fine things and said them well sometimes too. 'Andrea del Sarto' has always been one of my favourites. 'Pictor ignotus' means 'the un-known painter.' Browning always had a strong feeling for people and things that the world had overlooked or scorned. Do you remember the lines in 'Rabbi ben Ezra'[16] –

'Grow old along with me!
The best is yet to be,
The last of life, for which the first was made ...
[But] all, the world's coarse thumb
And finger failed to plumb,
So passed in making up the main account ...
All I could never be,
All men ignored in me,
This, I was worth, to God whose wheel the pitcher shaped.'

That's fine and courageous, isn't it? And yet many people (Sedgewick included) think of Browning as being only smug and self-satisfied.

I am delighted that Small heard and enjoyed my friends' singing. They really are fine people. I am so glad you liked them. But look here! You must not to be so lavish in your praise of me. You know what happened to the ambitious toad who got ideas of being an ox into his head. I don't want to burst with pride & vanity & that's just what is going to happen if you go on praising me.

I can't tell you how thrilled I am that you love Lawren and me so ferociously: I should hate to have Small *hate* me – or Emily either, for that matter.

The flowers you sent are still lovely. As I told you over the 'phone they were quite droopy when I opened the box but cold water revived them.

16 Dilworth is referring to 'Andrea del Sarto,' 'Pictor Ignotus,' and 'Rabbi Ben Ezra,' poems by Robert Browning (1812–89).

The honey flower is beautiful, the [freesia?] are as fragrant as can be and the lilies are opulent in beauty of form and perfume. The one that was opening so shyly is now a glorious trumpet. Their perfume fills the room. Both mother & Phylis[17] were delighted. Bless your heart, Small!

By the way, before I close this rambling note, what about the dedication of the Book to Sophie?[18] You remember we spoke of that – I think it is a fine & appropriate idea. How do you want the dedication worded? It should appear on the fly-page by itself. Would you like 'Dedicated to Sophie whom I loved etc' or, more simply, 'For Sophie ...'? Please word it yourself. It should be brief and yet convey your feeling for Sophie.

And now goodbye or 'au revoir' –

Yours affectionately,
I. Dilworth

Vancouver, B.C. [18 July 1941]

Dear Emily:
This is to be a really brief note – just a wind which I hope the Victoria Post Office will let you have before Sunday.

I was so thrilled to hear, when you spoke to me on the 'phone Wednesday, that I am now the legal guardian of Small.[19] Bless the child's ever-young heart! Nothing could give me greater joy than to give her whatever care she needs and is within my power and ability to give. I feel a little bit as Charles Lamb must have felt when he wrote his charming essay 'Dream Children.'[20] (There's that ambiguous word 'charmed.' Here it means gracious, sensitive, whimsical and wholly lovely.) By the way I have found great delight in Lamb's essays as perhaps you have – Everything he wrote was full of his own sensitive reactions to life – its tragedy, its beauty and its comedy too.

17 Phylis Dilworth (later Mrs W.W. Inglis) was Ira Dilworth's niece and his adopted daughter.
18 Sophie Frank (d. 1939), Carr's good friend, was a Salish woman from the Indian mission in North Vancouver.
19 Carr's child persona, from whom the title *The Book of Small* was derived.
20 Charles Lamb (1775–1834) was an English writer renowned more for his essays and literary criticism than for his poetry and drama. His essay 'Dream Children' is included in a collection of essays called *Essays of Elia* (1823).

I am not able to write you a full length account of my reactions to Bobtails[21] yet (I have had time to read the manuscript once only). The general effect for which you were trying is there. Punk and Loo[22] are real characters. Poor patient, hard-working Meg![23] Of course I *remember* her as I saw her often and again passing our house in Simcoe Street. [She], Sissy and Kip are all alone.[24] Gertie & Lorenzo[25] are admirably done (perhaps one or two details in 'Gertie' can be changed to give the picture more firmness). None of the humans in the stories have any real existence apart from their association with the Bobbies. It is a temptation to go on but I must not yield to it tonight.

The titles I suggested to Mr. Clarke were –
Totem Talk
Klee Wyck – Laughing One
Between Cedar and Salt Water
Ucluelet and Other West Coast Stories

I like both your suggestions for the Dedication – but I think I prefer, as you do, the simpler 'For Sophie.'

The coldest place I have found today is my tiny den with 'Juice of Life' looking down over my shoulder.

But now I must close & post this –

Yours sincerely,
Ira

July 18

21 'Bobtails,' a series of sketches about the sheepdogs Carr bred and raised in the 1920s, was eventually selected to form the second part of *The House of All Sorts* (1944).
22 Punk and Loo are old English bobtail sheepdogs who feature in the stories 'Punk,' 'Babies,' and 'Distemper' (*HS* 265–6, 281–2, 282–3).
23 'Meg' is the bobtail who appears in 'Poison' and 'Meg the Worker' (*HS* 271–2; 273–4).
24 These bobtails appear in the stories 'Kipling' (277) and 'Sissy's Job' (279) in *The House of All Sorts*.
25 These bobtails appear in 'Gertie' (283) and 'Lorenzo Was Registered' (278) in *The House of All Sorts*.

[14 August 1941]

Dear Miss Carr:
Bless Small's tender, sensitive heart – 'The Bishops's Blessing' has been with me ever since I had it the other evening.[26] What a power that girl has to find life and sense its realities! And what a joy that Emily is kind to her and lets her speak out now as 'the elders' did not always let her speak then! How she must enjoy being understood! She has lots more to say and I want to hear it all. She is my ward, you know. I hope you will use your influence with Emily and get her to encourage Small as much as possible.

I. Dilworth

Vancouver, B.C. [17 August 1941]

Dear Emily:
Here are the rest of the Bobtails. I did not get them finished in time for the Friday night mail. The notes are not, I think, worth very much, but such as they are I send them.

I was very much moved by 'Struck' as I read it last night for the third time. The experience is very vivid. As I have tried to say in my note on 'Struck' I think the concluding episode needs something – I am not sure what. Your judgment will *tell* you. The story of Adam is very strong and real and I believe it would make a good ending *if you* could indicate its relation to the other experiences.[27] Perhaps you don't want to do that – perhaps it is better as it stands and I am just suffering from one of my frequent blind spots. Perhaps I am deaf to the meaning which is shouting at me all the time. Perhaps you don't want it to have any meaning but just to be itself. It means something very definite to me – it means the persistence of your love for the Bobbies even after the kennels had been dispersed. If that's the real meaning I think you should indicate it

26 Dilworth is probably referring to 'The Blessing,' which appears in the first book of *The Book of Small*.
27 The sketch in which Adam is mentioned is 'Decision' (*HS*, 288–9).

in a few phrases or words, so that the deaf & blind & dumb among our readers (like me) will understand.

I have had a very quiet day – alone in my house. I have been reading Walt Whitman *nearly all* day. There is an amazing strength in his work: it makes many other poets' work seem pale and academic. What a poem that is – 'Crossing the Brooklyn Ferry' and 'Out of the Cradle Endlessly Rocking.'[28] At times I just could not keep from reading passages aloud. If anyone had heard or seen me I would have been judged daft at once – and, indeed, perhaps I am.

Hope you are keeping well and not too busy over your exhibition.

Affectionate regards to you both.

Yours as ever,
Ira.

Sunday Evening.
Aug. 17. 1941

---

218 St. Andrew
Aug 26 1941

Dear Ira:
Thank you for letter & poems[.] I am so sorry you are weary and troubled[.] I wish I could help. I wish that scallywag Small would jump inside your heart as she jumps suddenly into mine from nowhere – without warning – a streak of happiness coming without invite, going without warning. Do you know that you sent me a portrait of Small? Clearest I ever had of her

'It was not you, though you were near
  Though you were good to hear and see
It was not earth, it was not heaven
  It was *myself* that sang in me.'

28 'Crossing Brooklyn Ferry' and 'Out of the Cradle Endlessly Rocking' appear in *Leaves of Grass* (1891–2) by Walt Whitman (1819–92).

And yet Small & I never do seem the same 'person,' the same '*being*' perhaps, but two *persons* (and she much the nicer). I outgrew so many things that she keeps always.

Thank you for telling me about the anthology.[29] I'm so sorry that 'old johnny' was a fool. Courage, it will go through yet. *All the Oxford Press books can't be still-born!* It's too bad we are not specialitors of Detective Storm & Jazzy Crime[30] then maybe [we] would get over. Oh what a funny old world!!!! Oh! and here is something *serious*[:] look – you've got worries & are *very busy*[.] Wouldn't you like to wiggle out of my visit to you? *Honest Injun?* – I don't think you ought to have the extra of me & my work (book) dumped on you too just now & there is your family to settle in too. Oh, I wish you'd had holiday too away from *everything*[,] *a rest* to chase the tired out of you. Even when I think of Bobtails I feel greedy and shamed[.] You put lots of work in that.

Would I be disappointed? (not to come)? to Vancouver? *Well of course I would.* But I can take disappointments & I can't bear to see people overdriven. (Don't feel that way over Mr. Clarke[.] I'd like to drive a pin in him & set him on the run).

Summer has gone! Well – goodbye summer, goodbye, goodbye – the leaves rattle on the gravel, the birds are re-clothed after moult[.] If naked trees & new-rigged birds can face winter, so can I – my doves came home today – not so much fun loose in a rainy world. I'm as pleased as Noah (was)[.] Canaries & chip-monks are gone forever alas. I am glad you liked my pictures. Nan went home with one.[31] That's one less for the Ex.[32] The one that stood opposite studio door on the high chest. Lawren should be home soon?

29 Dilworth was working on a collection of poetry, *Anthology of Twentieth-Century Verse*, which was subsequently published by Clarke, Irwin & Company in 1945.

30 Carr may be referring to the work of Sax Rohmer, the English mystery writer who began writing popular fiction around 1910. During the 1920s and 1930s, there were periods when he was one of the most widely read and most highly paid magazine writers in the English language. One of his characters was Detective Storm Kennedy.

31 Nan Lawson Cheney or Anna Gertrude Lawson (1897–1985) was a Canadian artist who specialized in portraiture and became friends with Carr after she was introduced to her in Ottawa in the late 1920s. She was the first full-time medical artist at the University of British Columbia.

32 The 'Ex' was Carr's solo art exhibition, her fourth, held at the Vancouver Art Gallery between 21 October and 2 November 1941.

Mrs. Maran was in the studio the other day[.] She said '*Your* "little ladies"[33] were coming to Victoria 1st week in Sept.['] Are they?

Bless you & rest you[.] Goodnight.

Your loving friend
Emily

P.S. This M.S. is a scrap from the 'Biog.'[34] One of Small's joy-flutters (bigger photo of Small)
P.S.S. Take a drink of the Juice of Life Ira and get tonniked. Small
[on back of letter] Such note paper! I'm no lady!! Whatever is handiest when I write! Being particular stunts thought – sorry – brains limited.

Vancouver, B.C. [ca. 31 August 1941]

Dear Emily:
Just a short note to let you know how things are going on. In the first place, to begin with me and my – – ribs, they are progressing very well: in fact they are so much better that I can practically forget about them. By the way it would be horrible to have to be conscious of one's ribs or any other part of this 'muddy vesture'[35] which we call our body. What a miracle its patient working away without a thought from us. And then all of a sudden we do something or we fail to do something and the old buggy breaks down. So much about that subject – glad to be rid of it.

In the next place, we are all looking forward to your visit. Nan Cheney 'phoned me yesterday morning to tell me of the way in which they get Aunt Mary off the boat. They take their car down into the freight deck, because Aunt Mary doesn't like coming off in a wheel-chair. Well, if Nan Cheney can do it, I am sure I can and shall – that is if you prefer not to come off in a chair. But that is a mere detail which

33 Victoria Anderson and Viola Morris, two singers who referred to themselves as 'The English Duo,' came to Vancouver from Australia during the war. *The Heart of the Peacock* is dedicated to them (see Hembroff-Schleicher 1978, 287). They are referred to as the 'Little Ladies' in her correspondence.

34 'Biog' is Carr's term for her autobiography, which, at her request, was published posthumously as *Growing Pains* (1946).

35 This 'muddy vesture' is a reference to William Shakespeare's *The Merchant of Venice* (5.1.64).

will be solved when the moment arrives. Some details look so much larger in advance than they turn out to be actually. I am sure it will be the same in this case.

Have you decided when you are coming over to us? How many people (if any) do you want to see while you are here? You can see only Mother, Phylis, the maid and me if that is your wish. On the other hand, you might like to see a few people. Perhaps you have some friends you would like me to invite to see you. If so just let me know. I know Nan and Lawren will want to come in & the English singers.[36] Arthur Benjamin, the English pianist & composer,[37] who has now made Canada (Vancouver) his home is a great admirer of your work and would love to see you – so would Professor Gage.[38] But I know you want to rest and see the woods if possible. We must save plenty of time for that.

The main thing to remember is that, while you are here, our simple house is your home. You must let us know exactly what you would like and we shall try to meet your wishes. I hope you will be comfortable and happy.

Thanks so much, Emily, for your Friday letter. It was a joy. I read the first page as soon as it came and saved the rest for today. What a gift you have for penetrating the experiences of life and finding just the right word to say, or write, about them! You are very generous to say that my friendship has meant anything to you – no that's not the way to put it – I know you are sincere in this as [in] all other things and that you would not say things just to be generous & please me. You will never know what my association with you has meant to me. I want just to say that to you. Our friendship is one of those great, rich things in life which seem too great and wonderful to be true. I keep expecting to wake up and find that I have been dreaming. The fact that we did find each other is, as I said once before, one of these experiences which make[s] me believe in patterns, plans, direction in this existence which at times seems so jumbled and incoherent.

36 See note 33 on page 45.

37 Arthur Leslie Benjamin (1893–1960) was actually an Australian composer who came to London when he was eighteen to study at the Royal College of Music. He later settled in London, where he became a composer, pianist, and instructor of some repute. Benjamin came to Canada during the Second World War, during which time he was appointed conductor of the CBC Symphony Orchestra, a position he held until 1946.

38 Dilworth is referring to Professor Walter Gage (1922–78), who taught in the Department of Mathematics at the University of British Columbia.

I went to church this evening with you and Small[,] thanks to 'Gladness' & 'The Blessing'[39] and 'Juice of Life.'

I must close this note and sent it with Phylis: she is going to the post.

Hoping for good news of your visit and with affectionate good wishes.

Yours,
Ira.

Sunday, Aug. 31. '41.

Oct 22 1941
written Monday night

Dear Ira,
Stationary is one of the things that marks a true lady I've heard ??? – no lady me – would you prefer half a dozen politenesses on *real* vellum? Then return unopened as threatened, & I'll start a heart-to-heart correspondence with Max or Jack *or both.*[40] So there! I began this letter on even worse *paper* Tuesday evening after you had dickey-birdied back to Van. only to find the paper written on the other side. But I'll copy what I wrote because it was red-hot-written.

– 'Dear Ira, what can I say[?] The warmth and appreciation of your article flabbergast me![41] If I did not trust the sincerity of your heart I['d] say "blither!" & go kick myself. But I trust you so I feel like sneaking off somewhere to cry. I don't deserve it – no particular credit at all just to go straight on doing what you love to do[,] is it? God permitted me to be born in a glorious land and he gave me eyes to look with & a heart to feel[.] If the looking & the feeling of my eyes & heart have helped any-

39 'Blessing' appears as 'The Blessing' (*BS*, 37–40); 'Gladness' may refer to the sketch 'Singing' (*BS*, 41–8).

40 Max Maynard (1903–82) was a Victoria artist and teacher. He both exhibited and lectured at the Vancouver Art Gallery. Jack Shadbolt (1909–98) was originally from Victoria, although he moved to Vancouver in the early 1930s, where he taught at the Vancouver School of Art and was an active public lecturer. Carr's disdain for these artists emanated from her sense that they were condescending towards her. See Scott Watson's *Jack Shadbolt*, 19–21, 28.

41 Carr is probably referring to the advance copy of Dilworth's article, 'Emily Carr: Canadian Painter and Poet in Prose,' as it appeared in *Saturday Night* (8 Nov. 1941, 26)

one I'm gladder than glad and I thank God for letting me know splendid you[.] Knowing you has been a holy thing to me, wonderful niceness at the end of life like the bits of lemon peel we want to pick out of our cake, as the best to eat last. In my lonely years I used to pray [for] one friend that is real & won't wear out, one I can love & trust right through. I have had a few good friends, but they were not "yous" – an inspiration[,] a feeder of strong thoughts[,] your own or culled from great minds. Behind all I feel your belief in God, your belief in the beauty of the earth – your belief in Canada. Bless you.[']

[same letter] Wednesday. Oct. 22

(2) All day yesterday, I was minded to ask you minded to ask you [*sic*] to modify your praise in the article (the second one)[.] I pondered and went through the Biog.['s] first part again. It did not seem honest for me to accept all that. Lawren came in the evening & I put my trouble before him[.] He did not know the article. I just told him I was not as clever or capable as you gave the world to believe & believed yourself. 'That is not your business. Ira is writing that[,] not you. We artists cannot judge our work or ourselves. We have to leave the reaction to those it reacts on.' He was deliciously commonsense and my bother flattened out. He brought my nose back onto my face instead of poking where he showed me it did not belong. I accept his rebuke and push on. Lawren advised forgetting all about these things, these publishing pains. I shall & just thank God for my beloved trustors.

Lawren admired Lady Jane[42] *tremendously*[,] says she's a little beauty[,] was delighted at the meek way she went off to her little box without fuss or whimper. Everyone says 'you won't want to part with Jane when the time comes' but I don't feel one bit that way[.] I love & enjoy the little beast thoroughly but always there is an objective in my having her[,] anticipation in the joy she is going to give to a beloved old lady's last years[.] I hope Jane will not be too boisterous[.] She is so full of joy & vigor at present but the exuberant youth will tame down. Alice[43] is quite interested in Jane's education. Jane was always pulling the kindling out

42 Lady Jane – incorrectly referred to elsewhere as 'June' – was the spaniel Carr was raising for the Dilworth household.

43 Alice Carr (1869–1953), Emily Carr's sister. Carr had three other sisters, Edith (Dede), Clara (Tallie), and Elizabeth (Lizzie), and one brother, Richard, but Alice was the only surviving member of Carr's immediate family during the period of the exchange of these letters.

of the kitchen basket. Kindling sticks appeared in all corners of the house until I put spank-stick into Jane's vocabulary. Now she ignores that kindling-basket[.] She has mastered 'NO' and is pondering over 'gentle' and 'BAD.'

At 9:15 Sunday night I was mad[.] You had just finished the second reading of the 1st part of Sanctuary[,][44] the piece on 'birds[,]' when off went all our electricity. Black & a dead radio. The streets were still lit – different circuit but every house was black for one hour. I remained tuned in 'til the 9:30 gun went. How extraordinary to think Sanctuary was still in the air[,] still in my room[,] only needing the mechanical dipper to ladle it into my ears.

You will notice the Biog. as far as it goes is complete[.] The odd sections I sent as samples are there too[.] I have gone over them & done some cleaning and a few alterations so as to make them hang together more coherently. You'd better burn your first ones to save confusion (as varying editions of Cow Yard did)[.] I make no duplicate copies [until] *all* corrections have been made[,] all rotten spots removed, all faults ripened 'til they have bawled out & been removed[,] until you can read them[,] until miserables of wording or thought have quit pinching you. You don't want to double the mistakes. Don't you think I'm right? I don't think we need more than one set of Biog. I am only material – you the owner but I would like to have it clean & decent & intact. In a day or so I plunge into the next part of England.[45] Here Emily is a woman, though Small has not abdicated entirely. This part should be more mature with a more serious reaction to life and work. Also reaction to the land & people of my ancestry.

Date, ditto, 2.30 P.M.

Your note at noon. Thank you for your red-hotters re: Ex. I love red-hots[.] They sparkle. Perhaps the more mature reactions are more worth[while] & sedate. Emerson says we may think one thing one day &

44 *Sanctuary* was a CBC radio program that aired on Sunday evenings, during which time Dilworth would read selections of poetry. The poems were to provide a psychological retreat or 'sanctuary' from the turmoil of everyday life. Carr created her own 'sanctuary' – a cloth-bound notebook in which she collected the poetry that Dilworth sent her. Her book has been preserved at BCARS, Parnall Collection, MS 2763. See 'Last Will and Testament.'

45 Part 2 of *Growing Pains* deals with Carr's experiences in England, where she studied painting between 1899 and 1904. She suffered a breakdown in health and remained in the East Anglia Sanatorium at Naylands, Suffolk, until she recovered.

change the next on further consideration[46] but I think just glimpses show something truthful, a shine that perhaps wears off in pondering. I am so glad your first eye-full was pleasing. Lawren told me just how [al]most every picture was placed. Can't think how he could remember the pictures[.] I couldn't even though they were my own children. *You* remember the words of a quote of me better than I who wrote them. I remember the *thing* & I *meant* it when writing but I forget what words I pushed the thoughts out in[.]

Today is exquisite[.] I'm being exquisitely lazy giving mind & body a rest. (Writing you is not a labour it's just thinking in an easy ramble[.]) I got up late so I made it later. Cooked, Janed, Aviaried, and wriggled into bed again to write.

I'm so glad you like Jane[.] She's getting so good sitting out these glorious parting-with-summer-days in her little yard between the doves & me. She should learn gentleness & meekness from her nearness to the doves but be hanged if I think they are much less spit-firish than me. These glorious Autumn sunshines should give her a good winter start. Days in which Edna St. V. Millay[47] says the woods ache & sag and all but cry with color. World, world[48] – tell 'Bobbie'[49] to write me how he liked the Ex.

Love as ever from the 'Community'
Emily

P.S. Gee whiz! Alice will have to take this to the post on the wheelbarrow!

Oct. 26. [1941]

Dear Emily:
It is unthinkable that a week has passed since I wrote the first part of this

46 Carr is referring to 'Self-Reliance' by Ralph Waldo Emerson (1803–82).
47 Edna St Vincent Millay (1892–1950), an American poet who, in 1923, became the first woman to win the Pulitzer Prize for poetry.
48 'World, world' is a reference to the line 'World, World, I cannot get thee close enough!' from St Vincent Millay's poem 'God's World.'
49 Carr's nickname for Roy Dunlop, one of Ira Dilworth's employees.

letter[50] and that included in its crowded activity were two visits to Victoria & you. I should have sent the first part off – it is a shame to keep things lying around. Come to think of it – I wrote to you during the interval – a 'red-hot' as you called it after your exhibition. By the way, I am glad that you don't read all of my letters to Alice ever. Parts of them would not matter, but they wouldn't be interesting to anyone, just *words*. Most of them though [are] just specially for you. These letters are just a way of having a chat with pen and ink and paper.

Your beautiful letter came with the manuscripts of the Biography. I am sorry you were disturbed for even a moment about the things I said in my 2nd article. I meant every word of what I wrote. I did not feel that I had allowed the least bit of exaggeration to creep in. Someone is going to say these things of you and your work *afterwards* – I want to say them now so that you can hear them with your earthly ears.

I would like to have said publicly, but I did not dare, that working with you during the past two years has meant more to me than I can ever tell. It has helped me to realize a bit of myself and has given me a small share in a great piece of work for Canada. I think you know very well that I am a rather solitary person, in fact a *very* solitary person. It has always been difficult for me to let other people inside me atall. Once or twice before and *never to the same extent* I have known a true friendship. I thank God for letting our ways cross. It has been a grand, inspiring existence.

And now a bit of gossip! A friend of mine was at the Shadbolt's lecture.[51] He said that Jack took most of his time berating his audience & the world in general for not recognizing the *Canadian movement* – whatever that is. He kept the audience for one hour and forty minutes until my friends at any rate were tired out & bored to extinction. But that's not the big 'thing' – when the people arrived at the gallery a girl was at the door asking everyone to sign a sheet of paper. My friends did so and then what was their amazement to see the same girl rise, just as the chairman was beginning to introduce the great Jack, and say 'I protest! Why should Mr. Shadbolt a mere man attempt to explain the work of Emily Carr.' The poor chairman scarcely knew what to do & Shadbolt

50 Dilworth wrote a letter dated 19 October 1941 to which he appends the letter included here.

51 Shadbolt delivered a lecture at the Vancouver Art Gallery in which he both praised and criticized Carr's work (see *Vancouver Sun*, 25 Oct. 1941, 6).

had great difficulty getting started. Wasn't that an amazing thing to happen? The poor girl is quite 'touched': I have seen her several times when I have been at the Gallery. In this instance she spoke more truthfully than scores of people might with a reputation for wisdom & sanity. I hope she's not there next Friday or I may get scared and run out of the hall.

I think you are right about the manuscript of the Biog. We need only the one copy: I shall take great care of it.

What a thrill it was to have our book in my hands & tucked under my arm at last. I just would have burst if I had not had a chance to get over to Victoria to admire it with you. As I told you yesterday I have never before been so thrilled about a piece of work in which I had a part. I think the Press made an admirable job of the printing and general set-up of the book. I hope it will have a great success for their sakes and yours. As far as I (and I know you) am concerned the book's greatest possible success has come already in the working on it and getting it ready for publication. I honestly consider it as a great contribution to our Canadian letters. I know how eagerly Duncan Campbell Scott awaits its appearance. He must have a copy as soon as some are ready. I shall be anxious to know his reaction.

But now – talk about needing a wheelbarrow for your letter. This will need a special scow and I wouldn't blame you if you took two days to read it.

I must leave now for 'Sanctuary.' I shall think of you as I read. All the selections are from the poetry of Walter de-la Mare.[52] Sorry you missed 2nd half last week. I read 'Goat Paths' for you.[53]

Love to all three of you – Emily, Small & Jane – 'the three graces.'

Affectionately
Ira

52 Walter de la Mare (1873–1956) was an English poet and novelist.

53 'The Goat Paths' is a poem by James Stephens (1882–1950), an Irish poet and fiction writer.

[Typed] Vancouver, November 6th, 1941

Miss Emily Carr,
218 St. Andrews Street,
Victoria, B.C.

Dear Emily: –
This is a very formal sort of way to approach you but the subject is entirely business.

I had a letter from the Editor of the 'New World,' a Toronto publication, saying that Mr. Clarke had asked him to get in touch with me to secure permission to use the colour plates used in KLEE WYCK. Mr. Clarke mentioned this request to me in his letter which arrived yesterday. I have replied to both Mr. Clarke and the Editor of the 'New World' that as far as I am concerned, and I think I can speak for you, that we had no objection to the use of these plates provided the Oxford Press has none. Their use could be objectionable only from a commercial point of view and in these matters Mr. Clarke is the best judge. Therefore I have told the Editor of the 'New World' to make sure that he secures Mr. Clarke's permission. If he does I have said that we would have no objection.

Mr. Clarke tells me that the official date of publication of KLEE WYCK is November 7th. That is tomorrow. He says that copies should be in the bookstores in Vancouver by November 11th. I suppose that will mean that they will be in Victoria a week later!

[in ink] Love to you, Small & Lady Jane!
Yours sincerely,
I. Dilworth

Vancouver, B.C. [12 November 1941]

Dear Emily:
Well, 'Klee Wyck' has at last arrived properly clothed and, I am sure, in her right mind. The volume is most attractive, although I had my heart rather set on a black binding. (By the way, I hope you received your copy or copies today! One came for me with the compliments of the Press.

For fear you have not had yours I shall describe it a little.) The jacket is a great success with your village in rich colour. The background is black and the printing of [the] title is in the hand-done type we liked so much: it is in yellow. On the back they have printed excerpts from two reviews (the Sat. Night one and another from the 'Toronto Globe & Mail').[54] Best of all is your picture with Koko.[55] It is marvelous! I am thrilled to the soles of my feet. The bird is a rich brown, almost rust – it has a warm glow about it. The lettering is in gold. The title is from a hand-made block both on the front cover and on the back strip. I am sure you will like the whole set-up.

The local bookstores have copies today. When I went into Ireland and Allen's[56] and saw her there in her party dress just like a literary debutante, I had a lump in my throat to think she was completely grown-up. She was such a dear, engaging thing as an infant – difficult at times, temperamental about such things as naming! And what good times we had, you and I, watching her grow. Well, you would have been proud of her today. There she stood with an amazing amount of poise – not the least bit abashed by the company in which she found herself. Best seller novels, travel books, elaborate editions of this and that – all standing round her and she not one bit nervous, and yet, mind you, not a bit 'forward' either. She just between like the well-trained creature she is. As I say, you would have been proud of her.

The book-seller tells me he has had a good many orders and has had many 'phone calls enquiring when the book would be here. So, you see, she has really taken her bow.

Your letter is here and is a joy. I am glad you liked the 2nd article when you saw it in print and Davies' review too.[57] I was very glad to hear of Alice's reactions. Bess[58] told me Alice was delighted with Dr. Sedge-

54 The excerpts were probably taken from Robertson Davies's article, 'The Revelation of Emily Carr,' which appeared in *Saturday Night* on 8 November 1941, and from 'An Artist Loves the Indians,' which appeared in the *Globe and Mail* on the same date. Davies (1913–95) was a major Canadian novelist and journalist.

55 One of Carr's dogs.

56 A bookstore in Vancouver.

57 Dilworth is referring to his own article (see note 41, page 47) and Davies's review that appeared in *Saturday Night* (see note 54, above).

58 Bess Harris was a Canadian painter and an art critic for the *Canadian Bookman*. Formerly the wife of Fred Housser, she was Lawren Harris's second wife. Carr felt that Bess had not been forthcoming about her relationship with Harris and felt betrayed by her (see Walker, 34n18).

wick's review. They have all – Sedgewick, Davies, etc – been very generous in their references to me. And you are as usual too, too generous but I love it Emily and thank you for it. You know the real and great joy it has all been to me.

Thanks for the clipping from the Victoria Times.[59] First thing you know the Tourist Associations will be calling on you and making you into one of the 'sights' of Victoria. They will quite likely insist that you go down to Thunderbird Park (that awful thing across from the Capital Gardens)[60] and wave to people as they pass in sight-seeing busses from the Vancouver or Seattle boats.

Has Lady Jane expressed an opinion about 'Klee Wyck' yet[?] The chrysanthemums will approve of the colour of her binding.

Do take good care of yourself.

Affectionately yours
Ira.

Nov. 12. 1941

---

281 St. Andrews Street
Wednesday [19 November 1941]

Dear Ira,
I am a *chump*! I posted yours on *Monday* to CBC and forgot to *air* it, and the volume will draggle back after you've been home a month[,] slow as if it had *walked*. Ah me!!!! The world is too swift for we old fellows to keep up with entirely for sure[.] And yesterday's letter Alice whisked off with such swift friction my nose was hot. OOOOOOOOO!!!!!!!!! *IRA*!!! On behalf of the Victoria Business & Professional Women's Club[,][61] a box of *glorious* carnations [–] you should smell when I opened the box!!! If you only had one in your editorial button hole while you are cavourt-

59 Dilworth is probably referring to 'Emily Carr, Artist, Writes First Book' (*Victoria Times*, 8 Nov. 1941, 15).

60 In 1940 in Victoria, some totem poles were erected at the intersection of Douglas and Belleville, later known as Thunderbird Park, to preserve and display some of the Northwest Coast's rapidly deteriorating art.

61 In 1933, the Victoria Business and Professional Women's Club sent one of Carr's paintings, *Vanquished*, on her behalf to an exhibit in Amsterdam (see Blanchard 251).

ing round among the big men in the capital! And I've always slanged the B & P. women too & said they were 'no good' too. I'm rather a contemptible hussy and I have bursts of *awful shame* at things I've done & said now & then & I can't think how *anybody puts up with me.* I spanked Jane *good* yesterday and if you knew how I felt when she just *looked* and I spanked Jane for *real badness* & my club caricatures gave me that lovely forgiving look after my rounding on th[ose] B and P women for not *any* badness just for 'being *nothing*[,]' neither good nor bad, but *stupid.*

I've had a long Biog. write this morn. I'm in a London slum. Mrs. Radcliffe[62] (my London backbone) made me do district visiting (I was always jumping into something [with] both feet) & either sky high or drowning in woe – it has come on me with an overwhelming smack. How *tremendously* I hated London. I guess they'd put me down as a anti-English, traitor, rebellious, and insurrection[ist] and concentrate me by myself alone on another planet but I would not for the world be any other nationality *on earth than British* & they're marvelous but of course we must have faults & some of theirs I hate.

I sent Mr. Clarke's *'160' back,* express. I wonder if I did right about those beastly photos? I thought you *wanted* me to, so I did be took[63] but I wouldn't grin & I *wouldn't paint.* Mostly I held dogs & glowered. I do hope *Jane* comes out.

That Monday letter I sent long mail was the size of *your enormous* dictionary [–] some 'Trustor-Emily-Trust-business[.]' It'll keep. Have you heard any nasty things about our Klee Wyck? Surely *all* of her can't be good or do they shield us from the blow to start[?] Noon is past!!!!!!! It will be hardly worth getting up if I don't. Your Edna[64] thinks Jane is lovely & hopes she'll be there when she goes at Xmas to visit. I hope her manners will have steadied by then. This illness has unmannered what she had. She's the toughest, rowdy, poor lamb and *won't* learn that table level is not for dogs. Three times this day has she upped or offed with food.

Your two letters, one the address and one a nice long chat came this afternoon[.] Thank you. Edna said and I agree I never feel quite happy

62 Mrs Radcliffe is the pseudonym for Marion Redden, a Canadian by birth who resided in England and with whom Carr associated when she was in London (see Carr's 'Mrs. Radcliffe,' *GP* 137–46; Blanchard 78). Carr documents her district visiting in 'The Radcliffes' Art and District Visiting' (*GP* 196–204).

63 Carr allowed her photograph to be taken.

64 Edna, who married J.E.A. 'Jack' Parnall, was Ira Dilworth's niece.

'til you're downed. Edna was more enthusiastic than Phylis over Jane. I think perhaps she (P.) would have less patience with the pup.

This afternoon I had a brief but delightful little letter from Mrs. Clarke very enthused about Klee Wyck. I had felt a little [hurt] that neither had written but I guess they like her O.K. The 'University Women's Club' sent me a kind note too.[65] I am glad Flora Burns[66] wrote you. I think Ruth[67] *might have* [–] she knows K.W. owes all to you. Well, she can go to the devil! It is dark & foggy & Alice has gone to the Williamses. I hope they'll see she taxies home or Campbell brings her. They are such selfish fools those Williamses & *mean* as the devil himself.

Perhaps the Harrises are just paying back eat entertainments. I know Lawren used to loathe that sort of stuff[.] His work always came first. But since he married Bess – Bess likes posing a bit – charming hostess etc – I do not think she has strengthened him. Is it good for folks to be tooooo happy Ira? Isn't it a *little* dangerous[?] There is *nothing like work*[.] Vapor & fancy talk are brothers. Doctor Trapp[68] is real [–] that was a real night we had that night. I can't remember a great deal of what was said *but* the feel of it is with me still. They'll have an awful hop-about to recruit a whole core[.] It's well the old lady has pots of tin (very well off I believe) [.] Lawren *used* to be (Massey Harris)[69] but his expenses of late years must have been *enormous*[.] I believe he was very generous with his settlements on wife no. 1 & neither his son nor daughter are well off, & there is the other son to maintain I suppose.[70]

Bess had nothing[.] She & Fred[71] had all they could do I think.

65 See 'Varsity Women Honour Miss Carr,' *Victoria Daily Times*, 17 April 1937, 7. The letter to which she refers, dated 20 November 1941, has been preserved at BCARS, Parnall Collection, MS 2763, box 4, file 65.

66 Flora Burns (d. 1981) was one of Carr's earlier editors. She published two articles on Carr, 'Emily Carr' and 'Emily Carr and the Newcombe Collection.'

67 Dr Ruth Humphrey (1898–1984), an English professor at Victoria College (1927–45) and at the University of British Columbia (1945–63), edited Carr's early manuscripts until Dilworth became her sole editor.

68 Dr Ethlyn Trapp, a distinguished radiologist and close friend to Carr. She named her West Vancouver property Klee Wyck after Carr's book.

69 Lawren Harris was independently wealthy because he was an heir of the Massey-Harris Company.

70 Harris had three children with his first wife, Beatrice (Trixie) Phillips: Lawren Phillips, Margaret Anne (Peggie), and Howard Kilbourn.

71 Fred Housser, author of *A Canadian Art Movement: The Story of the Group of Seven* (1926), was an art critic who wrote variously on the Canadian art scene, the Group of Seven, and Walt Whitman.

Lawren is very generous natured, Bess a little tight, so maybe she makes him careful. I'm glad you took Bobtails East.

Interruption! – Flora Burns nearly driven me to drink – too nosey – worrying life out of me[,] going into extravagances and pushing me re: a maid[.] Well, I *got* to get one but Flora is absolutely undomestic[,] has no understanding & a perpetual giggle & says so much she can't possibly *mean* it all[.] I want to slap her. Well, it's my opportunity to post this *when* she goes. I just long to get into bed, & be mean & peevish. Alice stayed out 'til it was dark & thick fog[.] Those filthy Williamses ought to have seen her home into a cab & then Flora worries me with you ought & you ought & you ought like those damn Hennells.[72] Goodnight[.] That nervy giggle got me [–] the sooner I finish the sooner she'll get out[.] I got into bed & read sanctuaries[.]

Your nasty, Emily

Codicil O'clock *9.30* Sunday night[,] Nov 23 / 41

Thank you dear Ira, goodnight.
How beautiful, how crammed with loveliness Sanctuary was tonight. You read 'Crossing Brooklyn Ferry'[73] magnificently and the lovely 'Ease of the World' & the chrysanthemum[74] was just right for now too[.] Every poem struck beauty deep. Oh pity, pity, pity people who can't see beauty [&] pity those who *have none* to see. Dreadful squalid sordid places drowning in black that *men* have made blacker than night – why, why, *why do* men pack & mass into cities where the growing earth can't clean them with her renewing & perpetual rebuilding. Perhaps I am thinking of the slums round the old art school of Westminister & the airless desolation of the heart of London in old bio. days as I knew it. Perhaps I've never realized 'til *now* working on the Biog. how I *loathed* London. When I returned from some brief country excursion[,] how the factory outskirts, the smoke, grime, crowding people used to crush down on me, a condensed horror heavier than weight itself. Blacker than blackness, colder than coldness. 'Small' was not built for great cities. London nearly killed her[;] Paris nearly killed her[.] Doctors said in *both cities*

72 Alice Carr was a governess for Alexander Hennells, whose sons, Val and Paul, visited Alice frequently in later years.

73 'Crossing Brooklyn Ferry' appears in *Leaves of Grass.*

74 Bliss Carman (1861–1929) wrote 'Chrysanthemums.'

'get out or you will die,' 'I was a baby & a coward[.]' In those wild coast places out west there was *never* that desolation of utter loneliness crushing down upon one, like Small felt in London. – Again good night. In the cold before dawn you'll hoist away the clouds, sailing, sailing, rather wonderful, rather exhilarating. God keep you safe.

Emily

Sunday Morn [30 November 1941]

Dear Ira,
Phylis & Betty[75] came yesterday [–] nice girls! Lawren came too. His visit was rather hurried[.] He had to go to his mother. He took two sketches (canvases) back to submit to a Mrs. Fell's inspection.[76] It seems she likes 'Swirl'[77] (Lawren's picture) and wants it or something similar. He believes in this business of letting people hang pictures & decide (I *don't*[:] I either like or dislike) but I am quite willing to let people whom he know[s]. (Lawren is responsible for this.) Maxey-Square-jaw[78] is a different matter[.] *He* is *not* a responsible person. I would not let him loan out on his own and, Ira[,] while I think of it[,] when he sent in my acc.[,] there was no mention of the commission paid in by you. I know it had been [–] you told me. It was stated that I sold *4* pictures[,] but I was only credited with *paying the commission* on *3.* I wrote to Max mentioning that. The purchaser had *told me the commission was paid into the gallery* (the rest of the business was between purchaser & me). I am always *most particular* to see that the gallery always gets its commission (it is rather a trick of artists to elude it) and it should have been *acknowledge[d]* by the gallery on my statement. Don't you consider [it] so? He was mad being told but I *don't care*[.] He's max-square-jaw & I know his rotten business & I don't trust him[.] Maybe that % was credited maybe not, who's to

75 Possibly Betty Streatfield, from whom Carr saved a letter, which is preserved at BCARS, Parnall Collection, MS 2763, box 4, file 54.

76 (Mrs James P.) Ella May Fell was 'a Vancouver art patron, and a friend of the Harrises' (Walker 357). Carr refers here to two almost square canvases of Haida totem poles that she painted in 1941.

77 *Swirl* was painted in 1937 and exhibited for the Canadian Group of Painters exhibition in Toronto, November–December 1937.

78 Carr's nickname for Max Maynard.

know what pictures *were* returned to me & what not? He's not going to find *me* [an] easy fool. Lawren says he should certainly say Max *was* responsible for packing or at least overseeing. I told him (L.) in what shape they were crated[.]

But to return to 'Swirl[.]' Lawren offered to let Mrs. Fell have Swirl if it meant a sale. And he'd take something else. But he *likes* Swirl & I said *no*[,] let Mrs. F. choose another. I told Lawren 'Swirl' and 'Juice of Life' were *favourites of mine* & that was why I gave them to two people I loved. I wanted you both to have things I liked & was happy in the doing of, to remember me by. The money & Mrs. Fell can go to the devil or switch on to another (picture, not devil). L. said he was glad & would keep Swirl & if *you trade 'Juice'* I'll march straight over & hit you, now then!!

And here's more 'Trustor biz.' You know I meant to give 50 pictures to the West (Emily Carr Trust) and the business was *closed down* at 45. Lawren summed up it took about 30 canvases to make a showing (when my last show was hung). That only leaves 15 to raise funds on for the upkeep. And if I thought my Trustors were put to bother I['d] wither, dead or alive. My suggestion is *five* more are set aside, they can't go onto the Trust rigmarole (Heaven forbid Harry[79] be plagued with more codicils)[.] I'll hand them over as a *free gift right away now*, like the others are *already gifted*. Only, they'll have to *go out* of my studio[.] Either you or Lawren will have to *keep* them. For if I popped off they go int[o] the death-pot with the others, for death *duty*. I suggested that these five should be chosen by *you*. We (L. & I) chose the others & Lawren thought that a 'swell' suggestion (you to choose)[.] We decided however & I spoke for you too that the latest square[80] painted too late for our former choosing should be one to go with its mate. I said I *knew* you liked it too[,] specially too.

So that's that. You can quarrel over the housing[.] Lawren has such a [number?] of his own pictures & you[,] I should think[,] would be getting rather Emilish on the wall but I have to turn 'em out of studio to be *legal* & save bother to my beloved trustors later. And there'll be the clean fifty as my gift to the West (if the world is still a world when we stop warring).

Lawren is going to take his mother to Vancouver to live so I won't have any more of his nice often-visits. Don't *you* go and let them lasso

79 Harry (Henry Graham) Lawson, Carr's lawyer. He was the son of James Hill Lawson, Carr's guardian after her father's death.

80 Carr employs the term 'square' to refer to a canvas.

you in the East or I'll give right up & dig my grave under the big maple. You've both taught me to lean and now without a prop I'd flop. I'm peskily doddery [on] my *own two* feet[.] Once they were enough. You'll be rushing about on the double today[.] P[hylis] said you were going tonight but *you* said tomorrow. I shall of course listen to sanctuary. Maybe you will can yourself onto a disk. But I expect you'll give it to us fresh from the garden of your thoughts.

Jane is almost-quite herself & a little nicer than ever. I've *swore a swear* to answer my letters today[.] Mr. Clarke sent a Toronto 'Globe & Mail' article – no letter from him or Mrs. I am really grateful to Klee Wyck for the amusement and interest she has given Alice. I don't know *what* I wrote in Friday's letter[–] she whisked it off before I could see if it was lucid.

I took a short course from an artist once[.] He gave the class terrific subjects to draw on the spot out of their heads[.][81] Everyone said 'I can't! I don't know how!' He said, 'You'll be surprised how much you *do know.* How much more you have taken in than you realize' & you know, it *is so*[:] my writing has taught me so much about people & places that I'd only half-realized before[.] It's London now and students I'd half forgotten.[82] Back they troop fresh & exciting & I say to myself, 'Oh, why *didn't* I open my eyes a little wider then [to] things I only half took in.' My writing is curiously dateless. I had spells of thinking I'd keep a diary but I wrote long letters home instead[.] But they lent my letters round to some people I did not like and I got mad and quit writing beyond facts that were so dry, nobody was interested: don't you hate public 'common to all' letters? One never writes or talks the same to two people[,] do they? With most people you exchange *doings* not *thinkings.* I *can't* write *thoughts* to anyone I don't like[,] can you?

Finished my letters. Not so *arduous* [–] only *6 all told*[.] 2 Eastern, 2 Vancouver, (2 Victoria both from strangers). The two warmest & nicest were [from] Victoria Anderson and Viola Morris.[83] Thank you so much for letting me read yours. Spose I'd better keep [it] 'til your return.

81 Carr is probably referring to Mark Tobey (1890–1976), the American abstract expressionist painter.

82 Carr recalls students with whom she affiliated in 'St. Ives' (*GP* 220–35) and 'Bushey' (*GP* 236–43).

83 See the reference to the 'Little Ladies,' note 33, page 45. The letter from Anderson to which Carr refers has been preserved at BCARS, Parnall Collection, MS 2763, box 4, file 27.

People who mention K.W. always mention the foreword and your two articles. Mr. Gage says your prelude *could not be beaten* for goodness. [unsigned letter]

Saturday Night [6 December 1941]

Dear Ira –
How joyful to have my dear Trustor home again!! You will be in Van. on Sat. or Sunday I *expect*[.] Anyhow I'll have a 'blue-Monday' letter waiting to welcome you. Got yours yesterday air [–] 'airy-fairy exalted' [–] in which you said the air was bumpy. Oh I'd *hate* bumpy air worse than bumpy earth!

Came to bed at 5 P.M. – very tired – Dr. Lucas[84] looked in on me. Said he'd heard there was a 'party' in progress & looked in to see if he thought I'd *better* go[85] (Mrs. Lucas belongs to the University Women's Club) & is going to help me get out of troubles (pains better)[.] I am to stay in bed the day before & Mrs. Lucas (Dr.'s wife) is to keep a[n] eye on me – see I don't stay *too* long[.] I've never met her & I don't know which day party is yet.

I had such a nice kind letter from Mrs. McGeer[86] today. Friendly & genuine. I hope I shan't puff out with *more than fat.* Stick a pin in me like a dear if I get *too* puffy. But *I'm glad* they like our 'Klee Wyck.' [–] glad for *you* & *me* and *Canada* and *Mr. Clarke.* I long to see you & hear *all your newses.* But first before anything you *should* get into bed[,] drag the [sheet?] up over your head after putting one cork in each ear & catch up in sleep. Throw your worrying out the window (no peach tree under it to get spoiled like that woman's next door with one miserable mop) [.] Jane has a bounce & a lick all ready for you – Small has a bear's hug waiting.

Sunday – I am glad to see Sanctuary in the radio list for tonight – mind you[,] last Sunday I ha[d] the feel that you [were] home.

84 Dr Oscar C. Lucas was Carr's physician.

85 The University Women's Club honoured Carr with a party for her seventieth birthday.

86 Ada McGeer was a friend who subsequently worked for Dilworth (see Blanchard 281). Carr's response to McGeer's letter, dated 8 December 1941, has been preserved at BCARS, Accession number 93-5838-1. McGeer wrote 'The Emily Carr I Knew.'

I enclose your letter (Viola Morris) [,] also 'St. Paul's[.]'[87] It is not as good as I could wish [but] perhaps it will ripen further. I have no second copy so will you let me have it back to keep my sequence of sections clear[?]

Two ladies called on me today & left me a whole sheaf of tracts. They always enrage me like a bull. Once *some*one (maybe it was *you*?) used to pin one on my Simcoe street gate every morning. Finally, I bounced out thinking I'd spotted the perpetrator & nearly murdered a much astonished woman! Her baby had picked it off my gate[.] I had just caught the flutter of it out of the window & chased the innocent woman all down the street.

My new girl is devoted to Jane. I caught Alice calling her (Jane) '*darling*' the other day. This is your *blue-Monday* letter[;] the other was a *pink-Sunday*. I shall be listening in at 9.30.

As ever,
Small.

[7 December 1941]
9:30 Sunday Night.

Thank you Ira[,] goodnight.

Sanctuary was lovely. The first one (Wordsworth on Westminister bridge) [.] I'd just been in Westminister myself[88] – strange Holiness[89] I loved particularly.

Oh goodness[,] more war! It spreads & spreads – a badness, so *very* bad, eating up all the nations[.] What will be the end? – none of our business? Poor earth! When will it be that the beauty & tranquillity ([which] she is so full of under all this mess) shall straighten, calm it out.

My party is dated for Saturday next. The poor dears mean well – I'm to be carted to the function by the President who is a complete

87 'St. Paul's' appears in *Growing Pains* (Pt 2, 121–4).

88 William Wordsworth wrote 'Composed upon Westminister Bridge' (1802). Carr is also referring to the story she is writing for *Growing Pains* about her visit to Westminister.

89 'Strange Holiness' is a poem by Robert P. Tristram Coffin (1892–1955), a poet, novelist, and essayist who won the Pulitzer Prize in 1935 for the collection of poetry *Strange Holiness*.

stranger to me as are all of them except Ruth & Margaret Clay[90] (if they are there). Well, nothing for it but to (attire myself in the dress I split in Vancouver and all the courage I can muster) and *forget* about it 'til Saturday morning. Once I had to *talk* (art) to the Women's Canadian Club.[91] It was down in the Crystal Gardens[:][92] 500 women people. I took old Koko. It was marvelous the courage that little dog gave me. There was something special about Koko. An old dame in a magnificent fur coat grabbed little Koko onto her rich magnificent lap as I took my place but he politely but firmly slithered off[,] ran to the front of my shoes & sat there[,] a guard with his nose in the air. No army of soldiers could have given me the courage he did[.] There was something remarkable about Billie the Sheep dog & Koko the Griffon[,] such a courageous depth of unswerving loyalty[.] Either dogs' devotion to me was bigger [than to] himself[,] a love that brought out the very best that was in you[.] Some dogs are only sentimental in their love[.] It is selfish stomachy love. There was so much beyond that that it gave me the courage when the time came to give the order. K[oko] – his misery of years was too much [–] I could [do] it for [his] sake[.] God gave dominion over the creatures to us, a sacred trust to use or to abuse. Oh thank God for all the creatures – life – wasn't the description of that fox fire (in Sanctuary). Wonder how you will like St. Paul's & Westminister Abbey?[93] I'd just been toddling round Westminister myself – Abbey, slum, and art school[.] My schools always seemed to start off in slums[,] didn't they? Though, of course, we did ascend to the 'Mansion' in S.F.[94] You never told me how you liked that second lump of S.F. Maybe you never read it? (the mansion, the return home,

90 Margaret Clay (d. 1982) was director of the Vancouver Public Library (1924–52) and one of Carr's early editors and 'listening ladies' (see 'Alternative,' *GP* 363). She reviewed *Klee Wyck* for the *Canadian Historical Review* (1942) and wrote 'Emily Carr as I Knew Her' for the *Business and Professional Woman* (1959).

91 The talk, 'An Address,' to which Carr is referring was given on 4 March 1930 (see Hembroff-Schleicher, 1969: 34) and was published in *Fresh Seeing: Two Addresses by Emily Carr* (1972).

92 The Crystal Garden was constructed in Victoria in the mid-1920s by the Canadian Pacific Railway as a saltwater swimming pool for the Empress Hotel and the residents of Victoria.

93 'Westminister Abbey – the Architectural Museum' is a story from *Growing Pains* (Pt 2, 130–3).

94 S.F. refers to San Francisco; 'The Mansion' appears in *Growing Pains* (82–9).

the shock of Nellie's [McCormick's[95] death] & Ishbel's death & Mrs. Tucket[96] who loved her art better than her kids). I asked you once but you scuttled back to the 'Lily-field'[97] & 'the Hunch-back.'[98] I'm glad you did not *pretend* you'd read them[.] *Don't ever pretend* to me[.] By the way[,] aren't there *any adverse* crits on Klee Wyck? Surely there must be *some*[;] none have reached my ears[.] I want to know them. One learns so much by cuts of the whip even if they do hurt.

I'm enclosing [a] letter to Dr. Trapp. Don't know even her old address let alone new (if she's moved) [–] will you please? If posts get *much* worse with our *added* war[, we] will have to carry our own letters round 2ce per day – why write? Our *morning* delivery is *3 P.M.* [–] steady diet now. I enclose Dr. Trapp's letter for you to read[.] It's so nice.[99] You can read mine [–] answer too if you like. You are in it.

God keep you.
Yours
Emily

P.S. A lovely letter from D.C. Scott. He probably wrote to you.[100] Lawren sent me 2 copies of his article[.][101] I send you one (You may have seen it[.] Need not return it[.]) E.

95 Nellie McCormick was an American woman whom Carr befriended when she was studying in San Francisco ('Reasons,' *GP* 27–34). In 'Back to Canada,' the last story of Part 1 of *Growing Pains*, McCormick is described as having committed suicide and Ishbel Dane as having died in the 'Good Samaritan' hospital (90–6).

96 Mrs Tucket appears in *Growing Pains* ('Mrs. Tucket,' 331–3).

97 'Nellie and the Lily Field' (*GP* Pt. 2, 37–8).

98 An unidentified story.

99 Dr Trapp's letter to Carr has been preserved at BCARS, Parnall Collection, MS 2763, box 4, file 61.

100 Carr is referring to Scott's letter, dated 5 December 1941, in which he notes his preference for the sketch 'Sophie' and, more generally about her writing, that there 'is the sense of complete experience – the landscape – the sea[,] the forest . . . Description is not enough & you have the skill to conjure up the scene by the rhythm & balance of your sentences' (BCARS, Parnall Collection MS 2763, box 4, file 47).

101 The Harris article to which Carr refers is probably 'Emily Carr and Her Work.'

[Monday] Eve. [8 December 1941]

Dear Emily:
Here I am a most belated straggler of a writer! I have neglected you miserably but actually, Emily, my days ever since I reached the East have been feverish in the extreme. They have been filled to the brim and over it with meeting after meeting. There are so many details in connection with our work and so much policy and practise to be discussed and, if possible, straightened out that I *could* go on indefinitely but I have no intention of doing so. There is so much 'dumbness' and lack of courage in high places that I sometimes wonder we make any progress atall in this country. So many of our top people have limited or no imaginations, no sensitiveness, no appreciation of what can and must be done that they are constantly contributing their bit to our chaos.

I had lunch with Mr. Clarke the other day. Mr. Sandwell,[102] editor of the 'Saturday Night,' and Mr. Robertson Davies were there. It was a jolly little group which resolved itself with a Klee Wyck–Emily Carr admiration society. Mr. Sandwell and Mr. Davies were both full of good statements about 'Klee Wyck.'

You really should have seen the beautiful window in Simpson's store. It has there three large canvases and the original of 'Sophie' very well displayed. There are a number of copies of the book and the whole has a Christmasy background of trees etc. Mr. Clarke said they had taken a photograph of it and would send it to us.

The first edition of the work consisted of 2500 copies. Of these more than 1000 have been sold and it is some weeks before Christmas arrives. So the press are very well pleased. 'Klee Wyck' has gone over much better than they had dared to expect considering that it is a *first* book.

Mr. Clarke wants the manuscript of the second volume right away. They will publish it right away after Christmas he says. I have shown him most of the material and he is very pleased. I did not have time to read him 'Bobtails' but he is enthusiastic about the idea.

I was terribly sorry to hear of the business about Alice. What stupid people those are! Imagine them allowing her to go home in the dark at that hour. And Flora Burns must be a nosy, meddlesome nit-wit. If only

102 B.K. Sandwell (1876–1954) was the editor of *Saturday Night* between 1932 and 1952, an influential critic, and governor of the CBC between 1944 and 1947. His review of *The Book of Small* appeared in *Saturday Night* on 5 December 1942.

people would mind their own business how much simpler life would be for everyone.

I certainly did give Max a cheque for the commission on 'Tossed.' It was for $12.50, ten percent of the sale price. I can think of no reason why it was not included in the accounts sent to you. If Max has not done something about it when I get back West I shall certainly mention it to him.

I think your idea of putting aside 50 canvases is a good one. I shall be very proud to choose or *help choose* the remaining ones. I am very happy that you have included the new squares. As for housing the gift I am sure we shall have no difficulty about that. And no one can have 'Juice of Life' – not even you, altho' of course you have it in your heart and mind. Certainly Mrs. Fell can't have it. I was opposed to Lawren's suggestion that he let her have 'Swirl.' I think it would have been a great mistake.

Your two letters (one written on Nov. 24 & one on Nov. 27) arrived today. They were such a big spot of joy. I am so glad you heard 'Sanctuary.' I knew you would like the poems. 'Brooklyn Ferry' is a magnificent work.

I did not see the Scotts. They had left Ottawa before I arrived. I am going back to Ottawa tonight to spend tomorrow. Then I shall turn my nose westward with great relief. Two days in Winnipeg & then if I am not frozen I shall be off to Vancouver. I do not know when I shall get over to Victoria. Meanwhile heaps of love.

Yours affectionately,
Ira.

Scores of people have spoken of 'Klee Wyck.'

Tuesday morn [9 December 1941]

Dear Ira
Don't like war at all[,] do you[?] I thought of you so much[,] was so glad you were home (I *think you are*[.] I don't think it was your voice *canned* in Sanctuary Sunday night.) I expect responsibility & extra worries come through all this. I did hope you were not driving in the dark last night. How *wonderful* the radio is. How comforting the voice out of the black. I

thought the announcers were all *fine* trying to tell us true as they could without unnecessary alarm. After ours was off[,] I got an American station [–] such a nice programme. A poem of Walt Whitman among others[.] I can't make out if people are supposed to listen to radio or not[.][103] They tell one they'll be *on the air*, so I spose – of course I had the radio light all shaded. The cedars looked *particularly* solemn & lovely.

God bless you & keep you, Emily

Tuesday night
Oh my dear[,] how *glad* I was to get your *brief* note tonight 6:30 (no night boat last night) [.] I have thought of you constantly, positive that your job these days was overwhelming[.] The CBC are doing their job magnificently – I feel as if I loved every one of the staff but particularly most the ones behind holding the reins, cheerfully reassuring or [easing?] the scare. I just nearly break when you end up with 'O Canada' & 'God Save the King[.]' They seem[ed] to wrap Canada round safe last night in the black. I so often heard *your voice* in Sanctuary besides the Psalm. How unbearable stress times must be for those who have *nothing*[.] Goodness knows our faith is wobbledy enough[.] When I wobble extra in faith, I say to myself, 'Alright cut that all out of your life & where would you be?' and it is just unthinkable not to believe. 'While else withheld, withhold not from us belief in plan of thine in time and space.' etc. W.W.[104]

Tonight is more comfortable. I prepared [for the] blackout [in] my bedroom[,] kitchen & bathroom so we can have light. No time last night[.] We had to *black* with supper just cooked. Ate chops in fingers[,] couldn't see to cut it off bone. I am so thankful I have keep – a nice girl[,] willing & not afraid. I can send her a message & she helped me do the blackening – she does not sleep here[.] Lives a couple of blocks away[.] Goes at 6.30 or 7.00, comes at 7.30 A.M. How strangely quiet the world seems in the dark[.] I hope your mother is not frightened & troubled[.] Oh, I'm so glad you had safely 'planed' home[.] *Don't* roam around the city in your car in the dark, will you[?]

103 Carr is uncertain whether or not the enforced blackouts (for the war) include turning off the radio.

104 A line from Whitman's 'Song of the Universal' that reads as follows: 'In Thy ensemble, whatever else withheld withhold not from us, / Belief in plan of Thee enclosed in Time and Space, / Health, peace, salvation universal.'

And now good night. I'm *very* tired & going to sleep[.] I hope Small is snuggled to you close tonight[,] her arms round the 'pump'[105] that is her bomb-proof-shelter. God help you & keep you through these hectic weary days.

Yours
Small

Wednesday morn.
Thank you for making time for my brief note[.] It was so comfortable to know by visible eye that you were home. This is not a letter. You have not time for letters in among your other bothers. It is just Hello! & love from Small and Phyllis (new girl) is going to the post.
Cod. I doubt if there *was* a night boat – slept like a log & hope same of you. And the sun shines today. Blessings. S.

Thursday night [11 December 1941]

My dear Ira,
What a delight to get your special round 6 tonight[.] Thank you a thousand[.] You are so much in my thoughts, pushing, dragging, shoving at your big heavy duty-job. Thank God for men like you in big places & radio is an *enormous* place in the world now[:] grand men[,] not afraid[,] God-fearing. It means so *vitally* much to young people too to have men of your kind[.] Higher things & thoughts are so struck out of education & ridiculed[,] it is not *fair* to the next generation. I am sure you will feel keenly for those young Japanese students that have been under you[.] Theirs is a *horrible* place just now[,] crushed between two allegiances. I was so glad you told me about the man in Ontario enjoyin[g] 'Sanctuary[.]' I thought myself you were *even more than usually* grand in it last Sunday. It is a sadness to me these days that I have to go over & over a thing to retain it in my memory though it may impress me deeply at the time[.] Old things I remember with vivid clearness[,] present things I don't grip so quickly.

Oh pest – the Japs. I *wish* you could [come] to my party on Saturday.

105 Carr refers to the biological and emotional functions of the heart as, respectively, 'pumps' and 'feelers.'

You would be such a strength[.] Well I'll hang onto your spirit. Thanks for letting that come. Alice is going – an added responsibility – she is shy & looks *so dejected* when she is & gets so peeved with me over it. Still, I'm glad & surprised she *will* go at all[.] When I told her she was invited she flung out[,] 'I *shant* go [–] I *can't* see!' 'Well you don't have to!' I said 'but you can hear' & to my surprise[,] by not trying to press her[,] she seems quite keen now. I am afraid it's going to be rather big. I *am* glad people love Klee Wyck. I am so grateful to her for what she did to me when I was down and out, and for all she taught and brought to me (you etc) and for letting me show through her a bit of the woods & the Indians. I think I understand Lawren's use of the word resonance but I don't know *just* how to *say* it[.] Wouldn't it be like the clapper striking a bell – the woods & big thoughts of them striking on your heart and vibrating? Through the picture?

And tonight we are *normal* and it seems *almost* unnatural that three black nights were strange, thick & solid & still. No movement[,] no sound. The creatures gave me such courage. So perfectly *unmoved* & normal. War meant nothing to them & the seagulls sailing the sky[,] so unconscious of the mean things men are doing up in it[.] Only once I got the jitters, just a 'wee bit' as I got out of bed & did a section of the Biog & lost myself & steadied up. An uninteresting section that needed *thought* & enhancing. I am *so* glad you like her & feel she is coming to life. You will like the beginning better than the latter part[,] I expect[,] because of old 'Small[,]' your own ward. She writes those parts for me. I am glad you think I climbed over 'evil' successfully[.][106] I wanted [it] to be true & yet avoid being too sordid, face it without letting your reader gloat (I mean not that exactly) but read in print what he would not expect you [to] say with your tongue[.] I am doing London *sights* just now. All the time I was working[,] plodding at the rudiments of art[,] that other part of myself. What I saw & did must have been influencing my art through life I suppose. I do value having *you* to talk my work over with for I know you understand.

Jane! Don't say or *think* it is going to hurt me to give Jane up – little rascal! She has been a labor of love from the start. I have steadily looked forward to the time when she would bring joy & fun into your home[.] She is really a sweet pup. She is fairly clean now but *not perfect*[.] What arrangements can you have for a pen *under cover*? She should not run

106 'Evil' is a story in *Growing Pains* (Pt 1, 46–52).

out in *wet grass*. Pups at that age are very apt to get distemper if allowed to chill & get damp[.] Could you construct a pen [in] a little corner in your basement (not too near the furnace) [,] a warm sleeping box with a running space about it (into which you can put her frequently) [?] And whenever your mother wants to be rid of her & teach her[,] she must be penned there when necessary for her to go out & spank her if she yells. I chain her in my bedroom near the bed. She likes to be near me & the spank stick operates if she yells. It teaches her control too but she has [to] be loosed & put out every couple of hours or so. She is clean in her box at night now. We have about broken her of getting up on the table. But she is a terror for snitching[.] Today she climbed on a chair & onto the sewing machine then onto the bed and stole my heart-pills from the shelf. I found her with the bottle fortunately still unstoppered. Shoes, stockings, dusters, knitting wool. Everyone admires her for a little beauty[.] All men adore her. I think while this fearful weight & press of extra is upon you[,] she might be an added burden to arrange for. I'll keep her as long as you want. Only I want you to enjoy *some* of her happy pup-dom. If Ethel loves her like my girl you will have no bother. I never have to ask my girl to do anything for Jane[.] She just *loves* to serve her. She is a sweet child [who] loves the birds too. I miss old 'Pout[.]'[107] He was the one to be always on the watch for my every move. Sleep overtakes me – goodnight – don't be *too* disappointed over Saturday. I shall think about you a lot & love and bless you standing behind all your boys *& doing a grand job.* I would not have you add more tiredness to your plenty[,] even for my party. I'm so proud o[f] your job!

Morning News seems more cheerful. What a difference it makes.

Yours
Emily

3.30 A.M. Sunday morn [14 December 1941]

Dearest Guardian,
How wonderful our Birthday party was![108] I was terrifically happy. When Emily saw all those people she thought she was going to get the jitters.

107 One of Carr's dogs.
108 See 'Victoria Artist Honoured at Reception Today,' *Victoria Daily Times*, 13 Dec. 1941, 6

But *I* didn't[,] though I can't say what I *might* have felt if I hadn't seen my dear Guardian almost first thing[.] It was so comfortable to see my home right there.

Wasn't everybody *lovely*? And the dear flowers & the letters and best of all that lovely kiss you gave your Small in front of them all when you had finished reading (better than the whole bottle of Emily's heart pills).

I am so grateful to you for being there[.] It meant everything strong to Emily & to me.

Your Small

Noon Sunday
Cod. P.S. From Emily

Would you expect the child to sleep all through [the] night after such a day? – She didn't but she's O.K. & gloating over her room full of flowers[.] They are fresh & new as the morning. They are so lovely.
P.S.er The letters were marvelous[.] You shall read them.

Do tell me what to do about the *enormous* ones.
Do I write to Canadian Press & where & how?
" " " the Mayor and How[?][109]
" " " the Women's Canadian Club[?]
How about Lieutenant Governor[110] & Premier[111] [–] surely not?? Or how??? Indian Agents, yes of course. There were *20* letters in my mailbox.
P.S.*est* I am resting in my poems today. Small loves them. Snooze[,] poem[;] snooze[,] poem[.] That's the order of today.
Cod. P.S.erst. I've thought so often of that Indian boy looking at Sophie.
[on back of letter] Let me have the cutting back as it has the names of the societies present though I think *all* Victoria was represented except police[,] fireman & ministerial association. Mr. Laundry did for that.[112]

109 Andrew McGavin was the mayor of Victoria between 1936 and 1944.

110 William Culham Woodward was the lieutenant governor of British Columbia between 1941 and 1946.

111 John Hart was the premier of British Columbia between 1941 and 1947; he was not able to be present for Carr's birthday celebrations, but his wife attended on his behalf (see BCARS, Parnall Collection, MS 2763, his letter to Emily Carr, 10 December 1941, box 3, file 26).

112 The Reverend T.A. Laundry, whose wife, Ellen Laundry, acting president of Church of Our Lord, Ladies Aid, was also present (see BCARS, MS 2763 Parnall Collection, her letter to Carr, 19 December 1941, box 2, file 9, in which official birthday wishes are conveyed).

I liked that little beginning prayer[,] didn't you[?] We so seldom include God in functions these days.

Vancouver, B.C. [16 December 1941]

Dear Emily:
Yes, it was a wonderful party! I was so glad that I was able to be there. Your speech was absolutely marvelous. When I tell you I was completely amazed you will not misunderstand me, I am sure. Your voice was firm and full – not a shiver in it [–] and your straightforward statement of your gratitude and pleasure was exactly right. I was afraid you were going to be too tired but I was sure that if it did not do you a positive physical injury it would be a happy tiredness.

Mr. Laundry's little prayer of invocation was delightful. I agree that it was nice to begin that way. Mrs. Young's[113] arrangements all sprang from a desire to do the right, the kind thing. She is a bit of a fool at times but she means well. What a drove of people. I hardly remember what I did or said but that does not matter. I remember very clearly what I felt and that was a great joy that you were being so fittingly honoured. Of course, you could never be adequately or sufficiently honoured or thanked for the great things you have done for this beloved West of ours. But I am glad that our hometown made such a sincere and honest attempt to pay you a tribute.

Are you to answer letters and how? I am afraid I think you must answer them and I know your own sense of propriety will tell you how. I think every one of them will appreciate just a simple little personal note. Of course you will have to be formal in addressing the Lieutenant Governor as his Honour, the Mayor as His Worship and John Hart as the Honourable, the Prime Minister. Having got these kinds addressed, I always begin my letter 'Dear Sir' which I believe is quite correct. Letters of that sort always give me a pain in the neck but I am sure you will do them beautifully.

I hope Lady Jane is feeling better. We can take her any time that is convenient. You ask about our basement. We have a nice dry one and can have a bit of it enclosed for her. If she does not seem to like that she can

113 Mrs H.E. Young held the reception in Carr's honour at her home on Oliver Street, Oak Bay.

share the sunroom with the canary. We shall try to be good to her. Thanks for the warning about keeping her out of the wet grass. Please let us have other such suggestions: they will be very useful. You must tell me what she should have to eat. Mother was delighted with your letter and your comments on Jane. I am sure Ethel will like her and be good to her.

What a joy and comfort it is to know that you have a good maid at last. She seemed very nice when I saw her for a few minutes the other evening.

I am glad Mr. Clarke sent you a cheque. He asked me about doing so when I was in Toronto. You see it is just a payment in advance. There will be considerably more than that amount already credited to you as royalties. So you don't need to feel overwhelmed with gratitude. Of course it is kind of him to send the cheque in advance. He is essentially a kind person.

Thanks very much for sending the books back all duly autographed. I wish people would not make these demands upon you. I could not very well turn down these particular requests.

Well, Emily, I must say goodnight and take this to the post. Give Small a big hug for me. She really behaved marvelously at the party. I could see that she was enjoying it. But what a trick to carry off the birthday cake – oh, I know she will say it just happened to be in the car when we got home. I remember that other party when Lizzie was shamed right through.[114] But I do hope the child did not get a 'tummy' ache from eating too much of it. How happy she was about her flowers and they *were* lovely. It made my heart warm to have that brave red carnation pinned on my coat. Thank you, my dear. Saturday was almost as great a thrill to me as to you too.

Heaps of love –
Yours affectionately,
Ira

Dec. 16. 1941
Thanks for sending me the clipping.[115] It is very fine. The Canadian Press carried a long account of the affair on its wire service right across Canada.

Did you see Lawren? I saw him just as he was going into the boat Mon-

114 See note 5, p. 28.
115 See note 108, page 71.

day morning. I was seeing Gracie Fields off.[116] She had had breakfast with us at C.B.R.[117] But goodbye!

Tuesday – . [16 December 1941]

I hear of your bouncing down the ramp with gay 'Gracie' and am delighted that you 'looked bursting with vigor & cheer.' Lawren spent the evening. Just what I needed after Sun. & Mon. in bed. I was enough rested to be irritably restless but *too tired* to work. I feel like my flowers neither fresh nor dead[.] Those gold & white chrysanthemums (The 'Canadian Press' coffin full) were the most glorious shade I've ever seen[:] deep *pure gold*, not yellow, not tawny, but *gold*[.] So were my corsage rosebuds. Lawren was tickled over the party. Thought it a *huge joke*[,] *swell*!! He takes his mother to Vancouver today. Has all manner of 'staffs[.]' He's quite sure the Japs *won't* come – what a happy heart he has.

Today is perfectly grand glinting one's eyes out with shine – *too* sparkled. I feel like a leaf fluttered to earth and flat & sodden after the spin & whirl through the air. I believe I'm *glad* to be earthed again. The leaves must feel a little that way after having *sat* all their lives.

This (to quote you) is not a letter (I always *know* when you begin so[, the letter] will be quite sizable).

Is Carr St. to James Bay included in Book of Small?[118] If so, it needs peeling. Mrs. Fawcett's hundreds of fat curly children etc![119] I was driven to the party by Tommy McCormick's daughter. I wondered how she'd take the description of her mother-in-law with 'a voice so strong it could be heard on Carr St.[,] Princess Avenue and Birdcage Walk all at once.'[120] Still I loved Mrs. McConnell and respected her highly & hope the love showed through[.] You mentioned 'One Crow'[121] too once to

116 Gracie Fields (1898–1979) was a Lancashire born comedian and singer who conducted a nationwide tour of Canada to raise funds for the war.

117 CBR were the call letters of the Vancouver CBC station.

118 'From Carr Street to James' Bay' appears in *The Book of Small* (221–35).

119 Carr describes the Fawcetts, who have 'heavy, wide children with curls' in 'From Carr Street to James' Bay' (*BS* 223).

120 Mrs McConnell is described in 'From Carr Street to James' Bay' as having 'such a large voice you could hear it on Toronto Street, Princess Avenue and Michigan Street all at once' (184).

121 'One Crow' appears in Part 1 (titled 'Five Birds') of *The Heart of a Peacock* (8–21).

go in. It is childhood *but* you said [it] needed re-writing. Perhaps it would be best to save that for the collection of animals? (monkey, rat, vulture, crow, cat, coon, peacock, etc.)[122]

I posted *all* your books back[:] a 3 and a 2 bunch. I had a *silly* letter from a man called Hope Kerr – know him? Poets & artistics (Arts & Crafts & Victoria Authors etc) [.][123] 4 or five sheets of foam! I wrote up letters yesterday. The *most important*[,] your mother, Mrs. Young, Mr. Clarke, Parson Laundry, a blind woman and *old Holly Morley*[124] who sent me a *whole* pound of 'Liquorice all-sorts' on my birthday[.] Kick her roots on your way in tonight – prickly, almighty-pleased with herself, old scrag. SHE *LIKES* KLEE WYCK!!!!!!!!!!!? I am *not* a nice woman.

But I *am* your loving
Small.

P.S. Absence of codicils denotes humility & shame but I *don't care*[.] Some folks do rile – I'll quit spitting out – restrict myself to one *decorous* epistle *once* per month[,] eh?

Tuesday [23] Dec. [1941]
'For Christmas' [written on the back of the letter]

Dear Ira
A happy peaceful Christmas day at peace in your own self. Even if the big world 'yowls[,]' we each have a little world of our own in our own hearts to rule over and be happy in.

I am glad you left Jane tonight. I like to have her and I like to know I have not added to your already over-heavy burden by launching that whirligig on you. I always loved naughty kids better than goody-goodies.

122 These animals are the foundation for stories that eventually form part of *The Heart of a Peacock*.

123 The Island Arts and Crafts Society held an annual exhibition in Victoria to which Carr regularly contributed between 1911 and 1937. 'Victoria Authors' probably refers to the branch established in Victoria of the Canadian Authors Association in 1921.

124 The Morleys were Carr's neighbours.

Martyn (in the Biog)[125] *almost* made me quaver into love for him once when the 'Elder'[126] had told me I was the *black sheep* of the family & the only one that my mother felt anxiety over on her death bed. It made me feel bad but Martyn said, 'Well if you *were the bad one*, you may be sure your Mother loved you just a *little* more than the others.' That was *such a comfort* to me – I'd never thought of such a thing[,] only of mother being so disappointed in her bad child.

The Biog. is my Christmas present to you[.] Accept [it] as your *very own* with my love[.] It is far from finished[.] There is a lot more to London and then back to Canada yet to be done but you told me *not to hurry* it – so, I have been deliberate. I tried to dig. I have written it for Canadian Art – and for you[.] Its first writing was superficial – afraid to let go & show myself – a very dull document – I utterly *ignored* that M.S. in writing this[.] The only thing I bothered to follow was the headings. I had decided in the *first edition* what places & people I was going to write about & I have done so – parts may seem to you superfluous – cut out if so – parts I may want to re-write yet again. But I *want* to get it & complete [it] while my wits are clear and before the effort becomes impossible. You know how we *postpone* things[.] Two sections, 'St. Paul's' & 'Westminister Abbey[,]' you already have. I have made *no* duplicate copies of any of it & am destroying the old original as I write this. Having lost my confounded glasses has prevented my going over it for the 200000th time. There are doubtless many bad things that I can refine & simplify after it is once together. If you ever want to publish it you could 'edit' without me. I don't think there is anything for relatives to kick at[.] The Boultbee woman[127] was very fond of her aunts (except me) & thought them saints (me a devil). But Mrs. Boultbee's mother had seen enough of the Elder's domineering and autocratic rule over we younger children to *absolutely forbid* the Elder to lift a finger to *her* children. The nieces *only saw* her soft side. She was older & kinder then than when we were young.

Don't give old Biog thought now[.] You have all the thinking to do

125 'Martyn' is the pseudonym for William 'Mayo' Paddon, the son of Reverend Canon William Francis Locke Paddon (see Tippett 32–4). He proposed to Carr several times, but was turned down and subsequently married another woman (see 'Martyn,' *GP* 188–95).

126 The 'Elder' is Elizabeth Carr, one of Carr's older sisters.

127 Una Boultbee (Mrs Frank W.) was the daughter of Clara, Carr's eldest sister and the only sibling who married.

your head has room for. It makes me happy to give it into your keeping as done. I'm such a muddle-bag & loser.

God bless you and rest you, and give you peaceful quiet in your heart. No matter what may stir itself into 1942. Small says 'Give over Emily! I want my guardian's eye,' so – love from Emily

Beloved Guardian Ira
Here's a hug for Xmas and please 'Tossed' is my Xmas present to you. See me in it as you see Emily in Juice[.] I'll sing spring songs to you out of 'Tossed[.]'[128] Others may not hear them – you will & you'll try to shut me in the 'Book of Small' too but don't expect me to *stay* put in a frame or between the covers. I'm too kicky for that[.] Fold your arms across your front hard [–] Maybe then I'll keep still and stay put a few moments.

Always your loving
Small

Vancouver, B.C. Boxing Day, 1941

Dear Emily:
It is difficult if not completely impossible for me to tell you what your Christmas letter meant to me when it arrived yesterday. It was such a ray of beauty and comfort in the midst of the mad, swirling rush. You are so right about Christmas. Bewildered as we are and bedeviled by false standards we have allowed so much of the true character of the festival to be sacrificed and we have so often substituted mean, commercial, stupid show and noise for them that it is sometimes hard to keep the faith. But there are still faithful souls and loyal true hearts like yours and in these the world must find its true hope. We thought of you very often yesterday and spoke of you too – particularly when we gathered around our two pianos and sang the old carols – 'O Little Town of Bethlehem,' 'Away in a Manger,' 'It came upon the Midnight Clear,' 'While Shepherds Watched,' and then for you specially 'Breathe on me, Breath of God.' It was a beautiful evening in which my mother was supremely

128 Dilworth had paid the commission on *Tossed* earlier, but had not paid for the canvas itself. See Dilworth's letter of December 1941.

happy. After all what a great thing it is that Christmas comes with its memory of simple, deep things to turn our thoughts away from the trivialities of our fragmentary individual existence. You remember those lines of T.S. Eliot –

> 'We thank Thee for our little light that is dappled with shadow –
> And we thank Thee that darkness reminds us of Light.'[129]

And your generosity and Small's! How shall I speak of that. You have been far too generous already. I tell you once again that it is I who have always been in your debt – just knowing you would have been a great experience, but to be allowed to have some part in your work and to be taken into your confidence – that has been an experience of incalculable preciousness to me. I could never repay you both for that.

Your gift of the Biog., Emily, humbles me. I know how precious it is to you and how much it has meant to write it. I know too how fine it is and have a faint idea of what the revelation of yourself will mean to Canadian artists in the future. It thus becomes a sacred thing. I accept it with deep humility. I shall try to be worthy of the confidence and trust. It is so good of you, Emily. You must not weary yourself in the work of completing the Biog. Do not hurry it: let it come as it will.

Small's love and good wishes I accept with a free heart but, Emily, I must carry through my contract about the picture and send the money for it. You understand that I am not trying to pay for it – that I could never do, but I would feel guilty all my life if I felt I had fallen down in my part of that contract and it was a contract so awkwardly made too. 'Singing Spring Songs' – that's exactly what 'Tossed' has been doing (or Small in her) ever since I laid eyes on her. Last night 'Tossed' and 'Juice of Life' were lit only by tall tapers. The soft glow showed both to me in a new light. Mr. Gage remembered it in the case of 'Juice.' They are precious possessions the rich meaning of which no one will ever take away – not all the Mrs. Fells in the world – not Bess – not even Lawren. I feel they are mine in the truest sense.

'Klee Wyck' – what a run of prosperity she had! The stores here tell me they could have sold another hundred copies if they had been able to get them. Did you get a copy of her from the Oxford Press – very magnificent, all done up in a grand leather cover. I know this dress is a

129 Dilworth is referring to *The Rock* (1934) by T.S. Eliot (1888–1965).

costly one – but I much prefer her in her ordinary rich-coloured house dress, don't you? This new gown is the sort of starchy outfit people force themselves into for church, weddings, funerals and other often uncomfortable experiences. However you and I have seen her in a great variety of dresses – in fact in no dress atall and then we saw a beauty in her heart that no dress will ever be able to destroy. It was, of course, most thoughtful and generous of the Press to send this to me and I shall thank them for that. They must have done very well. I am sure nearly the whole of this first printing must be sold by now.

Lady Jane – Mother was thrilled with the picture – it is very good of you both. My niece Edna is coming over to us on Sunday or Monday. Would that be a good chance to send Jane[?] Mother is much better and the rush of Christmas is past. We are longing for Jane. So, if she is well & you wish to part with her, it can be arranged. I shall write to my sister by this same mail.

And now, dear Emily, goodnight and may God bless you and keep you strong. Your heart and hand have done great things for Canada: they have felt deeply into the life of things and have created sanctuaries for bewildered men and women to rest in. What greater achievement could anyone hope for?

With much love to you & Small –
Yours affectionately
Ira

Con. I. Talk about improving your handwriting in 1942. How about my awful scrawl? I am afraid it is incorrigible. I can read yours perfectly, so it doesn't need to change as far as I am concerned. D.

---

218 St. Andrews, Sunday morning after Xmas [28 December 1941]

Dear Ira
I was glad of your letter (special) yesterday morn. (This week we have got our *morning* mail around 4 P.M.) I don't know what Victoria (our post) is thinking of to tolerate a *morning* mail here before 2 at earliest when specialed. I seem to be the only one who *has* sent in protests (written & verbal) with the *unusual* business the P.O. is doing these days (& there is no *cheaping* of letter post) [.] They could surely put on *more men.* Oh After-Xmas! Oh after- [indecipherable]! Oh world! Oh war! Oh.

Diddle-dum-damn! (The Elder *raved* if I said *damn* in my youth.) But if [I] put *diddle-dum* in front of damn it went down smooth. Why? Ask the peculiar religious code of the house of Carr. But your letter – it *was nice.* I am so glad you had a lovely family time. Your house must have burst with music when you all got busy[:] two pianos, all your voices[,] Spring songs in Small's squeak, wait 'til Jane's soprano joins! How happy your mother must have been and how proud! That is something to be really proud of[,] children that you've made, real flesh & blood children! Made & spanked in pain. Oh dear man[.] I'm *not* nice and not good like you but I am in your letter – I am just old me as full of faults as a plum pudding is full of plums. Thank you for singing my 'work hymn' among the carols[.] It touched me deep and the kind wire too.

I stayed in bed all day after Xmas & most of yesterday – heart pains – I let the girl have a good deal of time off & did too much & poor old Alice has been *difficult* – her eye pain & I think she is worried that Dr. Ellington has closed his office [and] goes into [the] army. He told her some weeks back. There *might* be something he could do – an operation – a risk but a possibility & I think she was building. I wish he had said nothing. He told me she had cataract[s] as well as disease at the back of the eye. He said 'when I come back from the war – just a possibility – worth trying' – I suppose he meant her sight would be gone anyway – (this is strictly confidential. She has told no one but me & her 'Hennells.'). She is so terribly touchy – flies off the handle at *everything.* Yesterday I tried getting a cab and taking her out for an hour to see if I could brighten her. It was a lovely bright day but cold. To avoid bright sunlight we went to the Japanese gardens and oh it was so sad! She could not see the full sadness. I have been there in winter before when it was closed, but they gave me tea & it was filled with quiet winter peace. But this was desolation – sadness[,] everything barred. The broken fence gaped so we went in [–] all tables & benches & paraphernalia heaped in the poor old rotting tea houses[.] All the pot plants & birds & goldfish gone. Maybe it was *only shut* but there was a forlorn finality about it all that stank [of] war & bitterness. We went down into the middle of the garden and stood a minute there. Us two old wrecks, tottering & peering[,] went back to the cab & drove through Admirals Road house. The air was *nice*[.] Thick white frost was in the shadow parts of the woods – the dear woods were as marvelous as ever[.] Such vivid patches of unrivaled green moss that couldn't have throbbed one bit more green into its greenness (that's my own way of describing color *to myself.* I have always recorded it by '*throbs.*' I never heard any other artist describe it that way. But that's the way I *feel* it & I think you will understand, so I share my notion with you) but all underneath the somber tree shadows except for the brilliant moss were drabs & greys & browns mingled and lovely and promising, promising, no matter what *we did they'd* go on *doing*[.] No matter how we thwarted & destroyed[,] they'd go on growing and replenishing. Oh Ira[,] the most marvelous of all is *growth*[,] the unquenchable *spirit* of life and its bursting, tearing strength. Haven't you seen a tree root split a rock and you just looked *dumbfounded*[?]

Thank you for being glad about the Biog. being yours – What shall you call her? I called her first edition 'Growing Pains.' Ruth did not like it but could suggest no better[.] Maybe you will think of one[.] You understand[,] I know[,] that I would not want her published 'til '*Emily' is dead*[.] One would feel foolish and it would hamper one from writing so freely. Is it [a] compliment or otherwise to you that I don't mind your eye? It is that I think you understand. I am about through with the sordid side of my first glimpse of London now. Now comes England's country & perhaps *more developed Art sense.* English country is not so easy to me as my strong native wild land to write about. Very lovely in its tameness though. When you find time tell me, generally speaking[,] how she goes so far? I won't work *too* hard but I feel I *should* be getting on with her. The last phase will be most difficult & is the worst remembered, partly because it is *too new*[,] partly because my brain is old. Is it necessary to include my writing? Is the Biog *me* entire or just the story of my *painting*? Choose which you want.

Yes I got one of those *elegant* Klee Wycks. It is very good of Mr. Clarke but I feel a formal sedateness in that dress that is not Klee Wyck & excludes Small. I hope all his gift copies were not dressed so. What fools our booksellers are! Couldn't they see that Klee Wyck was selling (she sold early for sending out as Xmas presents[).] Why didn't the asses order more[?] I spose they scared-catted their orders to *half* a dozen. I think their usual limit is 2 volumes[.] Perhaps they got a few extra *jackets* to make a *display*[.]

There was a foolish write-up my maid cut out of the Times & brought this A.M. written by 'Rebe Edmonds.'[130] Very-would-be-Small. – I don't know where she got the tommy-rot she wrote. There was enough truth in it that she scraped up from my past & a good deal of lies she made up & a revolting picture of me. Gee whiz! My face newspapers frightfully. I

130 The article by Edmonds is titled 'Wanted ... More Emily Carr Stories.'

think this is one of that old sneak Knight's photographs.[131] Well I have only one eye in it & am as coarse as a fish-wife. If there was danger of my getting puffed up at all [from] the nice reviews[,] the newspaper pictures have completely stabbed the puff & let out the wind. But I don't mind – they *love* Klee Wyck. Rebe's thing is headed '*Wanted: More Emily Carr Stories*' & clamors for stories of my childhood & the animals. (Rebe was in Mrs. Shaw's literary class.[132] I attended *thousands* of years ago[.] She came several times to my studio and read a few of my early stories.) It is perhaps from these she draws her foolish descriptions. And I must tell you of another letter that pleased me and a card also that came from the 'Little Singing Ladies'[:] New York postmark, no letter, just [a] greeting card[.] Did you get one? The letter was from a missionary[.][133] She had read Klee Wyck[,] loved her & cried over her[.] She said there was one thing she felt like writing to the man in the East that he had *got wrong*[.] Miss Carr did *not hate* missionaries[.] She herself was one and had received many kindnesses & friendship from Miss Carr! I had rather dreaded when I got the letter to open it. Dreadfully dull old *ex-missionary* who frequented our house in her younger days.

And now Jane. – I don't [know] what to say[.] I must be very plain spoken. (I have not heard from your sister yet[.]) Jane appears in very *good health* and spirits! Oh! Lor!! Spirits!!!! But she has not entirely got over recurrences of looseness of bowels ever since she was ill[.] I have rung up the vet & kept her pretty well on butter milk & [a] very careful diet. Hoping to get her quite normal before shipping and the change of food etc. Some days she is about all right[,] some days not. She evidently got that beastly infection when at the kennel for spaying. He suggested I send her in but goodness knows what else she might get if I did. I think it just patient care & feeding. So maybe we'd better leave her a little? With your mother not well – you don't want to vex Ethel with extra. If you have a pen fixed in basement where Miss Jane can be safe from mis-

131 Harry Upperton Knight (1873–1973) specialized in portrait photography between 1918 and 1965. His photographs of Carr have been preserved in the City of Victoria Archives in the Harry Upperton Knight Fonds.

132 In the summer session of the Provincial Normal School in 1934, Carr attended writing classes that were conducted by Mrs N. deB. Shaw. Many of her stories she produced for the class were later used for *Klee Wyck*; at the time, she also wrote 'The Hully-up Paper,' which won first prize in the class (see Hembroff-Schleicher 1969, 278).

133 Letter from Ellen Millar to Emily Carr, 22 December 1942 (BCARS, Parnall Collection, MS 2763, box 4, file 25).

chief and where she could be free to do what she can't help[,] poor tyke[,] without dirtying the house[,] all right. This trouble has upset her manners shockingly. I hope it will soon pass. If I remember right[,] their fifth month was a bit hard on puppies. They cut some important *teeth* about that age & like half-grown children go scrawny & troublesome (not that she is scrawny in spite of low diet) – she has had a stye on her eye too. So perhaps you'd better do with cardboard Jane, cleanliness & no devilment for a wee bit longer??

Small's salute, Emily's love, Jane's bounce.
Emily

C.o.d. Did you deliver Dr. Trapp's letter?
C.o.d.d. Mrs. Brown sent me a lovely letter & a picture of Eric Brown.[134] It was addressed to me & intended to be sent nearly two years ago & got lost in a drawer. She was very pleased at your mention of Eric in your article in connection with my work. I think she & Milton Blackstone are the only ones in the East who have written about Klee Wyck[.] I rather expected to have heard from some of the artists – Lismer[,] Jackson, etc. They resent me a little – I'm a woman.
P.S. What a letter. Our writing books used to say 'Brevity is the soul of wit.'[135] I'm unwitting methinks. E.

[ca. 29 December 1941–1 January 1942]
9:30 Sunday night

Thank you, Ira, goodnight.

Your voice was *so sad* tonight[.] Why? Were you? Sad? I like the two poems (you did not give names or by whom)[,] the two just before 'the bells'[136] and the psalm to end up with. Sanctuary is *nice*[.] I look forward all week to it.

NEW YEAR'S DAY!!!! Happy New Year Ira dear – Happy in yourself

134 Mrs Brown was the wife of Eric Brown (1877–1939), who became the director of the National Gallery in 1912. He retained that position until his death, after which H.O. McCurry held the position.

135 A reference to William Shakespeare's *Hamlet* (2.2.90).

136 Possibly a reference to 'The Bells' by Edgar Allan Poe.

& in doing your best duty and serving no matter what the hullabaloo going on. God bless you. And last night came a *beautiful thing*[.] My eyes have feasted on her with my breakfast and the card said 'To Emily with love from "Macaroni"[137] and my "unc."' Thank you both for the love & the flower[.] It is *beautiful* & I love *it* & the *pair* of you. Oh it seems to me *flowers* were the exquisite first of all God's creation[,] a last bit of his own self thrown in for good measure. After the people[,] the beasts & the birds[,] then this silent, radiant harmless loveliness without flaw or naughtiness like the rest of us.

I put my light out at 5 to 12 & lay down to think a little into the New Year & I hardly know if I was here or there when 1941 came. It is always such a queer sliding feeling [–] something & everything passing with everything close & something more.

I doubt you've finished Sunday's 'whopper' (letter) yet & I'm not going to tax you with another[,] only there [is] a thing or two I *have* to say after I've hoped you are enjoying your visitors. I thought it so nice of Edna to think of me on a card and your sister ran in on Xmas with a piece of her cake[.] I loved her for the thought for me. What a nice family you have got. Alice and I drank port wine (she had a gift bottle) around 9 o'clock last night & toasted each other & the King, Queen, Churchill. 'Who else?' said Alice & I said 'Ira,' and 'his mother.' Said Alice '*And* Jane.' Then we both giggled because the creature had been the devil all day. Even Alice had approved of the spank stick[.] As a rule she only laughs at Jane's escapades and I heard my girl coddling Matilda into bed with 'You're worth 20 of *her* (sniff!)[.]' Poor little Jane[.] But we all forgive her the moment we've cleaned up and mended her rips & damages. I never knew so mischievous a person nor one so quick.

Ist *Now.* In a note from Mr. Clarke he said he *expected* (as far as he could foresee) to be out in *Early* January[.] Well, we know his foretold dates! He hurried to explain the check arriving on my birthday was chance *only*[.] Heavens he did not think I'd thought it a *birthday present*[,] did he!!! IInd What about the 'Book of Small'? There was still a lump at the end of little town[138] you wanted some reworking on[,] you thought [it] perhaps a bit too elaborated on[.] Would you like me to work over any of it by myself? Would I have the wit to cut out the *right* cuts? I am not *quite* sure what – but going over it again it might

137 A nickname for Phylis Dilworth.
138 'A Little Town and a Little Girl' is the second part to *The Book of Small*.

dawn on me & I know how crammed with work you *are*[.] *It might save you time.* I'm rather *scared* about 'Small[,]' d'you know[?] Scared in several ways. 1st all together it's an awful swallow of "*me*" in one lump[.] A story read at a time was different – (by the way[,] you & I are supposed to be 'airing' today aren't we? I *think* at 1.30) 2nd place How will people take Small after the delicious Indian people & the great wild[?] Land[,] won't she seem tame & footling? 3rd she is not quite so impersonal as the other & one feel[s] a little like having said things & bitten one's tongue after. Of course she is *not as bad* as the Biog[.] One would want to crawl into a hole if people mucked your face with *that* (while you still had a face) but to make the thing *honest* it is necessary to turn yourself inside out[,] isn't it? IIIrd About those 5 remaining pictures – they should be *chosen* & *got out of the studio*[.] If I died they'd simply drift automatically into the general 'stuff-left-behind' – I would like you to have chosen them[,] so would Lawren. *But I can do it myself* if you want? – I do not want to overload my trustors with work & worr[ies] over my leaving.

The New Year is *here*[.] I'm rested [and] have spent vast epochs in bed since [the] party. Written up my letters[.] Been working on 'cedars'[139] and getting things as clean as I can for a *fresh start*[,] painting & writing that is *awaiting the doing.* 'Klee Wyck's' page is turned. *Don't* let me *sit gloating*[.] Let me – *make me* – push on, forgetting behind and looking forward. The stretch ahead can't be *so great* a distance. *Be sure* to tell me, my Trustor, when I should stop[.] Watch for stupidity or weakness.

I read my poems a lot. Alice gave me a new 'Anthology of Modern Poetry'[140] on [my] Birthday & I have your galaxy of 'shorter poems' and best of all – my 'sanctuary poems[,]' the choicest of all. I never *tire* of them – they *hit* me hardest, so many of the poets twaddled about *surfacy* love – personal attributes, eyes hair & teeth etc & slur over the roots of the matter – the eternals[.] Whitman goes for them (brutally sometimes) but he gets them[,] doesn't he?

Wire just 'phoned through. 'Broadcast at 1 PM.' Thank you. We'll be

139 In 1942, Carr completed the canvas *Cedar*, which is now in the possession of the Vancouver Art Gallery.

140 Possibly *A New Anthology of Modern Verse, 1920–1940* (chosen and with an introduction by C. Day-Lewis and L.A.G. Strong), which was first published by Methuen in 1941 and reprinted in 1944.

listening – Bless you. You are a *big* man Ira and a good one. Bless you again and

my love,
Emily

C.o.d. The other day being most weary and *ratty*[,] that poised pondering pen of yours over these M.S. sheet[s] got [to] old Emily & she turned you to the wall (it was an old hang over from Small's youthful tricks. So many parson's pictures, missionaries & that smug old Aunt glowered from our home walls. Small was always being reprimanded for turning their face[s] in.) Well Small hadn't been hanging round too much while Emily was tired & cross but back she came bouncy lickety-split, faced you out & smacked old Emily (you surely felt a disturbance under your waistcoat?)[.] She's again in residence, your face is out-turned. Lady Jane is seraphic, Emily & all the 'community' over your chest thriving[.] Love Emily

Letters: 1942

Sunday [4 January 1942]

Dear Ira
I thought you would maybe be *here yesterday* – I thought so *harder* when the morning brought *no* letter for Sunday tho' I *did* have a precious little note with your mother's pillow on Saturday (only no *answering* letter for *epochs* of time. Why *me* write?) when those two lovely children brought it. Young girls *are* nice.

Thank you again for the cyclamen[.] It is *lovely*[.] Your mother's pillow touches me[.] All those stitches for *me*! It has been behind my very sore back ever since but today I shall write to her myself.

That Jane! After lying peaceful as a lily on my bosom for one hour she sneaks away and *demolishes my favourite dictionary.* The girls draped their stockings over with my picture dusters while they were here! & yet, she *can* be like a dream of love. Have had two days in bed with a *fierce* back-regular squaller!

Alice says 'Sanctuary' was proclaimed on CBC *yesterday* as to be *read by some strange person*[.] She forgot the name. Now why? Are you lazy, or absent, or is it a mistake??? Well if I don't like *he, she,* or *it* whatever – he'll go into the scrap-basket with the 'Choir' unless *maybe* he *beats you* – & then I'll hate him *worse* still[.] *No* I *won't* have him out-do you[,] he shant, & he *can't,* so there!

The day is perfect – singing sunshine. You'd never guess the world was evil. Oh Ira[,] she *isn't* but she must look pretty drab out there on the battlefields. And your New Year's note! I'm *so glad* you felt that way (love's ecstasy is stronger than war & upheavals)[.] Love & *friendship* – big, big things. Yours has meant so much – to Small & me[,] so *very* much. And I am glad we've meant something to you. Everyone is tremendously alone in this world when it comes right down to the core & there are so *few* cores that match – I often marvel *how* everybody comes to be so different when they see & hear, smell & eat the same things? Husbands & wives' lives perhaps are samish because – after all – I spose nature providing *them* with the common problem of making a next generation and they have that in common if nothing else. Life's terrific, isn't it? But husbands & wives seem to get *very* tired of each other sometimes even the ones that stick. Those widows & widowers who have to *try* to *remember* to be *sorry* when you can just feel the relief of their freedom. Mind you[,] marriage is *grand* if it's [the] right kind but apparently it's tricky & often disappointing. – Mrs. Radcliffe would say 'Dear one, Klee Wyck!' I think I'd better stop. Don't let me put you off the walnut tree etc. But *she must be beyond ordinarily nice*[.] Then I'll be *glad* for you.

Lawren says Mrs. Fell *likes* the canvas but can't decide *which* & he is going to ship the 'reject' with two of Besses to the Group Painters[1] show in Toronto[,] for which I am thankful to be saved the plague. Janette Cann[2] has not rung up to wish me New Years! Alice told her I had lumbago – she's probably right. Moving *is* rather awful[.] Anyhow *much* too awful to entertain old 'Em-Carr' – goodbye[.] A enormous hug from Small & a chaste salute from me. We both love you to bits.

Emily

C.O.D. If you've gone back on Sanctuary, I'll disinherit you! Maybe – we shall see –
C.O.D.D. I *think* 'Cedars' is coming at last!
C.O.D.D.D. Hello Guardian – Small!
C.O.D.D.D.D. My word[.] My first letter in 1942 does not look to me much improved in writing – sorry.

1 The Canadian Group of Painters formed in 1933 to carry on the legacy of Canadian painting that the Group of Seven initiated. Carr, a founding member of the Canadian Group, is referring to their exhibition that was held in Toronto from 6 February to 1 March 1942.

2 Jeanette Cann (1880–1956) taught English between 1921 and 1938 at Victoria College and was 'known for her extensive collection of colour reproductions and lantern slides of famous art works' (see Walker, 131n1).

9:30 Sunday Night [same letter]

Thank you Ira and goodnight

It *was you* and such a *nice* you *particularly so* Alice must have got mixed. She stayed late tonight & puttered round[,] turning off the water for frost. It was 9:15 before she left & suddenly I remembered & turned the dial. Who would it be? & it *was* my trustor & I was *glad.* I got the last 3 and all were *delightful*[.] 'Sweet as Eden' I have in *my* sanctuary & the 'Woodland Peace'[3] that came next & the little end one. Where do you find these *delicious* bits? All the places I love to explore and have mostly been to. Oh I'm so glad God gave me to love these things and gave to you the love of them too. Could *anything* else make up for what they gave us in life & have from our babyhood up given to us? How they have washed that grime out of things for us. I think the one really deep sorrow of my old age is that I cannot memorize any more. The poems in Sanctuary fill me with delight. They are vivid like a flash & then they are – not gone *exactly* but they've slipped their leash (the words sometimes even the theme). They have left delight behind but you know how one loves to *release* joy, go over & over it picking the words & thought over & over like the long good sucks of a candy – if you swallow it holus bolus it may satisfy your stomach but you want to keep the *flavor* of the very stuff it was made of on your tongue – appetite-satisfaction is not *enough*[.] *But watch me*[,] Trustor dear[.] If it comes that I babble on *but* get confused in my writing[,] *stop me*[.] Sometimes I'm afraid but I trust you[.]

I read a lot of Whitman today[:] 'Rolling Earth Song,' 'Out of the Cradle Endlessly Rocking,' 'Song of Universal,' 'Learned Astronomer'[4] & others[.] How he takes life in both hands[,] how every bit of him responds to the whole creation as if he'd been a great instrument and the universe making music with him[.]

I've written to you today. This is *not* a letter[,] it's thinking[.] Alice has me read Klee Wyck over & over to her[.] Seems to be the only thing she wants read to her and yet[,] Ira, I think she is *only* interested in the *story* side. She is a little scandalized & keeps saying '*I should not liked* to have done that or been there!' 3 nieces & 2 great-nieces have *mentioned* Klee

3 'Sweet as Eden is the air' is the first line of 'Woodland Peace,' a poem written by the English poet George Meredith (1828–1909).

4 'A Song of the Rolling Earth' appears in the poetry sequence 'Calamus' of Whitman's *Leaves of Grass*; 'Song of the Universal' appears in 'Birds of Passage'; 'When I Heard the Learn'd Astronomer' appears in 'By the Roadside.'

Wyck just in [the] same way. Nothing beyond lukewarm story past interest & hopes that she (K.W.) will bring in some *money*. Oh my *dear big trustor*[,] I am so glad & at peace that 'Small' & all my M.S. are yours[.] It would have hurt to leave my children in un[-]understanding hands. I'd rather have burned them than that. I don't *think* I ever minded the pictures *quite* so much. I *know* I did not mind the ridicule, like I would [mind] ridicule of [my] writing[,] but your *worded* thoughts are *so naked* – must be, to be honest[.] People pry into worded thoughts deeper than they do into painted ones[.] They have more in common with the medium. But oh it *isn't words* or *paint* it's *spirit*[.] *You understan*[*d*], bless you for understanding[.] *You* don't need *words* or *paint*[.] You take it from the things themselves[.] You understand the meanings[.] This old woman *loves you so* for it & Small never had a real flesh & blood guardian to love before & it isn't even the comfort of that *altogether*[,] it's spirit chumship[.] And yet Ira[,] don't you feel that the deeper down you burrow into *earth* things, the more of spirit you find?

I have not mentioned our New Year's reading[.] Thank you for the wire. Alice & I listened and we both thought you were *exceptional[ly] fine.* Your voice was strong & happy. I felt you put a great deal into them on New Year's day. You love canoe[5] – so do I. I shall never forget that particular night you read her & she was so vivid[,] she took me right back.

I'm trying an experiment *and* I have to *sing my work hymn*[6] *hard* for it – that's not true[,] one sings soft but *deep* – I am trying to write and paint the cedar sanctuary together. I would not tell another soul about it (not at this stage) – while you are feeling your way it is best *not* to talk of these things but *you* understand somewhat of my struggles & it's comforting to share. Don't expect much. Both M.S. & canvas may be dead failures but that failure may help one to see & *don't even to Lawren* mention it. Some things are too young to be spoken of. I shall miss Lawren's visits & he says he'll miss them too. I've loved them but there's always that old stick-in-a mud Theosophy[.][7] We only talk *art* not *life* like you & I do. I *love both my trustors very deeply*. Even if the Japs bust up everything & there was

5 'Canoe' is the last story to appear in *Klee Wyck* (84–6).

6 'Breathe on Me, Breath of God' (see Carr's letter, 28 December 1941).

7 Theosophy is a philosophical movement that relies heavily upon Eastern mysticism and that gained popularity in the early twentieth century, especially after the devastations of the First World War, when conventional Western religious thought was seen to have failed. Theosophy was seen as a viable alternative to and replacement for more traditional North American forms of religious thinking and became an influential and pervasive way of thinking among artists such as Lawren Harris.

nothing left 'to trust' & no Canada to trust it for[,] I'd thanks give unto death that I'd known you two men.

And now blessings and goodnight
Emily

C.O.D. What can I do! If I *don't* post Sunday[,] you don't get your 'blue Monday' and if I do[,] then it's before time to say my 'goodnight thank you[.]' If I do both[,] then it's too much. Life's difficult. S.

---

6 P.M. Thursday [8 January 1942]

Dear Ira
No *sight* of you no *sound* of you – I expect you are 'planing' home now. I waited for your call all day: But I understand – war, war, at the bottom of everything[,] d--m war. Dear Ira[,] thank you for your letters[.] They are so comforting, so true & stable[,] sticking up out of the mud of things. Oh the poems! I do love them[.] I *am* getting *so* much out of them and *will* get. It's the maid's day off[, so] I can read them aloud. I often read aloud Sanctuary at night when I'm shut up for the night – when Alice has gone home. It helps flavoring them to put the voice into the meaning as *well* and *seeing* the words[,] doesn't it? How *everything* helps *everything*[,] doesn't it[?] And *sometimes* this war *must* be helping the whole scheme of things[.] We can only see such snips & threads of things[.] Oh let's *try* to have *faith* but isn't it hard? *Big strong dear man* with such a load on you[.] God grant you calm underneath. I know your way just now *is* hard and the responsibility that has thrust itself upon you seems overwhelming sometimes: thank God for you *honest* men. I pray for the C.B.C. Every man & woman of it. Every sound it voices. Lassoing good & lassoing bad out of the air & you trying & trying to keep 'straight talk' and honesty before people[.] You are a *front* man now. I am *so* sorry you've been feeling poorly[.] We've had these colds that are not *quite* colds too – 'sniffalatums hitched to grunts' & the weather is *rotten. Don't* do *foolish* things and take what *rest* you can[.] I think about you a lot.

I've been ill – 6 days in bed (altogether) & I am still there a whole *bed full of pain* and a chair full of agitated Alice (meaning to be kind but she nearly drives me to drink when I'm sick)[.] She gets offended at everything & just *won't* let you *enjoy a good old misery to yourself.* Poor soul. Can't see there are times you know when all one wants is to turn your face to the wall. Even Small the merry knows that & leaves you alone. After 5 days of severe pain I sent for the Doctor[.] They are so busy these days, one hates to. He couldn't give the ailment a name but thinks it is muscular. It is mostly my back. He gave me 8 aspirins per day[,] sleeping draughts & some pain dope[,] for it is got quite quite out of hand but it's better[.] I had thought it was flu or lumbago but he said it was neither. I am to remain in bed for a bit. I don't care *if I can write.* First the pain was *too* bad & after that I was too dopey. But tonight I'm *really* better[.]

My little girl is very good, and *Alice likes her* which means a lot[.] Alice lets her do little 'helps' she has let no other girl do & is not so jealous as she usually is[.] It is getting increasingly difficult not to offend her. I wish I was nicer[,] Ira. The only way I can check myself from going nasty is by *seeming* 'off hand' because you *daren't* sympathize & you *daren't* ignore. I know her eyes have hurt a lot[.] She's so secretive[.] Sometimes I think we were *reared* stupidly on *hypocrisy* pride sensitiveness or something[,] I don't know what[.] I know how my sister always seemed so terribly *self*-conscious and self-righteous (perhaps I am too. I don't know) but I *do* know it has annoyed me in them[,] this self-consciousness. Oh well they've all always made me so blatantly aware how they all disapproved of me[,] every bit. A girl from the Old San Francisco days came to stay with me once[.] When we went to bed at night she used to roar & say 'Millie how can you, Millie you ought to be ashamed of yourself.['] She said it went on all day long[.] Alice was too indolent to care then. It was the other two. After they died she took up the tune for the three. Her tune was always not 'how can you,' but 'we (meaning the rest of them) always did this or that or never did that' – they bunched their religion & their manners & ways & clothes. I was always the *outcast* oddity and they were so *almighty superior*[.] Why *did* I do so & so? (This is *mad* little Small. Forgive her[,] just sometimes Small stamps & rants at the memory of all the smugness[.]) Don't hate your child[.] You know & Lawren knows that the woods & the beasts were Small's *real people*[,] Small's own folks – Oh Ira[,] *'God's Grandness'! What a jewel of a poem –*

'Because the Holy Ghost over the bent
  World broods with warm beast and with ah!
    Bright wings.'[8]

8 Carr mistakenly refers to the poem as 'God's Grandness'; the lines are from 'God's Grandeur' by Gerard Manley Hopkins (1844–89).

I glory in all four poems. I *wish* I could *memorize* them. Thank you so for sending them [to] me so I can read them over & over.

It is lovely of you to like Biog. What you have said heartens me to its finish. Don't bother with it now while you are so busy. As it is done[,] you shall have bits to relax you from more serious matters and perhaps *when the war's done*[,] we can go over it together (I think I'd rather clean M.S. with you than do anything else in the world) [.] Some strange thing seems to tie our hearts together then. I don't know what the cord is made of (its gossamer ties us to poetry too) only mine is snatching of twinkles of poetry. Yours is calm deep taking of wholes and laying them away in your soul. I love your soul[.] It is beautiful. Bless you. May your difficulties all be smoothed out. If I did not see or hear you today[,] I *knew* you were applying yourself to Canada's *big hard* jobs even in the middle of these silly noodles of men[.] Our land seems to abound in these timid nincompoops.

Those words in 'The Valley of Elwy' Ira[9]

'All the air things "wear" that build this world of Wales
Only the [intimate] does not correspond'

Doesn't that seem to apply to Canada? Don't you love 'In God's Grander'[?][10] ('And all is seared with trade bleared, smeared with toil; / And wears man's smudge & shares man's smell.')

I had a note from Viola and Victoria[,] just a few words for [a] New Year greet.[11] The address was (Henry Hudson Hotel West 37th St New York) & they ask about the new book[.] So many are asking about it & Klee Wyck. Christmas presents are bringing in their readers' comments now, every mail. It is strange to me that *no* adverse comments ever come! I thought there was *always some?* Wait 'til Klee Wyck gets your 'book of Small' to knock up against[.] Probably there will be some bickering between the two [of] them[.] Well she'll be on *your* head[.] She's yours[.] *It'll say so on the fly paper.* But the Biog. will be the *most yoursish* of all. If *ever she come comes to print* you'll have to fight *her* battle alone. No me to share the blame or the jokes.

9 These lines are from Hopkins's 'In the Valley of the Elwy.'

10 The lines, from Hopkins's 'God's Grandeur,' are as follows: 'And all is seared with trade; bleared, smeared with toil; / And wears man's smudge and shares man's smell: / the soil.'

11 Viola Morris and Victoria Anderson. See note 33, page 45.

Throw your cares out the window & *sleep* like a baby – goodnight.

Emily

C.O.D. Only Xmas flowers make my room so cheery. I had my bed turned round before so I could lie & watch the snow[.] It was *superlative* on the cedars ('world world' etc.)[12] but the snow is *too* cold to '*hold close*'!
C.O.D.D: Either you fib or you are a wizard. *I* can't read my *own writing[,] how can you?*
C.O.D.D.D. Writing this tonight so I can Biog. tomorrow morning.

Vancouver B.C. [ca. 10 January 1942]

Dear Emily:
I lived with you and the Bobtails all day Sunday. During the day I re-read the sketches and made some alterations in the text – mostly only unimportant things like punctuations & spellings. Occasionally I made suggestions of a more important kind such as the rearrangement of phrases or sentences. I asked my girl to make copies of the sketches with these changes in them. She has not quite finished: I shall send you the others as soon as they are done. These copies are merely working ones done on cheap paper. They may help you to agree or disagree with my pedantic opinions and when you are doing any further work on the sketches, as you said you would, they may be useful. They are doubtless full of typing errors – I note that my secretary has typed 'birches' for 'bitches.' Poor dear! She perhaps had so strict a Victorian bringing-up that she blushed as she did it.

I am returning the original yellow sheets with the copies. These will give you a basis for comparison and for measurement of *my meddling* (do keep them. I should like to have them if I may) To these I have attached a small statement of my reaction to each sketch. I have set down some further suggestions for you to consider.

Re-reading these sketches has convinced me even more of their value. Really the dogs became very real for me on Sunday. I actually wanted a Bobbie myself. You have succeeded in making them very attractive. What strength of character they had! How superior to most humans!

12 A reference to Edna St Vincent Millay's poem, 'God's World.'

As far as the 'Small' copies are concerned – like these, they were new working copies. We will use them as such when you come to Vancouver. Don't worry about them now.

I am glad the teeth are going so well – or should I say *coming*?

Your last letter was a delight. Thanks so much for 'Blessing'[13] – I felt a bit of the sacredness of it myself. How do you do it! It all seems so simple and is so strong and vivid.

This is a stupid, workaday sort of letter! I just haven't time to be myself this evening but I wanted to get these copies away & I know you will understand. I hope you will not think I have been presumptuous in my comments & suggestions re: the sketches. Of course not! It is silly to set that down even. I know that if you think they are not useful you will not use them and you know that I will not mind –

Affectionate regards to *you both.*
Yours as ever,
Ira.

NB. I am going to have a week away from the office. Thanks for your concern about my silly self. D.

Saturday night [10 January 1942]

Dear Editor
Before I roam on [and] on and side-track[,] here's a letter from Mr. Clarke received yesterday & here's a letter from Mr. Sandwell received today – for your consideration & I'd like them back please[.] Well, it sure doesn't take much of a letter to please Mr. Clarke if he calls my letters to him *interesting* (my last simply thanked him for my elegant Xmas book) but I was thundered under to think of 'Sir Humphrey Milford publisher'[14] even *thinking* about publishing the 'Book of Small' in England in war time. Also it looks as if there is to be a 2nd edition of K.W. I was written to from [a] University bookshop in Seattle asking where they could procure my book called 'Keewit.' They had been

13 Dilworth appears to be referring to the story 'The Blessing,' which appears in *The Book of Small.*

14 Sir Humphrey Milford was the editor for Oxford University Press in England.

asked for it & could not find it listed. I sent the note on to Mr. Clarke [and] also wrote the man the name of publishers.

Mr. Sandwell's letter speaks for himself[.] Isn't it nice? Aren't people nice about our book? Aren't you proud? A woman wrote from Ocean Talls sending her copy for autographs[.] She said 'Our K.W. book is a treasure particularly with my young boys (14-18)[.] They say you speak their language[.] They understand you[.] We eagerly await your next volume.' Isn't it wonderful[?] I don't think I feel conceited but I *am really* pleased for us both. I told that woman today 'I was glad she liked K.W.[,] that she had been a *happy* book, happy in *being liked*[,] happy in being *written*[,] happy in being *published*.' I did *not tell* that woman the happiest of all was that she introduced Ira & Emily to each other's real selves.

And now your 'dear special' – my Phyllis laid it on my chest with a smile that insinuated 'Here's sweet temper for the weekend.' Ira I think you *must* have my telephone number down *wrong*[.] My phone never rang all day[.] We were right by it all day[.] You know Alice has same address but different no. Did you call her? She might easily be up here or out[,] but not I and I was listening too. It would not have been too late. Alice *thinks* I go to sleep at 8.30 but really when I have seen her 100 times through the day[,] 7.30 to 8.30 is long enough for desultory conversation. She *won't* have radio or reading & I generally *am* yawning. But when she has gone I write or type a bit (she hears no sound) & read my poetries alive and *even*. I am waking from my dope now, been working on Biog today. Am quite O.K. again but had a long rather bad heart pains last night so am being lazy over Sunday. There is no rhyme nor reason to these things[.] There's no reason to worry as long as I can keep them in check with my pills[.] To get beyond that it means hypos and a nuisance. My back went better as suddenly as it came.

Jane loved the snow. She is getting as good as gold staying out in her dove-house pen for hours. Then Phyllis does me up in a sheet 'til I look ready for a barber to operate on & Jane has Jamborie 'til she's tired while stolid Tilly's eyes bulge scorn. How that dog despises Jane! Hip! Hip!!! We'll maybe get some licks at book of 'Small' in this week & I'll unearth all the 'likelies' for your choice of pictures. Mother Fell hasn't felled her choice yet, far as I know. I hope you were able to music at the Harrises tonight[.] You need the relaxation & music is such a joy to you[.] Tell me all about their house. Bess has written me 2 nice letters[,] one enclosing a friend's who she had sent you to – very enthused.

I was amused at dear little 'Major Macaroni[.]' I think all this (drilling) will help our young people[,] don't you? How proud you must be of her Ira. It is a grand *thing* to possess & raise a child[,] almost grander than having actually produced her[.] To accept the responsibility is a greater thing than to do well by something you can't help.

From her warm bed[,] Small went through all that exultation that used to fill her when the world [scaled?] up in [snow] & the dark heavy sky fell, before people trod it, before wind had tossed it & smoke smothered it, while the cedars hold it & the world is all muffled[.] Isn't it glorious! Thank you for letting me see Viola's letter. Those girls are very proud of you. It was a nice letter[.] I'm glad they heard your reading New Year's day. I answered Victoria's letter right away to catch them maybe before another [flight?]. Tomorrow is my dear bed-Sunday[.] I'll finish then – sleepy –

Jan 11. And it *is* tomorrow and Jane's 11th month Birthday[.] 'Merry Birthday Lady Jane!' May the spank-stick have an idle day. You shall have hamburger and a long gallop over my bed. And we'll send your cleanest lick & your biggest bounce to our 'community guardian' & ask him to get a pen ready in the basement so you can come as soon as we have made Mr. Hitler a little more uncomfortable & settled the Japs & have time to enjoy you.

Biog: = I'm visiting in a very grand house in London just now[.] 'Swanky,' not my own environment, and very amazed at everything![15] – London from a quite different angle. – By the way – I got a Xmas card from the Martyn (of almost 50 years ago)[.] It contained a pressed flower no words – he sends me one *every* year. Funny how I ran into him again. I forbade him to write for many years. He married very unhappily. Many years afterwards[,] I was staying in Berkeley Calif. & went over to S.F. to shop[.] Spent all my money & found myself stranded [with] no return fare across the Bay. – I looked up & there on a board was Martyn's name (Big Real estate)[.] I marched in and was told he was engaged [and] could see *no one.* I wrote 'Emily' on a card & sent [it] in – out bounced Martyn[,] eyes popping[.] 'Lend me a dollar please. I'm stuck!' He says I made a mistake not marrying him but I know I did *not.* – He made pots of money – created a whole town, but I'm *glad* I obeyed my heart and am me still. Love seems very cruel sometimes doesn't it? But if there wasn't any the world would be beastly.

Yours
Emily

15 Carr is possibly referring to the story titled 'London Tasted' (*GP* 205–9).

Wednesday – Friday [14–16 January 1942]

Dear Ira
That check *isn't mine.* No law of hereditary[,] no reputable lawyer (even Harry) could prove it belonged to me. The *material* belongs to Mr. Clarke[,] the *voice* belongs to you.[16] You both have *claims,* me *none.* What'll I do? Tell me. I'm sure it's yours or his or both. Don't lie to me *please* ... By the way people are always saying how *beautifully* you *did* the reading on New Year's day. – I knew it – Flora B. said you just gave yourself to it! An old girl neighbour said the same to Alice today & loads of people have said it. That check *is* yours. If you don't claim it I'll start a trust with it to buy you a tombstone!

Jane's a devil! In my bones I feel the Dilworth family *is going to hate me*! I'm humbled into the soil to see such manners come from *my raising*! [Luk?] is a princely gent – I *hope* you succeed better with the Walnut tree etc. & that reminds me. I dreamed last night that I was match-making. I engaged *you* to *Viola.* My two sisters[,] the little singing ladies & you were all in a great galleried building & I *did it.* Don't quite know how but I *arranged the engagement.* First I kissed *Victoria* then Viola (who was hilariously happy) then I ran down the balcony to you sitting quite alone. I kissed your forehead & wished *you* joy. But you never budged. It annoyed me that you did not go & kiss Viola. Seeing I'd engaged you by proclamation to the whole hall (though I think it was empty except for us) you did not appear to appreciate the trouble I had taken to fix things up for you one bit.

I am *quite* robust again & have worked like a black all day. Bless me. Mr. Clarke is as oliver-twistish as you over M.S. I'd have said there is almost as much in 'Little Town' (alone) as in 'K.W.'? I have heaps of things to talk about[.] If you *skip* me *next* time you come to Vic. I'll stalk in on your old meeting & say [to] them right there!! Remember I've proved myself a *public speaker.* So says Miss Small, & it's useless to ask letter questions[.] Your *next mail* answers always miscarry[.]

Next time I'm in town I shall buy one of those conversation books in a foreign language and answer my own askings. – and here I sit and it's 2 days hence that I have reached now. And I wonder if Mr. Clarke is kissing his family goodbye today. And I had a nice letter from Madam Fell

16 Carr is referring to the payment received for having her stories read over the radio.

enclosing a check for $250.00 for Red CEDAR. So there's your W.P. *gone*[.][17] You should have hurried[,] serves you right. You never tell me about *any* of our friends. I was thinking all were dead. Mr. Benjamin Mr. Gage Dr. Trapp[.] 'How Do – Goodbye' (your letters)[.] Maybe it's a limited (modern correspondence course)[:] shall I adopt it??? What a *teasing pig* I am. Don't mean a word of *any* of it. I've been hobnobbing with a *sow* in the Biog: (the sow of Tregenna wood)[.][18] Maybe she's influenced me. Here I wished I [had] been at Lawren's to listen in at the *big* talk. Was clearing our letters last night & came across a bunch of Bess *Housser's* to me[.] Made me feel like a swine[.] She used to *really love* me. In one she says 'that I tramped on her with *both* feet' (she was rather mean about returning a M.S. I had let her & Fred read[.] Put me off & I felt was *insincere* over the affair & over something else as well – that was when I told Lawren I did not trust her sincerity (not knowing they were in love & approaching the mix up). Oh dear[,] old letters often *shame* us. People have written me such *lovely* ones[,] *not* flattery[,] but *genuine* love & I'm such an unworthy beast & your mother hit square when she melted me into a 'spitfire[.]' Give her my love and ask her to start softening her heart towards Jane's iniquities, *right now*, so the poor wicked lamb can climb in. Mrs. Fell mixes Red Cedar with Klee Wyck in her mind. I am sorry if you are sorry she isn't in the trust – Biog: waits – goodbye. Hurry & come over. 'Big-hully-up-quick.' My 'phone is G1458 address 218 St Andrews, location James Bay, Province B.C. I'm me, a muddle up of Emily, Small, Klee Wyck & Mom, but always Your affectionate Emily

---

Sunday night [18 January 1942]

My dear
I have been through this[.][19] You will see I have made my notes in red[.] If they are wrong or unnecessary ignore my notes and cut out any sections you deem prosy & unnecessary to the whole[.] You know how

17 Carr means that, if Dilworth had still wanted the painting, he had lost the opportunity to purchase it.
18 Tregenna Wood was one of Carr's preferred painting locales when she studied in England.
19 Carr is referring to the manuscript of *The Book of Small*.

ignorant I am when it comes to constructions & literary value[.] There are only two rules that I know in writing = see the thing as *clear* as you can and try to *show* it never using *big* hard words where little ones will do. I don't *know enough* to know often good from bad parts[.] The ones you praise I always find are ones where I have let myself *go* 'til the thing has become a greater reality than myself[.] *After* that[,] one tries to tidy the phrases & words[.] Why did I hurry to be born so soon? Why didn't I manage it so that I happened along at a time when Professor Dilworth was teaching high s. in Victoria & had some literature cracked through my skull by a ruler or the back of a book or whatever his method was. Well I didn't[.] It's no good weeping over spilled literature, so I'll be thankful very thankful that I found him in time to guide the tail of my literary struggle. Forgive if my red notes have been presumptuous[,] ignore & cut. One page is missing (no. 8)[.] Should it be gone from your other copy too, don't worry[.] Let me have the *page before* & the *page after* & I could re-write the missing link[.] I know just what it was about. It introduces the Gregories & the customs house[20] & is quite incoherent without that link.

Yesterday I had a card from the Librarian of Congress, Washington D.C. saying they were cataloguing Klee Wyck & saw in my paintings [that] I am signed M. Emily & please give them my full name. Ruth was in and her eyes fell out to think K.W. was to be catalogued in Congress Library. I also had a Clarkian note[.] I won't bother you with it[.] He thanks me for sending him that Seattle bookstore's request & has dealt with it 'pending the completion of arrangements for an American edition of K.W.'??? Then he says 'my main purpose in writing this morning is to convey to you the very deep gratitude of Professor J.F. MacDonald[,][21] one of our outstanding critics in Canada' (probably he means he sent him a Xmas K.W.) ... Mr. Clarke continues after a dissertation on J.F. McDonald[,] 'When he praises Klee Wyck he means what he says. And I value his comments very highly indeed.' 'Am looking forward to seeing you middle of week after next.' His letter is dated Jan 15. Well that's that.

I can post M.S. tonight[.] P[hyllis] will take it to the post office for

20 The Gregorys, who live on the first floor of the Customs House, are described in 'Father's Store,' a story that appears in 'A Little Town and a Little Girl' (*BS* 139–43).

21 Perhaps a reference to J.A. McDonald, a professor in the Department of Romance Studies at the University of British Columbia, who wrote 'Emily Carr: Painter and Writer.'

weighing tomorrow. If my help is of any value do call on me[.] I have not much confidence in my decisions but when I know you are behind me in the final look-over[,] I wax brave & want to be of any help that spares your time. How curiously the mistakes elude you to the fourteenth & fifteenth going over. Cedars I did not get a look at today. I expect I shall tear my hair when I do[.] She has been sitting ripening or fomenting or whatever – I have gone over St. Ives today.[22] Found it *hard* to bring myself back to Little Town. I get so immersed in each as it comes along. The one before goes tame & driveling. I posted your school yesterday[.] I'm glad you have an *old* me watercolor[.][23] Funny[,] soon as I uncrated it[,] I decided it was yours *if* you wanted to have it. Educative subject? Well a half breed's school does not *quite* parallel a University!

Alice has been having great amusement from an old diary [from] 1907. She had had a spell of melancholy after cutting off a finger tip & suffering a lot. I was in Vancouver teaching & decided to take her to Alaska for a trip.[24] I wrote this diary on the way to make her laugh. We called it the 'funny book[.]' I would scratch down some trash with an illustration each night & we'd giggle. I unearthed it and read it to her the other night[.] She sat 'til 10 P.M. chuckling[,] said all the illustrations came back to her[,] said 'Did you show it to Ira?' (I found it along with those sketches I showed you)[.] 'He'd enjoy it[,] you must,' so some time when you are feeling melancholy you shall have it for your eye. She's funny[.] She has always pretended to be entirely indifferent to my work – *was* in painting[,] only interested in *nonsense* or society in which she comes[,] I spose.

Well. My mind is going so

Love
Goodbye

[same letter] 9:30 Sunday Night

Thank you Ira – goodnight

The readings were *particularly* lovely[,] I enjoyed them so. Silence and

22 'St. Ives' appears in *Growing Pains* (Pt 2, 220–35).

23 Carr is referring to her gift to Dilworth of the painting *Indian School at Lytton* (1910), which is now in the McCord Museum, Montreal.

24 Carr and her sister, Alice, travelled to Alaska in 1907.

'West Wind' particularly and 'The Silver Trumpeter' – Our West and 'Silence'[25] I felt my heart answering. Sanctuary is such *real* Sunday-ness. I am sure it settles *many* peacefully into quiet nights as it does me. The *beautiful* places! Oh the loveliness that we forget & neglect! Let them fade & get weak then something like poems or something speaking in nature jerks us back with shame to wonder how we came to forget. 'My Daffodils'[26] shared Sanctuary & heard the mention of their fellows. Don't let's call them golden[.] Why connect them with hard cold mettle? Let's call them illuminated not gold, their ethereal texture seems semi-embodied in light[,] just enough texture to whisper life to our touch. Don't you love the *coolness* of flowers[?] When they touch you their coolness seems to steady your warmth, even the swift passing is more lovely than stodgy changelessness[.] When fullness is reached they don't stay to gloat but pass on their rich heritage of fruiting & going on. And the Trumpeter[,] how grand that is, I love it. Some day, will you read the 'Song of the Rolling Earth' in Sanctuary?[27]
Yours Emily

P.S. Alice said a neighbour told her she heard such a beautiful programme Sunday night called Sanctuary read by Mr. Dilworth[.] Beautiful selections & *he read them so beautifully*[.] Alice told her 'Yes, I hear[d] that but last night I was writing & missed [it].' I had an *idea* she listened but she never let on. She goes off about 1/4 to 9 to her flat.

[same letter, ca. 22 January 1942] *Thursday*

I bet you've got flu! Backache, snuffles! Or else it's that 'high up C.B.C.' sitting on you. Thanks for letters returned. I have to answer Mr. Sandwell's. Letter from Mr. Clarke this A.M. Still in Toronto (was to have left a week ago). Someone in States wants an auto. of K.W. C. never mentioned West. 'Rosalind' came yesterday [with a] new bee in her bonnet – this time a 'bumble[.]' [She] is sending K.W. to *Queen Elizabeth! Lizzie & Rose.* She says Lizzie may be queen & she should now be preparing herself by studying the Indians of her domain!! What a woman! Her hus-

25 Perhaps Carr is referring to, respectively, Whitman's 'As I Ponder'd in Silence,' Shelley's 'Ode to the West Wind,' and Whitman's 'The Mystic Trumpeter.'

26 Carr is probably referring to 'Daffodils' by Wordsworth.

27 Carr is referring to 'A Song of the Rolling Earth,' which appears in the poetry sequence 'Calamus' of Whitman's *Leaves of Grass.*

band (not Lizzie's) was (before he died) the same[:] official. Whose job the sending of tokens to Royalty is & she knows *exactly how it's done & will do it*[.] I only have to get a K.W. and write a lovely beg-of-acceptance on the fly[.] Oh Lor! She says Mazo de la Roche[28] did & the Queen *received* her when she went to London[.] Well I have not that to fear – besides K.W. may be bounced before she reaches. Everything is submerged in Bio. I'm at it hard, just now I'm funeralizing Queen Victoria.[29] So you must excuse brevity[.] I'm *absorbed.* If you *have* got flu and roll in misery I'll wait 'til you get over the awfulest & send the funny book. But there is *nothing funny* in life while you are flu-ing. Take care & don't rush round *too hard before* or *too soon after. If you have* it I'm frightfully sorry[.] It's *so* beastly.

Lady Jane saintly last few days – weather magnificent – A[lice] comfortably easy.

Love, and be good
As always
Emily

Wed & Thursday (or thereabouts) [ca. 28–9 January 1942]

Dear Ira,
I love having a 'devoted flea.' I never experienced the *enjoyment* of one before. The more attention[,] the less I liked them. That C.B.R. Drat them!! They ought to provide you with a page to do the running. I am so glad you wrote. If people have to have tribulations there is *some* satisfaction in at least wishing them well en-route. I hate you sitting on clouds. What do *I* think of Mrs. D.C. Scott[?][30] Not much – very sweet to me – sent me *her poems.* I found neither her nor them thrilling. Why do men choose dolls? Well look out *you* don't. I'm told it is natural to choose one's opposite. Now pretty near *every* jack man that fancied *me* were sons of parsons & sanctimonious. And I was *always* like their little

28 Mazo de la Roche (1879–1961) was a Canadian novelist who acquired fame with a series of books that began with *Jalna* (1927).

29 'Queen Victoria' treats the Queen's death in 1901 (*GP*, Pt 2, 176–81).

30 Elise Aylen Scott (1904–1972), who married Duncan Campbell Scott in 1931, published some poetry and *The Night of the Lord* (1967), a spiritual biography.

sister who died young, 'til I was sick of it & felt I ought to be (died) [.] The world is so *queer.* – No the Biog: is *not* in Van. It's *not finished.* I am [doing the] final typing & find *millions* of changes to make[.] Maybe the beginning of the week? – I've been working at it hard. You shall have the 'Funny-book' for Sunday though & it is done up for mailing. Edythe Brand[31] came today[.] Fred is now in Ottawa[.] Edythe is here with pa[,] no accommodation in Ottawa. She was very nice. We've had Heaven weather. Alice has one of her air boys today: Val, the one I like & looking so nice in his 'aerial' togs.

I think you will find this session of Biog dull but one *must* pause their life a little[.] It is perhaps more the solid grind part of work. St. Ives. storm, – Bushey[32] – spring sweetness. I could have written the 'back in Canada' part *fine* the other night (round 3 A.M.) [but during] the night I had had heart pains and daren't. It was so clear and easy. I'd had 3 separate bouts of pain & was settled easy and was afraid to light up and [attempt it] for fear of return. It is going to be the hardest bit of the whole & had never seemed clear except that night [–] very annoying!!! Now it may *never* return[.] Wish I had *dared* the drat old heart. I always do[.] Here Alice brought her young flyer to see me & we've been discussing air. Well goodnight[.] I spose you are freezing in ugly Winnipeg tonight.

C.O.D. Good land! You need not worry fearing Lady Jane being *too meek*!!

[same letter. ca. 30 January 1942] Friday morn

Where are you? Just had letter from Mr. Clarke's sec. HE HAS LEFT!!!! Is spending a few days on the prairies en-route to coast[.] She says you *should* be seeing him in Victoria *some time* next week (dated Jan 28) [.] It is luck he *did* put off if you *had to fly away.* Hope you get home Saturday. Spose no[t] and we had *all choir* for Sanctuary!!! The thought knocks all my codicils blank!

Love
Me.

31 Edythe Brand (later, Edythe Hembroff-Schleicher) was an artist and the author of *Emily Carr: The Untold Story* (1978).

32 'Bushey' appears in *Growing Pains* (Pt 2, 290–49).

Epistle no. I
218 St Andrews 14th Feb [1942]

Dearest Ira –
There may be 1000 Iras in the world I do not know but I am *sure* mine is the dearest of them all. I have had a strangely wonderful morning. I had arrived in the Biog: at Lawren[33] and I pulled out a huge folder of his letters to me. I kept them[.] He was marvelously generous to me from the start of our friendship 'round about 1929–1930[,] opening the rich cupboards of his heart stored with art knowledge that I had never even dreamed of, [en]riched with his own perception[,] his inner struggles[,] his bigness[,] his love of lovely things[,] his struggles & hopes[,] high aims[,] patiently encouraging[,] showing[,] lifting the despondent failure of western me out of the slough [that] 'me & my thwarted Art' were wallowing in. How can I ever thank Lawren & You[,] my beloved trustors[,] for coming along, overtaking me without my seeking you, as I scrambled along in a not-too-easy way lugging canvases and M.S. I had not read Lawren's letters over for many years. They give me fresh light & inspiration[.] The lapse of years strengthens a lot of points in them. We have both developed in work & outlook[.] When I took this box of letters out of box[,] it was with the idea of clearing out, burning[.] They are almost all work, one artist to another[.] A few of the more personal where his unhappiness & bewilderment showed *just a little* I have destroyed in fairness to him[.] The working letters I'll perhaps rest in the 'box[.]' *You* would understand them[.] My *own* people would *not.* You know & love Lawren (& me I *think* a *little*?) [.] Canada is dear to you as it very obviously was to us in those letters & beautiful deep things are to you the same as to us[.] There is too one of the 9 [of] Bess['s] letters[,] warm loving & I think sincere[.] There are one or two from Fred. I shall send you one where he speaks of his unpublished book on Whitman.[34] There was a pathetic letter from a lovely German boy who I may have mentioned to you. Two German men[,] one an architect & on[e] an engineer[,] got a caravan & came out West from New York to see the world[.] They brought 'greeting[s]' to me from a woman artist in New

33 Carr is writing what subsequently becomes 'Lawren Harris' in *Growing Pains* (Pt 3, 340–52).

34 Fred Housser had written *The Whitmanic Attitude and the Creative Life* and 'Walt Whitman and North American Idealism.'

York (a German) whom Lawren had given me a letter of introduction to when I went to New York at [the] time of the Chicago fair.[35] They were out there a year or *so* later[,] expected to stay 2 days [but] remained 2 weeks & I saw them everyday & got very fond of them[.] We took the dogs & Walt Whitman & went into the woods & read him aloud[.] They went to California and there one died. I corresponded with this one for many years[,] once or twice a year. War nor anything (it was soon after 1st World War) could break the warm humanity of our regard & warm friendship. When he returned to Germany he was terribly ill[.] I hope he died before the agony of the 2nd War[.] He was too young to serve in the first. Oh Ira[,] there are places in life so much bigger & deeper than race, than ownership, than creeds, than anything else *but life.*

And here, your letter & your friend's letter enclosed. *Thank* you. It was indeed a lovely letter[.] How nice, men are so much nicer tha[n] I thought, once long ago. I used to be a man-hater once. Now I have far more men than women friends (tell me why did you in writing your 'me' say my work was very masculine? I have often wondered.)[36] I seem to get closer & deeper to them than to women??? Your friends' tribute to Klee Wyck moved me deeply. To have been permitted to give pleasure by writing & painting the plain simple things of my life fills one with the deepest gratitude, that these things spoke so that I might hear & in a language I understood even a little of. Dear Heart! 1 1/4 hour on me[.] How exhausting! Small shall be there & Emily this end. I'm glad we knew in time. Look here[,] you should not let me gabble on like a magpie. I *want to hear* about you & your work[.] It interests me greatly & I'm proud when you tell me any of your personal problems[.] It helps to unbottle ourselves[.] When (the 'etc-she')[37] comes[,] I shall fade[.] Tell me[,] won't you? I want to love her too & your heart is big enough [for] a faded shadow [who] won't take up much space. Glad you felt rested. Yes I slept like a top[.] It was a nice visit. I was very happy.

I have let Phyllis off to buy the wedding garments. She lights my fire

35 Katherine Dreier (1877–1952), president to the Société Anonyme, painter, lecturer, and writer (see 'New York,' *GP*, Pt 3, 325–39).

36 In a letter to Carr, dated 3 March 1942, Dilworth explains that the 'masculine' facet of her writing to which Carr here refers is related to the 'direct, frank quality' of her writing 'which men respect and admire' (BCARS, Parnall Collection, MS 2763, box 2, file 26).

37 'Etcetera' is the term Carr later derives in anticipation of a potential partner for Dilworth.

tomorrow & then is away for good. Dear child[,] she is very tender & thoughtful of me these days. I can't help feeling a little squashy. She thinks she's happy & I hope it is real – a dear little wife for any man, if they can both stick. I have not seen the boy. I so often think of that funny little Chinese girl I had (only 2 days[,] went home weeping with home-sickness) [.] She came in in a funny little white nighty & sat on the end of my bed blinking with sleep & so pretty. 'Miss Carr[,] do you believe in love? I don't' – Well *I do.* But I must say her little Oriental dissertation was comically straightforward & seems to straddle a lot of difficulties. I think we could a learn a heap from Orientals. But I think life without *real* love between man & wife would be Hell. Why this aside[?] I am answering your letter [or] perhaps St. Valentine has rattled me. Jane being gone I'd best go & beat up the walnut tree[.][38] Got her into training?

I am much encouraged over 'Cedar' [–] not a brush stroke more done[.] I had to lick that bear into shape for Mr. Clarke.[39] Always tell me if you have thoughts & things in your head re: my work[.] They help[.] I think I really have had as much or *more* help from the odd remarks of layman (provided he is honest) than from artists.

Just had a blow[.] My tenants are leaving to live in Penticton. They were with me in the Simcoe St house & went with my little house in Oscar St. soon as I bought it – splendid tenants – it means finding a new outfit. Houses are in demand[.] The trick is finding a good one like maids. Mother used to say 'there is as good fish in the sea as ever came out of it.' Maybe but it's getting the beasts on your hook. No I have not got 'Days in Woods' among my sanctuaries but I would like to.

Tomorrow I shall look at Cedars again and see if I can salvage anything.

I think your idea of black an[d] white illustrations as tail pieces are good (Book of Small).

I am so relieved all your household approve Jane. Dear little loving Jane & her wayward dirty little habits. Isn't the welcoming of a dog after your absence delicious? So wholehearted & spontaneous. Sara is very shy, *very sensitive,* very affection[ate] but I miss Jane's *overwhelm.* Thank goodness Ethel has lost her heart [–] and your dear Mother[:] Jane will

38 Carr is referring to the popular Gloucestershire rhyme, 'A woman, a spaniel and a walnut tree, / The more you beat them the better they be.'

39 Carr painted *The Laughing Bear* for *Klee Wyck,* although it was never used (see note from R.W.W. Robertson to W.H. Clarke, 3 September 1951, William Ready Division of the McMaster University Archives, box 19, file 12).

[be] gentle to her[.] I know they realize that some can't bear as much bursting exuberance as others. I am most pleased Major Macaroni responds. I was half afraid she might not. I have know[n] animals [to] have great influence over people. Maybe Jane will coax warmth & vibration among Macaroni's stillnesses. Not that stillness is not lovely[.] How I, or rather Small, always admired dignity & stillness & she such a flibbertigibbet! Thanks for the [she draws a heart] I can 'picture' it much better than Mrs. Crane's but it is *not* as the mottoed candy one – not the red-flamed pincushion one – & not 'the dreadful thing mother boiled for the cat!' Now for the cedar before the light goes.

Emily

C.O.D. I am appalled at the cheek of me. Apparently from Lawren's letters[,] I scolded & bawled his attitude[;] on some phases of ideas roared. I was older than he in years but so much littler in understanding & he took my opposition so kindly.

[same letter] 9:30 Sunday night
Thank you Ira[,] goodnight – a lovely sanctuary (all but the noise makers)[.] That 95 year-old soprano had the hiccups or something[,] a noise that did not belong came from some of her anatomy. She's like sour milk[,] just the green whey part. Not one of them *wants* to sing whey[,] do they[?] Wow! I'd rather hear a pencil scratching on a slate, but Sanctuary was *lovely* (the *poems*). W.W.[,] the Indian missionary (apples not so much)[.][40] Wasn't apple weak?

Bless you,
Small

Epistle no II (Sunday 7. P.M.) [15 February 1942]
[encircled] I swear not to write again for 1 month to let you catch up! Unless of course it's a matter of life and death.

40 Carr may be referring to 'Rich Days' by W.H. Davies (1871–1940), in which he writes of 'gallons of sweet cider seen / on trees in apples red and green.'

Dear Ira
Oh! Today's been just that – no more no less. No answers to my ad[vertisement] and Phyllis gone to her doom[,] poor little girl. I was mad with her at 8.30[,] resigned at 9.30[,] weepy at noon. Her last job was to (voluntarily) [–] when she was *entitled* to be beginning [bliss?] preparations on her own [–] run for the torch and help me in the intricate job of re-wiring & re-constructing my front doorbell[.] We did it – I turned it inside out with its innards exposed but its ring restored[.] It will be easier next time as we won't have to rip its inwardness out. I've had an ad[41] in but only a buxom Scotch Hussy who expected remunerations according to her size & the family she'd raised & who also had no use for 'critters' – meaning my menagerie.. I did not yearn towards her. A[lice] is *so difficult* when I am alone[.] Wants to do all the impossibles that she *can't* do and *won't heed* the things she can[.] She is not so deaf but lets herself slump into a far-offness unless you are *amusing* her. She simply seals up her senses & you could bellow your tongue off its pivot. I finished Mr. Clarke's bear and have the pictures all *crated* ready to be called for tomorrow[.] Did it alone after Phyllis left! Very proud of *me* am *I*. Mending doorbells[,] crating and a long afternoon rest have meant not much accomplished today. News is not nice today is it! I got so tired of this 'temporary' business[,] 'temporarily lost' they always say.

How was the lecture last evening? I was with you all the time[,] me & Small. Alice had a birthday party for 2 of her Hennell boys[,] a very nice dinner[,] just the 4 of us. They are very nice lads & *very nice* to her[.] Heavens she did enough for them in their childhood but people don't always remember. – You've moved. I tuned for Sanctuary[,] stupid of me to forget change of time[,] will have to postpone beauty sleep but am so glad it is later not earlier or I should have missed it.

This morning I was reading more of Lawren's letters[.] There's a tremendous pile and they are very fine. I hardly realized what they meant to my work in the transition stage[.] *How* he helped me[.] Rereading them gives me further illumination[.] What he tells me of his[,] what he says of mine[.] He *is* a fine man. They are such warm friendly help[.] I was so far off from *all* the workers[,] so totally on my own & rather bewildered[.] I had been through a period somewhere around 15 years[,] dormant[,] all the art smashed out of me flat. There are a few letters of Bess's too[,] warm loving letters & some from Fred. I am enclosing one about his Walt Whitman book I think may interest you[.] Of course they

41 Carr here means a woman responded to her advertisement for a new maid.

[–] L. & B. & F. [–] claimed W.W. was a Theosophist pure & simple whether he called himself that or not. I am sorting the letters over[.] Any that have anything personal[,] any hints which are now clear to me – though they were not at the time (as to his personal unhappiness) [–] things I see now but could not then[,] these I am burning. Nothing really in them but it seems fairer to him. The work letters I shall still keep. They would be of no interest to anyone but a worker or a seeker like yourself. They throw light on Lawren's work & on my own too. I think I shall cache them in 'the box' when sorted. Some day you might be interested to read them? Or bored? You could even let Lawren look over them & ask if you might[.] People who did not understand or love these things would think it stupid stuff & I'd rather they were burnt than that. There was a letter very happy following immediately on the bust up. It is rather pitiful[.] I guess both went through a bit of hell. Probably the whole thing was just unavoidable and right[.] Sometimes our judgments are so very petty & small, oh how *little* we are! How we splash around pretending we are whales & are really tadpoles.

I found something I had forgotten viz. Lawren tried to persuade me to write a Biog:[,] practically the thing I *am* doing[.] I remember jeering & saying 'Who'd want to read it?' & 'What had *I* to write about?' and dismissing it from my thoughts[.] Maybe it did not register *then*[,] maybe it sowed the idea[.] I don't know[.] I *thought* it was *really* because Eric Brown asked me to[,] said [if] I wouldn't[,] someone else would. I was amazed to see in these old letters it was just the type of thing he suggested. I told you I felt hurt when [he] suggested [it] some years or time [a]go. I sent it to him to crit the art part & he did not answer. I felt he was indifferent[.] If it's readable when finished[,] suppose you let him read it? In the view of these old letters I feel I ought to, if he is interested[.] Of course, as Bess is his now I spose she'd have to be included[.] Well I have so reduced the parts that would make me squirm & feel silly[.] I don't guess I'd mind[.] What do you think about it? I don't think I've left myself *too* naked[.] I couldn't bear the whole public & I'd hate the ridicule of *my own* relatives. Only one of my nieces commented on Klee Wyck[,] her comment (Mrs. Boultbee) 'that she'd only read a few pages[,] it was *too heavy* for her to hold in bed[.]' She'd always [be] in bed for something[,] potters in & out of hospital like the cuckoo in a clock. Too much money to spend on her fads. A *great* niece or two have mildly commented on K.W. However one buxom farm girl[,] Lillian Nicholles'[42] daughter[,] wrote me a short *real*

42 Lillian Nicholles had taught at Masset, where some of Nicholles's acquaintances assisted Carr when she travelled there to paint (see Tippett 107). The Nicholles are descendents of Clara Carr, Emily's sister.

letter[,] warm badly worded & *genuine.* Alice sent the Boultbee woman a copy[.] I did *not*[.] When I was poor & starting studio in Vancouver[,] she [–] a beautiful & popular bride [–] was very beastly to me[,] so I [have] always given her a wide berth[.] She adores Alice. She has always been mean & rude over my work (painting) & is a hypocrite like her pa was.

This brings me[,] Ira[,] to something I think I should be frank with my trustors in. Neither of you know how I stand financially[.] Neither of you like to ask but in arranging for the trust you *wonder*[,] so I'll try & tell you what my income is though it is a queer precarious affair & I often don't know myself.

My only *sure* income is a small house in Fairfield I traded my apartment for[,] rents for $25.00 per month. I have a few government bonds paying 2 or 2 ½ percent interest (round $10 or $12 a month I spose) and (this is a pill) Mrs. Boultbee gives Alice & I = Alice $35.00 per month[,] *me* $15.00[.] I hate taking from her when I feel – I don't trust her. – It happened this way – Her husband left her *very* rich [–] Braeborn mines[.] Well, years back she knew Lizzie & Alice had not any[thing] much & she gave them $15.00 a month each to spend on their gardens & little things. I did not speak to her for years[.] She told some lies & made trouble for me in Van. Well when Lizzie died she came over to weep and, to comfort Alice[,] I made up with Mrs. B. and she asked me to accept as a *goodwill gesture* the $15.00 per month she had been used to send Lizzie[.] I was terribly hard up at the time & to refuse would have upset the whole cart-load of kiss & makeup[.] Money meant nothing to her so I took it[,] which makes my income round fifty dollars per month. I have the upkeep & taxes of my Fairfield house[,] pay $15 a month to Alice for rent & $20 to a maid. But as you know I make a sale now & then, have been very lucky & there is Klee Wyck. These extras go into the bank to draw from because the 50 won't stretch when I keep a maid. With my rental for my flat & Una's & her bonds[,] Alice gets about $50.00 too[.] She owns her house[.] I have seriously considered withdrawing from Una's $15 – do you think I should? I expect she has fearful income tax & she spends her life running after cures in & out of hospitals[.] She hospitals for everything[.] She is very generous to her family[.] They are all poor. But if I did[,] she would probably rake up all the old fuss & if I don't I guess she thinks I'm rolling in wealth now K.W. has sold well – there[,] that's me & my pocket. Mr. Lawson our Guardian was honest as the day but *no investor*[.] Father left us comfortable and the old estate all clear but the 'Elder' never could keep in bounds. Between the two we only got a few hundreds out of the old place after everything was eaten up in taxes. If my sisters hadn't helped me [during] that long illness in England[, I] would have sent Small to the charity orphanage[.][43] How mad Lizzie used to be that my Art *was not profitable*[.] I remember Walter Nicholles coming to see my pictures once[.] He nearly but *not quite* bought one. Lizzie said 'Let him have them for *anything*[,] Millie[.] You'd be well rid of the stuff for even a dollar or two' (my entire Indian collection)[.] I felt dreadfully hurt[;] however Mr. Nicholles did *not* want them for even a 'dollar or two[.]' Maybe that is why I love *giving* them away now. *When* people love them, & *I like* the people[,] I want to give them far more than to sell.

Oh what a letter
Forgive
Emily

[encircled] N.B. Your *drawing* of a heart is simply *shocking*. You'll have to get someone to give you lessons in heart-drawing.
C.O.D. Hadn't you better have your secretary read[,] digest & give you extracts? Is your little English one that used to type me on the marry? Quitting??? But I guess you don't know punctuation question marks? Don't heed 'em.

[same letter] Epistle III

C.O.D. N.B. P.S. Thank you so for letting me read your letter[.] I love your friend & *he loves you very much*. How wonderful those sort of lasting friendships are. There is something in sharing those opening up years of one's life[,] when young things *wonder* together and have all life before them that connects the foundation[,] even if ways separate after. I think maybe men got them in a deeper sense than women. Women got so split up following the careers of their children & chasing 'round following their husbands: but men that have absorbed books & thoughts with other men & talked about deep things & planned life together have something firmer than a jelly-platform on which to sit down. Do you remember on the boat coming from Vancouver I told you [that] you had given me back *faith* in men? You did.

43 In 1903, Carr was diagnosed as suffering a 'nervous breakdown' and admitted to the East Anglia Sanatorium in England, where she convalesced for a period of fifteen months (see Blanchard 90).

Final C.O.D.: I shall *lick* the envelope *immediate[ly]* as prevention against further COD's.
N.B. I hear you *snort* 'Thank God for lick-glue!'

Vancouver, B.C.
Sunday Evening [ca. 22 February 1942]

Dear Emily:
It was a great joy to see you yesterday and have a chat even if it was only for a moment. I was sorry you were so tired – you have had such a lot of worry over that old Phyllis girl and her replacement. I do hope the new [girl] turns out well and proves to be capable and understanding. Few things can be more completely irritating than to have someone in the house who just will not or, perhaps, does not know how to adjust herself and help. I hope you won't have that experience.

The black and white of the little Church is lovely, Emily. It will fit marvelously into 'The Book of Small.' We called the sketch simply 'The Blessing.' Is that what you prefer or would you like to have it called 'The Bishop's Blessing'? Please let me know which you like best: the change can easily be made. What have you decided about 'From Carr Street to James' Bay'? Do you think it might fit into 'The Little Town' sequence – just after or just before 'Father's Store?'[44] It doesn't make a great difference: I think it would fit into the 'Little Town' very well indeed.

Thank you so much for your loving letter. Please do not apologize for the length of your letters *ever.* I look upon them as conversations and you know how I *love to talk.* As I said to you yesterday if you carry through your threat not to write to me for a month I shall 'cut you off with a shilling.' So there!

Fred's letter is a superb one. What a fine person he must have been! I like his directness and his honest, manly language. I was most interested in his comments on Walt W. and you see he did value your reactions. Bess has certainly been a lucky woman to have [had] two husbands such as Lawren & Fred. I wish I had known him.

I do not agree that Whitman was a Theosophist. It would be just as sensible to say that Wordsworth was one – and he wasn't. I think Whit-

44 'Father's Store' is the sixth story in 'A Little Town and a Little Girl' (*BS* 139–43).

man was much too honestly earthy and 'down to brass tacks' to be a Theosophist. Of course there may be passages in his poems where Lawren & Bess recognize ideas similar to their Theosophist ones, but that does not prove anything. All systems of beliefs and religions overlap and have often a great many things in common. I shall never forget what a great Chinese scholar once said to me at Harvard (he was a Buddhist). We were talking about religions (George Hayes was there too) – the Chinese scholar said that he could never accept Christianity and gave his reasons, 'but,' he said, 'what difference what we call our religion, or exactly what we believe? There are many paths to the top of a mountain. The important thing is not which path you choose, so much as that you arrive at the top.' That may be an extreme view but it has a great deal of truth in it. I find myself losing patience with people who insist on labeling things and thinking they know all about them. How many people keep on buying goods 'Made in Britain' merely because of the label which, of course, has or had a naming and significance but which is not necessarily the only token of excellence.

From your description of Lawren's letters they must be very fine. Certainly you should keep them. If the[y] contain wise things about art and life they should be preserved for posterity: we have woefully little wisdom and cannot afford to waste any or allow it to be destroyed. One of the great tragedies connected with wars is that so much that represents the finest and wisest achievement of men runs the risk of being destroyed. There are plenty of things which we could discard and we would be better of[f] if we courageously did discard them but some things seem to be said clearly only once. How unhappy we are if that statement (whether in paint, in marble, in building stone, in words) is lost.

I should love to see some of Lawren's letters but only when you think I should. The personal letters about his own joys & sorrows – those are difficult to decide about. I rather think you should leave them to be returned to him or destroy them. They might have some special value to him and some of them he might want to get into the hands of those who will search into his life to find if possible some clue to his power and his achievement.

Thank you for all the kind things you said about my simple talk. I am glad people liked it. It was sweet of Bess to write to you and such a glowing account of it too. Phylis & Walter were there. Walter said he thought it was the best talk I have ever given. There is no doubt it was the subject that inspired me.

It was good of you to take me into your confidence about your personal business affairs. I think, under the circumstances, canvases should be sold wherever a buyer can be found. The money should then be in trust but available for your own personal use if you need it: Lawren agrees with this view.

I certainly do not think you should have any qualms about taking money regularly from Mrs. Boultbee. I understand that she is very rich. After all, remember, Emily, you did not ask for it. She gets a certain satisfaction out of giving it to you. You could not refuse to take it without making a very disagreeable situation – disagreeable both for Alice & you. I am sure you have more than earned it and merit it many times multiplied. So, don't let me hear of your being foolish and allowing some passing whim to determine you to fly in the face of Providence: I have found even in my comparatively short existence that Providence wears some curious faces. 'God moves in a mysterious way' – I quote that seriously and without the slightest irreverence.

I understand so fully what you went through in connection with the property your father left you & your sisters. I had exactly the same experience. My Father left about $50,000 worth of real estate when he died – at least that is what it was assessed at. Almost immediately the slump came and the purely fictitious prices of boom days were out of all relation to the actual values. As a result I found myself hanging onto property for years, at first not wanting to sell it hoping its value would increase, and finally finding I could not sell it. But all the while it was eating up in taxes many times more than I was to realize for it.

I hope 'Klee Wyck' will continue to bring in some revenues – she has not done badly up to date. 'The Book of Small' may do even better. I know you do not like to think of your writing or your painting in terms of their cash value. But you cannot forget that aspect of things. It would be wrong if you did. 'The Good Workman is worthy of his hire'[45] – and you have been a good workman and the world has fallen far short of paying you adequately for your contributions to its enrichment. By the way, do you think Lizzie's passion for texts has descended upon me? This letter seems to be full of them, which means that it is getting preachy, which in turn means that it is time I said goodnight. No! it has to be good morning: it is after midnight now.

45 Dilworth is citing a biblical passage: 'And in the same house remain eating and drinking such things as they give: for the labourer is worthy of his hire' (Luke 10:7).

Please do me the honour of letting me know anything about your personal affairs when you think I can help.

Meanwhile accept my love in heaps – Jane would send hugs too but she is sleeping. She is marvelously well. She greeted me with all the impetuosity of a northern gale and all the warmth of a sunny day. You are quite right[.] There is nothing more delicious than the abandoned passion of such a welcome as she gives.

Yours devotedly
Ira.

[February 1942]

Dear Emily,
Here's a tiny little letter with a lot of important enclosures. You see that I am writing in pencil which means that I am feeling my greatness today, getting up into your class and Lawren's.[46]

First let's get the business over –

Yesterday brought me page proof of Small's book and the enclosed ideas for the jacket. The page proof I shall get through as quickly as possible and return it to Clarke. Quite likely it will accompany me on the 'plane on Sunday morning.

Clarke says he found your 'jacket' idea very interesting but that, after consultation with his engraver, he is certain they could not get anyone clever enough to carry out your idea effectively. He says that it has another disadvantage from their point of view, namely there is no space left for the title and your name. So, I guess that's that!

Clarke submits the two ideas which are enclosed. The small artist's sketch doesn't attract me atall. It would give the impression that the volume contained children's stories. In addition it has a definitely 'English' look about it. The other with Small's picture is in my opinion very good. It is in line with my own first idea. I like the old-fashioned wallpaper and wainscot-background. I do not like the quotation marks around *Small*. Mind you, I think they are useful in the design but I don't like their apology for the name Small. I have told Mr. C. this and have suggested

46 Carr and Harris almost invariably wrote their letters in pencil.

that in place of the quotation marks it might be just as effective to use small squares, circles or triangles or modified quotes set lower – I'll enclose a sketch if you won't laugh at it. In fact I'll send it anyway. But now what do you think of the ideas[?] – I am enclosing an envelope which you can use to send the samples off to me in Toronto with a brief note if you feel like writing. If you don't feel equal to it just have the nurse say that you either agree or don't agree with my opinion. Lawren saw the design and thinks it fine[.] So does Walter Gage.

And now to pleasanter things. Our visit on Tuesday was one of the very pleasantest we have had I think. It was marvelous to find you so cheerful again and I was most grateful to you for telling me what you did about your father. I think I understand even better than you believe and I had already guessed.

My dear I cannot tell you often enough that nothing I do for you is or ever has been a must. Everything is done because of that love and nice kind of friendship of which you wrote in one of your lovely letters from Mt. Douglas Park. No brother, sister, mother, father[,] sense of obligation, no bounden duty – just sincere friendship dictating the activity of mind and heart and hand.

So sorry you had *slumped* when you wrote yesterday. You must expect that, Emily, and don't grieve about it. Most of all don't apologize about telling me about it. Just write to me and let go of things. It often helps to tell somebody else about these things.

My next letter may be from the air.

God bless you and keep you strong is my prayer. I trust you will soon be well again.

Yours lovingly
Ira

N.B. I know how you must miss your birds – the doves cooing in the moonlight. You are a brick to take it so courageously. I should be in blue-black tantrums all the time if I were in your place. D.

---

9 A.M. Sunday [ca. 22 March 1942]

Dear Ira
What an exquisite parcel of joy you brought me yesterday in my lilies &

violets. I was conscious of them all night[.] They were on my bedside table & kept scooting the loveliest whiffs over to my nose[:]

O lovely lily clean
  Oh lily springing green
Oh lily bursting white
  Dear lily of delight

'Spring in my heart again that I may flower to men,' I am that 'Oh lovely lily clean[.]'[47] There is something to the smooth clear feel of a lily[.] Seems to me different to other flowers – *cleaner.* So, you loosed that dart of dearness in my room yesterday & here it is[,] winding in & out & about and cuddling 'round the dearest memories. Small is drunk with them. She's off to those glorious lily heavens among the scrub oak above Cadboro Bay (you remember those particular fields [–] the lilies' stems wer[e] redder there) & the fields of Cedar Hill & Mount Tolmie & the snarly little thickets on the north side of Beacon Hill where the oak scrub scratched your legs & tore your stockings & the cries [of] wild peacocks joined smells with the lilies & the meadow larks just yelled for joy & Small too. And this our own lily field that we waded through on the Sunday walks and the cow in the middle of it & later Small nearly grown, wandering back from S.F. and bringing poor Nellie McCormick with her to rest her bothered brain's hot worry among the mottled leaves & the piercing peace of the petaled lily's white. It all makes those lines 'World, world, I cannot hold thee close enough' (Edna St Vincent Millay) come bursting to you – and Small long[s] to give you a great hug & it's lucky you are not here or you'd get it! Emily knows & is always telling Small 'Ira doesn't *like* being touched.' Forgive the youngster. You see we've always had our creatures & hugging is one of the dearest ways of getting at them. Small always wanted to *feel* things *being alive.* You remember in Mrs. Crane how her hands shot out of their own accord to Mr. Crane & how she 'pulled the[m] back quick before Mr. Crane saw'?[48] Emily has always had to pull Small back for her own good[.] Sometimes she got hurt before the pull got her back.

And the violets too! Oh the *lovely violets*[.] How *can* one choose between flower & flower[?] Aren't you glad flowers have *cold* blood? It is far more thrilling than their being sticky & hot[.] I love to *feel* flowers as much as to *feel things being alive.*

47 From 'Everlasting Mercy' by the English poet John Masefield (1878–1967).
48 See 'Mrs. Crane' in *The Book of Small* (59–76).

Spring is back this morning after all that fuss & feather of cold last night. A horrid night for the boat trip. I believe today is ashamed of last night. It is so sunny & gentle. Alice came home at 9.30[,] very bright[.] She enjoys Una. Poor Una – I don't think she's very rich in other than money.

I will answer Lawren's letter today. I'll ship pictures tomorrow – Beloved Trustors[,] do *whatever you see fit* with your wards. As Lawren told me of the Klee Wyck crits (no business of mine) my job was the *making*[.] They have their own infinitesimal part to play in things[.] Maybe their work was only to *be* made[.] Whose is the little job? whose the big? – who knows? Thank you for sharing a little corner of your worries with me. It helps one to share a hurt[.] It is very uncomplimentary to friendship only to share the luscious spots. There is always a special flavor round the hard old stone & *I* think apple pits (if the apple is *sound*) are the most delightsome of all the apple[,] don't you? I'm so proud when critics allude to you (and many have) as being my 'close' friend.

Make it very clear to your mother, Ira, that when I write her it is with no thought of getting an answer & plaguing her with the effort. Just a message from her through you I love and to chatter to her of the little homey-things (the news she gets through others) – but little bits of me that her fingers weave into her knitting. My flowers & birds & dogs and my pride of the *friend* that is *her* son! What a *sublime* thing it must be to have made a man.

I hope this spring day is in your heart. The sun is touching my lilies & my violets. My room is full of their being stronger than their visible form.

Always your loving
Emily

Cod I: Sara is fine.
Cod II: Shall I send that little Oxford Press catalogue (post it to Miss Scott? Marionette? Library?[49]) [?] It is marked[.] She may want it or shall I send it to you in *Vancouver*? It has books marked as if she were making out her list.

49 A library in Victoria.

[25 March 1942]
[attached to following letter]

Dear Emily:
This is such a stupid letter when I read it this morning that I am tempted to burn it but there is no time to write another.

I am sorry I was not there when Small wanted to hug me. This is my birthday. Many happy returns!

Ira.

Vancouver, B.C.

My dear Emily:
What lovely letters! Three of them this week so far! You see I did not get your Saturday one until I came back from Victoria on Sunday – and, although we had talked most the points over, it was not like old, frost-bitten cabbage. It was fresh and true and sound and crisp and I loved it – and I never loved frozen cabbage – not to smell and I am sure I should not like it to taste. Of course I never tried it that way except as sauerkraut which my father always claimed must have a touch of frost: I never cared much for sauerkraut. I should rather have the tiniest of your letters than a barrelful of sauerkraut – Germans like it. Let's leave it to Mr. Hitler and his madmen. If that was all they wanted in the world[,] I wouldn't fight to hinder them from having it.

And the lilies – 'lovely lily clean' – they were absolutely charming. You know, Emily, it was pure selfishness on my part getting them and taking them to you and refusing to bring some of them to mother as you suggested I should. They fitted your bowl and the room and you so perfectly that I wanted to see them there and think of them there afterwards as I have done many times. It was the next best thing to seeing them starring the fresh green spring fields. Indeed I am not sure that it was not just as good. Yes I remember them with their dark red skins and more heavily mottled leaves. There were some like that in the oak scrub on Beacon Hill when we first went to Victoria before the broom supplanted them and the beds of yellow violets among their gray-green leaves and the gracious candelabras of the peacocks. What a glory that Hill was! In other places the lilies were so clear with traces of delicate green and their leaves were that heavenly almost translucent green.

Thank God, I have them in my memory so firm that nothing will ever be able to obliterate them. And thank God, they are in the 'Book of Small' and in the 'Biog.'

You are so absolutely right about the Indians, their life and their art. I agree that those things are gone – no, that is not right – they are done for all time and not to be done again. We should look upon them with great awe and respect and gratitude but we should not do what so many people do [–] try to make cheap imitations of them and wallow in sentimental twaddle about them. There are some remarkable statements in the introduction of one of Paul Elmer More's books – the introduction is in the form of a letter to my old Harvard professor, Irving Babbit.[50] More says – 'By some strange gift of fate, a few nations in the past have accomplished a work once for all and not to be repeated ... We cannot today – it is better so – reproduce the literature of Greece; we should shudder at the Roman sternness; to call ourselves disciples of Buddha or believers in Brahmin – as some unstable minds are prone to do – would be superstition and not spirituality. Yet to each of these peoples we may turn for strength and consolation; nay, we *must* turn to them if we would fortify our isolated life with the virtue and dignity of experience.' Don't you think that's fine, Emily – strong, manly, not cringing and weak but still ready to acknowledge and gain strength from the achievement of great human souls no matter where or when. If only we could capture some of that courageous spirit in this Canada of ours! But I am raving. You will be saying, 'Shut up, Ira' and I shall deserve it.

I am enclosing a letter which was sent to you in my care from Graham McInnes of the National Film Board.[51] He sent me a copy of the letter together with a long screed from himself to me. Now I know this idea may come as a surprise and shock to you. You may not wish to comply with his request atall – and in this case I think you must do whatever *you*

50 Paul Elmer More (1864–1937) was an American critic and scholar. He and Irving Babbitt (1865–1933), an American scholar and professor of French literature at Harvard (1912–33), were proponents of the New Humanism, a movement that advocated moderation and restraint as inspired by the classical traditions and literature.

51 McInnes, who worked for the National Film Board, wrote to both Emily Carr and Ira Dilworth simultaneously about the prospect of making a film about Carr and her paintings. They had made one on A.Y. Jackson's work shortly before. Dilworth continues the correspondence with McInnes and suggests that, after conversing with Carr, he felt that she would be willing to have the film made and that he was interested in helping 'to persuade Miss Carr to co-operate with the Film Board' (Dilworth to McInnes, 24 March 1942, BCARS, MS 2181, Inglis Collection, box 1).

want to do. I told Lawren about it and he said he would write to you and tell you what he knows of the Film Board's work. He recognizes that the Board is very anxious to do this. They want to honour your work. He thinks you should fall in line with their wishes. I am not so emphatic: I say you must suit *yourself* in this matter. Undoubtedly a film such as they wish to make would have great interest in two respects – it would be a record which might, like the Biog., be a source of inspiration and encouragement to young Canadian artists, it would draw attention to your work and (this is a third point) it would focus attention for a moment on the majestic loveliness of our British Columbia.

McInnes has asked me to help them with this project if you agree. I shall, of course, do anything I can for you and your work and Canada. I wrote to him and told him that I felt you must decide the question for yourself and that I did not feel you should be rushed into a decision. I also pointed out that I would not be able to do anything much about it until I returned from the East which might not be until the third week in April. I have a special suggestion to make about this plan, but I should like to talk to you about it, rather than to write about it and it will be valuable only if you agree to the idea first pronounced by the Film Board. So don't worry about the thing until you have had a chance to think it over. I shall go to Victoria & have a talk about the whole thing, sometime this week if possible – before I become too busy with plans & arrangements for my flight East. If we can come to a decision before I go away, I can discuss it further with them & give them your reactions in detail when I see them.

One more thing, Emily. Don't let the fact that they have done a film of A.Y. Jackson make any difference to you in arriving at a decision. I say that not because I want to influence you one way or the other but merely because the Film Board is serious in seeking to honour your work and this proposal should be viewed as fairly as possible. Is that an impertinent thing for me to say? I am afraid it is: after all I have no right to suppose that you would ever consider a proposal in any other way. But I know you are not like old A.Y.

The canvases arrived in their cases – everything seems to be in order. I have not opened the crates yet.

Thanks for Jane's certificate. Sorry you had any trouble about it. Jane gets more adorable every day.

The winter has been terrible – so cold – snowed last night more than any other time all winter.

Don't forget [the] singing ladies on Thursday at 6.30 over CBR.

Mother & Macaroni send love, Jane too, but I send the most of all. God bless you & keep you safe & well. How I wish I could help you with your worries!

Yours devotedly,
Ira.

Cod. This is being written at 1.00 am Wednesday March 25. So forgive the confused statements. D.

For blue Monday
Sunday 2 P.M. [ca. 29 March 1942]

Dear Ira
It'll have to be a jaundiced letter today[52] – white paper out – Small used up the last sheet of elegance writing to her 'best Beau.' Spring is really here today. I do hope she won't back-slide.

Didn't we have a lovely visit Thursday? Anyhow I thought so. The world *is* nice and *some* of the folks in it. (me and you and a few others – I leave you to fill in your own names[.] *Please* not the Sanctuary choir[.]) What about having them to supper when I come? Only give me warning so I can get Major Macaroni to do me some shopping[.] *Hat-pins* aren't rationed for steel are they??? Now to answer your P.M. – A.M. – Ira! You should remember your beauty-sleep[.] What *is* the good acquiring a 'waist' if you ruin the effect by sagging with weariness wrinkles? Don't mention sauerkraut[.] I spent a solitary Xmas at Kamloops once – weather *bitter* – I asked for a warm room in the hotel and they slept me on top of their stack of sauerkraut. I had to beg removal – the hotel was *decorated* for Xmas. I had a small table to myself in [the] dining room[.] It was specially decorated with an old spirea branch from which hung *intact* a *magnificent wasp's nest*!! I was scared the warmth would hatch the grubs.

Yes that *was* a beautiful quote about repeating & reproducing: I don't *think* I'd ever say 'Ira shut up!' I *like* raving. We have talked over the Graham McInnes letter. I suppose I *should* acknowledge the letter[.] Will get some notepaper tomorrow and give a brief 'think-it-over-answer[.]' For

52 Carr is writing on yellow paper.

[the] time-being perhaps you will have become a little more decided in your own mind for or against? (Which tail wags hardest?) The idea was *awful* to me at first – so was the birthday party – but I weathered that (even 'orated[,]' if you remember) and *enjoyed* it. Maybe the other wouldn't be *so hideous* if it had to be faced. Maybe it'd be *interesting* to see how these things are done? I feel *me* so 2ndary in importance to my *trustors* in the matter. And so very *very* unimportant in comparison to the *trust* itself. Not being sat a dead lump on its guardians' hands that I am willing to go the operation if they wish it. Bless you dear Ira. I know you'd spare me any hurt or shame being now such a recluse. I would not have to face 'grinners at my expense.' All I care is that the trust goes over – doesn't stick. Ira I am not blasé of all this kind warm receiving of the book & pictures. *Don't* think that I do not appreciate it. It warms one. But down below it seems to mean so little to what the *work itself has meant* to me. I have had so much the lion's share just in the effort of making. Scraps now & then are *very* sweet to the taste like the Indian boy whose eyes filled at [the] mention of Sophie & Walter Gage reading Klee Wyck over & over just because it spoke to him in some way & yours & Lawren's faith in the pictures & Flora going into the studio *mad at me* & saying 'the pictures took her mad away.' It's little things like that [that] make me *so* happy. I could burst & I know it is *all worthwhile* and part of life that has God in the middle of *everything*.

I listened to the New York Philharmonic concert (C.B.R.) today. I meant to dial a 'service' but I felt that [that] was just the same [–] prayer, music, painting, poetry – all worship – all resolve down to [the] same thing – there is nothing else in the universe but God. Call it this or that. The sifted out feel of *everything* is God. Life, life, life = GOD.

Rather drifted from my 'glamour-girl point'? I don't think *my* feelings should be consulted *too* much[.] If it's good for the *thing*[,] O.K. I'm willing if there was not much me, just animals, some shots of the best Trust pictures – in other words[,] *environment* rather than *personality*. O.K. I could see 'Canoe' gliding over the 'smoothness spread with light' but I would want *your* voice reading it. An unsympathetic, spectacular orator would make it unbearable. D'Sonoqua?[53] I don't know – those things were so real. I somehow *can't* imagine them being faked for photographing. If it was empty[,] just mechanical camera or if it catered to the spectacular[,] it would be *horrible*! Well you have a heap to see to and

53 'D'Sonoqua' appears in *Klee Wyck* (47–58).

bother with. *You* wish you could help with *my* worries[.] Oh my dear[,] you do more than you have any idea of. I just wish *I could help* with yours. I had not realized how big & heavy heading a job like yours was. All this shifting of men for national service & stenographers for matrimony must add to your difficulties horribly[.] Servant problem is a mere etc. It doesn't impact the whole machinery corporation but only one household if they are villain[ous] (helps)[.]

Your letter *wasn't stupid* & if you insist on such sayings I shall send a barrel-full of smacks to you C.O.D. (full of stories to weigh heavy too)[.] And oh! Please let me know what the Trust cost express[.] The Ira's were $6.00 you said. Let me know what the other was. I'd like to get that fixed before you go East. The money is right here to hand. That is my obligation, plain & honest[.] What happens later is Trust. I sincerely hope that your wards will be self-supporting & not kick up ructious.[54] Interruption – old fog[ey] missionary's sister-in-law phoning to tell me she has read Klee Wyck & it takes her right back to 'Ahouset'[55] where she lived at the mission one year with her brother. She is sending me some notes gathered up there by a teacher – I never was at Ahouset.

Ira you never answered about Miss Scott's book[.] I've a mind to post it to her[.] She may want it[,] being marked. I'm glad it was you [who] wrote Small's *feelers.* Atenea[56] or something – don't they call the stick-outs from a butterfly's nose? That it feels its way with? – our will-o'-wisp Small – now here, now not – did you find her (photo)[?] – (big Small) [?] – a Jap who was very proud of his new camera and [an] old student of the San Francisco Art school came into the classroom [and] asked permission to take it which I thought courteous (most whites would have snapped unasked). Everyone said it was the *best* picture of me I would ever have. I bought ½ doz. from him & I remember the polite way he asked permission to make for *himself* an extra print. I remember it was the morning after I had spent that awful night at the Raymonds (I forget the name[,] gave them in the Biog:) & slept with Aunt Rodgers with her wig on the bed-post & no teeth (the parrot place)[.]

Goodbye –
Emily

54 A word Carr has coined from the word 'ruction.'
55 Ahouset is a Nuu-chah-nulth reserve on the west coast of Vancouver Island.
56 Antenna.

218 St Andrews
Wednesday Night [1 April 1942]

Dear Ira
You haven't 'severed diplomatic relations' with me[,] have you? No, you are just on the high hop! Poor thing – in one way [the] train would be better for you than air – you'd *have* to stay sat for 2 ½ days instead of ripping through the heavens pitched from summer into winter and taking half the globe in one gulp. Is tough on the brain's digestion.

I had a letter from Mr. Clarke today and *no* mention of galley or 'Book of Small.' She might not exist. It was simply a note telling me negotiations with Farrar & Rinehart[57] are complete for the publication of 'Klee Wyck' & the 'Book of Small' – on 4th of June in Stat[e]s (civil & military emergencies permitting) [.] He gave me %ages etc.

They have an option on 'Book of Small' for 30 days from time they receive the final proofs from Oxford Press. I won't send you the letter[, since] there is nothing in it but that & [it] will only clutter your desk. Is Mrs. Clarke having a new baby[,] do you think? They seem very preoccupied, and *call* it *war-work* when apologizing for her negligence. My girl *seemed* nice[.] I liked her[.] Of course she only comes 4 times a week[,] 2 hours a time but if only she will *stick*! I shall manage nicely. I'm better – stronger on the pills.

I wrote Mr. McInnes – told him I was willing to abide by the decision of my trustees if and whatever they made. 10 P.M. Here come the little ladies!! – It was a lovely programme[.] It seems to me the little ladies' voices have gone sweeter. Ready to sleep now[.] Goodnight.

Cecil Laundry who is in the Post Office souping imbeciles out of income taxes seas *came* over an[d] souped me out of my tax mess. Found I did not have to tax *at all*. Fished out deprecations & repairs that exonerate me. Wasn't he a lamb? Nobody but a genie could have rescued me (all because I did not understand their fool wording[)] I expected to be *jailed* for not paying more & there I wasn't due for *any* – I'll go straight off & buy a bond! It isn't the money[,] it's the *tax fooling* that hurts. Cecil says it's been positively frantic[,] distracted persons all over the place, at tables with bottles of ink & worried women pouring out their entire family history & stomping on their hats for worry. It's cruel! & the Post Office is bedlam.

57 See the Introduction for an elaboration of Carr's interaction with this publisher.

Tomorrow [is] April 2nd and I am so sorry I forgot to fool you. I *over-did* Alice. Told her her old tom cat had 24 kittens on my front porch[.] Did she want them kept or drowned? I should not have said so many & the mangy brute *is* a tom. It'll teach me a lesson in moderation maybe[.]

Sara is *angelic.* A cherub pup. At four months she outdoes Jane in six-month manners & with half the whackings. Temperaments differ – Alice still insists 'but Jane was a lovely pup, I liked her animation.' Wonder if I shall see her much grown & will she remember me?

Well I spose I shall know when you spread your wings. Some Indians said Thunder-bird made thunder when he spread his wings & lightening when he winked his eyes. Bless you 'Man of Wrath,' I'm glad you *don't.* It will be rather wonderful flying through clean Easter spring clouds. I *think* you said you['ll] be taking off Easter Sunday? Anyhow blessings & peace be with you wherever, all the lovely Easter-ness and a quiet heart high above the troubles as your 'plane above the earth, and a happy successful solution of your businesses. There *may* be jam in the mails round Easter & my handmaiden *may* not be here Good Friday and Alice *may* not go to post[.] So anticipating *all the* 'mays[,]' I use preparedness.

As ever & for always
Yours lovingly
Emily & Small

[on back of letter] Mr. McInnes addressed you as 'Dr. Ira Dilworth[.]' It looked *very nice*[.] Could I? Or would it irritate you? Do you prefer Doctoring or Esquiring? Or alternate[?] Or both?

Good Friday Morn [3 April 1942]

Dear Ira
This [is] 'not a letter only a note' – hope you are more rested this lovely Good Friday morning. It was such joy seeing you yesterday. You had such a lot of newses and information (bulging like one of his majesty's mail sacks) and all good except that old Clarke's muddle up! And I am sure that will straighten out[.] It was probably just his fool reader[.] Goodness if *she* cheeked *you* & *he* backed *her*[,] I'd quit authoring & because he has first choice of me[,] I couldn't[.] I spose I couldn't

bounce to my *pet*? 'Ryerson Press'?[58] By the way ask Mr. C. if anything happened about 'Klee Wyck' for the soldiers & if old Mr. McCurry[59] got the *reproductions* of K.W. and if the studio magazine article ever came out? (K.W.'s reproductions were to come out in that[.]) The man might as well be dumb and have no hands to write with! *Resourceful* handless men write with their toes[,] I'm told!

I *do* hope my beloved trustors are in Toronto for the 'Trust' show.[60] I know it will exhibit better for their presences. I know you[.] In the gallery you will feel me parade between you[,] a hand on the strong arm of each. I was so terribly overcome the first time some of me hung there (in a 'Group Show') [.][61] I nearly died of embarras[sment]. Little did I think I'd ever have a show of my own or I'd have died *quite* off. Ira dear[,] you are so understanding (Bess would say you'd *been an artist* in a former incarnation)[.] Thank you for understanding how it felt clearing those 50 out of the studio. Nobody[,] *nobody* else did. Just you – it was just the wrench[.] I'm quite healed now & very happy about it all. And maybe I'll be let do a little more painting & there's the Biog: I'm working on her – *might* be *she*'ll be *done* when you'll come from the East. I feel she should get a wiggle on. It's *hard* digging down into the heart of my work & of Canadian life & feelings. Gee I wish I had a tractor & a stump puller!!!!!

I want to get this off so you will get it & (check for express eye) Sat. morn[.]

I shall be thinking of you doing a heavenly glide over B.C. Easter morn among the glory of the clouds. I think it will make your thoughts soar high – I know the prayers & love of *two* elderly women will be with you & I haven't a doubt there'll be young ones too (maybe even 'hussies' wishing you well) and all hoping for you a successful & happy

58 See the introduction regarding Ryerson Press's involvement in Carr's manuscripts.

59 H.O. McCurry (1887–1964) was the assistant director and secretary at the National Gallery of Canada between 1927 and 1939 and the director between 1939 and 1955. Carr explains their falling out as the result of her impatience with the arrangements made for shipping her art back from the National Gallery (BCARS, E.M. Hembroff-Schleicher Collection, MS 2792, letter from Emily Carr to Marius Barbeau, 5 May 1928, box 2, file 9).

60 Carr is likely referring to her February 1943 exhibition, which was derived from the original forty-five oil paintings of the Emily Carr Trust sent to the Art Gallery of Toronto during the war for their safekeeping.

61 Carr is referring to her participation as an invited contributor in the Group of Seven exhibition in April 1930 at the Art Gallery of Toronto.

trip[,] ease with your businesses & peace in your heart – &, see to it you come back with that holiday a *sure* thing[.]
God bless & keep you & bring you back safe & sound.

Lovingly Small & Emily

C.O.D: I'll specialize this so it won't clutter with Easter Cards & deliver 'round midsummer
C.O.D: II. Greeting[s] to the Clarkes & please don't read them my two last letters. E.

---

218 St. Andrews
April 6th, 1942

Dear Ira
Being *all* in a moil I write to calm myself – there are times when our sediment is all riled[,] not necessarily dirtying but disturbing us for the moment[.] Old perplexities[,] past & present arguing & shouting across intervening times. Feeling disappointments over promises unfulfilled, thoughts that blossomed but didn't fruit[,] dreamings that woke too soon[,] aspirations that sank & have lain in the mud bottom too waterlogged to hoist ever again. And others spiraling up with fresh bubble and new longings for being riled. I've been going over my letters (mostly Lawren's with the exception of Bess's occasional one)[.] I find all my hoarded letters are from *men* – I was supposed to be a man-hater!! He, he! I learned more from men, touched them closer[, have] been touched deeper by them than by women – queer me. I was always called a baby-hater too, yet babies always *came* to me[,] were not afraid! It would have hurt me dreadfully if they had been – animals & babies liking me burst me with satisfaction.

But the letters – Lawren's are splendid.[62] I don't know which to send you of them. I would send them to no one else. But as you know I have his permission[.] There is warm friendship & love between you two & I believe that both of you love me deeply. And it is because you have taken upon yourself the care of the burden of 'The Trust.' I feel you as well as

62 Lawren Harris's letters to Emily Carr are part of the Inglis Collection (MS 2181) at BCARS.

Lawren should know what went into its making[.] I shall[,] I think[,] let you have the letter bundle to browse among. There is repetition, always the insistent kindly push – work, work, always the cheering of my despair and discouragements. The delight that those men over there *believed in me,* had faith in what I was striving for, loved what I loved – Canada & things bigger than just money & glory in Art. Those letters show how weak & faltering I was & how Lawren knew the feel of weakness & the struggle necessary in his own work. Those letters are *worth* more than *my whole* Biog:[.] I had hoped to make some quotes from them but there is so much of value, I can't choose. As you read, save out & *mark* any you feel of special value to be put in Biog:[,] will you? – value to other seekers. You will see in how many he harps on 'the Biog idea.' Yet, I was quite unaware that probably he put the idea into my noddle originally, when I decided to write it.

There are a couple of letters also from a German man 'Gerrard Zeigler.'[63] Pathetic letters, read them. Oh the fine stuff in humanity and we let nationality drown it! I think I told you about those 2 German men [–] one an architect[,] one an engineer [–] who set out to see the world. One died in Arizona[,] this one returned a physical wreck. Both were mere boys during the other World War. They came out at a time when the world was still bitter against Germans and everyone who met them in my house said 'I am glad I met those *fine* young men[.] They make me feel different to all Germany.'

Well now you are in Toronto safe and sound, I hope. Winter again I spose! I hope you *snored* clear through your Winnipeg break & feel refreshed. We are calmly, restfully dull today.

To quote you 'This is not a letter only a note.'

Love and luck from a loving old woman and 'Small.'

---

218 St Andrews St
Ap[ril] 12, 1942

Dear Ira
Stan Caton & the *Choir* can Sanctuary the rest of the world[.] Tonight, I'll

63 Gerhart Ziegler, an acquaintance of Katherine Drier, visited Carr in Victoria with his friend Klaus for two weeks in 1930 (see Tippett 217).

Sanctuary you. I hope you've had a calm peaceful day with Lawren possibly? – Give the toes of those new shoes a chance to heal after scuffing them on Mr. Clarke's hard surface for the better part of a week. – I *wonder* if you reduced him to sensibility & in the end he pasted the bits of poor Small together again. She'll feel like hamburger 'til you do & he does.

Have been reading that poet of mine 'Song of the Rolling Earth.'
'The substantial words are in the ground & sea.
They are in *the air*[,] they are in you.
'The workmanship of souls is by those inaudible words of the earth
The Masters know the earth's words and use them more than
audible words.'[64]

I have been reading today Jacob Epstein's 'Let there be sculpture'[65] & somehow there seemed such connection in some way between sculpture – big modern sculpture – and the song of the rolling earth[:]

'The earth conveying a sentiment I utter & utter
I speak not yet if you hear me not of *what avail am* I to you?'

'I swear the earth shall be complete to him or her who shall be complete,

The earth remains jagged and broken to him or her who remains jagged & broken.' (How jagged & broken we all are at present?)

'Dictionaries of words that print cannot touch'[66] – Haven't you heard those unshaped unsounded words[,] Ira? Outdoors[,] specially in woods? The 'Song of the Rolling Earth' has always struck home in me.

Have you ever talked Whitman with Lawren, Ira?

Please will you word up for me the definition of lyric & epic? You know you told me that day we were going over pictures with Lawren[.] I have it in my mind that epic is a wholeness & lyric a piece[,] but I wish you'd give me a more particular definition.

11. PM. Oh how greedy I am[.] I have browsed on & on[.] Whitman, Browning – my sanctuaries & Stan & the Choir finished *long* ago & now *sleep* is here[.] I'll just read Edna St. Vincent Millay once again –

'Oh world I cannot hold the[e] close enough'
'World, world I cannot get thee *close* enough.'

64 'Song of the Rolling Earth' (I, 3–4, 15–16).

65 *Let There Be Sculpture*, by the American Expressionist (1880–1959) sculptor Jacob Epstein, was first published in 1940.

66 'Song of the Rolling Earth,' I, 25–6; III, 1–2; and III, 12, respectively.

[at the bottom of the page, with an arrow pointing to a smudge mark on the page] Sara's foot scampering over my bed.

And Oh – 'God's Grandeur!' So many lovely bits and bless you for sending to me these. Do you remember the last few lines of 'Goat Paths'[67] =

'I would think ['til] I had found
Something I can never find,
Something lying on the ground
In the bottom of my mind.'

Often when I am writing & things just half come & scoot away again, these goat-path lines haunt me.

I wrote your mother today[.] Knew she'd be missing you.

Always yours Emily

C.O.D. Monday and *lovely*[,] freshly subdued[,] no rampant glare but sweet *piercing* freshness striking crisp, the cool vitality of flower life which withers if touched by the hotness of our flesh.
C.O.D. Lucky Monday[,] Ira

Small.

Sunday, April 12 [1942, on 'Park Plaza, Toronto' notepaper]

Dear Emily:
Have you decided that I am dead? I should not be surprised if you had. Well very far from that I have been very busy. I am leaving today for Ottawa where I shall spend Monday and perhaps Tuesday. I am not sure whether or not I shall have to go to Montreal. If so I shall be there on Wednesday. I shall certainly be home in the West before Friday at the earliest.

Now for a brief recital of news –
1) Had dinner with Lawren and Bess or rather they had it with me. We had lots of excellent talk. Lawren is just the same grand person in

67 See note 53, page 52.

Toronto as he is in Vancouver – just as simple, just as honest, just as direct. He had not been able to see Baldwin[68] at that time but reported that the pictures have arrived – cases in good order so we shall expect the contents to be likewise. Lawren talked to Baldwin on the 'phone. Baldwin expressed [the] opinion that your exhibition should not come until next fall. Lawren will discuss [it] further with him. B. says the art season is over which seems to make no sense to me. They are thrilled to have the exhibition Lawren says.

Lawren & Bess plan to go to Montreal. They do not expect to be back in Vancouver for four weeks at least. Lawren says his mother's business is in good shape & is getting settled up very easily. I think they are finding Toronto & their friends here more attractive than they had anticipated but they still long to be back in B.C. I hope they are home when you visit us in Vancouver.

2) *Book of Small.* I spent all yesterday afternoon with Mr. Clarke. I had made a rearrangement of the Little Town material within itself which I think improves it, giving it a more obvious pattern. I left it with him and he promised to digest it. I shall discuss it with him when I spend a day in Toronto next week. I told him quite plainly that I was certain you would not agree to the arrangement they have suggested in the galley and that I would not ask you to agree. I am not sure what he will decide to do – he may propose some sort of compromise.

3) I shall see the Film Board people in Ottawa tomorrow and discuss your Vancouver career with them.[69]

We had a most awful blizzard of wind & snow on Wednesday night & all day Thursday. It was appalling but the snow has almost all gone & today is a lovely day.

Heaps of love to you, to Small & to Sara. I miss you all & Lady Jane.

Yours ever
Ira.

68 Martin Baldwin was the director of the Art Gallery of Toronto between 1932 and 1961.

69 In a letter to Carr dated 16 April 1942, Dilworth explains how he has met with members of the National Film Board, who showed him their A.Y. Jackson film as an example of their work. He reassures her that 'I have explained exactly what you are not willing to do and they have asked me to go ahead and prepare a creative plan on which a film might be based' (BCARS, Parnall Collection, MS 2763).

[on 'The Fort Garry, Winnipeg, Man.' letterhead]
Saturday, April 18, 1942.

Dear Emily:
Here I am on my way back home – indeed just half-way there. I shall leave on the same 'plane as this letter at 5 o'clock this afternoon and shall be in Vancouver before midnight if all goes well. If other plans have not been made, I shall be reading on Sanctuary tomorrow.

I had a long and rather trying interview with Clarke yesterday. I am glad to say that the result was satisfactory – he has agreed that the Book of Small proper and 'The Little Town' be kept separate. So there. Several things he has asked to be done – he wants us to take out some small repetitions in the Little Town. This can be done easily. More difficult perhaps he wants us to suggest new titles for some of the sections – more intriguing titles. He feels that the audience must be tickled into liking us. Some of the titles he wants to have changed are – Schools, Cathedral, Cemetery, Waterworks, Doctor and Dentist etc.[70] Will you think about them? I should have to go to Victoria some day next week & shall try to spend a few minutes with you.

Most serious of all – Mr. Clarke continues to dislike 'One Crow.' He thinks it shows a side of Small which 'is not in key' with the rest of her character as revealed in The Book of S. I have talked myself hoarse about it but he remains very firm. I think if we make a few changes in the story it may make it clearer & may remove the cause of his objection. Anyway I have done my best – my poor new shoes look quite scuffed – shabby.

Shall see you next week. Meantime heaps of love.

Yours ever
Ira

---

218 St Andrews Friday
Ap[ril] 24 / 42

Dear Ira
Perhaps it wasn't an overcoat[,] just a *warm* coat you put on to drive in.

70 The titles of the stories to which Dilworth refers were retained in *The Book of Small.*

It was a dark shade of navy – had a rough '[lumpy?]' surface[,] was double breasted. Perhaps you gave it away or it is in your cupboard[.] It was four years-old you said.

I loved seeing you Wednesday. Small jumped out of your waistcoat pocket or wriggled from under your sweater[.] Anyhow the little hussy came from somewhere & has remained perhaps leaving a scrap of herself like a nest egg in her permanent legal address. We seem to be thundering or is it practicing some new devilment for the benefit of Mr. Hitler?

Something bothers me a little about my proposed visit to Van. – turning you out of your own bed – Ferne & Mrs. S. were talking of how poorly you slept. To be listening through your sleep for your mother from upstairs to get up & come downstairs isn't so good as popping in from next door. Let me go upstairs this time[,] not oust you? I don't think I'd harm[.] I wouldn't up & down much, eh?

About 'One Crow.' I never thought much about Small in this story[.] I was trying to get at a place[,] a lone district where the little wild crow chooses human companionship even above freedom & his own kind & how something in his wild little black heart drew the love & *respect* of humans. I first called the story 'something unknown[.]' It was just as an odd story intended for the animal series. We wriggled it to Small later when we wanted material for Small. Don't feel sore if Mr. Clarke wants to kick it out. I [am] sorry he was sore & disappointed in that side of Small but Small had lots of sides, some of them *quite objectionable*[.] She was vindictive unforgiving capable of furious hating & sometimes altogether horrible. The crow was an honest-hearted merry trickster. You have no idea how deep he pecked his way into Small's heart[.] You remember him strutting up & down her carcass when she lay in the woods crying – mothering Small in her misery? That's why you are so dear[.] You understand that side of life. The love of animals & flowers.

Mr. C. took Sara kindly[,] even when she puddled on him. Maybe he's not *too* bad & he *did* agree about rescuing Small from Hamburg. So we'll let him have [his] way & chuck 'One Crow.' Only I don't want *your* book cut little. When you suggested re-moulding that other (I thought you said Shadow of Eagle[71] & that is *Indian*) maybe you[,] like me, confused it with 'Praying Chair'[72] – both duds – which I always did mix[.] But P.C.

71 Carr is referring to 'In the Shadow of the Eagle,' which appears in *The Heart of a Peacock* (89–109).

72 'The Praying Chair' appears in *The Book of Small* (49–58).

is small (the girl) [.] I've dragged her out & re-corseted her & I've pulled out some small *fragmentary* things[.] Might do now I've laid away Biog:[.] Rest may be good for her. I'll let you have the junk scraps at [the] beginning of the week[.] I intended tidying up a lot of oddments when Biog: was through[.] These will ease the job then. I don't want you disappointed over your Small book. Remember *I* give you *your own* copy autographed & be [thrilled?] & one crow can put his head under his wing & roost[,] *maybe* among the 'dear things' in the box (I'm living for a *long* time yet, I think[,] Ira) [.] But that box *is* comfortable. There is very little in it & that of no value but it hurts to think of unsupportive callous people tossing 'Old Aunt's' dear things round with curious laughs. Having a friend burn up your trash cleanly lovingly is comfortable. I spose a duplex person 'Artist & writer' is extra nuisancy[,] especially as the[y] *have* to hoard to make use of oddments to the end[.] Alice doesn't keep a scrap of *anything* – doesn't have to. She'll get out so tidily. Lizzie did too. Edith left an awful litter. Having the Biog: & knowing all my corners intimately better than anyone else[,] I just naturally lean on you[,] hoping I'm not too heavy. Thank you[,] dear editor[,] for battling for me in the East. Thank you too for telling me a little about your own business worrie[s]. I'm not wise but it's safe as a church – Sara is my only confidant and Sara's safe. Old Tilly is feeble-minded, shares confidences with anyone.

Hope you are enjoying the Lawren letters. If you have a blue or other gay pencil (not red) [,] mark anything you think should go in Biog[.] Those in red I have considered & used most of.

Cheer up over B. of S. Small herself is not depressed now (at first she was *scared*) [.] You know the longer I live[,] the more I feel every little thwart & annoyance has a *use* & meaning to us. If I smudge or spot or spoil in a painting[,] I work the blemish in & try to use it. Perhaps life is *not as queer* as we imagine. Do you remember in Song of Myself

'Oxen that rattle the yoke & chain or halt in the leafy shade
What is it that you express in your Eyes?
It seems to me more than all the print I have read in my life.'[73]

I took a journey in an ox-cart once up in Queen Charlotte I[slands]. The beasts rested periodically in the shade & I remember exactly that look, so baffling, in their eyes. A little few lines later W.W. writes

73 Walt Whitman, 'Song of Myself,' stanza 13, ll. 11–12.

'The wild gander leads his flock through the cool night
Ya-honk he says and sounds it down to me like an invitation
The pert may suppose it meaningless, but I listening close,
Find its purpose & place up there toward the wintry sky.'[74]

I believe that everything has [a] place in our lives and is to be used, even these tiresome little servant maids[.] I can see each one has taught me something as I look back & every animal I have ever had & every garden has planted loving memories in my heart and every sweetheart and every friend has taught me, and every pain & every ache [has] done something & some have to be repeated over & over before we heed[.] We *are* stubborn but I must get busy on my M.S. I only intended a scratch and here's a barrelful[,] a squirming unrelated mess – goodbye

Affectionately Emily

(over & page 2) Small's C.O.D.
Hello Guardian
Thank you and your boots for keeping me whole. Pat their scuffed noses for me. I'm home all except the little bit I leave in you to work like yeast in bread dough.
S's C.O.D. II. I always forget. Jane to be cut to 2 meals & a snack now – no more. She's grown & at a year only *one* per day – Sara has kicked off breakfast – gets 2 meals & afternoon tea. She's 4 months younger.
Emily's C.O.D. I. That maudlin sweet hour of prayer & your Sanctuary[.] What a difference[.] Bless you[.] I wish I could black that woman's eye.
E's C.O.D. II. Letter from Clarke just [came which] I enclose[.] Is this satisfactory[?] He seems pleased so I spose it is[.] I don't understand 'a straight royalty of 10%'[75] Emily

74 Ibid., stanza 14, ll. 1–4.

75 In his letter to Carr, dated 22 April 1942, Clarke specifically asks if 'you will accept a straight royalty of ten per cent. on his list price' (BCARS, Parnall Collection, MS 2763, box 4, file 30).

218 St Andrews
Tuesday morn [ca. 28 April 1942]

Dear Ira
Yours just come, special. Thank you for letting me know. Thank you for trusting me – helps the disappointment over too – so again it's hustle & bustle for you & if the C.B.C. rip you through the sky too! – Well they *couldn't* without splitting you in two & then both halves would be useless [–] one here[,] one there.

This filthy war! Now Alice tells me the Empress of Asia[76] [has] gone to the bottom – horrible! And the only thing to do – face the whole thing but look beyond it.

It is nice of people to want to see me. They are very kind – You know the ones I want to see. It is like coming home this time – last time I was *scared.* Afraid perhaps your mother & Phylis would not like me. Now I am *not* afraid of them. And I'm bringing a big paint-spotted apron to play with Jane in & spare my smocks. I don't care what you've done to her as long as you all love her.

I had a big work on the canvas of the little round tree yesterday[.] Took it to bed with me last night[.] I always know when I [am] working *earnestly* because I carry the one I'm working [on] to my bedroom & stick it up on a little shelf opposite my bed so I can see it with fresh eyes when I wake. I find lots of shortcomings that way. I am so happy that you like these canvases. It is specially nice of you to be good to your 'paint'-wards on top of all the 'write'-wards[.] Poor Ira – you required the capacity of a chick-brooder and I'm trembling anxious about the Biog: tail under your eye – I'm so queer (feeling) without her – tho' I don't think she was ever quite so *dear* to me as the 'Bobtails.'

Alice is[,] I think[,] really *looking forward* to the place *all to herself*[.] I am glad she won't be alone Wednesday night. I just told her extra business had cropped up for you[.] Maybe it's best for me to wait

Looks like rain.

May peace & blessing be in your heart over the worries of Wednesday. I shall think of y[ou] often. Sunday's Sanctuary is with me still. May I

76 The S.S. *Empress of Asia*, a British ship, was burned out by bombs on 5 February 1942.

someday have a copy of 'Cedars' and 'Flight of Wild Geese?'[77] I am bringing over the rest of L's letters for you.

All sorts of love 'til Thursday – NO only *one* sort – the best –

Always Emily
Small's C.O.D. – Mine too (love) your pocket-girl. S.

Friday morn [ca. 8 May 1942]

Beloved Editor,
I rushed Mr. Clarke's letter to you last night because for fear you *should* pop or hop over Saturday[,] then you would not get it 'til Monday. Well it was quite encouraging. Things seem to move. Small's cloth from the States to dress her in, and Wyckie no. II sailing to England & poking her nose into the States, and Mr. Clarke swallowing the whole crate of pictures! I'm sure I wrote him re: the other letter[,] Sir Humphrey Milford's offer[,] but I guess I sent it slow mail.

Well I am dying to know *if* you liked the bits of re-writing & oddments I sent you. I am so incompetent to judge myself. I spose it's because I write emotionally rather than by rules which I don't know[.] Two of those I *felt very* strongly[:] 'Mint' & 'Ducks.'[78] Do you know that[,] 'til I grew up[,] to pass a poultryces[79] & see dead ducks hanging up turned me deadly sick[?] That killing took place under the 'killing tree' in the cow yard[.] It was in the original 'Cow Yard.' Ruth cut it out as also she cut out 'Father is a Cannibal'[80] which was also in Cow Yard. Ira, *must* people always insist on glad merry things? Life is not like that as you intimated in your last letter. It's the downs that strengthen & assist the ups. I did not put in all the awfulness I might have. How Small passed through the kitchen as Bong[81] opened the oven door to baste the ducks & Small flopped on the kitchen floor[.] She just couldn't help it[.] Creatures meant so much to her yet I don't think she was very sentimental. Father thought it was nonsense, he

77 Carr is possibly referring to 'At the Cedars' by D.C. Scott and 'The Flight of the Geese' by C.G.D. Roberts (1860–1943).

78 'Mint' is an unpublished story and 'Ducks' appears as 'Ducks and Father and Mother' in 'Small and Her Creatures' (*HP* 153–4).

79 A poulterer.

80 'Father Is a Cannibal' appears in 'Small and Her Creatures' (*HP* 155–7).

81 Bong was the Carr family's Chinese family servant. See 'Servants' (*BS* 151–4).

raised most all our food. But I think the ducks showed him[,] for I was not allowed to look after the hens after that & the grown-ups had them for late dinner [while] we had tea in [the] nursery. I guess I'd have died to see the ducks dismembered at [the] table.

'Mint' I write just because it *was* mint and fairy-tales & school days & general happiness & loving & I put in a sprig of mint to speak to your nose[.] Praying Chair seemed to tell the 'Want' from beginning to fulfilment but maybe you'd duck at Small's *oldness* in the end. *Don't* be mad with Small for growing. It's a way life has. Oh my dear[,] what is this flesh of ours that grows old & fretted & ugly & aching. What *would* life be without the soul to back it.

I have not sent you any name suggestions[.] It is hard without the M.S. to refresh my mind. I do what I can over [the] week-end. My old body is paying me out for my day in the woods. Wednesday. Campbell took us[.] We went out at 1.30[.] They duped me & went for a drive to 6. P.M. A[lice] & Campbell. Oh Ira!!!!!! Just a little clearing all snarled with undergrowth around my silly feet and dead quiet & spring – I maybe found the end of the Biog: there. I found some lady-slippers & my *whole self* has been full of it all ever since[.] My soul self & body full of tiredness – gay enough 'til I got home[,] then the slump. And old Biog: wracking with tease. Alice's eyes [are] hurting from the outing[.] They are bad these days. Seems everything that suits me aggravates her – bum legs & all[,] I scuttle round the brush better than she[.] She never liked off a beaten track [–] a proper chair & a paved road. I plan to go into the woods a few times more while the spring, glowing the 'illumination[,]' is on. It is so fleeting[,] only a breath's-hold & it's off. But I haven't told all. Wild Geese – I am sure thousand upon thousands.

I heard you last night. Alice rushed up 'Ira's on the air!'

I found as many more letters of Lawren. I had separated the bunch & forgotten. You shall have them.

Love, always (really)
Small.

Monday [ca. 11 May 1942]
(Tuesday) [ca. 12 May 1942]

[at top of letter] P.S. Cod N.B. – Most of this is cancelled by a flesh and blood chin-chin yesterday[,] so spare your eye 'til X. [arrow points to sentence that begins with 'I know how I have to *sweat!*'] (Begins Here: Monday)

Dear Ira

I haven't *seen* you for *years*[,] *hear*[d] from you for *months* and it's *seconds* since I even *thought* of you. You might reward faithfulness with half a thought me-wards – the weather is getting *hot* and I know we are going to suffocate & I'd rather drown and something tells me you're blue? – it's Monday – the war looks beastly and I feel unsteady as an unsorted sack of mail[,] for my little friend (Carol)[82] is coming from the East[.] First she wrote she couldn't, then wired she would! I asked her for a month & wired fare yesterday and do hope it will restore her to activity and her wholesome useful life. Her family are so *delighted* at her having this chance & her doctor says splendid! I think it will do A. & I good too.

I wrote your mother yesterday[.] How is she? & what of the Major? *Don't be snippy*, I want the Dilworth newses. Didn't we agree to share our *goods & bads*? Not to be only ornamental friends?

The twins are up and doing[.] I will get my two pictures off to [the] gallery end of week (I hope) and am deep in 'No Man's land' (vulture)[.][83] If you don't like it *say* so but *I do*[.] It may have *serious faults* (born writer my hat! (N.Y. Times) I ain't!)[.][84] *I know how* I have to *sweat* to make my meanings *clear*. I've *always* liked my vulture story[.] I hope as far as humanly possible I went vulture so folks could *see* him[.] Love my uncle Tom[,] Ira[,] he was worth it. Sally & Billie & I sink to humdrum insignificance beside him. I feel it a privilege to have been permitted to live so close to his queerness for a spell. There was loyalty & nobility about him[.] He was more than a machine for the clearing up of carrion. Lawren read this story once, *long* ago[.] It was then *only* a *funny story* about a *queer beast*. I have deepened it since and now writing this to you has brought the experiences of Uncle Tom [a] little clearer to me still. Love Uncle Tom and *understand*.

Often when I write to you about my work[,] groaning on, sometimes irrelevantly, it is to clarify some muddle in my thoughts[.] Understand-

82 Carr perceived Carol Pearson (Williams), who wrote *Emily Carr as I Knew Her*, as a daughter.

83 The story appears as 'Uncle Tom' in 'Five Birds,' the first part of *The Heart of a Peacock* (22–4).

84 Carr is referring to a review that appeared in the *New York Times Book Review* titled 'Indian Ways' (7 June 1942) in which the reviewer claimed she was 'a natural-born writer ... [S]he writes with a brisk and sensitive originality.'

ing sympathetic ears & eyes help enormously. The day you told me about that little boy who put 3 crosses on the root-house roof I knew I'd find a sympathetic ear & it is very comfortable – thank you. I'm glad there is room for us *all* on the earth[,] no matter *how* queer an 'us.' If God made such a variety of flowers & trees, of course he made [a] variety of people too[,] just the rope he bunched us with is the same: individually so different! Some of us smell! (pleasurably[,] some disagreeably) –

Bless You – Now for Uncle Tom. = Tuesday night. How lovely it was to see you (and a *particularly nice* you yesterday[).] I've been trying to write to Mr. Clarke[.] Is there any nasty 'smelling' thing I could enclose that might 'hurry' an answer out of him? Do you think perhaps he may be waiting 'til that tin plate the Governor hands out *is* handed? Still you know he kept us dancing furiously on our hats a long time for K.W. to appear. Brother, let's elevate our uses and *pretend we don't care if she never* comes out, only then I'll be *so* shamed that your book fizzled on us. I've worked on 'Quiet' & clear today[.] I've put 'Ira Dilworth' as owner of 'The Clearing' on its back.[85] Lawren says those two can sit in storage in [the] Gallery 'til my fall show.

Small's Cods 1, 2, 3, 4, etc. Giggle with us a moment[,] Guardian! You me & Emily – if not[,] E. may turn rusty and you *said* I was to keep her cheered. You see, E. and I have had Alice in town (shopping & lunch). A's spirits were in dilapidation. 1st we roamed round 15 ct store & Kreskie's.

E. would pass slowly up the aisles making rambling comments. 'Here's potato parers, these are handkerchiefs – 5 cents & *very* ugly – castors, screws, gimlets, knives, string, wool, shoe polish, tooth-paste[,] glue, saucepans[,] underwear – now let's find hose-menders[.] (The new pups have bust all our combined garden-hoses) (Three busts to 1 foot)[.] Here are duckey children's sun-hats[,] little rosebuds all over but *very* poor quality – pretty teacups[.] Eh? 49 [cents] each[,] rather heavy but good floral design – some pink some yellow[.] So old Emily rambled on & on about the *use & looks & strength* of everything & if she moved more than 3 steps A. would lose her & fall into a lamp shade or butt into the candy cases. After they had filled a bag with junk such as can't be telephoned for & A. had bought household trifles that sounded useful or ornamental rolling off E.'s tongue[,] the old girls decided they

85 *The Clearing*, painted in 1942, is now in the possession of the National Gallery of Canada; it served as the frontispiece in *Growing Pains*.

were hungry & tired, so they braved the 'stop-go's' and got over [View Street] & A decided on Spencer's basement next for 3 lbs of butter. But, E. stuck at the stairs a *whole* block of underground walking before they got to butter counter.

'Couldn't you *phone* for the butter?'

'I like to see butter & *carry* it home[.] I'll meet you outside Terry's.' But as A. always went to wrong doors & missed meeting even when she had 2 eyes full of sight, E. did not want the risk of chasing round & round between Terry[']s 2 doors. So A. went into a fury and then dumb. They went to Terry's *early* to avoid 'lunch-rush.' In the middle of the floor a mean little bunch of waitresses (all new & in misfit smocks & caps left behind when their predecessors went military) were fighting as to whose tables were whose, while hungry people waited[.] When E had sat A. in a booth & read her the menu[,] the top half of E. kept oozing from their stall trying to arrest one of the wait-persons who occasionally came to the booth looked at them as if they were a menagerie & went away again[.] At last E. took to shouting her order at the back of each waitress but *nothing* happened except that A. got madder & said 'there is no rush, Millie!' Instead of all waitresses bringing all the orders E. had shouted[,] the meanest rattiest of them all brought us 5 paper table-napkins. E. asked if they might not have a glass of water to go with the napkins & the girl then offered a menu. When E. asked the 'wait' 'which food went with which' to make what was called the 'club luncheon[,]' the creature always began with 'I *imagine* this[.]' E. overboiled & (*I* think she'd done *well* to keep *under the lid that long*)[.] She roared 'I want to eat[,] *not* imagine!' So A. & E. came home hungry & *without* butter.

I spose it *is* war[,] Guardian? I did as you told me about 'giggling E. up[.]' The whole bother was that all the while she *wanted* to be with that Vulture Tom. – She[,] he & the typewriter are hob-knob now in her bedroom. I've left her there and am

Your *loving*
Small

A girl eater at Terry's had such lovely cheek-bones & pale eyes lighter than all the color in her face[.] I can't forget her. Strange vague thoughts were in her eyes. S.

Vancouver, B.C. [ca. 15 May 1942]

Dear Emily:
Thanks a million for your letters which have been grand this week (how do you ever get time from your work to do them?) and for your kindness in sending on Small's letters. The child is a dear and writes very well indeed. You must be kind to her, Emily. Her account of your visit to the 15-cent store and Terry's amused me no end. What an eye she has for the apparently trivial but really important details. Bless her dear heart and God keep her young and sensitive but protect her from being too much hurt by this cruel world and its messiness just now! Children are so easily hurt. Our Lord knew that when He said, 'Suffer the little children to come unto me.'[86] I like to think that He was remembering some experience when as a child he was hurt by some chance happening. He certainly gave a grim warning to the Hitlers of this world (who are not all in Germany) when he warned them against putting stumbling blocks in the way of little children and said it would be better for any one of them who did put a stumbling block in the way of a child that he were cast with a stone 'round his neck into the midst of the sea. Oh that all school teachers and parents knew what he meant when he said that. The eternal and ageless heart of the child! I sometimes think it is the very core of genius. Oh I know that wisdom must be added but so often one sees the gifted individual whose youth was bright with promise lose in the struggled for position, wealth, knowledge (book-learning) his tender heart and his sensitive powers of perception.

Uncle Tom is grand! You made me see him and love him[,] even though I have had time to read him only once. There are lots of suggestions which I should like to make and will – but basically the sketch is very well done.

Mr. Clarke's letters were fine. I would not suggest changing a word of it: I sent it on by airmail at once, so he should have it on Monday. I hope we get an answer 'plitty hully up quick.'

By the way, the bookstores here are making great preparations for special promotion of the sale of 'Klee Wyck' as soon as the announcement re the Governor General's medal is made public. I was in Ireland & Allan's Bookshop today and they are expecting a large shipment of

86 The words of Christ as they appear in Mark 10:14: 'Suffer the little children to come unto me and forbid them not.'

KWs next week to meet what they think may be a considerable demand [for] her. Ireland told me that the sales had stayed amazingly good for a Canadian book.

The contract came yesterday. I have thought about it a lot and the function of Biog. I am going to have supper with Lawren & Bess tomorrow night. I shall discuss the problem with Lawren: I know you won't mind. Wish you were going to be at Lawren's too. We shall think of you – you can be sure of that.

Mother is much better. She is up again and enjoyed our two days of sunshine.

Phylis is much happier now that she has made her decision. I am trying to find her a position in Vancouver – something that will occupy her full time in an organized, orderly way. Poor young thing! This is a hard time for them and, as you know, Phylis really is sensitive. Under all her calm surface she has kept a child's heart.

Now, my dear Emily, I must say goodnight and post this. I shall 'Special' it in the hope that it may reach you tomorrow. Love to you and Small –

Yours devotedly
Ira

NB. I am so glad your friend is coming to you for a visit. It was generous of you to make it possible. She must be *very* nice. D.
NB. I am not sure whether I have sent you these Sanctuaries or not. If I have, no matter – here are extra copies. If I have not, so much the better. Glad you are still enjoying 'Gitanjali.'[87] God bless you. D.

PURPLE MONDAY
218 St Andrews
25 minutes to 10 AM
Sunday [ca. 25 May 1942]

Good morning
You *deserve* a letter? Small & Emily in consultation say NO and duette a

87 Dilworth is referring to *Gitanjali*, the collection of poems by Rabindranath Tagore (1861–1941), who was a native of Bengal and who was awarded the Nobel Prize for Literature in 1913.

sniff. 'Is there anything to *answer*??? Only a[n] asking *type-written addressed* envelope containing only printed matter?' Are machines for recording *very* expensive[,] Ira? We should like to record the *magnitude of our combined* sniffs[.] '*NEWS*'? The weather is pretty nice this A.M. (we may as well get the worth out of our stamp). *Such thrilling* news about the weather – there has been so much wet in recent *years,* you know, tho' I must say we prefer wet to heat, but the dogs don't like it. That I think is *all* our news for the moment.

We met someone who met you strolling in the Vancouver Park recently. She said 'you hadn't aged much since we saw you.['] But I expect your handwriting *has* gone a deal feebler in the ages since last we read any. Hoping you are well & happy.

S. and E.

P.S. Our noses are in the air very high above our mouths. S.
P.S.S. I spose the tailor has taken in your waistcoat – doesn't seem very roomy. 'Small'

Tuesday [ca. 4 August 1942, Mount Douglas Park]

Dear Guardian
I'm so glad 'm'skeetoes' don't seek nutriment from bundles of memories like me[.] Poor old Emily's flesh is riddled with bumps that tease something *awful*! It is *cold* this morning[.] Autumn is eating up our only half-ripened summer. I hope she gets stomach-ache for her greedy impatience – Emily is O.K. with a blanket gown & her electric hot bag – Jane's plain bad[.][88] She's bust her collar, bust her chain, she busts everyone's heart & *wants the earth* but she's very happy[.] So is E. and loves her but none of them is as *free* as me.

E. & I went into the woods yesterday[,][89] a long walking & Mrs.

88 Carr had taken Jane with her for company.

89 In a letter written two days earlier, 2 August 1942, Carr describes her sketching trip to Mount Douglas Park woods (located in Cordova Bay Road, Gordon Head, Victoria), during which time she is bitten by mosquitoes: '2 more sketches yesterday and a walk (quite sizable) & the finding of a lively new spot can't be done today ... Oh the blessed woods! Waiting, waiting always waiting & we always rushing.'

Edwards[90] has decreed it's *bed* for E. today & E is meek. The cabin is nice with cedar trees for nurses – delicious nurses – who don't rustle starch, and chatter. Emily has *not* got the cedar rhythm yet nor their particular idiom. This place is full of cedars. Their colors are terribly sensitive to change of time & light[.] Sometimes they are bluish *cold* green, then they turn yellow *warm* green[,] sometimes their boughs flop heavy & sometimes float[,] then they are fairy as ferns & then down they droop, heavy as heartaches.[91] No wonder Emily despairs! Yesterday when she was hiding behind a great reddish purple cedar trunk on a trail across the park where no picnickers go – a solitary youth streaked by on a bicycle. 'Didn't see us' grimaced E. but at the turn the youth did & threw his bike down & came back.

'Painting[,] eh?'

E. glowered & grunted and the boy stood – E's eyes stung like mosquitoes. The boy didn't mind being stung[.] He really *wanted* to *know* & *see.* E. felt it, so she softened and he stayed most an hour maybe, he worked [on] the Gov. seed farm and was in earnest & they talked about 'growing[.]' He'd knocked round quite a bit & seen many places and Emily answered his questions about painting as best as she could & when he asked to come & see the picture again in her cabin she said 'no, she was busy here but he could come to the studio if he came to town & she'd show him some.' I was surprised because *you know* she's pretty crusty when working[,] Ira. She's a funny old windmill & creates frightfully as she whirls. There's a streak of iced sunshine across the floor now and outside the sunshine is being served with fog-sauce. Goodbye. I hope you're well. Here's a hug.

Small

P.S. Emily reads all her most beautiful Sanctuaries over & over here. I enjoy them with her. S.

90 Mrs Edwards was the proprietor of the tea-house, which was in close proximity to the cottage where Carr was staying (see Tippett 263).

91 Carr is likely referring to her oil-on-paper sketches of cedars that she made on the sketching trip and from which *Cedar Sanctuary* was later derived.

[ca. 16 September 1942, Mayfair Nursing Home[92]]

Dear Ira
Welcome home. And this time I won't leave a trail of stale letters to follow you like bitten buns after a Sunday school picnic[,] kicked here & kicked there. I'll send them to head-quarters & you can sort them from your *important* mail and read at leisure *when you don't forget.*

It's nice here[.] They are very good to me[.] Most the patients I'm told are 80 or 90 & have lost legs or wits or something, so I'm quite a girl & whole[.] I am to be allowed to *feed* myself one meal today[.] I've almost forgotten how to find the way to my own mouth with my own hand (that is supposed to be an effort). As for walking it is not even mentioned. I am still a 'flatter[.]' I'm told you & Mr. Clarke & Harry Lawson are on my chart as allowed visitors. But beyond Alice NO WOMEN (visitors). I back one window & the other shows nothing but shingles & the blind down. On the ceiling is an ugly oblong fixture with 2 dim lamp globes that is my new inspiration[,] but I have Joseph[93] & your glads still & some glorious zenias Myfanwy (Spencer Campbell)[94] sent me, big as plates & *such* colors!

Today is medal day[.] Will it be you or Mr. Clarke[,] I wonder:[95] poor two[,] I hope you don't hate it as much as I would. I wonder if the other Mr. & Miss will be there to grab theirs.[96] I wonder how soon I'll see you & Mr. Clarke *if* he comes to Vic. Perhaps I'll be too far away for your

92 Towards the end of August, 'a clot formed on [Carr's] heart' and, suffering greatly, she was 'rushed to the hospital' for a period of approximately ten days (Tippett 265). She was then transferred to the Mayfair Nursing Home, where she resided for five months.

93 A 'heavenly blue parakeet' (see Carr's letter to Ruth Humphrey, 3 August 1937 in Humphrey and Blissett, 109).

94 Myfanwy Pavelic (b.1916 as Myfanwy Spencer), a Canadian artist, was one of Carr's good friends. She was awarded the Order of Canada and is a member of the Royal Canadian Academy.

95 Carr's *Klee Wyck* received the Governor General's Award for non fiction in 1942. Clarke received the award on her behalf because she was too ill to attend the ceremony (see BCARS, Parnall Collection, MS 2763, letter from W.H. Clarke to Emily Carr, 16 September 1942, box 4, file 30).

96 That year, Alan Sullivan (1868–1947) won the Governor General's Award for fiction for *Three Came to Ville Marie* and Anne Marriot (b. 1913) won the award for poetry for *Calling Adventures!* Dilworth is credited with having introduced Marriot to modern poetry.

time here to visit. Jiggle me in somehow[.] I'll be here a whole month. Alice is expecting a lump of great-niece for a few days[.] She likes her so I'm glad. Val Hennell is on leave & is dear to her[.] He's a nice boy[,] my favourite of the Hennell tribe. She's been once[.] Val brought her. It's not far across the Park but I *told* her not to feel bound to come every day & wear herself. She really does love being alone in her house[,] that's one comfort. I wish she liked Sara. She does Tilly & her neighbors are kind if she lets them be.

I write a very little when too *completely bored.* 'Birds' grows slowly roaming my brain[.][97] I don't chase it. But when I get restless[,] I do a little bit & I have Gitanjali here[.] It is most beautiful and it soothes me and you promised me a *Sanctuary in hospital* [but] never sent it. Small was furious[,] sat on edge of your pocket & kicked your chest with her heels but I don't expect they felt on you. Emily understood that you were busy or wondered if it was the bad present males or mails & pretended she didn't care. But she did[.] My Sanctuaries are very comfortable[.] I brought them but they are out of reach in the cupboard with my typing things. This is from Tagore: –

'From the words of the poet men take what meanings please them; yet their last meaning points to thee.' Am tired – finish later.

Saturday Afternoon[.] Alice just come[.] No line from you[.] I'm *peeved*[.] You've been gone a *whole week*[.] There *is* an airmail service you know. I'm dying to know about you & Clarke's conference[.] You haven't kicked each other unconscious[,] I hope.

Mad but affectionately,
Emily

Monday [ca. 21 September 1942]

Dear Ira
It's come[98] & not much to look at – no more *gold* in it than in me. Looks as if made from the molten scrapings of a boil up of junk metal, and as if they were pressed out by the 100 second-handed round off hand like Sunday school tickets.

97 The early draft of 'More Birds,' the second section of *The Heart of a Peacock* (57–85).
98 Carr is referring to her Governor General's Award.

My name and & what for are scratched on in measly gilt letters. It wasn't worth your tails, white-front & fare from Toronto – glad you didn't go: what does one *do* with medals when they get them? Would you like it for a watch-fob? Now you've reduced[,] it would protect your whole middle in case a Jap-bomb hit you there[.] Well, a dead sparrow has lodged in the gutter of the house next door[.] I spose I shall have to lie and watch and *smell* it disintegrate[.] My nurse suggested we throw something to try & dislodge it. I offered my medal for a missile. Mrs. Clark[99] was much shocked. I know I *ought* to be ashamed. Some would give their eye-teeth for medals. I'm not blasé[.] *Don't believe that of me.* They just *don't interest* me & seem silly (like silver cups do) and yet, when a worthwhile commentator writes a *good* crit on my work, showing he *has read & got* it[,] or when someone speaks *deeply* of a picture[,] *I'm* terribly *pleased & proud*[.] *That* seems worthwhile[,] straight from them to you, *through your work.* I loved the understanding comments you made on the Mt. Douglas sketches & on 'Mother.'[100] I feel you'd got to the core of what I *tried* to do out there & it helped & pleased me a lot.

I have been wondering if I *ought* to have sent you my yesterday's letter? *Don't* hate me for doing so. I was boiling with rage – took heart pills etc – and why? When I *knew* it was lies. Only when *you* were not there to hit back, the ones who love you *must*[.] Old 'O' horrors'[101] looks like a kicked pup today. Mrs. Clark does not let her come into my room. If my nurse is off she sends the cook (a nice woman with *splendid hair*). Alice toddled all the way over to bring the medal. It wasn't her day[,] she only comes every 2nd day. Hasn't she aged lately? She is cheerful but losing in strength & sight. She is the frail but wiry kind[.] I'm afraid the recent antics of my heart have been very hard on her.

Mrs. Burrell (the nurse I had at home) came to see me today. She has been twice[.] She thinks I look much better & more rested. I typed a little (only 3 sheets) today & got tired[.] The table has to be adjusted[.] I did it in bed. Hope Major Macaroni is better[.] Tell your mother I'll write her soon – Mrs. Clark insists on long spells of doing 'nothingness[.]' I find it less tiring to both me & my eyes to *write* than to *read* much[.]

99 Mrs Clark was the head nurse at the Mayfair Nursing Home.

100 This story was recently published in *Opposite Contraries.*

101 Apparently, a letter by Dilworth was found and misconstrued by this nurse (although Carr was in possession of the letter, it remains unclear if the letter was addressed to her).

Don't hate me for being so *indifferent* & *stupid* over the medal[.] *Of course* I *am* pleased Klee Wyck went over but what one *has* done seems so poor & small compared to the '*going on*.' How's your anthology? If those old C.B.C.ers only provided some *efficient helpers* for their other heads instead of piling *more salaries* on top & ornamental chiefs[,] seems to me there'd be some sense – 'Small' is listed in the new book-list of the year.

Yours lovingly[,] Emily

P.S. Seems you don't want 'The Clearing' or you'd have claimed it. It has been *returned* to me – well, I can give it to the old Men's Home, eh?[102] E.

Vancouver, B.C.
Sunday Oct. 4 [1942] – 11.00 p.m.

Dear Emily:
I am so glad that there was no seat on the early 'plane yesterday and that I had time to go in to see you for even a few minutes. Sorry you were feeling 'low' but that is one of the characteristics of any kind of heart trouble. I do hope my visit didn't harm the precious pumping part of your heart. Wish I could give you a bit of my pumps: I am sure you could use it and I could spare it. But I have to be satisfied with sending you great quantities of my 'feeler' – perhaps that will help.

What a fine, understanding person Dr. Baillie is! It was very kind of him to go below and let us have our visit undisturbed. I had a chat with him as I came away. He is very anxious that you remain in the home for as long as possible. It really does seem best Emily and we shall just have to hope that the financial end of the thing will get looked after. I have faith that it will. You remember what Mr. Clarke told me – that if you wanted for money we must let him know and they would make further advances. So, my dear, don't worry. Things will work out somehow and worry and anxiety on your part will only complicate them.

You are so generous to think and worry about those pictures for Dr. Trapp, Mr. Gage and Mrs. McGeer. First time I am over again I shall try to

102 In a letter that followed a few days later, Emily confirms that Dilworth may take her painting *The Clearing* and that she 'was surprised when it came home' rather than going to him.

take time to go over to St. Andrews Street and choose them. Dr. Trapp & Walter will be thrilled to have them – so will Mrs. McGeer, of course.

I am taking the poems I mentioned in to be typed tomorrow. I shall send you part of the 'Melampus' by George Meredith.[103] It is rather difficult in parts but the central idea is clear enough, namely that Melampus learnt everything that was of any value in making him a useful person to his fellow men from the woods and the creatures of nature. There are some lovely thoughts and beautiful lines – for instance –

'For him the woods were a home and gave him the key
of knowledge, thirst for their treasures in herbs and flowers.
The secrets held by the creatures nearer than we
To earth he sought, and the link of their life with ours'!

I am going to send you also two poems by Evelyn Underhill.[104] She is an English poetess who takes a profoundly mystical attitude towards life and religion. Two of her poems are very lovely – 'Immanence' and 'Massa Cantata' – that title means a chanted or sung mass.

I share your disgust about the medal. It is a pretty cheap affair. But really, Emily, the honour behind it is great and you must try to think of that.

I share also your dislike of the English dandy cover for Small. She just won't have that. I should rather have her come out naked even if she does not see the light of publication until November and has to shiver in fog and rain. Better that than that she should be dressed up like a silly English prig – a sort of stupid volume for indolent *young ladies of fashion.* It won't do. So let's agree to talk hard to Mr. C. in favour of the green with Small's portrait in its gold medallion.

But it is late and I must get to bed. God bless you, Emily! And may he keep you always in his care. You remember that great expression – 'Underneath are the everlasting arms.'[105] I know you believe that. Oodles of love to you and Small –

Yours Ever,
Ira

N.B. I posted your letters for you.

103 'Melampus' appears in Meredith's *Poems and Lyrics of the Joy of Earth* (1883).

104 Evelyn Underhill (Mrs Stuart Moore, 1875–1941) was an English poet whose first significant book, *Mysticism,* was published in 1911.

105 A reference to Deuteronomy 33:27.

Saturday Night [ca. 10 October 1942]

Dear Ira,
It was nice to hear your voice on the programme today. I was surprised at your selection[.] It seemed almost as if it were part of Klee Wyck rather than 'Small[.]' I kept forgetting it wasn't. Well I've had a wonderful time[.] 3 splendid visits with Mr. Clarke[.] Goodness he *is* nice[.] And yesterday who should walk in but Dr. Trapp. And she came again today & is coming tomorrow[.] *Such* pleasures. Mrs. Clark is a dear[.] She knows those to let in & that do me good & those to *keep out* that excite & exhaust me. I am tired tonight but very happy[.] People *are* nice[,] Ira[.] To think I used to proclaim 'I *hated* men' & to find specimens of their kind so dear & good just shames me to the marrow. I told Dr. Trapp about 'the sketch' & asked if she'd like to go over and choose it herself. She said, 'No, I might if it was some people's choice but I would be *quite content with Ira's.*' I told her you were going to choose first opportunity that you had time. She did not tell me much about her new house[.] I spose people can't tell of their own as well as outsiders so you'll just *have* to[.] I want to hear all about it.

I had an exceedingly kind letter from Mrs. McGeer the other day[106] – Dr. Trapp brought me glorious red roses with a smell (the red rose smell) [.] I have a *lovely* new nurse (Mrs. Clark's regular head nurse who was away holidaying my first month here) [.] She is so competent[,] so nice to look upon & kind. I was prepared not to like her[.] Mrs. Clark cricked her up so high. But she is all & more.

Ira I love 'Melampus[.]' I do not find it difficult at all to comprehend. It has the same something which that other thing of Meredith's you sent me had [–] 'Woodland Peace[.]' That deep delight and intimacy with the small things of which the great whole is composed[.] I am thoroughly living in it. I liked the other selections tho' particularly the 'Little Things[.]'[107] I long for your anthology[.] I do so love your selection in poems.

106 The letter from McGeer to Emily Carr, dated 4 October 1942, is in BCARS, Parnall Collection, MS 2763, box 4, file 16.

107 An unclear reference, although possibly Carr is alluding to Kahlil Gibran's 'On Friendship,' a copy of which she kept in her personal 'Sanctuary' and which concludes with 'For in the dew of little things the heart finds its morning and is refreshed.'

Mr. Clarke spoke beautifully of *you* a number of times. I loved him for it. We had such *wonderful* talks. He is perfectly splendid & generous in the things he said of my work[,] Ira. We talked shop & more shop. I learned a whole lot of the publisher's difficulties that will[,] I hope[,] make me a heap more patient & sympathetic to them. He really has got that jacket to heart[.] He got a long wire this A.M. re: new suggestions. Yesterday[,] between us[,] we worked out a new one. After what the 'selling agents' said of the medallion I begged him *not* to use it[.] I could see his point[.] This is the one I drew up (I will enclose rough sketch) but meantime he gets this wire & eventually feels they should have some consideration (his printers) after all the trouble they have been to. He is airmailing mine & I fancy leaving it to them[.] He is so anxious Small shall *not tumble down.* He expects her to beat K.W. I do hope she does not flop on him. Well Ira[,] we discussed & discussed writing problems. It has been such an inspiration. He says he is itching to get busy on a 3rd book (animal)[.] I told him about Bobtails, Life of Woo, Uncle Tom, Peacock, Racoon, Even a Rat & Bravo[,] Mary Anne[.] I said I thought there was *almost more* than enough for a volume[.] I asked him to tell me *why* he did not like 'One Crow[.]' He said the other Small stories had not built up to it. Now he knows more[,] he understands the situation of Small then[,] but the public had not that background for the story[.] One Crow seems a M.S. rather left in the air[,] not quite fitted in yet[,] doesn't it? I told him about the Biog: & he said he'd like to publish it. And I told him it was *yours right now* and always and that *you knew* I did not want it published 'til after I was dead & he said he understood. I told him a little of its build-up & he was most interested. We discussed a name for it and he said 'not a Biog: name like Biog of E.C. or of an artist or like that[.]' He thought 'Growing Pains' rather suitable[;] however that is for you & he to fix when it comes. He was very interested in 'Birds[.]' I have the thing in the rough together & showed him the subtitles[.] He was amazed at the variety of them and wants to see it finished. I told him it may be *very weak* written under the circumstances (only fit for fire lighting)[.] But it had done good work in easing me over bad times & I was grateful to it, even if it did not amount to a row of pins. He told me also I must get Harry Lawson to write a letter to put with that copy of 'Sunday' that was put in the old desk (before any of my M.S. were published) stating it was but a *copy* & had no 'publishing rights' connected[.] He said then they could cause serious trouble by 3rd parties in later years[.] Harry is holidaying. I will see about it.

Well I blush to think *how* I chattered (& in my squeak voice too), but I feel very encouraged & happy. Ira you most *not* let me burden you with extra[.] I must try & help all I can in the preparation of this stuff[.] I know your dear 'feeler' is *huge & patient*[.] Oh my dear[,] it means a thousand times more than the pump[,] but Ira there is a *limit* to even your strength & endurance[.] All the *spare* time is squeezed out of your life. Let me help all I can. I know 'Woo's life' needs a *lot* of work[.] I had that typed by a Sprott-Shaw graduate[108] just out of school & she made a *bum* job, besides which I am sure I shall want to clean [it] up in parts. I have never read it through since she typed it. I would suggest I go through the thing cleaning as far as I can (you say I have got smoother in my writing) [.] Then when I have *done all I can* I'll send it to your eyes for punctuation etc & a final check up[,] like we did [at] the end of 'Little Town[,]' you remember. If only I can gain strength (I am better last few days) [.] I should be able to do quite a bit of work here[.] It is so quiet & Mrs. Clark keeps me free of *too many visitors* but she *does insist* in terrific *rest* spells. I fancy those recent animal stories won't want a *great deal of work if used* & Bobtails you checked well. I re-wrote parts so it would not need *very* much. Ira man[,] you are too precious to Canada (and to some individuals too) to go beyond your limit. Be *just to yourself* in matters of sleep & relaxation.

Yes. I *believe* 'underneath are the Everlasting Arms' but sometimes I wish we hadn't decorated God with suggestions of our *own mortality* arms, feet, eyes, etc. I like that verse (by whom I do not know) [:]

> 'I, God *surround thee like an atmosphere*
> Thou to thyself were never yet more near
> Seek not to shun me [–] whither wouldst thou fly?
> Nor go not out to find me. *I am here.*'[109]

Goodnight. Always yours lovingly, Emily

P.S. Mr. Clarke would *like* to see 'Mother' (I told him about writing it at Douglas Park) [.] I told him he *could ask* you. I left it to *you* to say yes or no. Don't let him *keep* it if you do. I told him you said it belonged to the Biog:
N.B. Here's a hug for my Guardian from 'Small.'
N.B. Don't misunderstand me. You have told me & I believe you that

108 Sprott-Shaw Community College in Vancouver.
109 From 'Out of the Silence,' by the English poet James Rhoades (1841–1923).

you never felt my work an imposition or a *must*[.] It is not that I doubt your generosity or love[,] it is only that you are so over-driven by C.B.C. & I understand. E.

Vancouver, B.C.
Saturday, Oct. 10, 1942

Dear Emily:
This is a brief week-end letter – just to assure you that I am still alive and to give you what little news there is. I am sending it *special* not because it is important but so that you may have it on Sunday. If I trust it to the regular mail you may not get it until Tuesday, Monday being a holiday.

Your letters came in due course and were most welcome as your letters always are. The second of them (replying to my stupid typewritten message) did, I must confess, give me a momentary pang. I am sorry that you allowed a thought of annoyance to lodge for even a moment in your mind. I thought you would understand that that message was not a letter really – it was written when I was in the midst of this mad whirl of the day's activities and was merely a means of conveying some information to you. It was dictated[;] its conclusion was, of course, my secretary's idea – it is the conventional closing which I did not dictate but which she put in. My pen and ink 'Kind regards' were added as my secretary looked over my shoulder impatient to get the mail signed and posted. I thought the circumstances would be so clear to you that you would forgive the formality.

And please do not think I resented your earlier letter's reference to etcetera – far from it. I know the motive which prompted you to write what you did and I was moved by your devoted care for my huge worthless self. I am afraid, Emily, the solution of my personal situation is not easy. In the first place, you see, there is quite a large and important area of my mind and nature where I am a rather solitary individual. Then there is my mother – while she lives I shall devote myself to care of her and that complicates matters in a way that I don't talk about. I have made it a positive principle of my life that no one else should become involved emotionally or otherwise (and through no fault of theirs) in my problems. I have had them with me for a long time and have had to adjust myself to them – and that has, perhaps, been good for me. Who am I that I should selfishly escape responsibilities? But, my gosh (as

Lawren would say) [,] I don't object to your mentioning them and even suggesting solutions. The fact that you have understood them and thereby penetrated part of my solitude and my mystery is further proof of how meaningful and real our friendship is.

And this is Thanksgiving week-end! Many people are wondering what they have to be thankful for. Well, I know what I have to thank God for. I have to thank Him (and I do) for my family and for the gift of a very small number of dear and loyal friends and chiefly for the great gift of our friendship and all it has brought me in rich associations. No one will ever know what it has meant to me. And I thank Him too for permitting me to do my small part for western Canada.

Mr. Clarke did not come to see me after he returned. I tried to get him on the 'phone several times but did not succeed until a couple of hours before he left on Thursday evening. Perhaps he is afraid of me or something. I am glad that you & he had such a satisfactory visit and that some progress was made in the planning of poor Small's overcoat – the winds are getting cold, November is a [chilly?] month. The dear child cannot go about naked or in flimsy clothing.

I asked Clarke to tell you I was reading an excerpt from 'The Book of Small.' I have just done so and not very well. I made one or two silly stumbles. Did you hear it?

I am going to Lawren's for dinner tonight. We shall think & talk much of you. So if your ears have been burning you'll know why.

Am sending some new poems which I hope you will like. Hope you will come to like 'Melampus' too and 'Immanence.'[110] They are favorites of mine.

And now be of good cheer. Hope your heart is better. Heaps of love to you & Small.

Yours *devotedly*
Ira

Sunday [ca. 11 October 1942]

My dear Guardian
Your special written Friday and 'specialed' [–] by & by soon the only way

110 Dilworth is referring to 'Immanence' by Evelyn Underhill.

to write will be to walk letters yourself [–] hoisted Emily considerably[.] Her both hearts (pumps & feeler) have been pretty poor last few days. To ease them she *wrote* hard on 'birds' which helped the feeler & hurt the pump. Consequence – typewriter confiscated after a long big pain. She was afraid that perhaps Phylis had something bad (you said she was temperatured) and that *you* were *mad* & would never write again and[,] until you did[,] *she* wouldn't. I hope you will *really* answer her letters as you promised (you don't *always* when you promise[,] you know) and it isn't always easy to be cheerful between 4 blue walls & a ceiling inside, and fog and a dead sparrow peering in the window.

You have been busy[.] It's no wonder you had no time to be a 'pill.' Sometimes we could attack that C.B.C. (head office as well as choir)[.] The nurses in this place fight something frightful. They are all good to Emily except 'O'Horror' who isn't allowed to come in E's room because Emily *hates* her dirty tongue and doesn't want O'Horror to touch her body.

Goodbye, love,
Small.

P.S. E. will write when she's spunked up a bit. She wasn't let 'sit up' today[.] After all[,] Dr. Baillie left it to Mrs. Clark's see, and Mrs. C's saw said 'NO.'

Pink Tuesday [ca. 13 October 1942]
(You couldn't have had blue Monday because it was Thanksgiving)

Dear Ira
I have spent Thanksgiving day writing this (A Kiss for Canada)[111] for my editor. I wonder if you will like it? It's true[,] *really* (not the way some writers say 'true' then write their *worst lies* & prove isn't true[)]. Your 'Sunday special' came yesterday[.] It was a dear letter[.] Thank you. I don't see eye to eye with you in *all* things, but you are a brick and I do honor you[.] There is only one person I think you are a *little* unfair to – yourself – bless you –

Don't I type *badly*? I don't *improve* one bit but rather *deprove*[.] It *is* a little improvement on my *handwriting*[.] I cannot understand both you & Mr. Clarke saying you have *no difficulty* over it. It gives *me* awful puz-

111 'Seventieth Birthday and a Kiss for Canada' appears in *Growing Pains* (Pt 3, 366–73).

zling & I simply *have to re-read* my letters over. I write quickly & leave out words & they don't make sense or put things hind before. The English language *is* crazy. Some same words mean 20 different things & others have 20 words meaning one – foolishness! Ach! Words! Why wasn't I born 30 years later and sat as a half-grown 'Small' under the stern eye of Professor Dilworth in his English class at Victoria High School? Would you have *thrashed* me? No, you'd have sent notes home & my big sister would have done it & I'd have gone to school next day hating you, & drawn hideous faces all over my text-books & you'd have sent *another* note & there'd have been *another* licking. Perhaps it's best I *was* born when I *was*[.] Now age permits me to love my best friends with propriety just as *hard as I like.* We are rather comical you know[,] you & I[.] My love for you is *something* like a mother's and your love for 'Small' is *rather* like a father's and our love for each other is friendship as deep as an ocean – goodnight.

Tuesday – Here's morning. Hope your whirl of business is not *too* speedy on this fine day. I spose the confounded holidaying of staff is about over? And still none for the head?? No time for *him* to 'sit and stare.' I love that poem 'Leisure'[112] that you sent me – I met with it some years ago in an anthology lent me by Margaret Clay to take out camping – I only committed a *little* of it to memory & wanted to come across it again and here it is. I loved all the poems & thank you & I go back & back to 'Melampus.' 'Immanence' too I love. Dr. Trapp *did* come again (3 visits[.] Wasn't she liberal in her short time?) [.] She had on lipstick!! Didn't know she wore it – but I love her all the same, though it did not go with her severe mannish hat. Funny[,] I sort of *knew* you'd be at Lawren's dining either Friday or Sat. night. You always wish I *could* be along too (fat old Emily as well as Small). I would not want to take part[.] I'd just sit and [knit?] like Bess. Dr. Trapp thinks Lawren *wonderful* & she evidently feels as *we* do about Bess[.] *Likes her* but –

Of course I understood about the *typed* letter & formal 'sincerely.' It was only my conscience worried me feeling perhaps I had *presumed* in my letter before. Mr. Clarke said he would be seeing you on Sunday[.] I hope he did[.] I think you are wrong in fancying he was eluding you. He spoke so affectionately of you[,] said 'I've known Ira 14 years[.] There are very few like him in the world. He has a hard job there in C.B.C.' & half to himself he said 'He needs our prayers.' That is the second man

112 'Leisure' was written by W.H. Davies.

who has said that to me – I told you before what Lawren wrote me at camp, he called it 'Blessing Ira[.]' Your friends do love you. Look at Walter Gage's devotion[.] That's why I love him[,] why I want to give him a sketch. Goodbye my dear[.] I got to be scrubbed! Land! How nurses do scrub! Seems to be their chief pleasure to wash you.

Emily

Sat Eve. [ca. 24 October 1942]

Oh my dear[,] I'm *furious*! Lend me your big boots to kick myself[.] I clean forgot your reading at 2 P.M. Now [it's] 5.30 and at my supper I remember[ed.] I'm so disgusted[.] Well, I've been drowned in The Pie,[113] that is the reason[.] I've *done* what I set out to do & it is all final typed and corrected. I have next week to re-read & will suffer agonies[.] I *know* it will be so plum full of shortcomings. I'll hate it & be so disappointed[,] so shamed and hold my breath 'til I get your verdict. *Remember Ira*[,] I'm sick but *can take it.* If I thought you would not *talk straight talk*[,] not tell me it should go into the fire & be done with it [–] *if that is how it strikes my Editor* [–] if I thought you gave me one inch of leeway because of my old heart[,] I'd be bound to *find out* & my trust in you would crack[:] *don't do that to me.* It would hurt much more than *honest condemnation* – if you find silly or sentimental bits as you read Pie – *score them out.* If you find it childish *silly*[,] *say so*[.] Next week will be culmination week[,] after that a flat & I start cleaning Woo[.] I'm trying to keep cool and that late scorching blaring sunshine nearly drives me crazy[.] I hate it[.] It always ferments me. My nice nurse has flown to Saskatchewan[.] Her father (that got horse trampled) is dying. I wish I hadn't missed that broadcast[.] What did you read?

Oh poor birds[.] I wish I could have done you justice! Poets have said lifting things about you[.] I did not *want* to make you drab & I'm afraid I have. Ira[,] good night[.] A great hug from your loving friend

Emily

113 'The Pie' is an early version of 'More Birds,' the third section of *The Heart of a Peacock.*

[ca. 3 November 1942]

Dear Emily:
It was marvelous to come home from Uncle Sam's Country and find The Pie waiting for me. It has given me very great pleasure, Emily[,] although that joy has been a little marred by knowing of your accident and relapse into pain again. I was terribly sorry to hear of your mishap but was glad to know from Mrs. Clark when I 'phoned last night that you were much better. I do hope it was not too painful[,] although I am afraid from what I heard that you must have suffered a great deal.

Now for a word about Pie – you say you are no pie-maker. I don't believe you. This is a most delicious pie. You must not run down your own culinary abilities. I have read the Pie twice and with the greatest pleasure – passages of it are very fine. As soon as I can get a moment I shall send you over detailed notes as I did for the 'Bobtails.' The introduction (Preface) is a masterpiece – so compact and economical of words and yet everything you needed to say is said – the mood of the whole work is set. 'When I was Little' is very fine – it brings back the mood and character of the child watching & loving birds very vividly. The first part is very movingly described – Small was with you when you wrote that. And poor old Lorne – you made him very real, what a proud beauty he must have been. I can't speak of them all – I just haven't time now. But I assure you they are very fine. 'A Debt,' 'Indian Bird Carving,' 'Sitka's Ravens,' 'Eagles of Skeena,' all are memorable.[114] Small was with you when you wrote 'Wild Geese,' 'Black Sunshine,' 'Height' and the delightfully humorous 'Smack for His Majesty.'[115] 'English Birds' and 'Bullfinches' are among the very best bits in the manuscript.[116] 'Sally and Jane' is a fine humourous sketch with oodles of insight.[117] I found 'Stern Parent' very amusing:[118] it is a fine strong bit of writing. Perhaps I was most of all moved by the little lyrics (they are really poems, Emily). 'Mystery,' 'Touch me Not,' 'House Birds' and especially 'Garden Gone

114 'A Debt,' 'Indian Bird Carving,' 'Sitka's Ravens,' and 'Eagles of Skeena River' appear in *The Heart of the Peacock* (respectively, 148–52; 83–5; 80–2; 59–61).

115 'Wild Geese,' 'Height,' and 'A Smack for His Majesty' appear in *The Heart of the Peacock* (65–6; 57–8; 222–3). 'Black Sunshine' is an unclear reference.

116 'English Birds' (published as 'Birds of England') and 'Bullfinches' appear in *The Heart of the Peacock* (70–2; 73–5).

117 'Sally and Jane' appears in *The Heart of the Peacock* (25–33).

118 'Stern Parent' appears in *The Heart of the Peacock* (67–9).

Wild' & 'Self-Contained.'[119] These are fine superb bits of expression. And what an excellent idea to end with Alice's sparrows![120] The reference to her blindness is so full of understanding and greater kindness that I know she will be pleased.

Well, again, you have taken me (and I am sure you will take many hundreds of other people) out of my stupid self and my humdrum existence and let me see something exquisite and beautiful – from the first jaw-dropping moment in Medicine's Grove to Walt Whitman's 'Mystic Trumpeter' the whole experience is packed with joy. Which doesn't mean that there aren't things I shall dare to criticize. For instance I don't think 'Fidelity' is as good as the earlier 'Heart of a Peacock'[121] and I think that you have driven the idea of the blindness of the tourists to the true beauty of Indian art a little too hard. But more of this again. Meanwhile thank you, Emily and God bless you. I hope you are better and that your pain is eased. Heaps love –

Love your friend
Ira

Monday pm. I shall send you Woo's Life tomorrow. It must be registered. How I wish I could give you about a pound of my heart – the pumper I mean. You have as much of my 'feeler' as you want. I am sure I have too much pumper – I could get along with less.

1037 Richardson St
Nov 6 [1942]

Dear Ira
Here's a red-hot[.] Drat that ass of an Ethel! Those fool girls as you say wanting to be 'in the swim.' Land sakes! The government is crazy to allow the whole works to go to pot so the young fools can kick their heels in idleness & draw payrolls & uniforms & feel domestic life a deg-

119 'Garden Gone Wild' appears *The Heart of the Peacock* (76–7). The other 'lyrics' to which Dilworth refers do not appear in the book.

120 Dilworth is referring to 'Alice's Sparrows,' which was later published in *The Heart of the Peacock* (78–9).

121 'Fidelity' appears to be a version of 'The Heart of a Peacock' (*HP* 3–7).

radation. All the asinine *home daughters* rush off red-crossing & falling over each other in *public works* instead of helping the situation out by running homes where domestic help can't be got. The whole thing is wrong & sickening & it's all very well for me to lie abed & rail. I wish I could help in your problem. Mrs. Clark was talking to the inspector of nursing homes & private hospitals. She says the nurse problem is acute as well as the domestic. I told her about your problem. She said the inspector said the *only* things to be got were *old* women mostly *past* work or girls disqualified for service by illness of one kind or another. This place is filled with *old* people. She turns down dozens. Most here stay for 5, 8, *10 years.* Here some [are] bedridden[,] some get up & go out just practically bored with nursing care. But with Phylis, Ferne & Edna, all able bodied[,] I do hope some solution will evolve. Let them share[,] Ira – it's just as much war work as making airplanes & stuff. *Don't* shoulder it *all* yourself (mind your own nose & business Emily) [.]

Mrs. Clark says 'Chatham House' is a *good* place if you were absolutely stuck (many nursing homes *are not*) [.] She says she could recommend it & you could use her name[.] She herself always gets people recommended or knows something about who[m] she takes & this place has a good name[.] I just give you this information for what it is worth. They say Van. General Hospital is in a terrible way[;] so is Jubilee for nurses. Old Mrs. Cameron the 84 year-old dying here has *not* gone yet poor soul. Been here 7 years.

I'm better[.] Less headache than for a week – (ever since my spell) [.] I can do a *little* work today first *time.* No typ[ing] for another week[.] Mrs. C. says she sees the writing does not harm but helps[,] providing I keep still & calm[.] So send along 'Woo[.]' I can correct & go over [it] easily[,] not like a lot of digging of new ground & I *should* be getting on with that stuff. I long to see your notes on the Pie. You are a 'Cuckoo bird' yourself *saying you* have nerve! Oh Ira[,] you *know* my *ignorance*[.] When I *get* anything it's just *luck* not *planning.* I'm not even *well-read.* I have a *terrific* veneration for learned ones. Those who have toiled through years of steady application & learned the rules of the game. Painting laws I have studied (not such a great deal of class work & set routine). What little I know I got mostly by remembering a little & forgetting a lot of the grind & letting my *own* self 'go' and it was my painting that taught me the little I acquired of writing knowledge – just an innate longing to 'hit' – it so often seems to me unfair I should receive praise for my stuff when I see people who strive so painstakingly hard & long & I know they have far more knowledge than I have. I have terrific veneration trust confidence in your criticism.

Why did Lawren's work change? I think[,] Ira[,] it was inevitable. I think it is part and parcel of Lawren's make up[.] He went through an awful *struggle* in the pause between.[122] The two were agonizing. He waited, inactive, longing for the new way. It *is* beautiful[,] Ira. Color[,] form[,] balance[,] dignity, space, depth, mystery, I see all that but I *don't* understand any more than I understand the vague weariness of his Theosophy[.] It is ether not blood. Lawren & Bess maybe can feed on ether where you & I need a thicker 'Juice of Life[.]' (By the way[,] how is juice? Does she feed you still?)

In 'Melampus' you remember 3rd verse: 'The prone, the flitting, who seek their food whither best ... [T]hey know the juice for [the] honey, juice for the silk ...' Maybe you & I want honey & Lawren silk from life juice? Lawren's abstracts move me deeply. I come back to my own and to his older school ones, as though they were a little clogged. I think I could tumble headlong into his way if it was not for their mechanical precision & this I know he strives for particularly (accuracy & precision) & they are the very things that repel me in work[.] Bess says he is doing wonderful new ones. I frankly admit I would be very sorry to see him *go back* to his old style[.] They had great beauty but now I feel them a little *forced.* I tell you frankly I am *not* satisfied at my own stopping point[.] (I wonder if I shall ever go sketching again Ira?) Maybe someone else will pick up the threads where I left off?

You did not mention your C.B.C. broken windows[.][123] *Don't* be afraid to tell me evils as well as goods. It was our bargain[,] you know, straight talk! Send 'Woo' soon. I miss the 'Birds,' my friend, but I'm glad I wrote it.

My dear you *won't* have to grow a beard now razors & blades are cut out??? If so give me kisses enough for the duration first[,] *please*[,] before [your] beard grows[.] There's all kinds of kisses – but hugs have only one kind. They work only from the *heart*[.] There are *no dirty*

122 Carr refers to the hiatus between two phases of Harris's painting styles.

123 Carr is referring to some dynamite blasts in downtown Vancouver, which the *Vancouver Sun* reported were the result of vandalism. The dynamite was placed behind two 'majestic 10-ton granite lions' that flanked the Vancouver Court House entrance and broke windows in 'Hotel Vancouver, in the Devonshire and Georgia Hotels, in the Court House itself and in another building on Howe Street' (*Vancouver Sun,* 4 Nov. 1942, 1).

hugs[.] A hug is an embodied encircled thing. There's a big one from Small. Hugs [are] spontaneous. Goodnight.

Emily

N.B. Did Mr. Clarke get bounced or busted on the way home? Never a word [from him] nor from his 'going-to-write' blow-bag lady (she [is] always *threatening* 12 months before she erupts)[.] I expect Small's clothes are held up for lack of cloth[.] Klee Wyck's were[,] you remember. Oh *clothe* the child in sackcloth & be done! I *know* the cover will be beastly. If – if – if – it's that jack-ass in a top hat & those three galloping bouncers[,] I'll – I'll – 'BUST'! GO SQUINT-EYED! BELLOW! AND *GIVE UP*!!!
P.S. E. says I'd best sign the P.S. – N.B.'s it's not ladylike. Your loving 'Small'
Emily & I are having fun in a game with your chrysanthemums. *I'm writing* it[,] me 'Small' (don't laugh)[.] I['m] using Emily's pencil & my thoughts[.] Doubt it ever comes to your eye but E. & I. are having fun. – Small.[124]

Sunday [8 November 1942]

Dear Ira
After you left they brought in your *lovely* chrysanthemums to me[.] Thank you my dear, they are *lovely* as the others were *gold*[.] So these are *light*[,] even in the night they glowed. I have watched them all day. Do you know (dictionary *truth*) 'Chrysanthemums' *means* '*flowers of gold*?' I did not know 'til after Small & I played our game[.] And now, a little lecture Mr. 'Man of Wrath'! And *no* 'back chat' please! – I've been sick a long *long* time. You have brought me such beautiful flowers for aeons of aeons and I've loved them but flowers are an *awful price these days*[.] They tell me they are *very* scarce. *Don't feel* you must because I am old & crocked and don't do it. It's like having a great sunflower visit me when you come in *yourself* (I've always loved sunflowers too). I heard people call S.F.s brazen & gross. Well some folks just *don't* know – Ira dear[,] to

124 Carr is referring to 'Small's Gold.' See Appendix B.

speak very plainly[,] I know the calls *business* men in high places must have made on them these days *are big* – a little pinch of love[,] a cheery word & a hug & *I'm rich* and a little wayside flower[,] a twig of cedar (not holly from Gov. St. Boulevard *nor from Mrs. Morley*) *PLEASE* but a sprig of our own cedars. These wee greeneries delight me to hold[.] No more big expensive posies *please.* I know you'll understand –

I will tell you a queerness I haven't told others. They'd think it soft. You know my eyes have burned & bothered a lot this sick week. The Clarkes' roses were by my bedside & [by the] 3rd day lost their exquisite crimson red & were gone purplish. Nurse had stated that [that] was their *last* day. Well I was in the near dark alone & took one from the vase just to hold its coolness close – I laid it on the smarting eye & it felt cool. Knowing its day was near done I held it close & took comfort in loving it. I held it about an hour & put it back in the vase *and* its original color and perfume were with it again[,] the purple gone[.] I took another & held it & the same happened. As though my life had revived it. They retained their color. I could tell those *two* 'til they were taken away *two days* later.

Alice was here yesterday and said you chose and Willie was crating *today.* I long to know what you took? I'd rather *you* than anyone handled my pictures. – It's sad to be still in life and yet not in it – & too it's a hard job for you. Thank you for doing it for me – there's a big picture on an easel I wanted to finish, I was getting a little [of] what I wanted, maybe I can *by & by.* Ira[,] between you & [me,] Lawren & I *don't* agree on some things[.] He lets pictures go here there & everywhere to let people see them in their homes & *keep* them *ages*[.] That Charlie Band[125] in Toronto *borrowed* almost everything Lawren ever painted (Lawren told me) and *never bought* one of Lawren's[.] He tried the stunt on me too but after a while *I* bucked. He was a mean man & lots of money[.] I say 'take 'em or leave 'em!' & I believe they sell better that way. Well I don't believe in people like old Miss Cann who buy their *pictures* to go with their *furniture* any more than I liked the Toronto woman who asked me to dine[.] She prided herself on her pictures (had a special shaded lamp reflector over every canvas)[.] Her dining room was entirely pigs foul & beefs in life & nauseated you with the pig foul & beef on your plate. I hope you did not have bother getting home scrap-books & 3 pictures! Why didn't you use that young rope ball I gave you last time? There was miles of it.

125 Charles S. Band had acquired a number of Carr's paintings.

Ira I don't want these people to think these pictures are Xmas presents[.] They weren't. Tell me *which* you took[.] I want the boys to have the two *small* board sketches just as mementos of me. The real reason is as well – their kindness to me[,] their loyalty to you & that they both *like* such things (not the *yous* but the pictures). Mrs. McGeer has shown me many kindnesses during my visits.

Give my love to Water Gage[.] He wrote me such a lovely letter about 'Small' [–] really appreciative [–] & spoke of how he *really* was enjoying his picture[.] I was so glad. I couldn't show *your* letters yesterday[.] There wasn't time for anything. Am better today[.] Hope this better spell lasts. Am weak as a rat again [and] want to get on with House of All Sorts[.] Was just getting on fine & now will have to re-sort & find where I am if want [to] be done before Xmas as I hoped. Don't know if it is good or bad[.] You see I have *no rules and standards*[.] I wish I had. You have to be my measure stick.

Mr. Clark[126] smokes vile dirty pipes[,] walks up & down lower hall puffing & the stink rises right to my room[.] It's strangling[.] I *have* to have an open window or door for oxygen. So I have to freeze because he stinks. He's a beast anyhow & she the 'typiest' of English. He's a ne'er-do-well who has always *lived on her*[,] spent her hard earnings – fool to marry him! Apparently all her men-kind were the same type[.] I'd turn the selfish varmint into the street but – I'm a vixen I spose, but I'd rather have had my sister's rope – a husband that *beat* me than the slithery worm anyhow! – It's almost time to listen to you. It's to be hoped your talk will be along peaceful ways. Sanctuary always did me good.

10 P.M. Thank you Ira, goodnight. It was lovely (except for the Choir)[.] I liked the selections[.] Isn't that little thing by Thom Hardy[127] about the kneeling cattle sweet? Only I wanted to talk about some of the things[.] Why does one question & question themselves & they get tongue-tied when the point comes? & it's not much good asking in writing[.] People go all round the question & not *at* it like the nigger who brought a spittoon brass & shiny & put it handy for the man but the

126 The husband of the head nurse, Mrs Clark.

127 Carr is probably referring to the poem 'The Oxen' by Thomas Hardy (1840–1928), an English poet and novelist. The line from the poem to which Carr seems to allude is 'If someone said on Christmas Eve, "Come; see the oxen kneel ..." I should go with him in the gloom, Hoping it might be so.'

man spit everywhere but *in* it[.] Finally he roared, 'If yas don't take that thing away I'll spit in it!'
Ira do you want me to go over Bobtails? R.S.V.P.

Lovingly, Emily & Small

Prince Rupert, B.C.
Nov. 14, 1942

Dear Small:
It seems very strange to be writing to you from Prince Rupert, but here I am and so this is where I must write from. After all it need not seem so strange because you were up here often with Emily, weren't you? I thought of you and Emily very often as I came up the Coast, especially as I was passing Alert Bay. Tell Emily the Indian Burial ground still stands – the real old one around the point before you reach the town and, of course, the show one too. I longed to get off the boat and roam among the deep mysterious woods as you must have done many times, but our boat did not land. We went in close to shore and a small gas boat came out to meet us. He had great difficulty because there was a furious wind blowing. When he went away towards the shore[,] he had a great load of mail and other sacks and one human being passenger.

There were two other reasons why I thought of you a great deal – I had *your* book with me and the lovely manuscript which you had written out in your own hand. Thank you so much, Small – the game of the chrysanthemums was a delightful one. How observant you are[,] my dear[,] and how vividly you remember every experience. You will never know how much your confidence and your love have meant to me, old bachelor stick-in-the-mud that I am. It has been a joy to get to know you and to help you say things to other people. Remember, though, other people may buy your books and think they have *you* but I know better – I know you won't desert my waistcoat pocket – at least I hope you won't. How marvelous those chrysanthemums became in your imaginative treatment! That manuscript will be one of my real treasures and *Emily* said I might want to *burn it.* Will she never learn that we understand and love each other – you (Small) and I?

The second big reason was that I had *your* book with me. It *is* beautiful, Small – more beautiful even than I had thought. Its form *is* very choice – Mr. Clarke did a very good job, didn't he? I know it's going to be popular. I believe there is a marvelous piece of our West in 'The Little Town' and I think the people of Canada will appreciate and love it.

I had great fun reading and re-reading Emily's manuscript 'The Pie.' It's grand, Small. Sometimes I think you must have helped her with it, particularly in the little 'poetic' bits, in 'A Garden Grown Wild' and in the beautiful account of English birds. I love 'Alice's Sparrows' and so will everyone who reads the manuscript.

But now, dear child, I must say goodnight and post this in time for tonight's boat. Give Emily one of your biggest hugs for me and keep a large share of my love for yourself.

Your devoted
Guardian

N.B. I shall not be home until Next Thursday. D.
P.S. I was embarrassed when I had to address your envelope, Small. I suddenly realized that *Miss* Small would not do, and certainly not Mrs. Small. Neither could I call you Small Carr, so, it had to be just Small. D.

Homeward Bound, Just past Alert Bay
Wednesday Afternoon [ca. 18 November 1942]

Dear Emily:
I have just finished writing my notes on 'The Pie.' I am not sure that they will be much or, indeed, any use. However, I promised to let you have them so I shall send them as soon as I can get the manuscript properly packaged and insured. I hope I can get them away tomorrow.

The manuscript has been a great joy to me. As I have told you before[,] parts of it are really extremely well done: they are as fine as anything in Small's book for instance (I hope Small will not be offended at this remark) – and the whole manuscript is evener in quality, I think, than anything except 'Klee Wyck' and 'Bobtails.'

I have suggested that some of the sections are so poetic in content & expression that we should try to give them 'free verse' form. I shall have them typed in that way and we can see what we think of the experiment. You may not like it atall. If you don't, I am sure you will say so at once.

From the mechanical point of view this is [by] far the best manuscript you have sent me – I mean 'first'-draft-to-reach-me manuscript. I have made a number of suggestions which will help on the formal, mechanical side. When you have studied them, and we have had a chance to discuss them and it has been decided to adopt or discard them, I shall have the whole manuscript typed. You must have no more mechanical worry about it.

There is one point I think I should mention. I think you are falling into the habit of using the dash too frequently. I do this myself. The result of overuse of it can easily be a style that is too staccato and gives the impression of too much nervous tension. The dash can be used effectively

1) To introduce a purely explanatory statement, or enumeration of details; for example, 'my sisters – Dede, Lizzie & Alice.'

2) To indicate a very dramatic break in the thought, or the passage of time, or a swinging of your thought. For instance, 'Grey bodies against golden stubble – delicious colour!' or 'he came home to find his wife and children gone – deserted!' or 'When Canada is peopled from end to end – then perhaps – not now – not yet.' Those are effective uses of the dash. It is well to beware of using it when a simple comma would do as well or better.

I have had a very successful trip. I caught a miserable cold at Prince Rupert and feel a bit 'groggy.' But that will pass. I have really had a wonderful rest on the boat going up and coming back down. We expect to arrive tomorrow morning at 7:30.

I shall be glad to be home. I know they have had an awkward time and I feel guilty to have been away. The woman who was to have come to us wrote two days before I left to say she had fallen and hurt her leg and would have to stay in her bed for three weeks. She 'hoped we would be able to get someone else.' Next day I 'phoned to say we would be glad to have her stay at our house and do what little she & her boy could. The people she had been staying with said she had *left that day to take a job in Chilliwack.* Aren't human beings simply impossible[?] I thought she might be alright too but these days such people can pick and choose and seem to have no sense of common decency atall. I do not know what poor Phylis has been able to do. Ethel was to leave last Monday. I hope they keep her washing dishes for the rest of the war, or peeling potatoes, or chopping up onions –

But enough of my miseries! I must go down to supper. I hope you have been well. I am sure you have had floods of compliments about

Small's Book. I am dying to know how Victoria takes it. The Marionette shop[128] had 35 copies the last day I was over.

Heaps of love to you and Small –
Your devoted friend
Ira

Sunday Morning
Nov. 22 [1942]

Dear Eye
Don't you think that's a sort of an *appropriate* name for a trustor and Guardian? Leaves out the 'wrath' part of you and leaves in the seeing (not that I have seen your wrath) [.] I'm better since I had that big howl. I hope your chest wasn't wetted right through. Next time come in a *bathing suit.* But I *hope* it won't be necessary[.] Who should hop in *right in the middle of my bath* but 'Small'! (a *little* draggledy but 'Small') Mrs. Clark and Mrs. Roy seemed glad to see her. (Don't know her[.] Of course no one does[.]) She'll probably be happy in & out of the weskit pocket today[.] What happens to her at night when you *take* your waistcoat off? Well Small & I have arranged to look steadily *forward* & *not* back[.] We have plenty of work on hand. Woo was finished & wrapped last night[.] Mrs. Clark will post & register her tomorrow[.] Don't be *sensitive about* hacking *out* all superfluous bits. I tried to give all Woo's angles and all sorts of people's reactions. I hope it is less dull than it was. I want it to be a real monk-*study*[.] How understanding & nice you are to all my creatures (memories) [.] You take them to heart as if they were *real* to *you*[.] I think sometimes it is easier to really share memory things with others than the *present*[.] I think I feel *your sister Pearl* closer & more real through the memory of her which you have shared with me than any of the rest of your family[.] I love her. I love her loyalty to you[.] She was just as much older than you as I was older than Dick.[129] I was not half as nice to my little brother[.] He left for school in the East when 13 or 14 & I only saw him once again for a few weeks in Santa Barbara[.] He was

128 The Marionette Book Shop was located at 1019 Douglas Street in Victoria.

129 Richard Carr, Emily's brother, was sent to a sanatorium in southern California in 1893 because he had been diagnosed with, and eventually died there of, tuberculosis.

tubercular[.] Was sent from school to South. I only got his full flavour later through his and his friends' letters about him and realized fully what a *lovely little boy he had been.* I remember most his clear clear blue eyes & their dark brown lashes. How often we don't *fully* appreciate things 'til they go.

Today I look forward to your help of 'Pie[.]' What splendid big pieces you gave me[.] I was so busy putting final ready on Woo[,] I would not allow myself more than a glance but the plates looked generously heaped. Thank you. I am most curious to know *how* you *blank verse*[.] I don't know what B.V. just is. In Sanctuary there is a thing called 'silence[.]' Blank verse I spose then is a formula? If they are blanked[,] will they go with the rest of pie that isn't blanked?

Dr. Trapp & Mrs. McGeer wrote to me[.][130] Both had read Small[.] Also Ferne wrote me a dear loving little note & left it with some flowers[.] She too had read Small (and '*blessed*' her)[.] I was pleased[.] So was Small. You didn't go & tell her I was sloppy[,] did you Eye[,] to make her write?

Harry came & I am glad I got at that will problem[.] He had *snarled* it[,] the M.S. part[.] That is straightened now *but* he has left my picture for *Alice* to will to *who she* wishes at her death & I *don't* want that. They'd be at the mercy of those stupid nieces & I'd crawl at the thought & I'm sure they would not want them anyhow (that is the residue of pictures after the trust had been taken out)[.] Of course the trust is over & done with[,] is yours & Lawren's[,] nothing of it in [the] will. The leavings (pictures) were trusted to Lawren & Willie Newcombe. But Harry says Alice can will them at her death[.] I would want her to have any money from *them during her life.* But not to hand the *pictures* themselves on. Harry has made you & himself executors (it used to be Alice but he said she find[s] signing etc difficult & advised [against] that)[.] He advises on account of death duties that the M.S.es remain as I wished – published or unpublished *unconditionally yours* at my death. I told him Alice might live 10 years or more & by that time the royalties may be all *worn out* & that I felt that unfair seeing it was *you* who had brought them to publication & helped me so and he agreed. So did Alice.

And maybe if Small's a flop Mr. Clarke won't want to publish 'Creature' or *any* more. Anyhow you & I have had joy out of them[.] That's

130 Dr Trapp's letter to Carr, dated 20 November 1942, has been preserved at BCARS, Parnall Collection, MS 2763, box 4, file 61.

the main thing[.] You never could have done for *money* what you did for *love of Small.* Bless you.

Hope your kitchen problems are clarifying. Poor Mrs. Clark is having an *awful* time with nurses and the house *full*[.] Nurses sick[,] nurses away[,] nurses with soldier sweethearts & no sense of obligation to their employers. She is far too good to them and us[,] foolishly good & *dreadfully* English. Very magnanimous towards *Canada*[.] Been out here for years & never been home[.] I bet she'd change her tune if she went back to live. It's the thing in me she *can't* swallow. I'm too Canadian[.] Otherwise she loves me & I can't swallow her English but am very fond of her.

You read 'Dr. Heal my Skin'[131] *beautifully*[.] I heard it & I loved *ducks* too.

Eye[,] I want when you have time (& I always feel a beast when I heap extras on to you) for you to go to [the] studio [and] fish out 'The Clearing[.]' Mrs. McGeer's and two of those smaller sketches are for Dick P. & *maybe* one for Roy Bobtail. Is he still [at] C.B.C.? You can set them together & then we'll get Willie *when* he has time to put them in the crate that Clear came home in & get them shipped to Van. & you could tie the M.S. into a bundle & let me have them here to sort[.] If I *feel better* by & by when Myfanwy comes home[,] *maybe* I can get her to get my paints & those Mt. Douglas sketches & do the few bits needing [work] *here*[.] My sketch bag has never been unpacked since Mt. Douglas[.] I rammed all sorts of things in after my valises were full[,] I remember[.] So it will be a putrid mess.

Love & hugs From Small & Emily

[23 November 1942]

Dear Emily:
I don't suppose you heard Dr. Sedgewick's review of the Book of Small tonight on CBR.[132] I am sorry I did not know he had chosen Small's

131 Carr is referring to 'Doctor and Dentist,' which appears in *The Book of Small* (199–203). Dr Helmcken, one of the main characters in the story, is referred to in jest as 'Dr. Heal-my-skin.'

132 Sedgewick gave a talk over CBR on 23 November 1942 (9:30 pm). A copy of his talk is in the McMaster University Archives, William Ready Division, Clarke, Irwin & Company Limited Fonds (box 19, file 17).

book to talk about this week. Had I known[,] I would have sent you word. In a way I am rather glad I didn't know because now you can't say I asked him to do it. He did it of his own free will which makes it all the better. I asked him if he would send you a copy of his talk and he said he would. I, of course, thanked him very much. You will be very pleased at the understanding things he said about the book. It will likely take him two or three days to get a copy made: so don't expect it too soon. He gave the book very high praise – compared it with 'Klee Wyck' and pointed out its difference from that book. He said it is alive with portraits of living people, that is[,] people who seem absolutely alive as one reads of them. He referred to you as 'Victoria's most distinguished citizen.' So, there! And all on his own which is very nice – don't you think so? He read very brief excerpts, one describing your Father (to whom he gave a lot of attention) and one describing Mrs. McConnell.[133]

Thanks for your two letters. I shall answer them later – no time just now. Meantime, however, there is nothing to forgive, my waistcoat was not wet through, I did not resent your 'howl' – that's what I'm for (a *howling tree,* just as the Jews in Jerusalem had a 'wailing wall') – and *I shall not forget Small and her book.* As a guardian, you see, I must assert my will-power and not let you or Small brow-beat me.

Saw Dr. Trapp for a moment at lunch today. She said she wrote to you last week.

Your picture at the Red Cross sale brought one of the highest prices, perhaps the highest. The only one that may have been higher was one of Lawren's: I am not sure of its final price. Yours brought in almost $55. Most of them went for $15 to $20. Bess's mountain one, which is one of the best of hers that I have seen, brought $17. Lawren thinks the sale was *very* successful. I am not sure what the final total for Red Cross was. When I see you I shall tell you all about old Mortimer Lamb's[134] efforts to secure your canvas but I understand he was outwitted by a Mrs. Henning who admires your work (both paint and write) very much and wanted this canvas to take back to England with her after the war.

133 Dilworth is probably referring to 'Father's Store' and 'James' Bay and Dallas Road' (*BS* 139–43; 115–18).

134 Harold Mortimer Lamb's letters from Carr are housed at BCARS, the Mortimer Lamb Collection, MS 2834. His article on Carr, 'A British Columbia Painter,' appeared in *Saturday Night* on 14 January 1933.

But now, goodnight! God bless you, Emily, and keep you well. Love to Small!

Your devoted friend
Ira

Monday evening
Nov. 23

Tuesday [ca. 24 November 1942]

Dear Eye
I loved your reading as you know I *always* do. Thank you for letting me know O.U.P[135] sent me 2 reviews[.] I don't know if I should send them to you or if they will be a bother because I want them back. And things one has to return are a nuisance. Still I *think* you'd like to see them. I have not read them to Alice yet[.] I hesitate to do so because I fancy she will a little resent some of the things said of the family – of the religion & my sisters being hard on me[,] particularly Edith and being unsympathetic towards my *art life.* I think these things would anger Alice[.] She would think it disloyal. Is it Eye? But it's no good trying to write if you are *not* honest. It's just sentimental goo. But Alice would like that. I only see Alice every 2 or three days[.] We have hardly mentioned The Book of Small. Mrs. Clark told her not to let me *read aloud* much. But I do read her a little of Small & Miss Wilson has read it to her[.] I have never talked to her about my 'flop fears.' I expect she thinks it *is* [a] *flop* as up to these two there *have* been no reviews to read her[.]

Somehow Eye[,] I can't talk about Small[.] Klee Wyck was different. I am fond of both Mrs. Clark & Mrs. Roy but I *never* mention Small to them nor do they mention the book to me. I keep my copy in a drawer[.] If anyone *asks* to see her[,] they go to the drawer & get her – few do ask. There is one thing makes me glad though (nobody but you will understand this). I feel she [–] Small [–] has sort of squared me with father[.] I had not realized how much of Father there was in the book[.] Of course all of her is stories before that brutal telling[136] &

135 Oxford University Press.

136 See the introduction, p. 14, for an explanation of the brutal telling.

the horrible crack up of Small's lively world which broke the fond[,] devoted relationship between us. I was bitterly unforgiving. It must have been dreadfully hurtful to Father. Knowing you[,] Ira[,] chased the bitterness out of Small. Small's being able to tell the deepest friend she ever had and that friend's understanding seemed to smooth away the old scar. If I have made people respect and honor Father through the book of Small[,] perhaps it has in some way atoned for all my years of bitterness: there is not much of Mother in the Book of Small[.] I suppose Father was the dominant element in our house at that time. But I loved Mother *best*[.] I think you will see that in the 'Portrait of My Mother'[137] that I gave you. I think perhaps that is the tenderest most loving bit of writing I have ever done. I *waited* to do it & I am glad I did it at Mount Douglas before my collapse[.] Whether she will ever be published or not I don't know[.] I'd like people to know my mother[.] You say she belongs in Biog: There was not anything to make right with mother like there was with Father[.] There was only love, no hurt.

The will is all fixed up & signed at last. I was shocked to find how muddled it was. It would have been in a big mess about the M.S. and not at all as I intended. *Half* you[,] half Alice! *No you* 'til Alice's death at all[.] I explained to Harry that Alice might live 10 years yet or more and by that time the royalties of my books might be all worn out[.] There's not much selling after a book's new is off[,] I expect? He did not approve of *half [and] half*[,] said it would send death-duty nosepokes into it & be bad & be a great trial to Alice[.] Harry had left Alice[,] Willie & Lawren in a mix over pictures too. So we had to settle that I have given her *now* that big canvas in my studio over the table. Lawren put [a] reserve of $500.00 on it[.] It is liable to sell some day[,] being of historic value. It is *hers* any time it sells or to *will* if she wants & where she wants but she is *out* of the other pictures and therefore *cannot will* them back to the nieces[.] Oh pshaw! Wills! But I['m] glad it is tided up[.] It was worse than no will.

I wonder if you will have to go north? I've been up in a chair doing a little rough type[.] My head is not too good for work.

How is your help doing? Did Phylis start her job today? What's the good of asking questions you don't answer??? That's nasty! You *are good* to me in your busy life *but is the* anthology getting anywhere??? Isn't Mrs.

137 See note 100, page 151.

Clarke an *awful* writer[,] *far* worse than *you* – as bad as *me.* There's a door going bang bang bang. I long to roam into the hall & *slam* it!

Goodnight[.] Your loving
Emily & Small

P.S. If you would prefer nose, mouth or ear[,] say so[.] I am adaptable. C.O.D. Carol wanted to be remembered to you[.] She is just a little jealous because she's so far off & you nearer. She loves Small but says she can't take the place of K.W. quite with her & so K.W. was their first love. Bill & Rolf like Small best[.] Joe sent me a dear little letter & a box of candy which he called a 'getting better present[.'] He is a dear little boy. I don't wonder Carol adores him. She is very truly fond of Bill. It is a thoroughly happy marriage but there seems a tremendous link between her and Joe.

[5 December 1942]

Dear Emily:
Here I am just to say a word before taking the boat for Prince Rupert!

Your letters with their enclosures came. My what grand eulogies the reviewers are showering upon our Small – but not too many. I do not think that Davies' review of B. of S. is as good as his review of K.W.[,] although he is certainly equally enthusiastic.[138] The book continues to sell very well indeed and people whom I meet continue to say how much they enjoy it. Gage is very keen about it. After my reading on Monday[,] a large number of people 'phoned. Two of them got in touch with me and asked where they could get the B. of S. I am enclosing the clippings which you sent to me. I know you will want to keep them.

Yes, Mrs. Clarke's writing is bad but I cannot talk: I am sure it is not worse than mine.

Yes, Phylis has been working for two weeks and enjoys her work very much indeed.

138 Dilworth's perception of the review is contradicted by a letter from Clarke, dated 7 September 1942, in which Clarke informs Carr that Davies had written to Clarke and asserted that *The Book of Small* was 'vastly superior' to *Klee Wyck* (BCARS, Parnall Collection, MS 2763, box 4, file 30).

Our woman is terrible but we are trying to put up with her. We have no choice in the matter. She is actually very good to mother which is a great virtue in her.

I am glad you told them of what you have felt in connection with the B. of Small's picture of your father. It is fine of you to feel that way. I think the picture of your father which the book contains is noble and strong – exacting and, perhaps, at times hard but nevertheless fine, strong, high-principled.

Harry Lawson sent me new agreements re: Trust. Have signed them and forwarded to Lawren.

And now God bless you & Small. I shall be thinking of you. Oodles of love –

Your devoted but more rushed-than-usual friend,
Ira

Sunday [ca. 20 December 1942]

Dear Ira
This may reach you for *this* Xmas[,] maybe not 'til NEXT. It strikes me [that it] is handy not having to be shifted 'til you've read from cover to cover.

I hope you will all have a lovely Xmas[,] peace in all your hearts[,] even if some of them do ache. I have not forgotten Ferne's boy is away. Give Ferne my love & your brother & Phylis. I just can't write letters this year but you know my loving capacity is unimpaired & Small's quite intact. Her sock made of cobweb[s] and hanging on the rail will fill with rain or dewdrops and completely *satisfy her*[.]

Alice waiting to post.

Great love from us both
S. & E.

Monday, actually day after Sunday
[ca. 21 December 1942]

You are a *dear* to bother about the pictures[.][139] Your choice is fine. I am quite satisfied the 'reserved' means nothing[.][140] I believe it *was* a woman who came long ago & never returned (thought better of it)[.] Just at first it hurt that I wasn't there that 1 ½ hours going over *my own pictures* with you but it quite passed [and] gave place to gratitude and joy that God had provided a 'you' – I just *couldn't* have let anyone else give away my pictures & I *think* you *enjoyed* giving them too?? I am glad Bobbie was pleased[.] Those things are so worthwhile[,] Ira[.] I am glad you liked the press notices[.] They were kind to our Small. I expect they are about through now[,] no hurry for the scrap-book. Keep it as long as you want – 'til you are less rushed – I am so grateful you did not have to be ashamed of Small as I thought you were going to be at first (when I howled so) – Small has had to be my Christmas present to *everybody* this year just as my mother gave me as a Christmas present to the family 71 years ago. I wish I'd been a mother. Yet, in one way I have been[,] haven't I? & I've felt the *pains* & the *joys* of it too.

Yes Saturday's visit was *lovely*. It did me so much good. I always got strength from you. Everybody about me knows it too and is glad to see you come as if you were a great bottle of magic medicine. When your hands hold mine they are so full of life's tingle. Goodness Ira[,] this thing called life! And we hurry through it without half absorbing it. Good land! Your special! Came at 11:30 *A.M.* They *must* have got a 'sprinter'!!!!

I'm at the 'house of all sorts' diving into the attics & corners & feelings and half-seeing the reasons *why* for lots of things and plumbing deeper into things I'd skimmed and[,] as usual[,] becoming *absorbed*[,] though my head and pump will only do *so much* at present! I *hope* you don't miss when you give strength[,] otherwise I'll stop taking.

Oh such a grand cyclamen (plant) just come *& who do you spose*

139 Dilworth had written to indicate what canvases he had chosen for Mrs Hamber, Dr Sedgewick, Mrs McGeer, and Mr. Dunlop.

140 Carr is referring to Dilworth's letter dated 21 December 1942 in which he claims that 'When I got home today I found written on the wood of the back in pencil – "Reserved for Mrs. Arnold Mather." Does that note still apply and should I not have brought this one?'

from??? Why old austere cut & dried Harry! Absolutely the very bed springs flopped under me!

And now this wicked time wasting must stop (your time) [.] Mine goes on [a] day by day level. I wish I *could* have located you an automatic 'letter reader' (no flesh & blood thank you) [–] just a mechanical dime pinched onto the envelope to decipher and annunciate. But I haven't heard of such [an] *invention* yet[.] When I do[,] I'll buy you one[.] Also an automatic hugger for all that hugging & donating you did for me[.] God bless you and your work.

The loving duplex
Emily & Small

P.S. Be happy for Xmas Ira. And *please don't* let my pocket [get] *too* tight. If you do[,] I'll empty my whole cobweb sack full of dew drops there and uncomfortable *you*! Small. So there! Small.

[ca. 28 December 1942]

Dear Emily:
Happy new year to you and Small! Give Small a great big hug from me. Yes, I am fortunate in knowing how real that child is, how impulsive, how full of the joy of life and how genuinely Canadian. And I ask God to bless her and keep her happy. I hope that 1943 will bring both you and her great joy and satisfaction. May it bring peace and some measure of security to the poor tortured world. Nature meant men to be so fine, so big, so generous – I am sure of it – and we have allowed ourselves to become so soiled and miserable! But we must not lose our faith. I still believe that there is 'one divine, far-off event towards which the whole creation moves.' But it moves slowly, sometimes almost imperceptibly; it is set back by great world-shaking cataclysms, tragedy, war. But such checks are not permanent. We must look beyond them and here and now we must keep some quiet places in our minds and spirits where things can be created – thoughts, literary expressions, paintings, etc – which will turn men's eyes from the surface details which at times are so absorbing that they seem the only facts – will turn their eyes to look into the centre of all things where all manifestations of life and art merge into one great essential being. You have been and are doing this always

(perhaps oftenest unconsciously) in your painting & in your writing. 'The Clearing' where the two meet for a moment has been so lovely since I brought it home. I have just feasted my eyes & spirit on it, Emily (I hope you don't think that sounds sentimental). Under the freshness and the tenderness of the spring landscape which you have depicted in that canvas I sense a peace, almost a serenity – as if, for the moment at any rate, the thing had been found. The canvas soothes & rests me. There is not the movement in it that I feel in so many of your paintings but it is full of vitality. In this case, the life is (for me at any rate) not in movement but in the glowing light which makes the young trees in their tender green pulsate, in the brooding sky, in the shadowy, mystery of the background. But what use are words? I love 'The Clearing' – it moves me tremendously.

I hope you have not been worried by our request for a message.[141] I know my statement was vague – as a matter of fact the statement I had from the East was vague. That's why I wanted to discuss it with you – and then I was such a numbskull as to forget all about messages & CBC in the joy of Christmas. If your message comes tomorrow we shall try to have it recorded & sent East. If it doesn't come tomorrow it will be too late. In any case don't worry about it.

And now this must get posted or you won't get it until 1943. Once again oodles & oodles of love & hugs to you & Small –

Ever your devoted friend
Ira

PTO [*written on the back of the letter*]
nos.
1. 'Oodles' are very good things. They have nothing to do with *noodles.* They are a special unit for measuring very vast quantities or distances – something like, 'million-billion-trillion' tons of miles of – so there!
2. No, Walter is not dead but very much absorbed in himself & his work just now – so much so that I have seen very little of him.

141 Dilworth wrote (23 Dec. 1942) to ask if she would participate in a CBC program called *Our Canada: The Arts Grows Up*, scheduled for 3 January 1943 and for which 'a number of people outstanding in literature and painting and music' would speak. Lawren Harris and Dorothy Livesay were also giving messages.

3. Am invited to Lawren's for New Year's Eve – Sedgewick & his mother to be there – rather dread it. I hope Small will go with me. We'll drink your health. D.

Bed – Wednesday [ca. 30 December 1942]

Dear Ira
I am 'shame-hot' – hot enough to boil the Pacific Ocean! The M.S. I sent you was *so rotten*! I knew what I wanted to say but was hurried – suddenly realizing New Year's day was a *holiday* & it *must* be got off *today*, if going. Myfanwy carried it right down to the boat[.] She was waiting while I typed it (and how badly!) [.] I ought to have gone over it 3 times more and without *anyone there.* Don't mind scrapping it[.] I shall understand. I should have got to it *at once* when you spoke of it[.] I waited for Xmas[,] then I was so tied up with All Sorts. Myfanwy went over to the studio & brought my Mt. Douglas sketches & paint bag. I want to *try* and dab paint on the white spots where the clips were over the paper when I worked. They would then be passable for mounting[.] In spring *maybe* I could carry some of them further. I shall be glad to see them again. She routed out my paints & brushes & got my gasoline. Such a beastly day too. Slush & snow! Ugh. I was *very unpleasant* to everyone while I wrote it & typed[,] let my dinner go cold[,] told nurses to 'shut up[,]' snubbed Mrs. Clark, and kept Myfanwy waiting ages, and everyone was *so kind & forgiving*, re-heated my dinner while I tumbled into bed and *slept* an hour, shoes, gown and all. There are times when I *am most un-nice.*

Ira I have not heard from Bobtail since he got his picture. Before that I wrote thanking him for Dr. Sedgewick's talk and in the letter I told him my name for him was 'Bobtail' and I told him *why* and that it was really a compliment. I told him it was because he was so loyal that first time when I was in a *fret with you* because you hadn't done something or other & he stuck up for you & made me ashamed. I can't help wondering if he is hurt at the nickname. The reason I told him was that the last time I was over, you invited him up & Phylis & one of the [Schuyers?] or some girl saw him coming & said with a laugh 'Here is Bobtail[.]' I did not want the boy to think I had made a joke of him behind his back should it ever come to his ears[.] So that was the reason I told him.

I had a greeting card from the faithful Martyn (of Biog:) [.] It is fifty years since he asked me to marry him. Poor Martyn. When I met him (after 35 years again) [,] he told me he thought I had made a *mistake*[.] You see I was poor & had to *work hard.* He had done *well* and was *rich* but unhappily married. Not living with his wife but supporting her liberally: I do *not* think I made a mistake. To be married without love would be hell. When people do it they deserve what they get! Where would Small & Klee Wyck and my painting have gone? I *was* poor but I was *happy*[.] He wasn't – poor chap – but I could not have made him happy though he would not have given sister Dede[142] the satisfaction of *beating* me. I also had 3 letters from the north[.] All people who had *just read Klee Wyck* [and who] hadn't even *heard* of Small. Goodnight – I sleep – you should get my letter & M.S. tomorrow morn. I *specialed* it – forgive its muddle & repeats & badness – what time is the broadcast Sunday? I'd like to hear Lawren's and the others. Hope Phylis' cold is better.

Your loving friend
Emily.

P.S. This is goodbye 1942 letter[.] Small & I are looking back through 42[.] It has had sadness & gladness both. It had Jane and Sara[.] It had our visit to Vancouver[.] It had Mt. Douglas trip & Carol's visit[.] It had *some* sight left to Alice (we were afraid it would have gone sooner) [.] It had 'Small' & the Gov. Gen. medal. It had lots of kindness[.] It had our happy friendship with its delightful interchange of thoughts & speech[,] written and spoken. Your kind visits that gave me strength. Yes it has been a *happy* year in spite of crockiness & goodbyes to dear things which instead of groaning over I shall than[k] God I had so long. (Birds camping trip etc[.]) May the New Year to you be overflowing with blessings and peace in your heart[,] belovedest friend – in they bring your New Year letter! What a lovely one[.] Thank you for its courage and cheer. Ira[,] do you believe in the second coming of Christ in person coming to rule on this earth? The Bible states it definitely but I somehow can't *count on it as a fact.* Perhaps I have a lazy mind. I put it away in the same pigeonhole of my thoughts & beliefs as death, as things *beyond* our comprehension, the ones that 'eye hath not seen nor

142 Edith Carr.

ear heard,'[143] unexplainable, as growing (us, plants, animals) everything to its full *limit*[,] each kind of flower so high, each beast so big, each is so wise. And beyond that is none of our business. One just *can't* see so why waste the energy we should be putting into every corner of our reach now to grab at vagaries beyond our present comprehension[?] Perhaps that is a lazy stupid way? There'd be no inventors if the world was filled with me's. I did not think your thoughts of The Clearing *sentimental* but very dear & genuine and I rejoice that it gives you soothing and rest.

It was funny how I had searched for the Biog: ending and then[,] when I was not thinking about it at all[,] I found it right there & the wild geese flew over and there was spring and ladies slippers! And such happiness in me!! As you say[,] Ira[,] the *thing* seemed found & never another though[t] came to add to the Biog:[.] After working at it for so long it suddenly was finished. It seemed the most natural thing in the world to give it to *you*[,] otherwise I should very likely have destroyed it. There was not anyone else I'd have cared to leave it to. Do you think[,] Ira[,] if it is ever published it would be nice as [a] dedication to put just = 'To Canada'? or 'For Canada'? & I'd like The Clearing as the *very last*[,] the tail piece. It is not ususal to put a full picture that way but if you wished you might add a footnote explaining why it was so done.

By the way, I have *somewhere* a very nice photo of *Woo.* I have also a good photograph of *Adam.* Would they be good for 'Creatures'?? Did I by chance give the one of Woo to you [w]hen I gave you that job lot of me[?] Did you ever find the San Francisco photo of me I sent when I sent you the one of Small[?] It was considered the best I ever had taken[,] was done in the Art School in S.F. by a Jap. A snapshot.

Hope my M.S. was in time. You did not date your letter but said it *must* be in by tomorrow or be too late. Well if it was[,] I'll just know it wasn't to be. So! Sir Editor[,] you go to lots of dinner parties!! Sure Small will be there tonight. Sipping the toast wine, nibbling tidbits, chuckling, and don't you be surprised if you feel kicky heels under your waistcoat. They'll be tickling to attack Dr. Sedgewick's shins[,] he with his false

143 The quotation from Isaiah 64:4 reads as follows: 'For since the beginning of the world men have not heard, nor perceived by ear, neither has the eye seen, O God, beside thee, what he hath prepared for him that waiteth for him' and appears again in 1 Corinthians 2:9: 'But as it is written, Eye has not seen, nor ear heard, neither have entered into the heart of man, the things which God has prepared for them that love him.'

promises[.][144] I have no use for him[.] He can puff & he can blow[.] I'd rather have kept promises & reliability.

And now Happy New Year. Be good to yourself and to Phylis (and see that she's good to you). Joseph is singing you a message[,] so is the white cyclamen (mutely) [.] So am I, untidily & wordily.

Here's a hug and a cheeky message from Small.

Lovingly
Emily

P.S.S. Dear Guardian. How *can* Emily hug *me*? Go stand in front of a mirror & hug yourself! We think 'ooodles' are *very nice*[.] Send them often. We like you *loving* better than *devoted.* You can be *devoted* to beer or football or plum-pudding or cold baths but '*loving*' pertains to pumps & feelers[.] Ooooodles of loving from us both[,] enough to drown and oust every woe sneaking round 1943. Your Small

144 Carr was irritated with Sedgewick because he had taken considerably longer than promised to read her manuscript and send her his response.

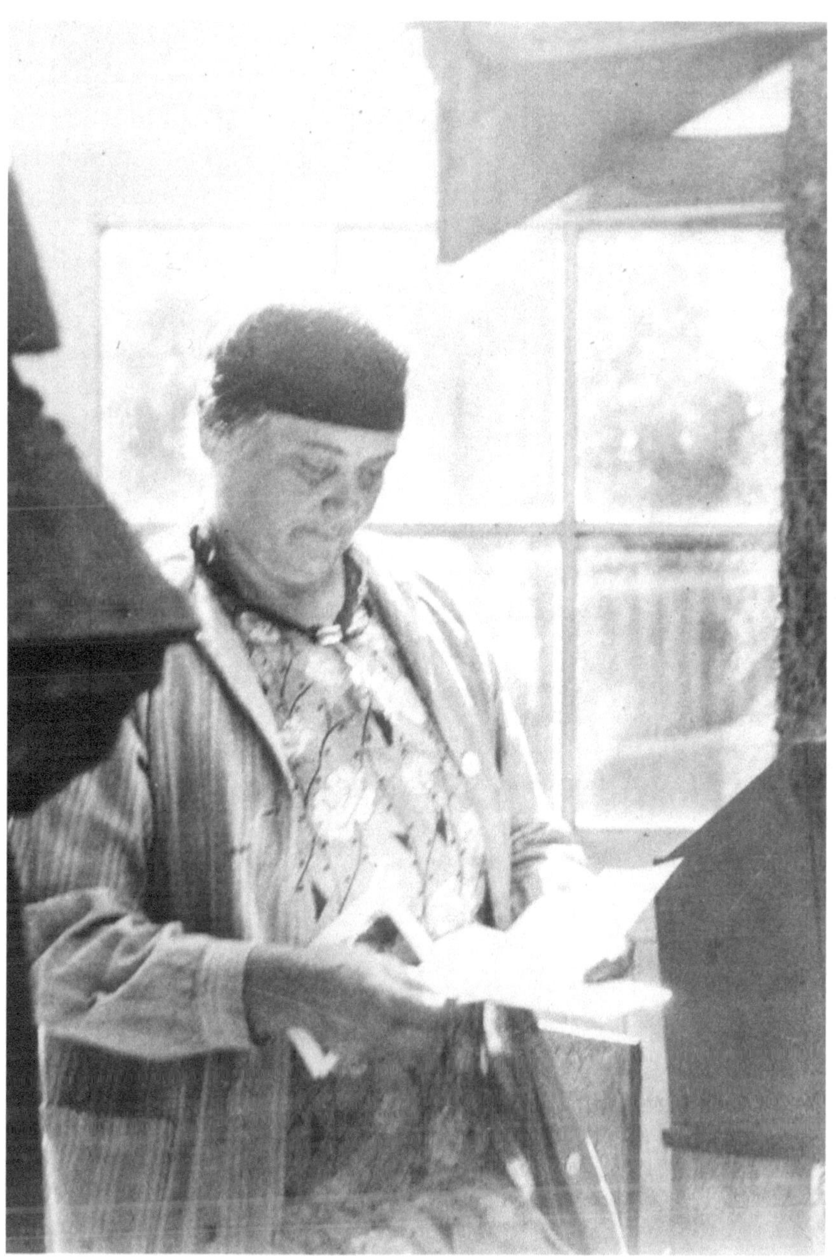

Emily Carr reading a letter, 1930

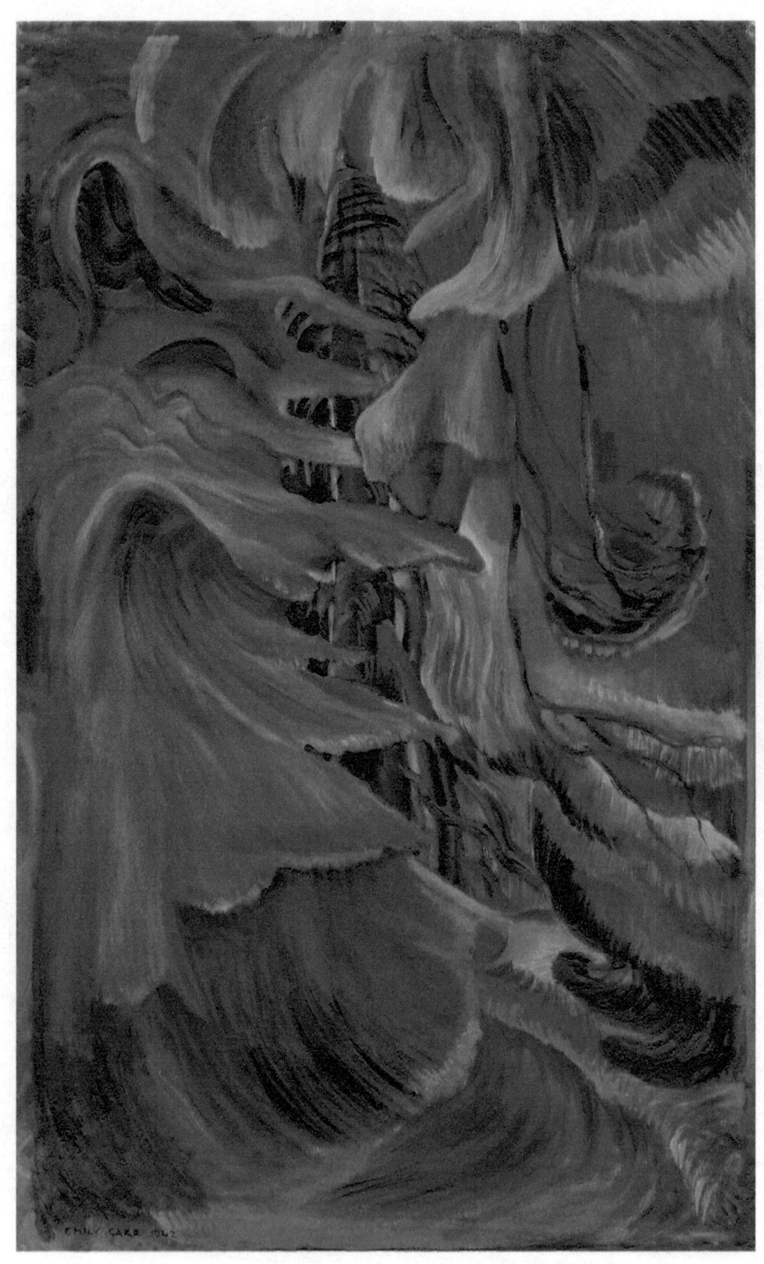

Emily Carr, *Cedar*, 1942 (oil on canvas, 112.0 x 69.0 cm)

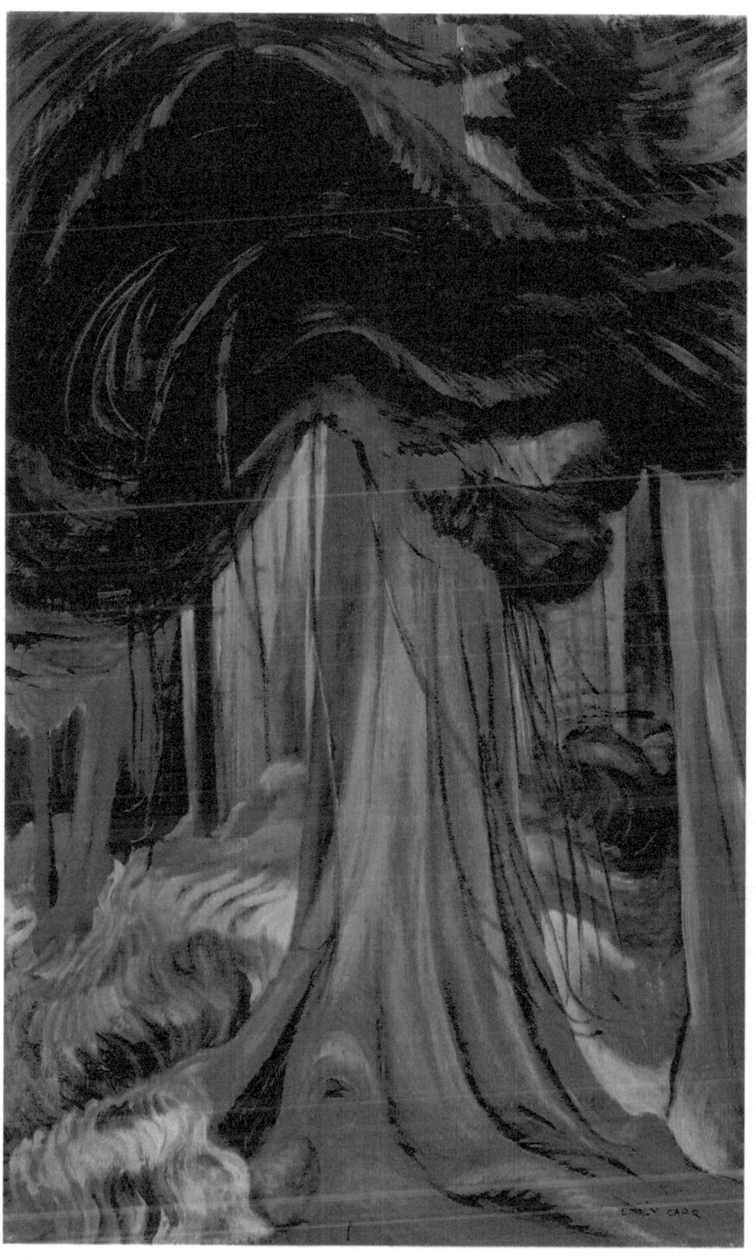

Emily Carr, *The Red Cedar*, 1931–3 (oil on canvas, 111.0 x 68.5 cm)

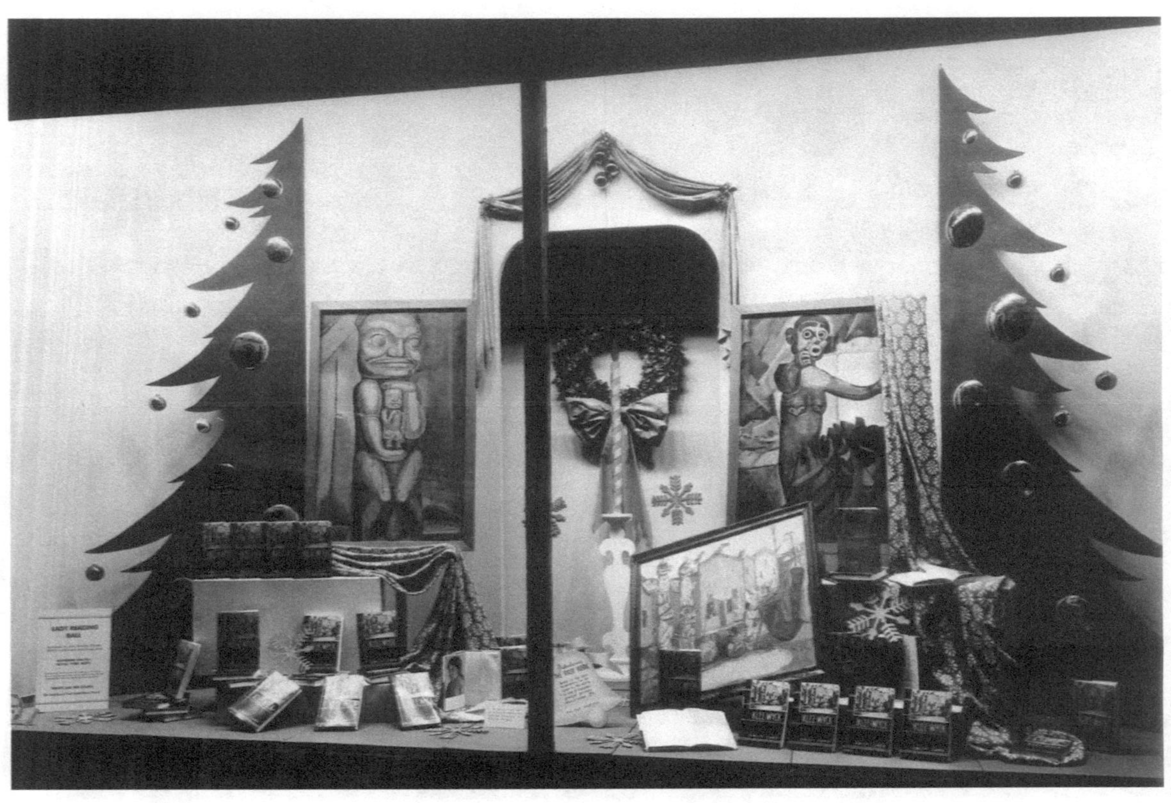

Window display in the book section of a department store, Toronto, for Emily Carr's *Klee Wyck*, 1941

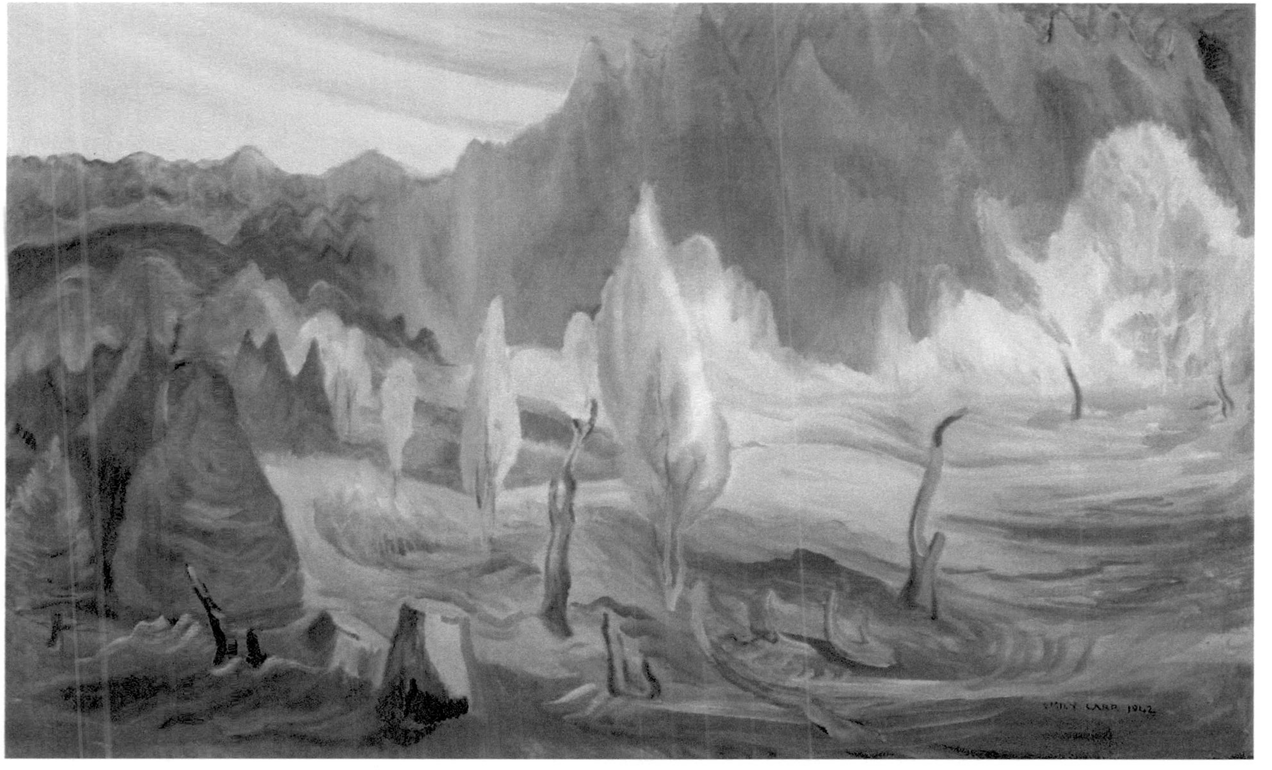

Emily Carr, *Clearing*, 1942 (oil on canvas, 68.6 x 111.8 cm)

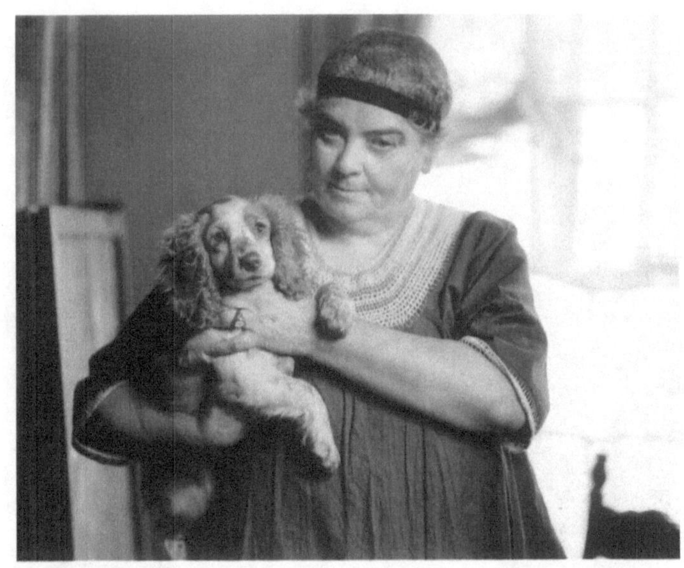

'Lady Jane, the dog, and Emily Carr wish Ira Dilworth a Merry Christmas,' 1942

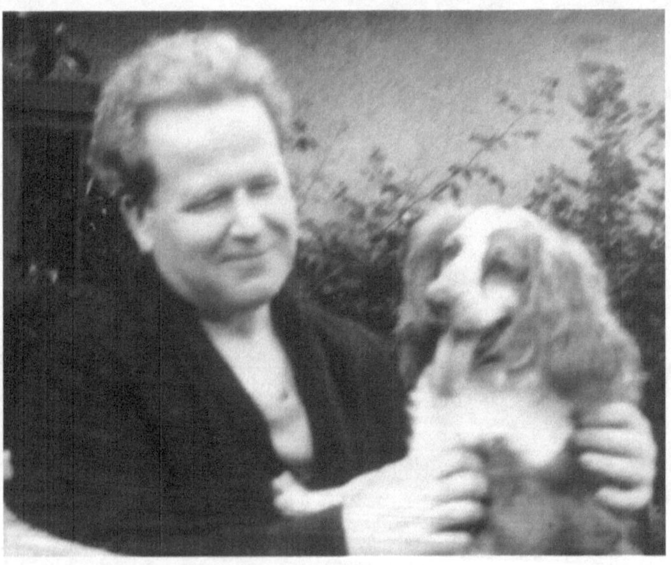

'Lady Jane, the dog, with Ira Dilworth' (attached to a copy of Walt Whitman's *Leaves of Grass*, dedicated to Carr by Dilworth), no date

on a bicicle. "Diddent see us" grunted E. but at the turn the youth did & threw his bike down & came back.

"Painting, eh?"

E. glowered & grunted, and the boy stood — Em's eyes stung like musquitoes. the boy diddent mind being stung he really wanted to know & see. E. felt it, so she softened, and he stayed most an hour maybe, he worked on the Gov. seed farm and was in earnest. & they talked about "growing" he'd knocked round quite a bit & seen many places and Emily answered his questions abt painting as best as she could. & when he asked to come & see the picture again in her cabin she said "no, she was busy here but he could come to the studio if he came to town & she'd show him some." I was surprised because you know she's pretty crusty [illegible] Ira. she's a funny old windmill & creaks frightfully as she whirls. there's a streak of iced sunshine across the floor now and outside the sunshine is being served with fog-sauce.

Goodbye I hope you're well. here's a hug.

Small.

P.S. Emily reads all the most beautiful Sanctuaries over & over here. I enjoy them with her.

S.

Copy of Carr's letter to Ira Dilworth, dated Tuesday, ca. 4 August 1942

Dear Emily:

Yes, it was a 'delicious' visit. I enjoyed every minute of it in spite of the fact that I was sorry to find you feeling so low in spirits. I was sorry too (more than I can tell you) that I had contributed to your feeling of depression. As I told you on Tuesday my failure to mention your suggestion about dedicating "Pause" to me was certainly not because I did not want you to do so. It was just that there were so many things I wanted to say in my one letter that that got over-looked for the moment. I don't suppose you can understand that. I hope you can and will accept it as an honest explanation. In accepting it you need not forgive my stupid clumsiness unless you wish. You must do just what seems best to you about the dedication of "Pause". I would be deeply honoured and touched to have it dedicated to me but I must not be greedy. There are, I am sure, others who would feel the honour of such a dedication too.

I have spent my spare time all week getting "The Pie" typed and checked. It is

Copy of Dilworth's letter to Emily Carr, envelope postmarked 2 October 1943.

Letters: 1943

[ca. 3 January 1943; attached to letter of 3 January]

Dear Small:
I think you had better burn this letter before Emily reads it. It is a crabby, ill-tempered, irritable letter. But, then, Emily said I might howl on her occasionally if I wished – all about stupid people in the CBC and –

But goodbye, don't be too severe in judging.
Your loving Guardian

Vancouver, B.C.
Jan. 3. 1943

Dear Emily:
I have just heard the programme 'Our Canada – the Arts Grows Up.' I just got into the house five minutes before it began. I must say I was very much disappointed in the programme – too many words, and words, and words. If it had not been for you and Lawren and Ned Pratt[1] at the beginning[,] the programme would have been a complete flop. Your message was honestly the best of all. I was mortified that they cut the first part of it. I recorded the whole message with the exception of the two short paragraphs at the bottom of the second page. The first page

1 E.J. Pratt (1882–1964) was a major Canadian poet who was also a professor and literary critic. His collections of poetry include *Newfoundland Verse* (1923) and *The Titanic* (1935).

was so fine. I liked what you said about it being useless to talk about making a Canadian art – that Canada would make her own art if the artists would only allow themselves to be used by Canada. It made me mad to have producers in Toronto cut that out. I suppose they thought the idea did not fit in with the things which so many of the people gave us. They couldn't have cut it just to save time. They certainly seemed to have plenty of time – those gabbers in the Toronto studio wanted lots of it with this humming and hawing[.] Really I am just annoyed about the whole thing, Emily. I hope you were not too much upset and that you realized that I would not have been so stupid as to cut all that first part out of your message. It was extraordinarily kind of you to agree to do the thing atall and it really was the best. It had true Canadian flavour and *said* something even if its poor head was cut off.

But this has been a day of disappointments. I was so sorry to have missed seeing you when I was in Victoria this morning. I had to go over to see Mrs. [McCheney?]. She lives, as you know, out in Garden [Head?]. I spent the whole morning with her. I had only 20 minutes to speak with poor mother and had to be satisfied with just sending you a telephone message which is far from satisfactory. I hope next time I am over I shall have more time. It was good to hear from Mrs. Clark that you were well. She said she would give you my messages.

I had a very nice long letter from Mr. Bill Clarke of Toronto on Saturday. He is very pleased with the success of 'The Book of Small.' It has gone very well he says. The first printing is practically all sold out – and they printed 4000 copies which he says is more than they ever print in a first edition. He says there have been dozens of reviews and most flattering in their praise of the work. So he has every reason to be proud and pleased.

Hasn't it been most peculiar weather? I hate this raw cold. It was beautiful on the boat this afternoon – at least I should say the mountains and the sky were beautiful. Mount Baker and the adjoining mountains were really superb. We saw them so clearly from the boat as we came out of Active Pass. It was bitterly cold, however[,] and there were millions of people on board. I think all the soldiers and sailors & airmen in Canada must have been holidaying in Victoria and took that boat home. Hundreds of people seemed not to be able to get even a seat. Fortunately I got a cabin and was able to get away from the crowd and rest a little.

I am sorry this has been such a disagreeable letter. I seem to have nothing but grouches. I should put it in the fire and burn it up. But I will let you do that. You perhaps got disgusted long before this and stopped reading.

Accept my apologies on behalf of the CBC for mutilating your message. I am going to send the complete text of it to Mr. Clarke. I sent him a telegram asking him to listen. I wish I had read it more effectively. My voice seemed to be colourless and lacking in colour – perhaps it always is.

But I will put a full stop to this rambling, ill-tempered note and let you get on to more interesting things.

I shall answer your beautiful New Year's letters when I am in a better mood.

Ooooodles of love to you and Small from your crabbed but devoted friend and guardian

Ira.

Why wasn't Duncan Campbell Scott in our programme[,] I wonder? That seems an inexplicable omission. Oh, those Toronto idiots!!!

Sunday [ca. 10 January 1943]

Dear Eye!!!!!
There now! I just *did* it to make you mad! I'm *completely horrible* tonight. My blue has been deepening all day 'til it's *navy.* I haven't a thing to be low about (except homesickness & a headache) either! Just threatened Mrs. Clark to 'cry or die' and she only says 'which first?' I could have done with a visitor today. And Ruth had to go & come exactly at 3, just as I had turned Mrs. Clarke's Book Review on.[2] Ruth had her sniffly kid along & said she *couldn't* stay a minute & talked Mrs. Clarke down for *five.* I can't read much these days[.] My eyes prickle & burn. I dreamt about *you* & *me* & *Small* last night. You were both *stupid*[.] We were all up in the attic of the 'house of all sorts[.]' I was quite interested [in] looking at Small and thinking to myself [that] I have never seen her physical self before[.] She had *yellow* hair – and was about the age of Small on the book-cover[.] Her eyes were open but she did not move (neither dead nor asleep)[.] You were beyond 'Small' but you did not answer when I spoke to you[.] You had reams & reams of M.S. & were turning

2 Irene Clarke was reviewing *The Book of Small* over the radio.

the pages over & over[.] In fact I couldn't get anything out of either of you & was provoked: I know just what *made* the dream. I got the Bobtail M.S. off to you yesterday, [and] I'd been sweating on 'House of All Sorts' & writing about the *Attic Eagles*[3] up there & had been talking to Flora about Small in the book[.] It's all logical but *please be more amiable* next time you visit my dreams & for goodness sake I hope Small is not *that* dumb. I don't think much of 'House of All Sorts.' Prepare to find it stupid. I enclose a huge spiel Edythe Brand sent me [which] she said [was] from the 'Evening Paper[.]' They are in Ottawa so I spose it's [from an] Ottawa paper. Bill C. has not written me in ages. Not this *year.* I'm sick of being sick, Ira[.] That awful hanker for the woods is on me. I guess I miss Myfanwy too, she's been coming *every day.* Yes, I've read Lawren's article in [the] Gallery bulletin. I think some radios of him would be fine. Had a letter from Humphrey Toms in which he says 'Your Guardian Angels L. Harris & I. Dilworth are fine' & he is glad I'm in such good hands (me & my works).[4] Swore I'd get some Xmas letters answered & I haven't tackled *one.* I believe if I could climb out on the fire escape & stand on my head it would help some. If someone *would* only do something nasty[.] They are all too kind[.] I did snap at one nurse last night[.] She's a rough cow and was scrubbing my back so hard I bellowed 'Please to remember you are not scrubbing the *kitchen floor*!' She's one of the smug kind who is *always* prating [about] self-righteousness. There! *Hate me if you want to*!! I know I'm a *cat*[,] no *cuddle-puss* either – a *spit-cat!* I feel a little better now! But I don't expect you want 'oodles' tonight. So just plain goodnight[,] Ira

From (horrid) Emily.

Saturday night [ca. 16 January 1943]

Dear Ira
Where are you? I *can't* help feeling anxious because the weather has been so awful. I hear there were no planes west of Winnipeg for two

3 'Attic Eagles' appears in *The House of All Sorts* (200–1).

4 Humphrey Toms (1913–83), a good friend of Carr. The letter to which she refers, postmarked 8 January 1943, has been preserved at BCARS, Parnall Collection, MS 2763, box 4, file 60.

days. Perhaps you took the train or waited[,] perhaps you're *not* home yet? – I worried since Tuesday & prayed God to help keep you safe. I wish I knew you were home – the weather has moderated here today[,] brought sunshine. I am afraid there is a lot of suffering & anxiety with [the] fuel shortage.

Sunday 12 AM. Your special just come. Bless you for it, it is such a relief to know you *are* home. I was always thinking of you & my half was always saying to your half of Small 'warm at *least* his pocket Small, keep his pump from freezing.' Gee whiz! What a curse the old pump in our kitchen [was] when they froze! *Have you got fuel*? R.S.V.P.

Mrs. Clark groans & wonders but keeps us *fairly* warm – Alice has my woodpile to fall back on if her own fails (You remember she refused to stock up more than one cord at a time?[)] & she is not frozen up. I haven't seen her these 10 days. Too slippery. I got Mrs. Clark to *forbid* her to come. Willie Newcombe has been good. She sounded cheerful when I 'phoned.

Oh I am afraid there is heaps of suffering. Aren't you glad your mother was safe here with Ferne while you were away? It seemed so rotten her being turned out because of maid trouble, but, if *that* and the *cold snap* & you *away* had happened *all at once*!!!!!!

I *do want to* see you so. *Don't be too hurried* next time but – there is the C.B.C. and your mother. I know – just friends mustn't be *unreasonable*[.] I am *so grateful* you are safe. It must have been *beastly beastly*! Cold, delays, discomfort. Everybody ought to move to the *tropics*! I wish Baldwin would move to somewhere even *hotter*[,] the fool! I'll do what I can with the mess (for your sake & Lawren's not for his) but it won't be much.[5] I don't know one date in my life. I had no '*periods*' that *I* know of nor any direct planning of *how* I was going to or did work. I just *went on*, the other stuff is all *jargon*[.] When art sinks to *jargon* it's *dead*. Art should grow and become, just as a cabbage heads up. Baaaaaaaa! For the Maxies & Jackies & bleating Baldwins, who are too busy hoodwink[ing] & *impressing* the public to grow or let grow. I will *try* to be co-operative[,] Eye dear. But how can I date when I *haven't* any? We'll probably forget all about it if you do come, like we forgot the radio. So I'll get busy & figure first. I take it you did *not* see Bill? You have never mentioned him[.]

5 Carr is in part responding to Dilworth's letter, dated 15 January 1943, in which he mentions that he has met Martin Baldwin and that, for an exhibition scheduled for February 1943, the latter required 'a lot of information concerning the approximate times of painting the various canvases in the Trust Collection.'

Well[,] how could you do everything? Has he got Woo? I'm *drowned* in House-of-all-Sorts. There's lots more to do (cleaning) yet but I think I have got all the material together *if* something else doesn't pop into my noddle[,] as 2 nights ago [when] a thought came [at] 3 A.M. and had to be wrote (just a note which filled out in the morning but would have been gone if I hadn't nabbed [it]!)[.] It was about our old maple tree stump left in the ground to die after the top had been sawn off & the house built over her but she *wouldn't.* I may have mentioned her in Bobtails[.] Anyhow she seemed to belong to the foundation under House of A.S. as much as the top attic which I slept in & had two huge spread eagles painted on the underside of the roof.[6] My typer is coming tomorrow. I have [got lots] to prepare[,] so must not be too long-winded apart from you being just too tired to read splather. – Mrs. Clark looks like a 90 year-old floor mop. Some of the old ladies have been ructious[.] They are half-wit & can't understand tea rations & she has spoilt them so, tea 2000 times a day & now they are rearing in wrath at the cut. I feel mean about Mrs. Clark. This love business is awful[,] Ira! I don't mean 'orful' in the slang sense but awe-full – so unmanageable. You can't compel and you can't forbid it – it's never even in give and take & the one that gets most feels so *mean if they can't* give – Mrs. Clark *loves* me *despite* my Canadian-ness[.] I am indifferent to her *because* of her Englishness[.] I *can't* swallow the lilt she effects[,] this my *deeear* hypocrisy stuff to the old girls[.] I *know* she could strangle this 'darling Tommy[,]' the husband I know she despises more than adores. She's jealous of my nurses, jealous of my *love for you even.* When your special came today[,] she said 'I'm *so* glad *deeear*[.] You've been worrying.' Then kissing me she said 'fifty of *my* letters would not have lit your face like that. I love you so much but you don't love me much "dear."' 'How could I help loving you when you are so good to me?' I said, but I knew what she said was true. Love *can* be unfair.

I've been loved furiously & not able to pay back & I've loved furiously with cold response. But there just isn't anything to be done about it! There is such great joy in *giving* love that I spose the compensation works out with absolute justice but giving indifference in return for warmth does make one feel *mean.* People love different sides of people[.] Take Myfanwy & Carol. I *love* both those girls but from entirely different standpoints. Carol & I meet very humanly. Our main tie is

6 See 'Attic Eagles' (*HS* 200–1).

through creatures. She is fond of art, in a way[,] but has no comprehension of art's *bigness.* She is fond of poetry but *sentimental* poetry.

Myfanwy & I meet in the last two but I do not imagine (we have never discussed it) she has much comprehension of animal life. Oh well everything is a jumble & the jumbledst jumble is loving! I don't see it one squint clearer than Small did 72 years ago. Besides the fashion of love is all changed from what i[t] was then anyhow.

Now for that Baldwin nonsense or is he wisdom with his dates & periods and my dissertations folly? I'll put my cork in & read his stuff –

I never read such a rigmarole of tommy rot in my life!! The only lucid statement he makes is no 1. = 'I very much enjoyed your visit.' I *couldn't* for the life of me tell what year I began to paint or *what year I shall stop.* Yes, in the Biog: I told of a dog drawn on a paper bag & put away with father's papers = (drawn by Emily aged 8). By careful deduction from birth date *I could period* the dog but unfortunately I don't know what happened to him. I haven't any idea which pictures were painted between which dates. I only *named* pictures because it was necessary when they went out to Ex. for catalogues. He (an ex-architect[,] Lawren told me) seems to know so much more about my periods & years than I do. He had better play his "chromat chords" in major tones' to suit himself at the expense of my work – to the devil with him! I'm not a museum. And I *won't* be a *datery* – sorry! – I'll put something neat & clean onto a different sheet that you can send him if you want to rather than be shamed.

Yours lovingly,
Emily

P.S. How do you like my dress of leather[?] Look almost like a bible[,] don't I? Small

---

Sunday Evening [ca. 31 January 1943]

Letters are answered
  letters are not:
No answer so good
  as those RED HOT. E.C.

Dear Trustor:
I am almost ashamed to confess and perhaps you won't believe! – but since seeing you on Wednesday I have been *very* ill[.] Nurse specially hand-fed & all the miserable rest. You know you thought[,] so did I[,] that I was [quite?] fine Wednesday[.] I seemed quite *overflowing* some days before[.] I spose this is an aftermath[.] I began to cough that night & felt pretty bad[.] I told them my chest was being *noisy* & I had pain there but Mrs. C. was sore with me & did not come near all day & nothing was done[,] so I coughed through that day & 2 nights & fed myself heart pills by the *dozen*. Friday morn, night-nurse found me very ill & I sent word to Mrs. Clark[.] I wanted to see Dr. Baillie. I thought it was either acute bronchitis or pneumonia[.] Mrs. C. evidently did too. But apparently it was [my] *heart*[.] I wonder you couldn't hear me breathe in Van. Awful racket. I'm pretty noisy yet but better & writing, not to tell you this but because I *want to say things*. What was it you'd said you'd be[, a] howling tree? Well 'let me howl.' But I'm not weepy now, Small's here & staying on her job pretty well – she knows & I know[,] Ira[,] that we've got to make hay while sun shines[.] Emily is pretty tough but *you* never know where the kick is going to strike next[.] Those Mt. Douglas sketches want finishing (only little bits here & there) & there's the M.S. Mrs. Whitfield is coming tomorrow but I shan't be able to dictate[.] I'll give her some of House of A.S. to take home[.] Also she could finish Bobtails at home if they come tomorrow[.] If not[,] what do you say to sending me over the three Bird stories with them[:] Peacock, Uncle Tom, & Crow (Crow is already done[,] you say) [?] Peacock is print clean[.] I think if the 3 bird stories went in with Woo & Bobtails and the 3 animals stories were kept over for a volume of (Pie, Flowers – Cat – Coon – and Rat) [,][7] it would make [a] good contribution & prevent repetition as the 'bird' comes again in 'Pie.' If you sent Uncle Tom, Peacock & Crow[,] then we could give that combination to Clarke at one sending & it I think would fill a volume[.] And I think the other combination would fill another volume. You know how he fusses[.] If you sent the six[,] he might pick the ones which would overlap with the pie.

I had such a nice letter from Kenneth Macrae (Vancouver lawyer)[8]

7 'Cat,' 'Coon' and 'Rat' are references to 'Some Animals,' the second section of *The Heart of a Peacock*, which contains the stories titled 'Balance,' 'Even a Rat ...' and 'Bravo, Mary Anne!' (37–40, 41–7, 48–54).

8 The letter from Kenneth Macrae to Emily Carr, dated 28 January 1943, has been archived at BCARS, the Parnall Collection, MS 2763, box 4, file 19.

yesterday[.] He was a boyfriend of mine in our teens. He wrote about 'Small' so warmly. He is the boy whose mother sent him to tell me my sister had killed my dog 'watch' in 'Praying Chair' (I called the old mother 'a not understanding old woman'). He is also a great friend of Alfred Langley, the small boy who gave the party. Kenneth said he'd sent a copy to him[.] He lives 48 miles out of Vancouver & knew he'd love it.

I have had more men than women writ[ing,] loving *Small*[.] Eye[,] *I don't think* I'm conceited. I don't feel like it but I *am so* happy about K.W. & Small[.] Of course I've liked and been *amazed* at their kind reception by men & women of education[,] but it is the plain simple souls who *touch* me deepest[.] Last night the nurse who watched me through the night read Small all night[.] She is a gentle middle-aged little woman[,] rather foreign in accent (*might* be Swedish or Danish or something)[.] She specialed me when I had the stroke[.] When she came in[,] she laid her hand on my arm & said 'Oh I've loved your "Klee Wyck" so' and last night[,] every time I'd look across[,] she was bent under the lamp smiling little quiet smiles with Small. She'd forgotten Emily in the bed & was quite unaware that Small was there inside Emily & watching & very much alive. And I was glad we'd written Small. Every letter I get says 'write us some more[.] They help these dark war days.' – Ferne wrote me 'she forgot everything else when she was reading Small[.]' Don't think me a conceited beast for being happy that *our* Small has helped – you're glad aren't you? There's another thing I wanted to tell you – early in K.W.'s reviews[,] I don't remember which one[, someone] said such a nice thing[.] It touched me & I've tried to live up to his opinion. It was when Miss Missionary & I were alone at the wild Tanoo & the Indians way off beyond the reefs.

'Miss Missionary wanted the tent all fastened up tight to keep everything out but I wanted everything open to feel the trees & life near.' The commen[tator] said 'he thought that told my life[.] I had opened it [up] to things?' Maybe I'd done that unconsciously[,] loving outdoor things so, but since then I've tried to. I never had to try with creatures & nature – people were always harder. My sisters always said I was *narrow* & *intolerant*[.] Lately I have tried to keep my flaps open – I think these little enforced pauses in life & artistry must be for a purpose[.] I'm *trying* to use them to creep towards something bigger. This is a *desolate* place[.] With the exception of *2 beds*[,] everyone here has crept here *to die*[,] 7, 9, 10 years[.] There is no general sitting room. 3 old women & a man on this floor (besides me) are confined (3 are up & about) to the four walls of their own room – don't even have the fun of fighting among themselves[.] They aren't sick[.] They're just *waiting*. All have money and relatives who put them out of the way here. Mrs. C. *feeds* them well but[,] oh Eye, there's more to life than a stomach. They crawl down the hall surreptitiously peeping into each other's rooms but they *don't know* each other[,] don't speak – 3 meals (good ones) per day[.] Wow! It's the saddest place I was ever in when Dr. B. classed me here as an *indefinitely*[.] Wow. Wow. Wow! Then I get these kick backs – I've really been very *grateful to this place* but I just don't want to go on & on years & *years* here. I've set my *hopes* on March – but – there I've wailed!

Forgive Your loving Small

P.S. I signed Guardian. E's all right[,] just homesick[.] Shame to her! Mr. Baird is here from Toronto [–] husband of the nasty woman who upset Carol so. E. *won't* see him!

Vancouver, B.C.,
Friday pm. Feb. 5 [1943]

Dear Emily:
I hope Mrs. Clark gave you my message yesterday. I was terribly sorry that I was not able to go in to see you when I was in Victoria. I was over for so short a time and had so many duties to attend to that it was quite impossible for me to do so.

I got in touch with Dr. Baillie to find out how you were. He told me that you were planning to leave the Nursing Home and go back to 218 St. Andrews Street. That news has worried me. I know you have been growing discouraged and restless. You mentioned something of this in your last letter but I had no idea your discontent had grown to such proportions. I *am* sorry. The Home seemed such a comfortable place that I was hoping that you could remain there until you were really well enough to go to your own house. I realize the irritations that you have experienced there but I knew also, as you do, how difficult it will be to arrange for your comfort at St. Andrews Street. I do hope it will be possible for you to make some arrangements and adjustments so that you can stay in at the Nursing Home. Do try again to 'stick it out.' Oh, I know you are going to say that it is easy for *me* to *talk* but you have to *live* in the situation. I assure you I realize that, but I am trying to balance all the considerations as objectively as possible and the scale does seem to me to be weighed in favour of staying on at the Nursing Home. Pray forgive me if you think I am meddling unnecessarily, Emily. You know that I am thinking only of your comfort and happiness. I know it is difficult but everything is difficult these days.

It has been a very disagreeable day – cold and dark with torrents of rain falling. I hope we don't have any more snow. Many people who could not get fuel suffered bitterly during the last snowstorm. We were very fortunate but we will be out of coal by the end of next week. The dealers have promised to bring me some by the middle of the week but one can never be quite sure.

Now I must get to bed and have some sleep. Oodles of love to both of you.

Your devoted friend
Ira

Mayfair N.H. Tuesday Feb 9, 1943

Belovedest Trustor & Editor,
I shrivel to know you aren't well and *me pestering* you with details and manuscripts[.] Is *it that damn flu*?? There [have] been such heaps about and your worry over your mother & the coal situation. I wish she could have made up her mind to remain with Ferne 'til the weather was more certain – *and* the *coal*. But I know she is *never* happy quite away from you. The M.S. came this morning and I am sorting. I'm afraid they've given you a nuisance on top of all the rest of your worries. I don't know why you sent you sent [*sic*] the 'Mint' 'Buttercup & Daisies' etc. M.S.[s] that came back from Clarke? And it seems to me Crow is unnecessary to change if they've got it *already*[.] The only one I want now is *Uncle Tom*[.] You told me at the time it needed going over[,] once the whole of Bob-tails is assembled (I seem to have just oddments as if she had jumbled the sections all up. It was in two parts[:] first I. the kennels & house & Bobbies[;] 2nd half[,] the pups & buyers.[9] It was like in two halves rather like the 2 parts of [the] Book of Small. Well when the rest comes[,] I can sort them[.] Meanwhile I will have these to get on with &

9 Carr is referring to the organization of the early version of *The House of All Sorts*.

Mrs. Whitfield says she'd rather take them home to do in odd times during her housework. Why send me Bravo[,] Mary Anne! Balance[,] and Even a Rat just now? Those I suggest would go into the Pie etc later. But *Uncle Tom, Peacock, & Crow in with creatures. Uncle Tom* and the balance of Bobtails is all I need *now. Has Woo gone to Clarke*? I had a letter from Mrs. Clarke today[.][10] She did not mention it. It was just a chatty letter[,] no news.

Thanks for [the] write up of [the] Gallery show. I never heard one word of Montreal or London. Wonder if they were a flop[.] I should think they'd have written you or Lawren[.] No word from Myfanwy for a *long* time.

Am settled here for another month and working *very hard* on Biog: Will stop that and attend to Bobtails at once. Alice was bitterly disappointed and cried yesterday[.] That always upsets me so I plunged into work[.] Mrs. C. has swung back to the kissing and deeeering[.] I like to '*dear*' & *be deared by those I love.* I love to kiss and be kissed *by those I love.* This other stuff cheapens and nauseates – interruption!! An old lady a Mrs. Corcoran bringing a letter she received from her son [–] a doctor in Newfoundland [–] to read me[,] full of the *joy* he'd had in reading Small. He had evidently digested it pretty thoroughly & it had brought back his youth in Victoria very vividly[.] It was a lovely letter & of course genuine[,] as he never expected it to meet *my* eye. Take care of yourself Ira and *don't* curse me and my M.S. I just *couldn't bear that* nor could I bear a M.S. to go out without first having your eye thrown over it[.] It gives me a feel[ing] of safety and rightness. Miss Harman or Hangman or something (Bill's office) is coming West, here in two weeks[.] Mrs. C says wasn't it she [who] did those fool corrections [that] made us so *mad* once?

Always lovingly
Emily

P.S. Me too, Small – I'm standing by – Emily is uppish again. What with her daffodils & Joseph & me. I hope I am not too gossamer in the *pocket* to be a comfort. Take care & if it *is* flu[,] be *decent to yourself* & give it a chance. Small.
C.O.D. We had a little dratted snow yesterday.

10 The letter, dated 2 February 1943, is preserved at BCARS, Parnall Collection, MS 2763, box 4, file 31.

C.O.D.D. Dr. Baillie is stupendous on fees. $3.00 per time for *one beastly* handshake [–] sends in every 3 months so the amount looks *enormous* & *is*. Ooodles & a hug. E.S.

Thursday night [ca. 18 February 1943]

Dear my Guardian
It's Small.

Emily not only let me sniff the violets[,] I was *in* the bunch all middled in between freesias & violets, ready to bounce out at the silly old girl and chase her tears round the block. You see[,] Eye[,] when spring comes with a gallop, like it's doing now[,] Emily drags her chain & kicks up the dickens of a dust & [al]most pulls her kennel over & she doesn't learn wisdom with years for wanting woods. Oh Eye dear[,] *we're going home*! At last, at last, next time you see us it will be there – the maple tree & the cedars – there won't be any birds but Joseph & outside Chippee & Tilly won't be there but we're going to be very practical & Emily can get her feet on the dirt & creep round the house instead of just getting into bed from the other side which is all the variety there is here. Of course she'll miss some things (care & waiting on) & you see[,] I couldn't always be in the nursing Home[.] These dry crusts of old women chased me clean off sometimes. Emily is *really stronger* a lot for the long rest in bed. Her heart is lots better[,] though it likes to kick up a little sometimes just to remind her she has one & it still pumps.

Thank you for our lovely flowers. I wish your nose was here to smell them.

A thousand kiss[es] & a million hugs from
Small

P.S. Do you know *maybe* Emily will paint when she gets back to the studio[.] Myfanwy brought her stuff over here but she hasn't *once* used it. She's been very lazy[.] Only one M.S. and a piece cleaned up.

Home Tuesday [ca. 23 February 1943]

Dear Ira
It's Small – such a happy me at being home. The ambulance hearse wasn't bad – still a night & a day 'spry' – very good to Emily – Doctor Baillie is a hen but you & I know Emily has a tougher heart than they think. She says to tell you she'll try & be patient & have courage[,] Ira & to thank [you] for your dear brave letters & strength that she has leant on & felt so comfortable [with]. The kind things you said about the Mt. Douglas sketches helped her enormously. Thank you for your understanding and your love & prayers for Emily.

Always your loving 'pocketgirl'
Small

Saturday night [ca. 27 February 1943]

Dear Ira –
Anthology finished! Hooorahh I *am* so glad. I know you have sweated & been very weary. When Bill & I were discussing the shape of M.S. last time (I mean getting them sent off in *good* shape, good *type*) I said 'Ira's are' & Bill said 'You bet they are – perfect.' Well good luck go with the anthology. I look forward to it so. Bill always speaks so lovingly[,] so admiringly of you[.] So does Irene. They hold you in the highest esteem. They've been here today[.] Irene came in morning and both in afternoon. They've been so *nice* this time. Harry is kicking up ructious[,] giving Bill a lot of worry about O.U.P not being 'incorporated.' It's been going [on] almost 500 years[.] Harry is a stick-jaw. You remember how he was over the Trust? I do want to leave everything right & straight (seems to me to concern you more than me)[.] Bill sent to his Bank to get a paper with the seal of the *Lord Mayor of London* stating what was what & what right he has to being he. Sometimes I could kick the head off Harry[,] old dear tho' he is! & I know [he is] looking out for my interests[.] I *am so* glad you were here over the contract[.] Ugh! I hate business! Bill approves the M.S. 'Tom.' He left [it] in at hotel but is going to send it[.] Doesn't want it altered. Then Mrs. Whitfield is going to pick it up Monday and type it for me. Bill hasn't read Woo & Bobtails.

Today they rummaged through that case of watercolours which I've always been going to show you and as yet, no time! – How could I in that 'sick-house'? Cooped up for months? Bill & Irene were thrilled. You know Lawren was too. They kept asking 'Has Ira seen this and that?' We will attack it some day. I am in my *work* pinafores again! And have cleaned my paint pallette & I *am* stronger (pain on and off) but I think that will go on 'til I'm coffined. But oh it's *lovely* to be home. I did not feel *quite* human at Mrs. Clark's. My house is comfortably in order *but* Mrs. Malcombe is going! She claims it's her feet have given out but she has a chance to go into a *store* again which she says is what she likes so. ...... Damm! Darn! And all over again!! She'll find more foot work in a store, I'll bet. She has always said she was quite satisfied with my wage [of] $30.00 but she like[s] *meeting* people – oh well – I'll advertise again[.] She was so suitable[:] good cook, economical, kindly. And she did set the place *going* again[.] They're *all alike*[;] don't know *what* they want except change[,] change – novelty. I've made everything so cosy for her[,] done everything I know how to make her happy[.] She says housekeeping is *beneath* her level. She takes exception too to the fact that when I am *writing* I am *silent*. To the *devil with them all*[.] Oh, how I do miss not having the silent companionship of a dog! I'm glad your birthday was nice. Bless Bobbie, how nice of him! But I knew that first night he called upon me he was devoted to you. Victoria wrote *me* too. So they evidently were not in Vancouver for long. She said so[.] Ira, that last month in the nursing home did something to me[,] aged me, got me *down*[.] I let the miseries of three old women & the last leg of the old man eat into *me* and Mrs. Clark's hypocrisy bit me too. To work it off[,] I've written a 10 page M.S. 'Indefinitely[.]'[11] I thought[,] like writing 'Pie[,]' it would clear the bother out of my system and I think it has. It [–] the M.S. [–] is just old age on that upper floor. Three of the patients I *never saw*[.] I pieced them together like jig-saws from odds and ends that nurses let fall, from their *empty* rooms (when they were out I saw 3 of the 4) [,] from what their windows looked out onto & what they had & what I heard through the walls – their slippered feet sloppering down the hall – because you love your mother a lot & me a little[,] I don't think I'll show you the M.S. It might sadden you and our age weigh you. The M.S. has done its work & you'll find it in your box someday perhaps. I think it was good for me to face it & write it out. Old Mrs. Clark would not like it[,] though she & the nurses are scarcely mentioned[.] It

11 An unpublished manuscript.

has all to do with 'oldness' & being put away *indefinitely.* Eye dear[,] you remember what I said on the Nanaimo Boat? Forgive me and bless you for the dear loyal son you are. I was thinking of your mother's *lonesomeness* and I *have* seen old ladies very happy in homes but Mrs. Clark's was a jail – solitary confinement – not a soul year after year. 3 meals on a tray in your *own* room. They couldn't even quarrel with anyone. They just lost all incentive[.] They became *things*[,] nothing else, even cruelty would have waked resentment. For *them*[,] there was nothing to wake anything. You are a dear son. I'm glad your mother liked my letter. I just *wanted to write it,* wanted to thank her for *making* you, like people thank me for *making* K.W. & Small[.]

Off again! You gadfly!! I *hope* it will be more comfortable than [the] last trip was. Take Small to keep your heart warm and pinch her if she's sassy[.] Your letter this A.M. (special) was lovely.

Thank you for all your loving care and your visits while I was in the N. Home. It *is* good to be home[.] I *wish* Mrs. Malcombe was staying on. Don't worry[,] my dear[,] something will turn up and at least the house is in order. God bless your every step & smooth the beastly worries. Clarke says the anthology is going to be *very fine*[.]

My choicest love[,] oodles of it
Emily

P.S. My love & hugs too. Small.
Sunday: Clarke's gone by noon boat[.] Both here this A.M.[,] so loving & kind. I am lucky.

Toronto, Ont. [on Canadian Pacific Hotels letterhead]
Friday, April 16, 1943

Dear Emily:
At the end of a very busy, crowded day and before my 'plane leaves I want to tell you of the happenings of this day in which you and Small were honoured. In the first place, believe it or not, it snowed heavily from early morning until five o'clock this afternoon. Sometimes it was coming down so thick and fast that you could hardly see across the street. I thought that there would be no one at the meeting to hear me speak this a.m. But what was my surprise to find a room very well filled with an extremely interest-

ing, alert-looking audience. (It was the University Women's Club.) Everybody there was a professor herself, a wife of a president or dean or professor and[,] had it not been for the warm spot over my heart where Small kept watch and for the sprig of your cedar[,] [12] I think I might have got cold feet and run out on the good ladies. They said the talk went very well. What interested me most was the very sincere interest of the audience in you & your work. I talked very much as I did at the University. I read the first page of 'Biog.,' 'A Cup of Tea'[13] and 'Canoe.' During 'Canoe' you could have heard a pin drop (even though the room was covered with a luxurious deep carpet). I was entertained to lunch after the talk and found that my first impression of the women was justified. They *were* intelligent and were sincerely interested.

Well, four o'clock came. By this time, snow had fallen to a depth of almost five inches & was continuing to fall. In spite of this the rooms at the Oxford Press were packed with people – and were they swells!!! – the premier's wife who brought her husband's regrets at not being able to come, the Chancellor of the University of Toronto, the President of the University, Canon Coady,[14] what seemed like dozens of professors and their wives. It was all very, very nice. Delicious refreshments were served and I was asked to speak briefly about your work and read. I read the description of Chinese servants in Victoria and of Bong, 'White Currants' and the 'The Heart of the Peacock.'[15] I thanked the people for coming and told them that I realized that they were there to pay homage to *you* and so I thanked them in your absence but on your behalf. Poor Bill Clarke had had to go to New York and the weather was so bad today that he could not get back to Toronto. I was very much disappointed. After the reception, Irene, her brother John Irwin and his wife took me to dinner.

And now here I am at 9:30 pm, tired but distinctly happy. I was proud

12 Carr refers to this 'sprig of cedar' in an inscription in one of her copies of Walt Whitman's *Leaves of Grass* (MS 2763, Parnall Collection). She writes: 'This sprig of cedar went to Toronto and saw him through his talk on me.' The sprig is attached to the book by a paper clip. The book itself had been a gift from Dilworth, in which he wrote, 'For Emily, in gratitude for her visiting us in Vancouver – a great joy to us – and I am particularly glad she brought Small. I.D. Sept. 21, 1941.'

13 'A Cup of Tea' appears in the second part of *The Book of Small* (157–9).

14 The Premier of Ontario was George D. Conant (1942–3); the chancellor of the University of Toronto was the Hon. Sir William Mulock (1924–44); and the president of the University was Henry John Cody (1932–45).

15 These stories are, respectively, 'East and West' (*BS* 155–6), 'White Currants' (*BS* 77–80), and 'The Heart of a Peacock' (*HP* 3–7).

of you & the books. You would have been proud too to hear the deeply appreciative things that people said about you and then Small was thrilled and behaved like a lamb all day except once when an effusive member of Canadian Authors Assoc'n came up to gush. Small almost shrieked in my ear, 'Now's your chance, Eye – kick her in the shins!' I was afraid the authoress would hear but she didn't: she was too full of her own importance and the fact that *she* has written poems which she wishes to send to me to read.

How marvelous our maid is! I wired you on Wednesday asking for the first page of 'Biog.' It arrived yesterday (Thursday) before noon. Thank you so much, Emily. It made a deep impression on those who heard it.

Your letters have been wonderful – and Small's too. They have helped me so very much. Thank you, old dear! I hope your Shanks [is] still running about your house making things comfortable for you. I shall try to get over to see you sometime very soon. I am very anxious to get home to mother. Poor dear, I am afraid her accident shook her up badly.

And now it's almost time for my 'plane to go. So I shall say goodnight. God bless you both. Oodles of love –

Your devoted friend
Ira

P.S. Am returning 'Biog' first page. It must be kept together and if I take it back with me, there's no telling what may become of it. D.
P.S. 2 I am returning the sprig of cedars. It has been on a long journey. The sprig of ribes which came some days ago cheered me up. D.

Tuesday night [ca. 11 May 1943]

My dear old Eye
Yours just come, answer red-hot[,] though I sent you a little note (or rather Small did) this A.M. which you won't get because now you've flown. Oh my dear[,] don't think I was annoyed [or] hurt?[16] Perhaps a

16 Carr is responding to Dilworth's letter, dated 10 May 1943, in which he asserts that he is 'sorry that you were annoyed at not hearing from me' and that she was 'getting information concerning my activities from Lawren.' His two letters prior to this one had not arrived when Carr had written her letter.

little at the long long silence[.] You see[,] I did not get your other *card* 'til Wednesday when you were *supposed* to be home again by then. The letter has *not come yet*[.][17] Oh this damn war! Making everything into soup. A letter from Africa[,] a letter from Winnipeg[,] both telling today of *impossibilities* of *everything*[.] Oh it's all so wrong and crooked – forgive me if I sounded peeved and hateful and you shamed me so by telling me of your mother's cheerful patience in her suffering. She has a 15 years heavier burden of years than me & sometimes I am so rebellious, so lacking in faith, faith in God, faith in humans, faith in life, faith in myself. I'm nothing but a bowl of *mush.* If I'd had a son like you[,] I wonder if I'd have been strong-hearted like your mother? I wish I *had.* Oh I'm so sorry you are so weary[.] I don't wonder[.]

It's just wretched[,] all this worry & rushing over the earth. Dear Eye, God keep you. The earth so still and beautiful, and us so wracked. Myfanwy was over this weekend[.] Poor child[,] she too has her troubles[.] When she told me hers[,] I wriggled with shame that I had thought *mine* hard. I'm old, nearly done, she has a long way to go yet[.] I had felt *hurt* that she had only dropped me one little line ever since she went to Van. (there you see again my *little* faith.) I *was* annoyed with her but with you[,] *no* & you'd need not 'hope I *don't* hate you' because I *don't think* I could. My heart *told me* you were overwrought, so did Small[.] I have been rather desolate (not seen Alice for *3 whole days*). Says she is not coming again[.] *Resents* my working[.] I suggested she brought her braille up & worked in [the] studio where I painted but no – expects me to drop everything & *cackle about nothings by the hour* & I've so little breath these heavy days (cardiac asthma on top of angina. Feel as if you are going to smother[.] It's beastly). So you see[,] no you, no Alice, no creatures. Well there it *is* and forgive & *never* call me 'annoyed[,]' leastways, not with you[.] Your mother *does* have a loving family[.] That helps a lot. I am so glad your sister-in-law is being so good & Ferne is wonderful. You do not mention the Indian maid? Shanks is not bad, she is nice to Alice too, knows a good deal through having a blind Mother. She's a little nosy & I never discuss *family* affairs with my help. She sees my – what *I'm up against* though – and she says when I roar it's because she *is trying* & she admits her *shortcomings* and she says I'm *never never* mean. I'm so glad! I *never* roar at Alice like that [–] It's just [I] *can't* talk[,] being too tired[,] that annoys Alice during the few days of her absenting herself. I've got such

17 She is referring to a postcard Dilworth sent her from Chicago, dated 6 May 1943.

a lot of work done (both twins busy)[.] Work is *necessary* to keep my head & heart cool[.] The exhibition is coming on fine[.][18] I [have] done lots to those sketches & the sweet deeps of Mt. Douglas Park are so soothing.

Yes my fuchsia[,] my big lemon verbena[,] the fancy brown tree and one of the big tub hydrangeas are *all dead.* Did you ever get the ladies slippers I sent you for your mother 3 Sundays ago?

I don't think warm weather is *ever* coming. Today is thunder & heavy rain & such *bitter winds day* after day[.] I can't lie on the porch as I'd like too[.] *Too cold*[.] Well I'm making hay while sun shines (while Alice sulks rather)[.] Shanks is rather a cow in [the] studio[.] Still, tho' she makes me squirm[,] I *can* call on her help[.] She's willing[.] Her idea of an artist is the cheap novel kind in wild Paris studios. Guess she's rather disappointed in old me as an artist, but I *believe* she loves me a little as me. And now I've been awake since 3 A.M. I never know how the night will be so here's a great bear hug & Small & I will pray as hard as we know how for your peace of mind and safety. I hope she went with you. She's sneaking around here a little too again.

Always your loving two –
Small & Emily

P.S. It was good of *you to take time to write. Lawren is fine but he isn't you.*

[Envelope postmarked 28 May 1943]

Dear Emily:
This will be a very brief note – just to say how glad I was to see you and chat with you again yesterday and how very much I hope you are feeling better. I am afraid I stayed too long and tired you out. It is always such a temptation to stay on and on – Your nurse will have to equip herself with hard-toed shoes or with some sort of device for picking me up bodily and throwing me out at the first indication that you are feeling weary. What a horrible business that old asthma is! I do hope warmer weather will cure it.

18 Carr held a solo art exhibition at the Vancouver Art Gallery, 11–24 June 1943.

It was a great joy to [see] your last year's paintings again. I was afraid you would think I was being just a stupid admirer yesterday as I said of one after the other, 'That's lovely (or beautiful), Emily!' But there wasn't anything more to say. I am amazed all over again by the great beauty of that work. As I told you yesterday I have sometimes wondered during the interval since I saw them (almost wet from your brush last year) whether I was swept off my feet by the emotion of the moment and I have been almost afraid to see them again for fear I might find them less wonderful than I thought. But yesterday's view of them dispelled the fear. They are finer than I thought. They are really very impressive, Emily. I hope you will call the series just Mount Douglas Summer, 1942, or Summer in Mount Douglas Woods, 1942. You have really captured the true spirit of that lovely forest as I have known it in many hikes into its vast solemnity and as I remember catching a glimpse of it as we drove through it one afternoon on the way to Mrs. McClung's.[19] It is not sadness or sombreness that pervades your paintings of last August. It is the quiet solemnity which characterises those woods. I felt it yesterday just as I felt it when I first saw the sketches – there is a calmness that is absolutely beautiful. I shall be most interested in Lawren's reaction to the paintings although nothing can alter my opinion of them and my reaction to them.

I was quite overwhelmed by your generosity in wishing me to have one of them. It is too much, Emily! And yet you know there is nothing [that] would give me greater pleasure. If I am to have one I wish you would help me to choose it. I must have seemed dumb and stupid yesterday – dumb as Miss Cann. But I just couldn't choose. My mind was to[o] bewildered by the riches spread out before it and it was torn too by concern for the fact that you were so uncomfortable. Anyone of them that you would choose would be a priceless possession for me. But I shall look again when I am over next week – as I hope to be.

I think your idea of dedicating the Biog. to Lawren is absolutely right. The other alternative is fine but I am convinced that your first idea is better. Lawren would appreciate it deeply. I'll mention it to him as you suggested I should.

And now goodnight. I want to post this in time to reach you tomorrow. Oodles of love. Small *hasn't been with me* today. (It's been a tough

19 Nellie Letitia (Mooney) McClung (1873–1951) was renowned for her early-twentieth-century books of popular fiction and for her involvement in the cause of women's rights.

day, lots of elephants tramping over me.) So I hope she has been with you.

Ever your devoted & admiring friend
Ira.

P.S. Mother was very touched that you remembered her. She said, 'And the poor dear is so sick herself.'

Tuesday Night [ca. 22 June 1943]

Dear *Old* Eye
Thank you for your letter[,] for taking the time & thought and the answering it required. Oh my dear[,] I ache for the weariness and trouble you are all going through[.] You are in my thoughts always. I know how close the link between your mother and yourself is. I know the comfort she gets from having you with her but *my dear* you *cannot* go all day and all night too without breaking[.] You are bone-tired to start with[.] No holiday for *ages*[,] rushing all over the earth for C.B.C. You *must* have sleep[.] Couldn't you get a *night* nurse? Your room right next[,] she could call you at an instant's notice. Your mother may linger a *long* while yet. Conserve your strength that you may not break and so be unable [to] help her to the end. What vitality there must be in her being. Poor Ferne. Torn in two ways too. Oh *I wish I could help.* I understand so well what you mean (about in[-]law). Thank goodness for your sister-in-law's efficiency but – good land[,] for a *mere man*[,] you are a *marvelous* housekeeper *and no flattery*!! My dear[,] what I said in my letter to your mother was not compliments or too generous[.] It was true. Your mother *knows* it and I know she'd love to *hear* it. You are so specially hers[.] If I was a young woman[,] she might not be so pleased[,] might even dub me a 'hussy.' But I talk to her about the son she made as she might talk to me of a picture I had painted, that would please me, and I am so glad if my little letters [are] enclosed in yours so that you can read them or not as you see fit and at the right moment when she is resting easy [to] give her a moment's pleasure or diversion from her weariness. If you see they bore or weary her[,] *don't* read them.

I am very distressed that your little Indian girl is going. What shall you do? Would you like me to put an ad in [the] Colonist & interview anyone who applied[,] see if they'd go to Vancouver? Some might. There do seem more here than there[.] I always get *some* answers[.] Shanks would be *no good* to you. She *can't* cook & is so *intensely* stupid but she *is* kind & sweet-tempered and [–] believe it or not! [–] loves me. I eat pounds of 'humble pie' after losing my temper entirely[,] for she is trying. You can't imagine. I yell directions from bed 365 times 365. If you are loud and nasty she heeds, sweet & easy – you might just as well crawl into your grave and drag the dirt over you as direct anyone as dumb as a plate!

I hope you are at Lawren's this minute which will mean that your mother is easy and you are availing yourself of the friendship of a true and dear fellow being. Mr. Carl[20] of the Museum and Mayor (I think he said) King of Education Dept called on me today[.] Mayor King lugged along a huge parcel of sketches done by Kitsilano School students[,] illustrations of Klee Wyck[.] They were horrid and they shamed me because I felt such a failure[,] as though I'd given a wrong impression in K.W. of Indians[.] They were undeniably Maxey and Jacksie things[,] were all show off[,] no observation[,] no Indian feeling[.] Just *one* child or 2 had shown a hint of having observed a canoe & shore-line (in 'Canoe') [.] I was horribly frank[.] I told the men I hated the drawings.

Mayor King wore a black wig over very grey spiky bristles & had a scrub brush moustache[,] pepper & salt (like your new business suit) [,] and his face was red. Mr. Carl caught a mouse on the chipmunk's box by hand & took it back to the museum alive in a little box in his pocket.[21] I showed a few pictures[.] The sketches embarrassed them (no like) but a few Indian ones restored them. We parted after [a] 1 ½ hour session on good terms and my voice held out.

Hope I see the little ladies. I'd love to tip Delisle[22] and Valley Thornton[23] out of a boat into [a] neck deep mud-puddle. Nobody but you, Lawren, Grigsby[24] and one semi-idiot poetess have mentioned my

20 Dr G. Clifford Carl, who wrote for the *Victoria Times*, was director of the B.C. Provincial Museum.

21 Mr Carl wrote Carr that the mouse did not survive (see William Ready Division of the McMaster University Archives, Clarke-Irwin Fonds, box 19).

22 J. Delisle Parker, in addition to being an artist, became an art critic for the *Vancouver Daily Province* in 1940, for which he published 'a weekly column under the by-line "Palette" ' (Walker 5 n.3).

23 Carr is referring to Mildred Valley Thornton's article 'New Carr Show at Gallery,' which appeared in the *Vancouver Sun* on (16 June 1943).

24 A.S. Grigsby was the secretary-treasurer at the Vancouver Art Gallery between 1931 and 1944 and the secretary-curator between 1944 and 1947.

Van Ex. Do I care? I *don't think* so. It's the last – none of the folks I know over there seem to have gone. Only relatives? Oh! *Of course not*[.] Well I'd sooner you went your six times and got a feeling of refreshment from them than Vancouver's 6000 had turned up their noses as if there'd been smells & bad. Dr. Baillie came today[.] He says his three daughters are *staunch Canadians*[.]

Now it's time to take a vile dose[.] Bitter as gall & smelly as the James Bay mud flats of old.[25] That is supposed to lullaby me into sleep. By the way[,] does your Phylis write songs? I see something by Phylis Dilworth listed in the C.B.C. programme.

Goodnight indeed[.] Rest to all your household. But Eye[,] think about a night nurse (not to take your place) but just to prepare you by rest for the next day. I know those sinking weaknesses are almost worse than pain. Yet how we cling to that last fibre of life is just innate in our being. Living, dying, life[.] Oh Eye[,] we don't know anything do we?

'Darest thou now oh soul walk out with me?'
'All lies undreamed of in that far
off inexplicable land where neither
ground is for the feet nor path to follow.'[26]

Like you I thank God for Whitman[.] Like you I pray that your mother may pass quickly and peacefully & I pray that you may be supported. Here is a heart full of love (2 of them, Small's and mine)[.] Two big hugs and a few tears

Always[,] *Us.*

Tuesday [ca. 29 June 1943]

Dear Eye
I was afraid that was the reason [for] your silence. I feel so deeply for you (watcher and watched)[.] Yes thank God if there is no pain[,]

25 The Empress Hotel is now located on what was once known as the James Bay mud flats.
26 'Darest Thou Now O Soul' comes from 'Whispers of Heavenly Death' in Whitman's *Leaves of Grass*. The lines Carr cites actually read as follows: 'Darest thou now O soul, / Walk out with me toward the unknown region, / Where neither ground is for the feet nor any path to follow?' The third stanza includes the line 'All waits undream'd of in that region, that inaccessible land.'

though that terrible weakness is agony[.] Can't the Doctor give her some easement that will calm her into oblivion for a rest period now and again?

And your girl gone. Oh I wish I was young and strong to come and help. I wish Edna was there instead of in the East while her husband is taking training.

Glad you got to Lawren's[.] Your letter cleared up a point. I thought he was asking if he might send my two borrowed for B.C. summer show & Seattle[,][27] though he meant that B.C. show might go over. From your letter I see it was *my* show: I have not had a word from Grigsby since the show. Had no idea any more than one was sold.[28] But for you & Lawren[,] my trustors[,] Walter Gage & Ada McGeer[, the] show seemed I found to fall pretty flat & those foul write ups! Better leave the paper flat without type than be smudged over by Delisles & Valley Thorntons[.] This is not a letter[,] only a hug from Small. My dear[,] I do not expect letters in this time of stress & weariness. I write you because it is *all I can do* – and pray[.] Your Sunday letter came this morn. Never let my letters bother your mother[. If they] give her a moment's amusement, alright, I'm glad[.] Give her a beautiful kiss for me. Summer has come to Victoria.

Every kind of love (every *nice* kind)
From Small and Emily

[ca. 2 July 1943]

Dear My Guardian – It's Small.
E. left this page for me. E. and I. wish we could help you these heavy days and nights. I'm always as close as your waistcoat but I can't always get under your hyde[.] It is very tough. Sometimes you tighten up and seem as if you wanted to keep *everyone* out (even your own self) and the love and sympathy of so many is wrapping you round just now too. Don't roll us off like water on new paint leaving us to sink into the dirt and dry up.

27 In addition to her solo exhibition at the Vancouver Art Gallery, Carr also had a solo exhibition at the Seattle Art Museum in August 1943.

28 Carr is responding to a letter by Dilworth (ca. 21 June 1943) in which he asserts that a number of her paintings had been sold.

Our wasps are all gone![29] They used a terrific poison squirt and the wasps were tough & persistent. E. just got a letter from Irene. That wretched English refugee child has followed *scarlet* with *chicken pox.* Mrs. C. was just sending Bill & the youngsters away[.] He seems far from well. E. hasn't been very well last day or two[.] This is not a letter. Only a hug.

Love & a kiss to your mother from us & don't go *and keep it* (you keeper of kisses that has to be reminded). Here's a thousand for yourself

From Small

P.S. If you can't accommodate 1000[,] put them in an envelope & send them to Jane[.] We often think of her. Small
N.B. This is a blue Monday[.] Will you get it I wonder[?] S

Friday, July 2, 1943

Dear Emily:
Once again an apology for not writing sooner and thanks for your last letters! You are so understanding and kind that first thing you know I will be taking advantage of your generosity.

Mother still lingers, getting weaker and weaker. She has been almost completely unconscious since Tuesday night. She hears our voices occasionally when we call her and once or twice yesterday she recognized Ferne & me – there was just a slight flicker of recognition in her eyes. But she has not been able to speak, to form intelligible words. Poor dear! It's such a shame. I just can't see any reason for it atall. She has lived fully and well: she is ready to go, eager to be away. Her whole soul and personality seem to have turned another way (as Lawren says) and when she hears our voices and gives any sign of consciousness it is as if she came back from a great distance. It is cruel, Emily, very cruel to have her fight on day after day like this. And she has been so infinitely patient! We shall never forget the experience of that patience.

29 In a letter dated 26 June 1943, Carr writes about how wasps had made a '*most curious nest*' between 'the walls at the side of the big studio window' (BCARS, Inglis Collection, MS 2763).

She was not well enough to understand your last letter. I could not read it to her. It was a clear, kind letter. I liked it so much.

And now I must close this brief note.

Oodles and oodles of love,

As Ever
Ira.

Saturday [the date is in Dilworth's handwriting] July 3, 1943

Dear Ira
Your letter written Friday and received today made me cry and cry[,] not only about your mother but for you too. Oh Eye[,] you must not let this inexplicable thing crack your faith. It is[,] I know[,] bitter to watch and not feel rebellious[.] Your faith has been so strong[.] Your mother leant on it, so do I. Don't let it give an inch.

Be thankful for the oblivion that has fallen upon her[,] wiping out that agony of weakness. Don't try and pull her back to it. Maybe Pearl, her husband[,] and others are now helping her from Beyond, more than the children she loves so much on earth can. Frankly I do not know *what to expect* when we die (whether we recognize [it] or whether we don't). I just rest on 'Eye hath not seen ear heard nor hath entered into the heart of man.'[30]

From what you say I think she must be more there now than here and I earnestly pray for her release[.] I do not think people suffer when unconscious. I know those three unconscious days in St. Joseph's (thrombosis time) were just blank[.] No remembrance of discomfort or pain (& they say it is awful pain)[.] I am so glad Ferne is with you. So wait [as] quietly as you can and rest back on your faith[.] Think how dreadful it would be if you had none[.] But you had a good mother

I wish I was Small and could come to comfort you. But I'm only me and sometimes, I a little envy your mother being so nearly over. I'm not so old as she but not so *patient* either.

Remember Browning's –

30 See note 143 on page 185.

'Sudden the worst turns the best to the brave,
  The black minutes at end
And the elements' rage[,] the fiend-voices that rave
Shall dwindle[,] shall blend
Shall change, shall become first a peace out of pain
  Then a light' ... [31]

And that line of Whitman 'the beautiful touch of Death, soothing and *benumbing* a few moments[,] for reasons.'[32] But here me quoting quotes to *you* the Arch-Quoter, millions on your tongue tip. Call them to your comfort now[,] else where is the good of poetry? No mistake [–] it hits the bull's eye straighter than prose. And *you* make such beautiful selections. I remember the two occasions I sat near the radio in your sitting room opposite your mother listening to 'Sanctuary.' How proud she was hearing the voice she loved[,] sending those beautiful thoughts over the air to thousands of listeners.

Write when it eases you to do so[.] I am always wondering how it is and praying for her release, but *don't feel it necessary* to apologize when you *just can't*[.] I understand.

Be the soul brave and sweet that your Mother bore and was so proud of. Kiss her for me. Courage[.] Blessings[.]

Always[,] Emily (Small)

Monday [ca. 9 July 1943]

Dear Ira

Oh I am so glad[,] so glad her rest came at last. We who loved her can't help crying a little but it is for ourselves the tears are sad, not for her. Of course her place will never be filled in your heart. One only has one mother[.] But generation follows generation and so it must be. You had a long, long spell of being mothered and then you were able to turn round and mother her many many years. (I only had my mother 'til I was 12 and oh how I needed her after that) but[,] like me[,] you *too had*

31 The quotation is from Browning's 'Prospice.'
32 From stanza twelve of Whitman's 'Poems of Joy' (*Leaves of Grass*).

a good mother[,] a very dear one[.] She was permitted to fulfill her years, and Ira[,] after that[,] life becomes a burden.

The last few weeks have been terrible for you[,] I know[.] I've ached for you. Now dear man[,] stand calmly and look at your quiet dead. It is a holy beautiful healing thing to do – to see that afterglow which comes briefly over a face obliterating the lines of pain & care

'Birthless and deathless and changeless
    Remaineth the spirit forever
Death hath not changed it at all
    Dead though the face of it seems.'[33]
God comfort you.

Always lovingly Emily-Small

Page (1) Thursday July 29 43
218 St. Andrews St. Victoria

Dear Eye
Oh it's finished at last! It tried so hard to beat me[,] but Small came in at the finish and that helped. I *hope* she is going to stay[.] I was overjoyed to hear she'd been round your back garden too. Another thing that cheered me too when 2 days ago Dr. Baillie told me the *tears* had *legitimate cause* and *reason.*[34] Same cause that has robbed me of appetite for months because *everything* tasted so bitter & horrid. I feel much better[,] since I know *it was not just flabby give in.* Anyhow[,] I do hope next time you come to this house[,] Small clothed and in her right mind will be here to greet you.

I had a *long* handwritten letter from Bill and one from Irene. I'm afraid they'd take you *weeks* to read, I've only half-digested them myself[.] They are still away in the country[.] Bill's lumbago [is] better but he is evidently not right yet. Both wrote so kindly. Irene says they *both love me*[.] I am so glad. Bill says[,] owing to wartime production worries[,] he does

33 This passage was written by Sir Edwin Arnold (1832–1904), a British poet and journalist who wrote *The Light of Asia* (1879) and *The Light of the World* (1891). The last line is 'Dead though the house of it seems!'

34 In a letter dated 18 July 1943, Carr explains that she is weeping incessantly and without apparent reason.

not think 'creatures' can be put through for the Xmas trade (may have to stand off a year) [.] He has some thought of putting out 'Heart of a Peacock' [as] a little booklet and is considering that book of colour plates but says he will discuss when they come out *in the autumn.*[35]

'Book of Small' comes out in England next month[.] Sir Humphrey Milford likes it *very much.* Well when I have read their letters more carefully[,] or perhaps next time I *see* you[,] we could read them[.] I feel you are *too busy* these days to plough through that very difficult handwriting[.] Let me have Clarke's statement on K.W. & Book of S. some time[,] will you? Ferne came yesterday[.] I enjoyed her[.] It was tantalizing to get my teeth nearly into you and find the old 'Potentates' gnawing on the other end. Your letter made up for a lot though.

Goodnight[.] I hope those dreadful men will come & go without reducing you to a blown egg.

Please let Lawren see Biog: [as] soon as he gets back. If you *do have time* run over 'Green' & 'Wild Geese[.]'[36] Both are short & both gave me *much* trouble (at least my head wouldn't work) [.] I'd like your eye to run over those two before Lawren[.] Dr. Baillie suggested I *quit* for a bit but I said 'I was afraid to for fear I couldn't begin again[.]' His answer was 'Miss Emily[,] there will always be *one more* thing beyond the last to finish.' I am contemplating an assault on the studio. Capt. Ross Hamilton never paid for his picture[.] Said he'd send check *next* day[.] I think that will be 6 Sundays ago.

Ooodles on oodles on oodles
From your loving 'fliend'[37]

P.S. Me too Guardian. I'm often in your garden[.] Do you remember you likened Jane to me? How is Jane? Ooodles of love and a mammoth hug[.] It won't hurt because you know what I'm made of[,] so spose you hug yourself & say[']from Small![']
P.S. The foreword is beautiful[.] Thank you. I kept the original [and] made a new copy for you.

35 Clarke endeavoured to appease Carr's concerns about the sales of her books. He also expressed concern about publishing 'Woo' and 'Bobtails' and, instead, suggested publishing 'The Heart of a Peacock' on its own (William Clarke to Emily Carr, 27 July 1943, Parnall Collection, MS 2763, box 2, file 10).

36 'Green' and 'Wild Geese' are stories that appear in *Growing Pains* (Pt 3, 353–5, 378–81).

37 Carr is referring to Sophie's term for Carr, as described in 'Sophie' (*KW* 41).

P.S. Friday morn[.] Thought I'd better not bust the law by enclosing letter in Registered parcel.

Thought I'd landed a find in a smart young boy to fix my woodpile[.] After 2 hours work[,] he's gone home with a *stomach*[-ache] & goes away tomorrow for 2 weeks[.] Oh help! Shanks gets more & more worse[,] forgets everything & moreover is now saucy if reminded. Whatever you tell her to do[,] she does the direct opposite[.] It *is* aggravating & has turned very nasty when re: told. I do try to put up with her & be easy. She *uses* not one shred of common sense. I have to oversee *every scrap* of cooking. She can't even make a yeast powder biscuit[,] yet she kept house 30 years for her husband. (Poor man) She either lets the fire *out* or she wastes great quantities of fuel roasting me. Life isn't *all* easy[,] is it? The Clarkes[,] it seems[,] have had a terrible lot of illness[.] Irene says she has neuritis in her hands[,] hence her writing – *it's awful.* Bill's in bed too (writing) [.] You and I are not the only ones[.] Your writing is *good* when you know it[.] It's funny[,] the bigger the man[, the] smaller he writes. Ira[,] I'd rather like Bill & Irene to *see* Biog:[.] What do you say? I'd like my *live* ears to hear their comment[s] & Lawren's[.] For the rest I don't care[.] What do you say? I have not said anything to them & the Biog is *yours* not mine[.] I mean just send it over for them to read with [the] understanding it comes *right back to your keeping*[.] I think they'd appreciate it & they have been kind. She liked the bit you read so much (baptism) & I'd like their reactions to it as a *whole.* Bill says K.W. (& Small) *did* pay their publication [but] not much more[:] 'the books are still selling & will continue to sell for years and years in other editions[.] On their performance to date there is not the slightest ground for disappointment or even discouragement. I wish they had sold ten times as *many* copies, but I never for one moment expected them to do any such thing. On the other hand[,] I shall be greatly amazed if they do not sell ten times as many as they have sold already. Books are permanent investments if they are as good as yours are.'[38] Bill says also Sir Humphrey regards the objection of Mr. Lawson to [the] form of contract which he prepared some months ago & discuss[ed] with us on last visit as justified in part[.] He has consented [to] his solicitors who suggest no re-drafting of the form of contract but a *new power of attorney* for Mr. Clarke which would be satisfactory to Mr. Lawson[.] 'I'm sorry creatures is not to come out this year but I sort of expect it too.' (Me) Irene does not mention it

38 BCARS, Parnall Collection, MS 2763, letter from William H. Clarke to Emily Carr, 27 July 1943, box 2, file 10.

but says she has been working on Woo. (You know when here her only comment was she'd have liked some words in Woo's life expanded[,] see if I could better them.) I hope she does not let the Harman woman mess them like they tried to do Small. If you & I ever have a chance for a long talk[,] I want to ask my Editor a heap of questions but I don't want to bother his over-taxed noddle these days. I don't feel happy when my work goes out other than direct from my Editor's eye, yet[,] Eye[,] I *do* think I'm more independent than I was at first[,] don't you?

Take care of yourself these busy days & bless you.

Your *fliend* always with love
Emily-Small

P.S. I'm right here guardian. – Small.
Irene asked me some time ago (for the Women's Art Association) if I could find them an Indian picture[.] $50.00 was limit the Club had & they did not like to offer that. I asked Irene *if she* thought I should present them with one. She said I was to consult *YOU* but her advice was *no*[,] take their fifty as a matter of course.[39] I will look one out so I told you I am going to try[,] now the Biog: is off my chest[,] to do a little stock-taking in the studio. I do not see why you should be hammered by questions or thoughts[.] Still I do like to feel you believed me. Talk about being solitary[.] I sometimes feel like a country road rambling on & on with twisting and *no* lights. I wish Lawren & Bess were taking you off on their mountain trip[.] That glory air[,] Lawren's society & being out of C.B.C's reach *would* do you good. I wonder what last night's 1.30 to 3:30 A.M. house of parliament call was for[.] Can't go see the poor old sleepy heads pulled from their beauty sleeps. Oh what horrible times[.] It sickens one. Everybody is nearly crazy like the wasps when the engineer was squirting their nest & they buzzed 'til they tumbled & you couldn't help feeling sorry for them, even for wasps.[40] Emily

39 Irene Clarke's (undated) letter to which Carr refers and in which Clarke suggests she consult Dilworth has been preserved at BCARS, Parnall Collection, MS 2763, box 2, file 10. See also her letter to Carr, 25 November 1953, in which she argues that the Women's Art and Lyceum Club ought to pay Carr $50 for her canvas.

40 See Carr's letter dated 2 July 1943.

Wednesday Aug 4 / 43

Dear Eye
It *was* good to get your letter yesterday and the few words of warm praise for Biog:[.] Am I conceited? You see it was so, so long since you'd given me good[,] bad or indifferent on anything I'd written[.] ('Small['s] Gold[,]' *I think*[,] was the last, months & months ago at Mrs. Clark's[.]) I knew you were frightfully busy and worried[,] so I slipped the little I wrote (4 smallish ones which I don't think you may care for particularly[,] there is not much of Small in them). I thought to myself 'perhaps Ira is wearied of my writing[.'] It is all so much the same (all sort of biographical)[.] You see I have to *experience* things to make my work vivid. So I can understand people might tire of it[.] It is now 7 or 8 months since I sent you '*House of All Sorts.*' I asked you once after several weeks after at Mr. Clarke's if you had read it and you said about 3/4. I gathered [you] were not satisfied with the start. I have mentioned it in letters a couple of times since[,] but you have ignored the question. We agreed on the policy of Indian 'straight talk,' so I came to the conclusion it was probably one of two things[:] either you had lost the M.S. or else you found it *bad* and hesitated to tell me so. Please tell me my dear[,] *please straight talk*[.] It may be you've just *forgotten all about it.* I have myself lost the M.S. 'Cedars[.]' You did give it back to me to work on[,] didn't you? There were a few bits in House of A.S. I liked[.] If available[,] send it back to me & I will salvage & re-write. I would doubtless find much wrong after all these months anyhow.

Now man[,] listen to me! *Don't you ever let me hear such things as you said about the Biog's forword.* I may be ignorant but I *do* know the difference in scholarly English and words caught just by ear with no basic rules behind them, like mine. Time & again[,] different people have said of your lecturing or your writing 'I always like listening to Mr. Dilworth[.] He uses such good English![']' So there!

No. I *added* nothing to Biog: I only tried to simplify sentences & make meanings plainer[.] I did rewrite 'Green' & 'Wild Geese' because I thought them too important to be so shoddily expressed. I am so very, *very* glad you found them 'swell.'

I will be glad when this old 'Board' have done with you and gone home and you can get the rest & quiet you need. I hope you go into high air, away from the coast Take a few pet books and hide from beastly humans[.] Take Small too. I can't holiday her any more[.] She was so crazy happy over our camp too. Harry Lawson has gone to the mountains for 3 weeks, Lawren to the [hills?], Ruth for all summer, Margaret Clay, Flora, everyone holidaying! For one wild moment my wings beat rebelliously. *I wanted to go* too. I even thought of asking Dr. Baillie (just some tiny distance). But I guess I'll spare breath. Nights have been very bad lately. Next thing I know I'[ll] be [riding?] in the ambulance[.] I'll just stay put and go on with my tidying up[.] Only some days *I can handle work at all*[.] I don't know really how long I can *endure* Shanks[.] She gets worse & worse[.] I'm so sick of thinking for her[,] of going into the kitchen & cooking *her* meals (for myself I have *no* appetite)[.] The only thing I can trust her to cook without supervision is porridge. So when I feel too awfully bad to stand over the stove I just say 'oatmeal porridge' and leave her to it. But it's too bad, I pay a good wage $30.00 & there is little to do here. Yesterday I *did* rebel. I crawled into bed after finding (tho' she'd been to town that day) she had let us run out of *everything, even porridge*[.] I said you can make any filthy mess you like for supper and eat it too but, if you can't keep your wits about you and take a little care of me & my house[,] I *must try & get* someone who can. She does not want to go, it scares her. She knows no one would put up with her. I rang her sister up to see if I could get any clue why she was such a fool[.] Her sister said 'I know what you are up against, I had her with me 5 years [until] we could not stand [it] any more[.] I told her she must go off on her own & I advise you to do the same.'

Yet when after 4 months of daily telling she does the things *all wrong* and acts so surprised when you correct her[,] I find if I just bang my fist down & roar 'Mrs. Shanks!' not one other word[,] she goes ahead & does what I've repeated so often, showing she *can* if she puts her wits on it[.] But oh you don't know how trying it is & the worst thing possible to upset my fool heart. If I change I might [find] someone with *all the common sense* but *not kind*[.] She snoops so dreadfully too[,] the keenest ears I have ever come across. I have no privacy. I really should not pay $30.00 per month for the work in *this* house and *get out of my bed to cook for her.*

I am slowly digging into odd corners and portfolios[.] Oh *never never never* be an artist[,] Eye! The stuff that collects around them[.] I'm having royal bonfires & mind you have no hesitation in bonfiring the contents of your box. But it is nice to know I can put in there things I may want to use to the end of my sensibility & not burn them today to want them tomorrow. I am glad you agree about the Clarkes & the Biog: I hope that Harman woman keeps her nose out of it. I'd like Bill's & Irene's reaction [and] also Lawren's[.] Of course that goes for Bess but I don't give a twopenny damn about her opinion[.]

Don't envy Lawren[,] Eye. Lawren *is fine*[,] so is his money-freedom but, *you are finer*[.] You are right out in the battle line, leading men. Lawren & Bess have a vaguely lovely world. You have not got 2 wives (at least *I hope not*) [.] I have no doubts[,] although she was troublesome[,] she must turn over uncomfortably in his conscience as the mother of his 3 children. What I would love to see *you* have is a house & garden *of your own*: if I ever thought old Biog: would turn up trumps & contribute towards that aim[.] My! How happy I would be. I'd love to see you *own* not a pretentious mansion but a home & garden. Luck to the parties and love to yourself – I had thought to *say* most [of] this letter when you came over but when –? If you come over the 11th with the big pots[,] they'll keep you busy and there is Ferne too[.] These days you will want to be a brotherly comforter to her. So bless you, bless you, bless you, and if that holiday *does not come this time*[,] I'll come marching over if (I have to climb over my own corpse to do so) and shoo you out.

If you *should see fit* to drop me a line[,] *answer about my work House of A.S. etc etc.* I'll be grateful. But don't if it riles you. I've waited a *long* time[,] I can wait still. What happens to Phylis when you go away? Have you help[?] Is your brother & [his] wife still there?

As always your loving
Emily & Small

Small's P.S. Em's about squeezed me out[,] Eye! All right[,] old Em[.] I can go to Board meetings[,] big dinners & you can't. Old stick-in-a-mud Emily: listen for my chuckle[,] Eye[,] and don't let them poke beastly liquor down you, big pots or no big pots. If you have to make a speech[,] put your hand on your waistcoat pocket & I'll give a little tickle to help. Your loving Small.
P.S.S. Shanks put up a *good* lunch[.] All Em. did was make the gravy (in bed). Shows Shanks *can* if she *has a mind to.* Yesterday Em. was giving her feet a good soak and scrub & Shanks gave her her *tooth*brush to scrub them with. S.

[Undated letter; envelope postmarked 5 August 1943]

Dear Emily:
Thanks for your letter which has just arrived! The spring of lemon verbena was lovely. For a moment it filled the air with its indescribable

sweetness. I am so glad that old root did not perish in the hard winter cold. It will soon be a big shrub again. My cutting did not survive the winter. It grew quite well last summer and full but the cold was too much for it. But as I told you before two of the lady slippers sent up leaves – no flowers. They may come next year.

Yes, I often wish I could get a small place of my own – just a garden which need not be a fancy one and a small house where I could have my pictures, my books and my piano. Everyone should have a place for his *household gods.* Without it one seems constantly to be simply a border or a tourist. Some day I may manage to get such a place. I rather fancy having a place outside the city where I could spend the week-end and *my holidays*!!

Sure, I'm going to have a holiday. I am going to go away somewhere, find a hole, get into it and pull the hole in after me. I shall certainly take Small along. And by the way she is going to be at all the Board Meetings and at the dinners and other functions. I don't suppose she has told you: after all we have to have a few little things to ourselves.

And now about 'House of all Sorts' – it's a shame, Emily, that I have taken so long about it. Of course I haven't lost it. I wanted to do careful notes in all the sections as I did on 'Bobtails' and I started & got halfway through when time failed me. I shall finish up what I can and send it over to you by Monday next. Don't think it's a disagreeable labour: it is a real joy always to be working on your mss. but you know that you cannot do creative work unless you have time and place of mind to give yourself wholly to what you have in hand. Now, when I'm reading and trying to analyse work that I care anything about the same thing is true. It may sound presumptuous but I do have to live the thing over, create it for myself if my judgment is to be worth anything atall. If H. of A.S. arrives on Monday without notes you'll know that it was just because I could not get the time and leisurely detachment necessary to write them.

My brother & his wife are still with us. They are a great comfort. I am sorry Shanks is such a stupid. I know she tries your patience sorely. But it's impossible to get better keep these days. Oodles & oodles –

Yours ever
Ira

[ca. 5 August 1943; written on a tiny piece of paper]

Dear Small:
I am using this thin paper in the hopes that this note may miss Emily and so not make her jealous and annoyed.

I do want you to come to the Board meetings and to the dinners (one in Vancouver & one in Victoria). There'll be some fearful swells there – Archbishops, Bishops, Generals, Major Generals, Chief Justices and so on but who cares? They'll be funny and stupid perhaps but it will help to have you along –

Take care of Emily and don't let Shanks put her toothbrush to such bad uses.

Your loving guardian.

Wednesday [18 August 1943]

Dear Eye
Have your pajamas a breast-pocket? I hope so (those I made for the red X had). Small often seeks sanctuary when E. is depressed in long wakeful hours. 2 A.M. to 6 is a long time to kick round sleepless when you've taken all the sleep-pills allowed for that night. The night before last I resorted to writing *twice*[,] one hour at a time. Sometimes it puts me off. Dr. knows (and approves)[.] I am getting on with 'We paused, The Birds Sang on.'[41] Another week will see her *through* (with luck). I wonder how you will find her? There is a lot about death and dying but I *do not* think it is a *sad M.S.* It will be ready when you come back *but when are* you going? Or have you gone? *You promised I should know.* I am fearfully proud of you. I got my C.B.C. programme today[ ] How grandly they spoke of your work for the Western network. And what a young happy picture of you! It is a grand work you are doing: I read your talk with great interest. I'm very *proud of knowing Ira Dilworth*[.] I spose they

41 This manuscript eventually comes to be published under the title *Pause*. In a letter dated 8 August 1943 she explains why she considers the title 'We Paused, the Birds Sang On': 'I had thought of "Pause[,]" now I think maybe it's "The Birds sang on!![")] In almost every section the birds come (and they sang all through the pause).'

stirred up heaps & *heaps* of *more* work for you. But they *must* know every machine needs rest (even Men-of-War-boats are scraped & painted occasionally). I'm better[.] Dr. said so today[.] Seems he'd been worried over a swollen vein in my neck & it's got better[.] He is 'guinea-pigging' several other heart cases now & seems rather pleased with himself.

Yesterday an *awful* woman (2 of them) came from Regina[.] She is a friend of Grace Campbell (author of Thorn Apple Tree)[.][42] She 'phoned & I told her a *short* visit as I'd been ill. Well after about 1/4 of an hour of the *two* of them[,] she told the other to go & do her business & come back round [after] about ½ hour (which she couldn't have done if it was in town). I said ['] *Oh please no!* I can't talk that long! ['] Then she produced a great sack full of extracts[,] some from Small[,] some K.W. & read them to me. Then a long M.S. that Grace Campbell gave her (a very dry uninteresting old woman soliloquy-ing) [.] It was long & I slumped. She kept it up for an hour. I couldn't even *listen*[.] I said '*Please please* go! I'm *so tired* & the Dr. says he'd rather I *worked* than entertained visitors[.'] She suddenly became aware *I was done.* She said 'Are you alone?' 'Yes, my housekeeper is out.' Then she declared 'she did not think she should leave me! She had not realized I was so ill' & I said 'Oh *do please go*[,] then I can go to bed.' The last I remember of her is her lips pressing a clammy *kiss* on my brow. Her name was Dolan[43] and I hope I never see her again[.] She left me a daft poem written by herself too. Goodness, goodness, Ira! Some females is fools! How Dr. Baillie laughed when I told him but he said she *was a fool.* And it was all I *could do* & he was glad *I told her to go.* Well I hope you are picking up after your successes & exertions & if you *have* gone away – well I hope you'll have a *splendid* rest and come back as nice as you look in the C.B.C. schedule programme. Don't forget to give Lawren the Biog: if my last letter *was* snippy – forgive. I've been a *very crotchety old woman lately*[.] Seemed like I felt too *mean all over* to be decent[.] Haven't been in my garden for 2 weeks.

Always your loving old guinea-pig!
Emily –

P.S. *It's Small*[,] *Guardian.* Em is not lying[.] She has been *real mean*[.] I

42 Grace MacLennan Grant Campbell (1895–1965) published *Thorn-Apple Tree* in 1942.

43 Possibly Mabel Dolan (Mrs G.R. Dolan), who wrote a letter to Carr on 4 June 1943 in which she mentions that she wrote a review of Grace Campbell's *Thorn-Apple Tree* (BCARS, Parnall Collection, MS 2763, box 3, file 5).

am glad you wore my cedar in your lapel[.] The little Doctor said you did. Emily's mad with little Doctor because she thought her last crit was stupid & worse than none at all. Small.
N.B. The glads have come out right to the tip-tops.

---

218 St Andrews [ca. August 1943]

Dear Ira
Has the bird already flown? I *was* glad to see you before you went[.] The new suit is nice. I think Small will travel very comfortably and I hope you will. It is a nuisance for you that they bother you about those beastly 'write-ups[.]' This thought has come to me[:] why not use the formula adopted by that wise old cockatoo Sally. 'Sally is a Sally.'[44] = 'Emily is Emily[.]' I tried to teach the bird 'Sally is a fool' because she would not talk but Sally changed it to suit herself[:] 'Sally is a Sally' and there you had the whole of her[.] 'Emily is Emily' enough for Ottawa[.] McCurry loathes me.[45] I 'sassed' him years ago for being (smart & overbearing) [.] He was then Eric Brown's secretary. Eric was fond of me & good to my work. McCurry never forgave me. I've never kowtowed to him. He would agree 'Emily is Emily.'

Give up, let the world & the C.B.C. go hang! They have drained you[.] Go out & fill up again on the things you love[,] beautiful things[,] nature[.] Don't carry the C.B.C. with you on your chest (it would crush Small too) [.] Be good[.] Take care of yourself & get the full good of your trip & take as *long as you can.* You have 4 years holiday coming to you.

Goodbye[.] Always your loving Emily-Small.

P.S. I am better these 2 days. Shankses day out Thursday seemed to restore me[.] Combating her stupidity got wearisome. E
P.S.S. I'm ready[,] Belovedest Guardian. 'Small.'
N.B. I think Alice was more touched by 'Pause' than by anything I had ever written. Perhaps she had never realized that 18 months in my life[.] She had even forgotten how long I was in that purgatory.[46] Beyond her

44 This anecdote about Sally is also documented in 'Vancouver' (*GP* 277).
45 See note 59, page 129.
46 Carr is referring to the period she spent in the East Anglia Sanatorium in England.

eye trouble[,] she has never been ill in her life. A long smooth life. Yet as she reads the ups & downs & struggles of mine[,] she is a little resentful[.] Bitter little things she says to me & to others show jealousy[.] She forgets I had to kick & struggle[.] Things were not easy won while she was leading a placid, unheeding life[, the] 'path of least resistance[,]' always and scolding & scorning my turbulence.

Sicamous, B.C.
Saturday, Aug. 28. '43

Dear Emily:
Well, here I am off on my holiday or more correctly here *we* are[,] for Small is quite definitely here with me. We got off the train here at 7 this morning. This is the junction point for the Okanagan. We have to wait until almost 11 o'clock for the other train. But I don't mind that. It is beautiful here. The lake is really lovely with clean pebbly beach and the mountains coming down sheer and sharp into the water. Small doesn't mind it either. First thing when we got out of the train[,] she spied a flock of mallard ducks. There were 25 of them. (I counted them: I find Small is not strong with figures.) They were sitting on the lovely pebbly beach except four or five who were swimming in the water. One of these was just sitting in the water, sleeping with his head under his wing. Small loved him and went down to see him at once. She has been snooping around down there at the water's edge ever since. I hope she gets back in time for the train[,] altho' I am sure she would be quite happy to stay right here for a week and so would I.

Thanks for your letter, Emily. You must not take too much trouble over 'Pause' before I see it. I am very curious to read it: the title is really most intriguing. I think it is a stroke of genius. I like to read your mss. just as they come. You don't need to polish them for the first reading, so don't worry about it: send it along and let me have a look at it. I wish I had it with me on my holiday.

You are both right and wrong about 'Klee Wyck.' You are wrong to think that its style is not wholly yours. Every bit of that book is yours[,] almost more than the 'Book of Small': You are right in thinking that little roughnesses may have been smoothed out in our work together on the ms. Our minds rubbed each other and helped each other. But the original part, the creative part is wholly yours. It is in your finest style as are many parts of B. of S. For example, 'Time,' 'Sunday,' 'Loyalty,' 'The Bishop's Blessing.' I think every writer finds that it is impossible to sustain a uniform quality in writing. (And I am sure you know that is true of the painter too.) Some things turn out to be more completely incandescent, growing, luminous than others. It is part of the great mystery of creative genius and the way in which it works. One sees it clearly in the greatest poets – Hardy, Whitman, Wordsworth, even Shakespeare. And the strangest thing is that poets have usually been unable to distinguish accurately between what seems to the world the finest and what seems less fine. Wordsworth was a good example of this. When asked to read his verse he usually chose selections which now seem so much below his highest achievement that they are scarcely read atall. Browning said

'All I aspired to be
All men ignored in me
That was I worth to God
Whose hand the pitcher shaped'[47]

Well, goodbye for now. Oodles of love. I must go out & get Small –

Ever yours,
Ira

---

218 St Andrews St Sept 12 43

Dear Eye – It's Small.
Thank you for taking me on your holiday. We did have a good time didn't we? Especially on Dilworth mountain. I loved it and the old ranch. And Emily enjoyed it through me tho' almost too sick to enjoy anything just then[.] She asked 'Did you see the old root-house where the little boy set the three crosses at Easter? Did you see the paths of stone, the alters on the hillside?' Did I Eye? Or have they been cleared away?

I came back to Emily for just a minute [–] once Eye[.] Perhaps you were dozing & did not notice me slip from my sanctuary. Emily was in a different room[.] She did not know I had come[.] Doctor Baillie was sitting by her bedside & her eyes were shut[.] When I kissed her cheek it

47 The lines are not quoted correctly. See note 16, page 39 on Browning.

twisted up a little with the tickle & Dr. B. said 'Good! I see a little light glinting through.' E. opened her eyes & as she'd commenced the grin[,] she had to finish it. So she rummaged her brain for some small foolishness of Shanks to tell Dr. B. It would never do to let him know about Small. That joke is just yours & mine & Emily's. He isn't going to be let in. Only you & I & E. know it was made a *really legal* joke when Harry fixed E's will & made me yours & I wasn't printed then & so scared about it and it was such a comfort to have a Guardian.

Emily was mad when she discovered you had such a short holiday. She said 'All those little male & female scrubs in C.B.C. got 3 whole weeks for themselves & the director only 3 days!' But she was glad the three days were happy looking over the old familiar places.

We wonder how you like 'Pause[.]' Let us have a general red-hot reaction [as] soon as you *can*[,] even if you are not able to scrutinize it correctively *for ages.* E. hopes you won't mind having so much death in it. To ring true she had to. She thinks it goes a little deepe[r] than House of A.S. What do you think? And she says[,] would you like to have its dedication? If ever published[,] it won't be 'til she's dead & by then people will have forgotten Small's dedication was yours. But perhaps it's too much death for you to want it. If you don't answer soon she'll know & say no more. Writings don't have to *have* a dedication[,] do they? It can just be blank.

Heres hugs & oodles from us both.
Your loving Emily & Small

P.S. This funny little scrap is one of my vows made more than 60 years ago & written in my own handwriting (I wrote clearer then than now[,] didn't I?) [.] I need to write my vows to help impress them[.] E. found this in the leaves of an old school book. V.O.N. still hypoing E. twice a day. Small.

[ca. September 1943]

Dear Eye
Thanks for special[.] No I was not mad at you[.] Maybe just a wee bit sad at you that you felt you must apologize as if you had neglected a *duty*[.] Also that so often lately you have told me you were too sad to write & phone[.] My *old* dear letters that you wrote to me and I wrote to you are

not obligations[,] at least on my side they are not[.] As I told your mother in very truth 'I love to write to Ira.' It is as though a bubble burst in my heart (the feeler) and released something that wanted to fly to you – my letters to you have always been not an 'ought but a want to' & I hoped yours to me were the same[,] written not only for each other but to ease ourselves too. I could not write the *same letter to two* people no matter if I thought I loved them all equal. I would write a different letter to you than to Lawren or Bill or Myfanwy or Carol[.] Don't you see what I mean Eye? A letter to be a correspondence must be a spontaneous loving outpour from one to another[.] How can you 'respond' if there is not a 'co'? If I thought I pushed myself over your conscience to squeeze a letter out of you, I would not enjoy it[.] When it came[,] it would just be a business deal or an advertisement instead of a privilege of friendship. Perhaps I have been selfish and tired you[?] If so[,] forgive me. It was such a relief & also such a joy to get an answer. I have felt very alone with Alice so difficult lately & Shanks such a fool. And it's a long long time since you & I had a good *long* talk[,] isn't it[?] I am not complaining. I know you are pushed beyond the limit. I only say write when you *want* to: you know it is a joy to me. And I know you will come when you can. Damn Hitler! His war makes for *so many* extras[.] I would like to have talked House of AS & Pause over with you[.] Maybe some day there will be the chance. I think I see what you mean by caricaturing instead of characterizing[.] I expect that is a natural trait of mine[:] too wholesale over laughing, over crying, over hating, and over loving, but I *don't think* I over-stressed the 'cure'/the over-feeding & the red tape[.] Over one point[,] I felt a little sore. You wrote me two letters since you got 'Pause' & totally *ignored* the dedication[.] Perhaps you did not read the enclosed few lines. Small & I said you might feel it sad & not want it[,] in which case your silence would answer for you. If you wanted it[,] I asked you to say so red-hot. Somehow I had a little different feeling about Pause[.] It had cost me blood & tears[.] I wanted to give it to you. I had thought of two other people but it would not be quite the same[.] They only know my crust. So I think I [will] just leave her undedicated. Living 'Pause' scorched my heart[.] I would not want her to have an un-understanding Godparent. I am *rather* sorry I suggested Lawren & Bess read Biog. He pretended he was keen & said he'd write me his candid opinion. I could have just let him have the section 'Lawren Harris'[48] which I did feel he had a right to see.

48 See 'Lawren Harris' (*GP*, Pt 3, 340–52).

Bill & Irene sent such a kind wire[.] I don't know how they knew I was in hospital[.] Also a *lovely* box of roses & reviews they one or both expect now to come out in November (West). I did tell you [about it] in 'Pause.' I was ill, very ill (did not know I was hospital ill then)[.] You made no allusion or comment in your letter[.] The wonder came to me[:] had you read the letter? A postcard Bobbie sent me from the North took a whole month to come.

I sent Shanks to gather 2 sprigs of lemon verbena & she mutilated the whole root[.] You can't trust the fool with sense anywhere[.] Dr. Baillie says my present condition is partly due to starvation. Shanks would not bother to cook & I was too sick to get out of bed & do it for her & I had no appetite[.] There was plenty of good food provided. I told her she could cook it for herself or starve. But I dare not get rid of the useless thing[.] There is nothing else [and] she does not want to go. O I wish – that's cowardly.

Goodbye old *old* dear. Here's a great hug [Carr draws a big circle][.] As little San 'Jenny' said 'Let[']s us be enormous friends to the end.'[49]

Always your loving Emily & Small

P.S. Me too[,] you bet. If you are mad with Emily[,] take it out on me. Such a smart pinch. People will think you have a bee in your pocket or your fountain pen has leaked. I'm a bad child[,] you know[.] Guardian. Loving Small

---

[This letter is written at the end of one written by Irene Clarke, dated 27 September 1943]

Irene alludes here to last time she was out [in Vancouver.] She (not Bill) had read Woo's life[.] She told me then her only complaint was that she felt in some places things in Woo's life should have been more fully amplified & explained[,] carried *further.* I said & asked 'if she marked such places[,] I'd see if [I] could expand them a little[.]' Nothing was ever said of expanding *Bobtails.* If that satisfied *my Editor*[,] it is good enough for her. The more I think of 'The Pie[,]' the better I think the idea of your idea in making it a Xmas book rather than Peacock alone. I

49 In 'Jenny,' she says 'Let's be friends. Enormous friends' (*P* 622).

do not remember anything particularly personal that would shudder me under the public eye during life.

Far as I can think now (have no copies) [,] the only ones I'd *feel delicate over* would be 'Mother,' Biog: & your own personal ones[,] 'Small's Gold' & 'Kiss for Canada' & possibly 'Man, Woman, Dark[.]' The last little one I tucked into your trunk *not* typed[.] It is one of those tiny unexplained experiences that just might happen to men & women[,] millions of them (not love experience) [,] something in the make-up of a man and the make-up of a woman clicking. Something telling me that man remembered the incident as I did. A little kindness that came out of the blackness of night. Kindness & trust accepted & *given*[.] The kindness that is asleep down at the core of all that is *natural* and[,] being natural[,] is therefore *great*[,] but which convention, vice & sex have perverted. The blurred forms in the dark knowing neither form[,] feature[,] nor name of each other but recognizing what was greater *than* these – and the story padded with the sensible natural sagacity of the Bobbies[.] Must I write this to you? *You* know, but not everyone knows[.] There are things beyond explanation that have deep meaning[.] But back to M.S. You know the odd one or two that I would feel *too* personal for publication which I like afterwards[.] They are yours & at your death I'd rather they went to a man's keeping than a woman's[.] A man would understand better, but goodness knows! Etcetera may be an authoress in her own right or a publisheress & then it's up to you. Harry brought me the revised contracts to sign yesterday[.] I'm tied up pretty tight. I wanted to ask you & forgot to yesterday [–] R.S.V.P. [–] 'Can I destroy *old* copies of *unpublished* & *uncorrected* M.S.?' I use them for preliminary writing paper but see no sense of keeping even *decently* typed copies of Book of Small material. (Uncorrected finals) only make confusion[.] Who's going to plough through them? Not *I* [.] I shall tackle that job when strong enough (tidying up the M.S. pigeon holes) in studio. Eye[,] I had 7 seven HOURS SLEEP after your visit that night[.] I woke a different woman. They kept coming in & looking[.] They said, afraid to wake me & see if I *was all* right[.] My clock was so astonished it fell on its back & lost 20 minutes & my teeth slipped under the bed. 'Small's Gold' had been put into the cooler or I'd have thought they'd worked a spell on me. Perhaps it was Dr. Dilworth! Anyhow it was a *good* sleep & what a lovely visit! Small held the gold ball in her hand 'til she went to sleep[.] She's flittering round among the bloom all day. They took me down & the first floor (in my bed) & cardio radiographed my silly heart. I asked the nurse 'Can you see all the people I love in there?' but she said 'No!'

I am sorry you have to make one of those beastly East Trips. I spose this time you will fry[.] Last time you froze[.]

Something I saw in the Radio Programme scared me too, yet[,] Eye[,] I want always the highest of honor for you[.] You know that[,] don't you?

Always yours lovingly
Emily

P.S. Me too. Small. I'm taking out my most cobwebby dresses for the Eastern heat. Or shall I wear one of those batting dresses that fit like fish scales?

[Envelope postmarked 2 October 1943]

Dear Emily:
Yes, it was a 'delicious' visit. I enjoyed every minute of it in spite of the fact that I was sorry to find you feeling so low in spirits. I was sorry too (more than I can tell you) that I had contributed to your feelings of depression. As I told you on Tuesday my failure to mention your suggestion about dedicating 'Pause' to me was certainly not because I did not want you to do so. It was just that there were so many things I wanted to say in *one* letter that that got overlooked for the moment. I don't suppose you can understand that. I hope you can and will accept it as an honest explanation. In accepting it you need not forgive my stupid clumsiness unless you wish. You must do just what seems best to you about the dedication of 'Pause.' I would be deeply honoured and touched to have it dedicated to me but I must not be greedy. There are, I am sure, others who would feel the honour of such a dedication too.

I have spent my spare time all week getting 'The Pie' typed and checked. It is ready now to send off airmail to the Press. I have had two clean typed copies made. I shall send one to you and I shall keep your original in the meantime in case any points are to be discussed with Clarke. Of course, I have no idea what decision Bill may arrive at as far as publishing 'The Pie' just now is concerned. I still think it a fine ms.

What a long letter from Irene – not much in it but obviously kind and generous in intention. So she & Bill plan to come out this Fall. I'll believe it when I see them. I should think she'd be afraid to go traveling:

she always seems to fall ill when they're about half-way home. Wasn't she ill in Edmonton when they came West last time?

Now for one or two things in your letter –

1) 'Man, Woman, Dark' sounds most interesting. Thank you for putting [it] in the box in the meantime. Your letter description of this experience is extremely well expressed.

2) Be careful of destroying papers etc that may be of interest. If you have a lot of duplicates or definitely discarded *first-tries* [of] something, they can be destroyed but things that had not been finished should be kept[,] however fragmentary and incomplete. You never know when you may be inspired to go back to an idea and develop it – and when you do[,] an early sketch may give you a point of departure. Remember, my dear, that the great Italian composer of opera, Verdi, did his most original and, in many respects, his most significant work after he was 80 years old.

3) About Lawren and 'Biog,' please don't blame Lawren – it is not his fault. We were going to read it (or parts of it at least) together. Well, the opportunity has never arisen. I am going to his house for dinner tonight and have told him I am taking 'Biog.' I shall have it for him to read and I know he will do so. He has spoken of it several times. You must not think that he is not interested.

I 'phoned Mrs. Hamber today. She is definitely taking the 'Indian Cemetery.' She wants another but has not decided which yet. She says she will call at my office early next week to pick up the picture and leave her check for its price – $50.

I was very glad to hear you had enjoyed a good sleep. That would help a great deal. I hope you are feeling much better.

I must stop now and go home to pile in a load of wood – I think it's going to rain.

Oodles of love to you & Small –
Yours as ever
Ira.

P.S. I can't possibly tell you how touched I was at your wishing me to have your ring. I shall cherish it always but you must keep it with you for the present. D.

Monday [ca. 4 October 1943]

Dear Ira
Your special delivered yesterday afternoon was a real joy[.] It was like your old ones. And I'll admit that though I hid bravely[,] told you not to feel you *ought* to write[,] but I *was* bitterly lonesome getting over weekends without one, which shows I am selfish & unreasonable when you are so very busy! And here's a great woozy hug for *fixing* 'The Pie' all [in] your spare time!! That's a shame! Clean copies!!! Thank you Eye [Carr draws a swirling line with the word 'hug' underneath it]. I hope Bill can put it through[.] So many have groaned at not getting their Xmas book this year[.] The Pie may be as too long as Peacock [or] too short. I wrote Irene [that] you'd told me of the suggestion & I was delighted.

Of course I've forgiven you about Pause. I am so glad you *want* it.[50] My other two ideas were Dr. Baillie and Bill & Irene. Dr. Baillie knew the San (had spent a weekend there with Sally Bottle) but I did not really *want* any of those people[.] I wanted *you* & when I thought you did *not want her* decided to let her go naked[.] I'm glad you want her. I *might* give House of A.S. dedication to Bill & Irene[.] What do you think? Irene was taken ill on [the] way back from Quebec & had to stop off in Montreal to recover[.] I forgot about Edmonton. But they don't seem healthy that family. I fancy they are the kind brought up with thermometers in their mouths like Ruth's child.

I mark what you say about the M.S.es[.] Will sort best I can when I get home[.] You will grin when I say I have made a few feeble scratchings towards *something else.* A few stray thoughts but head not up to much yet. Dr. B. says for me there'll always be a *next* one just beyond the last. Perhaps but I *have* to go much slower & check & recheck[.] Am curious to know *what* Irene has found re: Bobtails. As I said before if they were O.K. to pass you[,] I'm not having her or Hangman mess them up[.] I have never been happy that the Bobtails did not go *back* to your eye after Mrs. Whitfield typed it[.] Of course you *had* checked it & Bill *seemed* in a hurry for it. So it was to gain time I sent it direct. I take it your brother &

50 Carr has attached to this letter a sample dedicatory page, with the title *Pause,* and the following: 'To my beloved friend and Editor Ira Dilworth but for whose encouragement & kindness my stories might have been born and died in a bureau drawer.' She notes, 'cut out the frill & just put 'To Ira' if you like it better' [although] the rest is true & is meant.'

sister-in-law are away & you and Phylis [are] keeping house[.] Oh these scrabbly war days[.]

Millions of ooodles. From your loving
Emily & Small

When do you fly? I send special for fear immanent. E. God bless your wings. E.

Wednesday afternoon Hospital Room 306 [ca. 6 Oct. 1943]

Dear Eye
Believe it or not[,] I'm *working*. Still in bed. I brought in an old exercise book and a thought or two began to wiggle[.] I told Dr. B. and he called me a 'bad old thing.' All the same he says he'll hate to see the day when another something isn't hanging ahead of me to do.

Alice came to see me today[,] 2nd time[.] Last time it upset me to see her so blind & frail[.] Today she looked better & was cheery[.]

The 'gold ones' still cheer me. One day they took a half-hearted notion to die & the next had perked[.] We all remarked on it. – Lawren wrote me this morning and loves the Biog: he said he was going to write me as he progressed with it[.] They had only got to end of 1st part S.F. Says they [have] been fearfully busy and he *won't* read it in little pieces[.] He wants whole evenings full to browse over it. He did not offer any comment from Lady Bess. I forgot to enclose the enclosure in last letter[.] I feel so happy that 'Biog:' and 'Pause' are both *specially* your own. My new write is a hodge-podge. It is at *present* called 'Hundreds & Thousands[.]' Did you have those tiny tiny colored candies [that] you sprinkled over birthday cakes or rolled soft chocolates in 'til they coated like barnacles? 'Liquorice all sorts' fix a few among the plain for effect too[.] Each one of the hundreds & thousands is too small to call a candy but they do wake the color of drab chocolate up and add interest to its sweetness. These little jottings are *too small* to call stories. They are just little isolated incidences told as *clean cut & briefly* as I can. Each a separate little unit with a thought tied up in it[.] They will [be] here & there picked from my 70 years[.] I wish I did not *have* to *live* things to make them alive. Bill Clarke said when I lamented about so much 1st person[:] 'It was *not me*. They were things that might be anybody.['] It will be a thing I can pick up and lay down to finish other things when I go home[,] each little unit individual. Does the idea seem to you good?

Maybe you'll be gone when this comes to you[.] Hurry back! Good luck and good business. Carol & her husband are talking of selling their Eastern farm & coming West to farm. Carol wants to be near me. She says there is good demand for farms for swank buyers in the East now & they have improved & modernized theirs[.] I would not advise one way or another[.] I'd love to have her near but[,] well[,] I think Western farming is hard going.

Goodbye old *old* dear. If you *should* be contemplating a weekend letter[,] better send it to 218 St Andrews[.] Dr. has not said when yet but I hope it isn't the hearse again. I'm sure walking would be less harmful than their dirty stretcher.

[ca. 8 October 1943]

Dear Emily,

Just a tiny note to accompany the ms. of 'The Pie.' I sent the Press copy to Mr. Clarke earlier this week. You will notice that there are still many typing errors. These girls are hopeless! My note concerning the order of the selections may surprise you. Perhaps you want the sections to go in the order they had when you sent me the ms. – if so, that's alright. If you have not a definite preference for that order I think we should discuss the matter. I believe a better order could be devised – by that I mean one that will capture the reader's interest earlier in the book. Some of the sketches are stronger than others – notably 'English Song Birds,' 'Ravens of Sitka,' 'Eagles of Skeena,' 'Gardens Gone Wild.'[51] It occurs to me that one of these might come earlier in the volume. Now, that does not mean that I think the other sections weak or uninteresting. They are just not quite as arresting and that is an important consideration in planning a book.

You will notice that there is no copy of 'Heart of a Peacock.' It should come in before 'A Smack for His Majesty.'[52] Clarke has the copy of the 'H. of a P.'

51 See note 119, page 163 and note 114, page 162.
52 See note 115, page 162.

I was at Lawren's for dinner on Tuesday evening. He has read the first part of the 'Biog' and is very enthusiastic about it. He asked me to read aloud to him several sections – 'Baptized,' 'The Roarats,' 'Mrs. Tucket' and 'The Lily Field.'[53] He was very impressed with them. But he will doubtless write you about this himself.

I don't think you like Autumn very much. I do – always have, I suppose partly because the season in the Okanagan Valley is so rich and beautiful. As Keats said it is truly the 'season of mists and mellow fruitfulness.'[54] The past three weeks have been absolutely beautiful in Vancouver as far as weather is concerned.

Hope you are feeling better and happier –

Oodles of love –
Yours devotedly
Ira.

Friday a.m.
Oct. 8. 1943
NB. I am not going East until early in November – don't know date yet. D.
NB. As I told you I have kept the original ms. of 'The Pie.' If and when you want it for reference it is here in safe-keeping. D.

Friday later.
Your letter has just come. Thank you, Emily, for the dedication of 'Pause' – it is beautifully worded and far too generous. I shall have it just as you have written it. I am glad now & always shall be glad to be known as your 'beloved friend' – Glad Lawren wrote about 'Biog.' He's a dear person. D.

Jubilee Hospital Sunday [ca. 10 October 1943]

Dear Ira
Your letter & M.S. 'Pie' received yesterday, thank you ever so much[.]

53 These stories later appear as 'Baptism,' 'The Roarats,' 'Mrs. Tucket,' and 'Nellie and the Lily Field' in *Growing Pains* (3–4, 53–8, 73–7, 37–8).
54 Dilworth is quoting from 'To Autumn' by John Keats (1795–1821).

Good of you to have the clean copies made. Don't you want me when I've read the one you sent me to send it back to you? My originals are such sights! It would be easier for you if Bill *accepts* the idea of publishing & argues. I hope he won't turn it down. As always when a M.S. has gone out of my mind for some time[,] I feel disappointment meeting it again since its writing[.] I have re-written Biog: 'House of All Sorts[,]' 'Pause' & several oddments[.] You finish each on a bounce of high hope and send it off but somehow when you confront it after a while again your balloon has pricked. I spose it's just natural causes. Thank God I have a 'beloved Editor' to fall back on or there'd be no courage left in me. The support of your knowledge & kindness is ever behind me. That reminds me re: dedication[.] Shouldn't I have put Professor or Dr. Ira Dilworth? (After Beloved friend & Editor?) Or D.D. or M.A.[?] I never am quite sure of your titles but I want you to have all that's coming to you.

I am better and *lots* more cheerful[,] thank you. Have not taken that depressing stuff for some time now[.] It takes a while to work it out of your system[.] My breathing has wonderfully cleared up & I am stronger[.] Still 2 hypos per day and 100000 pills for heart. I have sat half an hour last two days on my own private porch. It was lovely being under the sky again. Yesterday was too cold in A.M.[,] too roasting in afternoon[,] so I sat after supper between 5–6. There is an absolutely healthy great oak tree right in front. It seems so strong & grand to be in the middle of all we sick weak things. When one looks at this great hive of menders for weak bodies[,] these cheerful busy workers[,] & realizes all the pain these walls see & hear dying everyday & night[,] new babies arriving with an indignant squawk and such agony to their mothers [–] it makes one think a good deal[,] Ira. Leaves one in a maze at the marvel and the mystery of creation.

Dr. Baillie says he is going to take me home (himself) on Wednesday. Oh I'm so glad not to go in the hearse & be borne by the greasy pork butchers who bore me in. I look forward to going home & dread it a little too. Perhaps I'd better write some of 'Small's' vows. re: good temper? Did you get the one I pinned into her letter some little while back? 'I will be good tempered when I go home from school?' I think the separation has been good[.] Alice has been 3 times to see me & been loving & sweet. Here she has to submit to railings of Dr. & nurse & doesn't *blame* me[.] She sees a little too what I have to put up with Shanks day after day.

Shanks *considers herself a very tactful* person and is really like a cow playing on a harp!

You are right[.] I do *not like* those freeze and burn autumn days & nights. I have always hated low burning sun glare. *How you did love your Okanagan Valley!* I am glad you read bits of Biog: to Lawren[.] I think I can see why he got you to. Your reading clarifies & adds. Bless you both[.] Thank you for considering me worth reading. A V.O.N. nurse came into my room[.] She looked at you on the wall. 'Ira Dilworth, my but he can read poetry[.] I never heard anyone read it like him,' she said. I will show you the letter Lawren wrote me when he came to the end of the first part. He too liked Nellie & the Lily field. He liked the Roarats where you liked 'Gladness' which he did not notice. Does lady Bess approve the Biog:? Fred would have but Bess was ever a little on the snoot re: my writing.

No. I had no particular arrangement for the Pie. I see what you mean by putting those stronger ones earlier. I put the 'First Birds Nest' & the 'Debt' at the beginning because they were childhood and I stuck the English Birds well back because I wanted the Canadian flavour to come first. I guess 'Eagles' & 'Ravens' could come after 'a debt' & then I expect that silly 'Hangman' will go & topsy-turvy & upset our apple cart. If you go East in early Nov & Clarkes come West you cross in the air. But maybe you'll be there & back before they are here.

The priest came to see me[.] You know I forgot his name. He was very ill for a year in St. Paul's, Vancouver (& fought with the sisters like cats)[.] He had arthritis & suffered terribly but he got his own way[.] The Doctor sided with him & routed the mad sister – we talked about everything *but religion.* The day before a presbyterian missionary called on me (collusion). Today I asked the nurse if she was unloading a Jewish Rabbi on me? I always did tremble over parsons[.] Most every man who wanted me to marry him was a parson's son.

'Hundreds & Thousands' grows – 50 little stories or incidents[,] most of them are roughly suggested. Plenty of typing (rough copies for corrections corrections corrections) when I get home.

Eye, I did like your blank verse arrangement of 'love' in Pic. I wish I knew how to verse.

I'm tired. Goodbye[.] Oodles

Emily

P.S. It's Small, my oodles too & hugs, guardian[.] It is good to know how you are still 'ours devotedly[.]' You hadn't said so lately.
N.B. Dr Trapp said she was planning to come to Vic weekend in Sept.

She, Mrs. McGeer, Nan[,] *nobody* except you & Lawren write me from Van now. Do you ever see or hear of Jane[?][55] R.S.V.P. Emily

---

Hospital Tuesday[.] I hope your Thanksgave [went] well yesterday [ca. 12 October 1943]

Eye
I'm so happy I just *must* write this A.M. I got Lawren's second chunk of crit on Biog: I couldn't tell you all he said[.] I'd blush too hard[.] I knew *you* liked 'Biog:' & I thought that was all that mattered 'til I died. But you once said 'You wanted my flesh & blood live ears to hear it' and perhaps I *am vain* enough to be glad to have heard Lawren's crit too. Between you & me[,] Ira – no I *won't*[;] yes I *will* – (you know what I think about your crits so I don't have to) but I value Lawren's too & I'm glad to have his opinion as an artist critic. It took my breath a bit[.] I did not expect such praise. I am going to send you the letters presently but *please* send them back or I'll sow *you* [–] or is it sue you? Anyhow I'd like to have them to read when I have the weeps or am low & down[.] Your last two 'golden ones' are going to see me through hospital (two weeks today since you were here)[.] It is a quiet dull day[.] Yesterday roared with wind & blew me nearly out of bed[.] Today was much easier to bear. I could not even sit on my balcony. They say I'm a *good* patient & they're *sorry* to see me go. My nurse says 'I'm her *very favourite* of all her patients.' See how cocky with conceit your Small has puffed since she got pretty letters! This is only 'fit for a garbage pail letter[.]' It's sure not worth a 4 ct stamp. But we are always

Lovingly[,] Emily & Small

P.S. I'm afraid I picked up some of my fat again here[.] Don't care if I've got strength & been patched & feel fairly sea-worthy again.
[on the side of the letter] Don't be mad with Lawren for contributing to my conceit – hug! I'm only pleased[,] not really vain. E.

55 In a letter dated 13 September 1942, Dilworth wrote that he had decided to give up the dog Lady Jane.

218 St Andrews St [ca. 12 October 1943]

Dear Ira

Patched again and home! But please excuse another letter so *quick* on top of last[.] It is business, so please *don't* garbage pail it. It is Lawren's letters which I enclose (please return) [.] Only that way (letters) can you understand I think what I'm up against and you see[,] my dear[,] that Biog: it is *not mine* any longer[,] it's *yours* & before I alter it[, it] *must* be with *your* consent. I think I see Lawren's *points.* They are all in the tail (the alterations) [.] I see what he means about bringing in New York & I have (come across a bit of writing when packing for hospital) a bit of description of my impressions of N.Y. written at the time[.] It is not of much value but with a little adding too & bits of remembrance [it] would be helpful. It is dated New York April 24 1930[.] I was in N.Y. one week besides another spent on Long Island where I left Koko with my friends while I went to Martha Washington hotel & saw New Y. & some picture galleries & exhibitions. I did not study there but I see what L. means by reactions to the 3 great cities[,] London, Paris & N.Y.

2nd Lawren think[s] the Biog: incomplete without something of my *writing* coming in. I thought it was only the story of my *painting.* He thinks it should be the rounded circle of my *life.* I *did* not mention how I used writing (towards the end) *to help my painting* but not as a thing of itself[.] It seemed unnecessary to me & to make my life two-tailed. What do you think 'Beloved Editor?' *No. 3* Lawren thinks I should do just what I tried to *avoid.* Give a spiel on the praise my work had received. But why tell you all this[?] You will see for yourself what he says. If I do bring in that birthday party[,] do you mind if I culminate *my pride* in the 'Kiss for Canada' given at the end of the Birthday Party readings of Klee Wyck by a master-Canadian professor? Before my townspeople publicly? I do see where he is right after stressing all the kicks and rebuffs of the West. I should acknowledge their their [*sic*] kind turn & tribute. It is so hard not to sound & feel braggish doing this. Lawren's words[,] '*Face it quietly*[.] You are part of the Canadian creative life[,]' touch me & turn my protesting mute as his advice at the publication of Klee Wyck touched me. 'It is none of your business[.] The artist does the work[.] The reviewer does his[.] Take your nose out where it does not belong.'

Good gracious Eye[.] Lawren & Bess did lap it up (BIOG)! (At least I have had no word or message from Bess[.] Lawren says *we* so I spose they read it together[.]) Altogether I am *astounded* that it seems to have made so deep an appeal to them. He thinks 3rd part *too* short for the other two? Well *old* (dear) Eye[,] what? It is yours. Does it *please* you for me to enlarge[?] Do you agree? I would have to have it back to fit in my pieces. I can't for the life of me remember the last line of 'Are you saved' that he says has the kick of a mule in it?[56]

I'm too *tired* to rest so thought I'd best write you[.] Too weary to wrestle with M.S. When bodily rested[,] I'll buck up in brain I hope. In meanwhile Lawren's reaction to Biog: has amazed, pleased & exhausted me. Write *when you can* (I know you will & I ought not to ask).

I am homesick tonight for the hospital and the nurses and the electric switch that winked if you needed anything. Shanks and Alice gave me kindly welcome. And again I putter along the crookedy way meaning to be careful because for fear of the glass hearse & dirty decrepit stretcher bearers! I'd wish I'd lost 100 more lbs when Dr. Baillie & Shanks were boosting me up the veranda steps. My legs aren't worth a nickle the pair. Small's cobwebby ones can do more kicking & stronger. 'Never mind[.] Use the other end' says the Doctor[,] cheerily tapping his head. Oh, I hope it hangs out (head)[.]

A million kisses from Small and a bear's hug from me. Goodnight

Your loving Emily-Small

Morning P.S. A good night [–] 5 hours *straight sleep* after I write you & Lawren off my chest – longest sleep for ages. Shanks is really trying[.] I talked seriously to her in the hospital & told her she *must try* or *go*[,] that she proved she *could* if she put her mind on it & did what she was *told*[.] She will *not* but goes *her own foolish* way. She does seem really *glad* to have me home. It is dull & *very* cold[.]

Hope Mrs. Hamber came through[.] I don't know the lady but from experience & her foolish letter I take her to be very untrustworthy over statements & promises.

Eye[,] *are* things getting any easier? Don't think you are not *very often* in my thoughts day & night knowing how you still listen & watch and then remember. Mothers like yours & like mine last in memory *all our lifetime* and the memory gets sweeter & sweeter with the years. You'll be amazed at how the little wee incidents come back[,] some stray word or

56 'Are You Saved?' appears in *Growing Pains* (Pt 2, 168–75).

caress when you were a tiny chap[.] It is so[,] I know by experience. Her love clings[.] Bless you always

Emily

[ca. 13 October 1943]

Dear Emily:
Thanks for your lovely letter which came with yesterday's mail – it was a peach! I can see from it that you were feeling much better and I hope that has continued. You said you were going home with Dr. Baillie today – so I am taking a chance and sending this letter to St. Andrews Street. If all has gone as planned you will be in *your own* house under your own maple tree at this very moment. I know how good that will be. I hope Shanks will be more bearable and reasonable. Poor Alice, I am sure she means to be kind. I know from her deep concern when you were ill before that she really has a deep love for you. It is perhaps hard for her to show it consistently: she lives so much *to* herself and *in* herself.

I am more interested in what you have told me about 'Hundreds and Thousands.' I shall be very glad to see it when you are ready to send it over. Don't worry too much about first corrections, and it is not necessary to have it all typed out 'clean' before it comes to me. You know I have no difficulty reading your ms. So send it along when you want to. By the way I don't want you to send back the copy of 'The Pie.' It will perhaps save time for me to have the *original* to refer to if Clarke decides to publish [it] and wishes to argue some point or other. I shall keep the original carefully and send it to you either when the Press has decided not to publish it or when the pains of publication are over.

Yes, Lawren was really very much moved by the 'Biog.' He brought it back to me yesterday and beamed all over in his most boyish, enthusiastic style when he discussed it with me. He said he had written a long letter to you about it. He told me some of the suggestions he had made. They seemed very sensible particularly the suggestion about expanding the 3rd section.[57] I see what he is driving at. I shall be glad to know what he said in detail. He told me he hoped you would not take his remarks

57 *Growing Pains*, Carr's 'Biog.' is divided into three sections.

amiss – he *thinks the 'Biog' is your best writing*, thinks it will be very impressive when published.

Bess expressed herself as being very much impressed by the Biog when I was at their house last week. They had then finished only the 1st section. She was very enthusiastic about the parts I read.

No, you must please not alter the Dedication of 'Pause.' I should not want Professor or Doctor or even Mr. and certainly not my degrees – just Ira Dilworth with the grand description 'beloved friend.' That is simple and direct and pleases me more than any flourish of academic or other titles could possibly do.

Mrs. Hamber promised to call for her picture early last week. She has not come yet. Mrs. Fell would like to buy it. I am almost tempted to 'phone Mrs. Hamber & say that someone else is interested in buying it and that it is not now available for her. But, of course, that is not possible. Mrs. Fell could scarcely buy it under those circumstances because she is a great friend of Mrs. Hamber's. Oh, these people with money in pots make me furious! They can be and often are so arrogant.

I am going East on Oct. 31. I think I shall be away for a short time only. Meantime I am going to Seattle & Portland to speak. I am leaving on Oct. 22 and shall be away until Oct. 27. I have to speak four times. All this spouting seems to me pretty useless. Why people want it is a mystery to me. I am to speak on Canadian Radio [– –] Radio as an international agency in the establishment of peace or goodwill and on my work in B.C. Sunday night, Oct. 25[.] The speech is to be in the Civic Theatre at Portland. I am rather terrified at the prospect. I hope I get home alive.

Oodles of love to you & Small. Yes, I saw Small's resolution – I know how hard she and you try to be patient in a world that is very, very dear and wonderful but fearfully muddled at times and hard to understand.

Yours devotedly,
Ira.

NB. I have not seen Jane but I heard from her last week. She is well and her present owners are very fond of her. D.

218. Nov 1/43

Dear Ira,
Thank you for sparing the minute for my special. I know well how busy you are every day these days and[,] with an away of several days and a going so soon again[,] it's extras & job & jobs. Old C.B.C. keeps you on the hop! Small says to tell you she's sorry she couldn't send you her sprig of courage for Toronto, no one to pick it for her[.] Em *bad* with cold. Shanks sniffing & *afraid* to go outside the door[.] Alice [has a] cold too. I hope Small was in her sanctuary & helped. Glad the speeches were successful. I've been writing about *you* all afternoon (Biog extension)[.] I hope you won't be angry[.] It's all honest true my dear[.] It shows your care & kindness the day of the party & the support I felt in knowing you were there to appeal to when I did not just know how to act. I guess I did show that I loved and honored you – you don't mind the world knowing that[,] do you? Well no one sees it before you do & you may cut out anything you *don't like*[.] It's just honest[,] *not palaver*[;] every word *meant*[.] No sentimental gymnastics.

A baby doctor came to see me yesterday (I don't mean a maternity man) but 6 yards of infancy (he looked very young)[.] Dr. Baillie is away[.] He told the young chap to keep an eye on me. So he just looked in. And there was me smelling like a doughnut fry[,] all done up in my old 'dog kennel remedy' [–] 'hot bacon grease[.]' My chest was so badly burned with mustard plasters I couldn't do any more. The infant was shocked at the row going on in my chest works & my cough. He laughed about the bacon fat & prescribed a *most filthy cough* mixture[.] Told me not to talk & to *take care*[.] Such a cold on top of what I had already could easily swipe me out, too much strain on heart[.] Fiddle-diddle Eye! That old organ of mine must be a 'tough' to have gone through all it has. I expect I [will] outwear Roosevelt and Churchill and the old ducks yet.

I had the most *extraordinary* letter yesterday. I'll enclose it. If you see Bill before you leave after receiving it[,] show it to him. It was forwarded by the Press. It was from Nigeria West Africa. Ruth says she thinks it is from a negro. I thought it was from a lunatic[.] I am amazed it ever reached the Press & me. Those Clarkes are tombstones! You have time to make 5 more trips East & back before they'll turn up. Irene writes 'three words of promises regarding a *tremendous* letter to follow' & 'Bill is always writing the end of the week *full* particulars' regarding Peacock. Neither he nor she have ever mentioned [the] word 'Pie' to me and still address to 'Jubilee Hospital' [–] why not to 'Ross Bay'?[58] That might be more permanent still.

I've added 40 pages to Biog: good land! Well you can cut all you like. Only it seemed I had so much to get in each piece. You may find lots of inessentials[.] I really enjoyed writing the bits & they came fresh & strong[.] Things I'd have thought might have gone from my mind came back. I had those few notes on New York's *buildings* & hotel but nothing about the people & exhibitions[.] Those just clearly visualized as I wrote (& no make ups either). One thing will be a little bothersome[.] I want to *end on Wild Geese* which means I shall have to go back to my painting after the publication of Small & K.W. Do you know, it was a *great* disappointment to me 'Bobtails' could not come this fall. I'd like to have seen how people take her so different again from my other two. Irene has never sent back Woo. She was to have *months* ago. Maybe we *won't* send Biog:[.] She seemed quite *surprised* when I asked her to register Woo as posts were bad these days & we only had one copy of things now. I'd be mad if they lost or kept your Biog: *indefinitely*[,] wouldn't you?

Always your loving Emily

P.S.S. 'Me too Small' and oodles and a sack full of hugs.
N.B. Come back soon & come to see us[.] We need you. S.

[ca. 6 November 1943]

Dear Eye
It's Small, a happy Small, so heavy[,] had such woe-letters lately[.] Emily says 'we'd better write & give you a happy one.' It was Emily's girls rousted out the happy (K.W. & me). Flora Burns came to see me today[.] She told me of a mother who had lost her young son in the war[.] She is heart-broken and they can't rouse her[.] She went to spend the weekend with Flora but Flora said she could find nothing to interest her in conversation[.] At last some mention was made of Early

58 Carr is referring to the Ross Bay Cemetery, where the Carr family plot and her burial place are located.

Victoria & she read the woman some extracts from Small[.] These seemed to interest & please[.] She kept saying 'go on, don't stop reading.' Flora said 'There is another book too Klee Wyck – it is about the coast and Indians.' The woman replied 'Folk[lore] does not interest me.' F. said 'this isn't exactly folk[lore,] it's experiences' & she read her 'Sophie.' The woman was absorbed[.] She asked if she might take K.W. to her room for the night. The next day was Sunday & the woman came from her room at 12.30 with K.W. finished. She said it had lifted her into a different world. It seemed to have roused her as nothing had done since her son's death. She left carrying me (book of Small under her arm)[.] It's so funny watching the reaction of the two books on different people[.]

(EMILY) Dear Eye[,] now Small has her chatter blown off I can maybe get a word edgewise. Dear Bill has come & gone. What a sweet gentle soul he is. He stayed with me 2 hours Sunday & an hour today & we talked & talked. I don't expect he said anything different to what he said to you (only I haven't heard of your visit with [him] yet)[.] I told him my suggestion of putting Bobtails, 'Even a Rat[,]' 'Balance[,]' 'Bravo Mary Anne,' 'Peacock,' 'Uncle Tom' & 'One Crow' into one volume. I thought The Pie and Woo might be united in one book[.] He said you had some of that lot so I hope they turned up[.] I know you let Bill have 'Heart of a Peacock:' I have never beyond 'Bobtails' *ever* sent a thing to Bill or anybody[,] only to you since the days when Ruth & Flora used to read proofs for me[.][59] I think you will find them at home[.] I remember your telling me Walter Gage read 'Even a Rat' aloud to you. He said (Clarke) I had taken him up wrong[.] He did not mean Biog: must be the *next* thing done but he felt Bobtails was not big enough for a book & he wasn't satisfied with Woo. Did not feel Woo & Bobtails went together quite. He agreed with you that a Biog: should be last. *But* he said he *would* like *me* to hear what sort of a reception Biog: would have. He thinks (from what he has heard) Biog: beats K.W. & Small & the rest[.] Well, time will tell. Anyway he told me *why* he was anxious to get the stuff arranged for the rotation. Looks to me like I'll have to prolong my stay on this planet if I'm to wait for Biog: & they come out at one per year. Sir Humphrey is very pleased with Small & she's the only *Canadian* book to be printed in war-time England (I had thought he meant by their house) but he says by any publishing house.

59 See notes 66 and 67 on page 57 for biographical information on Flora Burns and Ruth Humphrey.

This afternoon came a lovely cyclamen from Irene & Bill's[.] No wonder I'm happy and isn't it lovely to see a man & wife appreciating each other & loving their children & being so useful in the world. He says he goes away leaving things in her capable hands quite satisfied[.] She must be quite remarkable & I want to hug them both all over again. Aren't there times when you want to hug the whole world? (excluding the Shankses) Bill's visits brisked me & made me want to put forth new effort to get better & work.

This afternoon came a letter from Lawren & I am so amused at the differences in your judgments of the new parts[.] Lawren does not think New York adds an iota to the Biog: On the other hand he thinks 'transition' *valuable* and he says 'Your tributes to Ira in the new additions are to my mind *just right.* I am so glad they & he are in it.'[60] I am too[.] Ira, the end had puzzled me from the beginning. I know *you ought to be there* neither sentimentally nor sloppily but *you belonged* there a stout sort of pillar to cling to. Only, I *was* afraid to say *too* much or *too* little. I am proud in my book to tell the whole world that I loved you well, you and all you stood for in my work and the 'Kiss for Canada' seemed to nail it into the right spot. He calls the '70th Birthday and the Kiss for Canada' a delight and a joy (Lawren).

Haven't been very well. Those repeated hypo stabs got my flesh riled.

Bill says you're house hunting. I'd like to hit the C.B.R. Don't get a great big one that is a worry to keep up[,] just room for the 2 pianos[,] Phylis & you and a not too big a garden & then there's that old gas problem if you go further out. 'Oh, that we were as snails & carried our homes on our backs.' I'm tired now[.] Goodnight.

Always your loving Emily (hug) [Carr draws a swirl]

[ca. December 1943]

Belovedest Guardian –

It's Small! and I'm writing with our new Xmas pen which came too soon. Em. says I can have first go. She's been in bed a week, tried getting up today but it was not a success. Your Prince Rupert letter and *my* old trip

60 The story in *Growing Pains* that deals with Dilworth's role as editor is 'Alternative' (356–65).

up Skeena did so much to bring things clear & fresh[.] These calm quiet eagles *so strong*[.] Did you notice the turn of their heads. Such a twist of power! I've thought of you a lot – that always was a beastly, rough road. But I guess it's worse now than when only ½ finished when I took it[.]

Ada McGeer wrote me a few days ago[.] She said 'You['re] looking *very* tired.' Em. & I wish so that we could help[.] There is 'tired' for work & 'tired' for sickness and they are a mean pair. Though work weariness is the most satisfactory because you are getting somewhere. Em. says she's deteriorated a heap since she gave up animal & creatures about the house[.] Often she cries about it (when there is no one but me to see)[.] You see [it] is [that] I'm the little of her[.] She doesn't need to mind me because I know what she's made of and all her faults. I'm quite firm with her. I say 'you old baby. You had beasts for 70 years & you can't expect oldness not to punish and hurt somewhere.' Oh Eye can you hardly bear to be a human with such awful things going on as are in the world[?] It's just unbelievable.

Yesterday quite a nice woman (even if she was 'English[')] came to see *me*[,] 'Small.' She'd read the book[,] came all the way in from Cadboro Bay to look up 'Small's' growing up spot[.] Got it all wrong but wrote to tell me she loved Small[.] So I sent a polite reply & she was so pleased to get the letter. She came into town again and brought me her last sweetpeas from her garden. I saw her but was not able to talk much. So she asked to come again. There are nice people in the world, even *some English.*

We have not done any work for over a week[,] not even *thought* work. Em. can't *bear that*[.] She is as foolish as me then – only able to use thoughts feelings hands feet & tongues[.] Em. feels so useless and shamed[.] Victoria Anderson wrote me the other day.

I wonder if Bill is home yet?? Irene's *long* letter now 4 o[r] 5 months overdue has *not come* yet [–] only a promissory note! I think they are very happy in each other[,] don't you[?] It must be fine to be like that, not always snap & snarl. The world *is so* queer.

Em's got a bee in her bonnet but it may find a hole & buzz out without doing any harm[.] I think Lawren backed by you *put* the bee there. You see you said I made no secret of Victoria & Vancouver loathing my doings & it was only fair to tell later of their decency to K.W. & me. Well Em. has never gone out of her way to meet them[,] has not shown (pictures) in Victoria for *years*[.] Well certain people have *tried by hook & crook* to get into my studio to look-see & I have not been helpful. Of course the pictures are in the main gone[.] Still I *have* the odd few & lots of sketches. I wondered if it would give them a little more gracious memory of me[.] Also there have been quite a few come to *look for Small's roots* & if I was to throw the studio open to the public (general newspaper invite) [,] would it be decent? I asked Alice & she approved but not in my present condition[.] Of course I'd have to ask Dr. Baillie[.] He's interested in my work & believes in it[.] He says it is my life & he knows how unthinkable life would be without it for me. The affair would be a bit of a squirm & I [would] give *no tea*[.] Those interested drop in[,] look round & fall out[,] Alice & I sitting there like two old stuffed pelicans in full moult. Those 'Small' worriers could look out the back window & see the back of Small's old home & the spot where the *pig pen* stood, which was at Alice's back door. What do you think? No[,] Trustor? Praps no one would come!!!!

This woman yesterday said she'd seen several mentions in *English* papers of Small & Klee Wyck & [some]body said they should [be included] among the *classics*!!! I wish that darned old Irene would send clippings.
Goodnight Guardian[,] Goodnight Trustor. God give you rest.

Sunday. Hope you had a better night than me[.] Sat upright from midnight 'til 7[,] couldn't breath lying down. Couldn't sleep sitting up [for] fear of tumbling out of bed. It is not pretty[,] life under these circumstances[.] I've slept most all day in cow's grease. We look [like] rain but we neither rain nor snow[,] only look like it.

Love & goodbye & love from
Me & Emily & me
As ever, us!

[ca. December 1943]

Dear Old Eye,
Thank God for a night's sleep! (assisted sleep) But oh so welcome. Dr. Baillie & a hypo help & a triple dose of 'bitters.' I'm an old coward the way I set to 'look' before I seize & drink those burning bitters, awful! The last 3 nights had been a case of sitting bolt upright for breathing & pain[,] sitting 'til you tumble over from exhaustion. Dr. Baillie says no

'open studio' just now[,] says the idea is good but put it off 'til after Xmas so . . . we'll postpone the moult.

Have your ears been burning? The nice ear (I believe it's the right) because two of your girl-friends have been discussing you & *not* unfavourabl[y]. Dr. Trapp no less & old me! Dr. T. was here *3* hours. I put her in with the men clan as visitors[,] calm and sane & healing[.] I was up for first time & clothed in the studio[.] We talked about many things[,] among others the Biog:[.] I told her of Mr. Clarke's visit[.] That started it – & she wanted to know when 'Creatures' was coming out? & I said Clarke said he couldn't & on top of that wanted to pub. the Biog. She said she wished it would come out, then she said she understood how I felt but she said *she would* like to hear some of it *right now*[.] 'Not mine' I said[,] just the Clarkes' & Lawren['s] & Bess['s.] I said 'Ira says its pub. rests with *my* decision and I know I can trust him[.]' I am going to make one concession though[,] Eye[,] made to you – because I know you like Dr. Trapp. *Should you get the opportunity & wish to read a chapter here & there* to her (Biog) (I could trust you as to your picks) to Dr. alone[,] O.K. with me. *Not before Mrs. Collishaw or her girls[,] not before Phylis and her friends.* Not before *the McGeers & their friends* but just you & her or you & Lawren & Bess & her. If it would do you & the Dr. any happiness[,] I'd like to give that happiness & raise the ban. But from what I hear your time & hers are so chock-jam of your jobs you have no time for anything extra except brushing your teeth. So I doubt you have time & doubt still more a whole flock of others would be roused.

I've invented a marvelous device for sitting on my front to sleep. You see I could not breathe lying back so I dressed my little old camp stool (been with me everywhere for 50 years) up in a little cushion & case to work it over my knee & lie on my forehead. I got so exhausted I toppled out of bed sitting straight up. Dr. Baillie wanted a week of hospital care but I begged off[.] I told him his speaking to Alice had made a great difference. Telling her not to fly into rages if I *could not* rouse out of the dope when she came in first thing in morn. Nor talk for hours if I had no voice[.] She gets so jealous if I talk to you or Mr. Clarke or Dr. Trapp without exhaustion but you see you are quiet interesting & don't expect me to do it all. She[,] poor dear[,] *wants entertainment* & offends if I don't chatter nothings by the hour.

Dr. Baillie is all twisted in his advice[.] First he says work, *work* up to 'til your *last breath*[,] it keeps you going in your life[.] Next turn it's rest, rest, rest, & there I am stuck in the middle that's been so bad these last two weeks – not able to work – it makes yours & Lawren's job more *particular* & more *unpleasant*[.] It is not easy for you to come to me and say 'Quit Emily[.]' I'm trusting you all the same & perhaps it will come naturally and I shall tell myself like I did over the painting. That's why I gave Bill 'Wild Geese' and the 'Birthday Party' to read[.] He said he found no [flaw] & it was some of my recentest[.] I wish I could talk 'Man, Woman and Dark' over with you. I want to see you dreadfully but I know[.] I understand. I said to Bill[, ']Ira is so busy[,] I hardly have the face to send him a M.S.['] Bill said 'If I can help you[,] Emily[,] when you want an M.S. read[,'] then I came to with a pop! 'Oh I couldn't do that[.] Ira'd be hurt if I did not send them direct to him.' Was I right?

I never felt quite right about not sending 'Bobtails' to you after her final typing & you put that little reproof 'I *do like to see the M.S. before they go off.*' Of course you *had* made its corrections but I think perhaps that queered 'Bobtails' & I'm sorry the Clarkes have her & 'Woo.' Mrs. Clarke & Miss Hangman messing her over I do not like[.] I wish we had her back. I'll never do it again unless you tell me to. Do you consider 'Woo' & 'Bobtails' *weaker* writing than K.W. & Small? What kicks me is Bill's being so keen on Biog: being published right away when he said it was *impossible* owing to war to publish 'Creatures' this year.

Now for my *disgusting bitter draught*[.] Is it the Lord paying my tongue back for all the mean things she ever said or the bitter thoughts? May your night be calm & restful.

The other night I dreamt I came back from (where?) [.] And the 'one' I told of when in Biog: I said I 'discovered love & Poetry' [–] the one who did *not want my* love [–] was trying on my ring[.][61] It had a black band all round the middle of the gold. I was angry[.] I said 'that is not yours' & I snatched it [back.] He declared it *was his*[.] '*It is not!*' I gave it to Ira[.] Well it has moved to a bigger yet finger [for] the third has shrunk too small. I told Dr. Trapp she'd stolen my fat[.] I thought her looking so well & much fatter[.] She said it was a small hat. She looked very nice & pretty little hat & fur coat & it was lovely having her[.] I forgot all about my grievance[.] I told them I'd felt ugly & you & others said how busy she'd been.

E & S.

61 Carr never identifies this person by name. See Blanchard 74.

218 St Andrews St. Xmas Dec 18

Dear Ira

This shabby little gift, crudely bound in a piece of my favourite dressing gowns, comes to wish you well, and carr[ies] my love and Small's[.] 'Vesty'[62] was read first on a camping trip to Cowitchan Lake with 2 other girls[.] Perhaps you will find inspiration[,] unconscious inspirations[,] from her in Emily's own writing? I don't know[.] I never voluntarily set out to make them. I just loved the Vesty people like I love Indians perhaps. I got homesick for them in the San & sent home for her & Vesty went the rounds in 'Pause' & caused many a laugh. I wouldn't let her knock round an auction room & I *couldn't* put her in the fire. Missionaries have called her 'vulgar & profane[.]' I have heard polite correct women 'see no object in having written her' but I do & I think you will like her.

I hope you will have a serene Christmas[.] I know what a 'miss' will be in your heart all the day. I have never seen your brothers but I know this last little one of hers was *very* dear to your mother[.] Though she loved all her children[,] how many little things she told me about when her family was young and how proud she was of you all. But I know[,] my dear[,] you would not wish her back[.] Old age[,] even if love full[,] *is very full of weariness* when the strength is gone. And how you piled love and tenderness on her to the very last moment! Some pass through the last struggle so easily and some so hard. Why? I'm glad 1943 is just about gone[.] She was a cruel year[.] She seemed to hurt from all sides & be cruel.

I posted your book yesterday[.] What a filthy pea-green jacket America put on K.W. They did not change the inside coloring. Bill sent me a birthday wire, said one only of Small's reviews had got across. *Of course* the Clarkes have all had flu again. Mrs. & 2 kids[,] now I spose Bill [and] other child & maid will take their turns.

God bless you over the Xmas season my dear. Don't be lonely. Lots of people love you. There was no letter today & know you are *very busy* & the *mail's awful*[.] But *don't* promise & not fulfil – that hurts.

Hold the acorns in your hand while you read[.] I made these mark-

62 *Vesty of the Basins: A Novel* by Sarah P. McLean Greene (1898). The copy to which Carr refers is covered in a floral patterned fabric and inscribed as follows: 'Ira Dilworth, with love from Small and Emily' (BCARS, Parnall Collection, MS 2763).

ers, I love the feel of smooth skin & the marvel of knowing you are holding the *whole make up of a great oak* tree in your hand. My jabbing darning needle has probably killed the germ of life but it *was* there once and perfect[.] Give to Phylis the season's greeting[s]. I expect one of two things will happen[:] you will dine with Lawren and Bess or[,] if able to get away[,] go to Ferne's.

I am not working[,] have not for the last month. God keep you and bless you.

Your loving two
Emily and Small

P.S. You did not say if I 'planed East with you last time[.] I did[,] but did you feel me?

Letters: 1944

Sunday [ca. 12 January 1944]

Dear Eye
You are not a very sympathetic person[,] are you[?] The 'sores and abscesses' you dismiss (after a couple of days as *hoping* were quite well *long gone*) were a two weeks' solid agony of hot fomentations & lancings[.] I should not have mentioned them only I spose I am particularly shut-off from all human beings & I over-burst to my Trustor. People who have not been through illness cannot tell what it is[,] how should they be able. Alice is the same (except for suffering with her eyes, she has never been ill)[.] I have felt for a while now [that] you were rather bored with Emily's ailments & Emily's M.S. I know you've been *dreadfully busy* & now house hunting as well. That cry in one of your recent letters startled me[.] You said, (I forget the words exactly) 'there were limits to which a human *could* go.' It was a cry of utter tiredness and I was angry with myself for having contributed to your overburden: be *honest* with me. I and my work have been the last straw sometimes[,] eh? Well dear[,] I must try & stand on my own two wobbledy feet and leave my maladies to take care of themselves[.] Drat them & my rebellious spirit. Ah! and, well[,] I *thought* you *liked* me to send the M.S. to you *first*[,] not to anyone else & since the days of Ruth & Flora's crits[,] I have always chose so. However there won't be many (if any) more now[.] So we need not bother: oh I've always *wanted quick death*[.] This year after year of early going & coming back to go all over it again has been –

To all intents and purposes I *am* dead[.] *Now* people have accepted the books & pictures of me *as* me, they forget the old derelict shelved away. My visitors (except for the occasional *stranger*) are nil & I have cut my correspondence down to a minimum (only those I love)[.] Old age is lonely & bitter when it has to be taken sip by sip to the dregs. Suddenly there will be a little clatter of crying[,] a few flowers and I'll be put away. Queer how the soul seems to go off & hide[,] leave[s] the struggle to the today[.] At times 'to us belong the courses of continual change[.] We pass through the darkness and the light of this world but thou art ever the same' (from that lovely little prayer you sent me with the rest at New Year)[.] I think I am passing through one of the *darks* just now?

The Earth always wants us[,] is always ready to incorporate us back into herself. But the beyond demurs[,] so the soul hides & leaves the body to get along in its waiting [the] best way she can. I can't & won't believe there is nothing but the physical return to the earthly ground.

I can well understand your engrossing excitement in house hunting. I spose it's your first self-hunt. Before[,] you have always been selecting for a home that would [suffice] *all* your family[.] Of course I know next to nothing of its location or layout[,] only the wild garden[.] I hope it will be a very very happy home for you.

Lovingly as always[,] Emily

Has Small died? She seems as remote as the dodo bird. E.

Jubilee Hospital, Thursday
Jan. 1944

Dear Ira
I can't write but my heart has cried out since your last letter[,] its weariness and disheart. It made me ache, especially when I felt I had added to it by me & my darned old work. Blot [it] out of your consciousness. What if you did not do Biog:[?] I'm not dead yet[.] Of course flesh has limitations[,] so much[,] so many[,] only the skin deep of me gets ruffled[.] Underneath is quite still & full of love & trust in you.

It's been a work of hard going. Morphine & all the other horrors[.] There seems such a terrible lump of me to melt away before I can disappear[,] such a tenacious me[.] I have my sanctuaries in with me but have been too sick to read them or even think, but [I] lay my hand among the cool papers & can feel their good[.]

God bless & keep you calm[.] Eye dear[,] perhaps I am writing you oftener than you know[.] If I don't see you ever again[,] you & Lawren[,] you know you have my love[.] Give it to Bill & Irene love if you write[.] I can't write them.

Your note just come[.] Ah it is the beastly flu has got you, I suppose! You are in the middle of it[.] God heal & help you[.] Let us pray for trust & patience for each other[.] Take care of yourself[.] See a Dr. & don't take risks[.] Let the old C.B.C. sit up & take notice. No my dear[,] the hospital is overcrowded & attendents awful[,] also food. They are all doing beyond [what they are] able. Oh the *weariness* of the flesh! Small is cuddling you[,] close to you. I did not know Alice wrote you[,] poor girl. She has been up every day[.] Some days they did not let me see her or I was asleep – don't I know that awful sleeplessness?

Get better soon. Remember all the Small fry took care of themselves[.] Now it's your turn.

Always your loving Emily & Small

Vancouver, February 4th, 1944. [Typed]
Mr. W.H. Clarke, Oxford University Press,
University Ave., Toronto, Ontario

Dear Bill: –
This will acknowledge your letter of January 27th in which you have asked me to do something about getting together Emily Carr's manuscripts.

Miss Carr is at present in the hospital again. She has been very miserable for the past two or three weeks. I went to see her when I was in Victoria on Wednesday and we had a long discussion about the manuscripts which should be made available. May I set down the result of that conversation for you?

1) Miss Carr is very strongly of the opinion that the autobiography should not be published just now. In this opinion I concur. I feel that it would be very difficult to publish anything further after the autobiography had come out. There is a finality about it which would make it impossible logically to publish anything subsequently.

2) The manuscripts which now exist and are unpublished are as follows:
a) 'Bobtails'

b) 'The Life of Woo'
c) 'The Pie'
d) 'The House of All Sorts' – this manuscript is not entirely complete. Miss Carr wishes to revise it. It is in the condition, however, where you could read it.
e) 'Pause – The Birds Sang On' – this manuscript also is not completed. Miss Carr wishes to revise it in the light of some suggestions that I have made.
f) A number of short manuscripts which are more or less in final form:
'Uncle Tom'
'Balance' (the story of a coon)
'The Heart of a Peacock' (not the version in 'The Pie')
'Mary Anne, The Push Cat'
'One Crow[']' (not the version included in 'The Pie')
'Even a Rat'
'Ducks, and a Father and Mother'
'Father is a Cannibal'
'Curly Coat'
'Mint'
'The Little Street'
g) 'Wildflowers' – these are very brief sketches of British Columbia wildflowers. Some of them are beautifully done.

This list which I have made up from memory contains everything that I can remember which is any considerable size and is ready or nearly ready for publication.

Miss Carr is very anxious to have 'Bobtails' published. She feels that it was written with a very deep purpose and that in it she really succeeded in doing what she had set out to achieve. I agree with this opinion. The manuscript, when I first read it, was for me very moving. Emily set herself the task of exploring the lives and characters of her sheep dogs and of making these as clear as she possibly could for other people. She avoided making the animals talk because she did not wish to give them any human qualities but she did want to show the inter-dependence between herself and the dogs and to reveal the beauty and strength of these creatures. I believe the book would have a very considerable appeal for people in general and a quite extraordinary appeal for animal lovers. Emily suggests that an animal volume might be published containing 'The Bobtails,' 'Heart of a Peacock,' 'Balance,' 'Mary Anne, The Push Cat,' 'One Crow,' 'Uncle Tom' and 'Even a Rat.'

I have just had word that you are coming to Vancouver on Saturday. I hope we will have time then to discuss this matter very thoroughly.

Kindest personal regards. Yours sincerely,
I. Dilworth

Hospital March 2 / 44 (Small's letter)

Dear Eye –
It's Small – thank you for permission to roam your garden – I'll tell you a secret – I *did* do so before I asked & even if you'd said *no*[,] I would have because I know your heart is kind. I've told Emily all about your garden (she knows about your heart or at least part of it). And we both love the garden – better because it is wild[.] Don't tame it *too* much[.] Only[,] of course[,] dead unhealthy stuff must be cut out & we're tickled pink that our tree will grow there[1] and when you are digging & hacking with an axe[,] we'll think of & bless you[.] And isn't the music grand that's going to float out of those windows into the garden. You, Phylis[,] Mr. Benjamin & Lawren, even the trees will love it. And when both Em. and you have black moods so I *can't* stick round, I'll have a refuge in the garden. I can climb into our tree & maybe I'll be singing & you'll hear (if you listen)[.] Emily is coming out of the black. She is only gray now[.] Dr. Baillie says the air is doing more for her (going out and the rest) than all the doctors' medicines in the world. Everyone says she looks quite different since she was put out. The seagulls come right to E's window now & the hospital thinks her appetite has improved[.] She hates her food as much as ever but the seagulls' appetite is as good as it ever was & they come to the window and get it.

Always your loving
Small

1 In a letter, dated ca. February 1944, Carr offers Dilworth money to purchase a tree on her behalf.

Friday [ca. 17 March 1944]

Dear Eye,

I'm glad you read my letter from Mr. Clarke[.] One followed next day from Hangman with a book she wanted epigraphed. She's a fool. I wrote Bill last night, found it very exhausting putting my weight on it[.] I was too tired to do one to you as I intended or to make a copy of Bill's to send you[.] My breath simply wouldn't go round. I told Bill I wanted to be cooperative but on one point was adamant & you & I were in agreement on the matter = Biog: I also asked that he read the material & return promptly as my time for work may be short & I want House of A. Sorts & Pause to go over with your notes & *please* not to allow Hangman to take your notes from their [place?] or switch the M.S. sections as she did before[.] Perhaps you'll think I was wrong but I tried to give the impression we were satisfied to send for Bill & Irene's perusal but weren't keen on Hangman's (even if she did send me a box of candy for Xmas)[.] Do you remember her hat? Oh I'm so sorry my papers were not in better order but it is hard keeping them in order & working on them day by day or worse still getting them out to work on & being too rotten – Pause! I just had my first lesson in using the Hypo Harpoon on myself[.] You have to plunge the needle to its hilt & *straight in* & press the nob 'til all the [medication?] is poked into your arterial veins. I pinched so hard, I bruised my leg (you can't do your own arms because you need both hands.) Oh I'll get used to it! I wish I could have it *every* hour[.] It only lasts for one hour & you have to wait *3* hours for another. I am scheduled to have it 4 times a day but permitted to ask & have it every 4 hours when bad instead of 8 hours. – A little woman[,] a stranger brought me (because of K.W. Small & my pictures) a bunch of violets & freesia yesterday[,] a delight of smell during the long bumpy night of pain, dark, and gasps[.]

I am afraid Clarke has again stirred up just what I wanted to sleep. I did not want *you worried with my M.S. during this time of stress in C.B.C.* I'm so sorry & after all the bother probably the Clarkes will let it lie dormant for months. In the Pigeon Holes (studio just by bedroom door) were a muddle of old copies & I think a few good. You remember I asked you about destroying old copies? I asked Bill *again* for 'Woo.' I said I'd like to re-write parts[.] But [in] Bobtails I had purposely left [the] human element out except where the buyers influenced the dogs during their first year[,] which I usually followed up[.] Do you know I believe the

Clarkes would like better that gooey mush of *sentimentality* having the animals *talk* & *think* & be utterly un-animal. Well they won't get that mush out of me. Dr. Baillie is frightfully keen on my Bobtails[.] He is a dog lover[,] has one of his own & he wanted to see 'Pause' too [in the] worst way when I was writing it, but I sent it straight to you. If my brains will only stick together I want to get 'Indefinitely' finished (gone over)[.] I have it here with me but my head *won't* work yet. You've got such a lot to forgive in me[.] Please do. You are so truly a 'Dilworth' and I a *not-true*-to-type Carr. Nobody except Mother ever seemed quite sure about me & I remember once she said, 'Child you are like your Aunt Nancy[.]' Where Aunt Nancy hailed from or went to I don't know, never heard of her before or since[.] Anyhow I was pleased at being *like something* and I knew I was mother's little black 'crow' (that was a saying of hers[:] 'every old crow thinks her little ones the blackest') and now this little crow, grown old, stands very much on the moult[,] her years tucked under one wing & her pain tucked under the other waiting & wondering[,] looking over wistfully.

I used to wonder what people who were uncertainly facing death thought about it[.] They seldom mentioned it & I often wished they would (we are rather cowardly about that thing). Now I look on it very much as I used to looking out on going out into the woods in the van in old days[,] busying myself in the preparation of leaving things as straight as I can & leaving the new camp to be itself when I get there.

Knowing it will be all right, the gold & jasper and sardis bigness doesn't appeal to me much, nor the exact setting[.] Do you remember those Sanctuary words of Manley Hopkins?

> 'Oh morning at the brown
> brink Eastward, springs –
> Because the Holy Ghost over the bent
> World broods with warm breast and with ah
> Bright wings.'[2]

I am glad I have lived through this hour[.] At one time the game did not seem worth the candle[.] One Saturday afternoon Dr. Baillie & Mrs. Walton (head nurse) came to my room. [T]hey had a great bunch of chrysanthemums Dr. B had brought. He stood looking down at me[,] not smiling nor trying to make me smile as was his usual way[.] It is about the only time I've seen his face without a smile. I liked it best that

2 From 'God's Grandeur' by Gerard Manley Hopkins.

way and it told me a lot about the probable condition of me[.] My body was a state of misery[.] Well – here I be! I get better but never quite catch up. Lizzie with same trouble went so directly & quickly. Perhaps her spirit was in better shape to go.

I'm sorry about your box[.] You see I was just too sick to fix it[.] I [placed?] lots of things in at last to keep them from Shank's prying. I've had *7* of these rush visits to hospital in last *6* years. Last time I was really [ill?] but when I went home I got out work again. The Dr. said 'You don't know how relieved I was to get you into hospital that night[.]' I often think of your mother when I lie awake at night and imagine how glad she must have been to hear your footstep in the hall & know you were close[.] She must have rejoiced in having born you. Eye[,] don't ever envy Lawren. I agree with you he is a prince in his own right[,] a grand person[,] but he has nothing on you[.] Lawren had money & his Art, his wife & family. I love Lawren & think him fine. But in places he is weaker than you are. Your mother would not have changed sons neither would I have changed my 'friend of friends.'

Have had another day with the old needle[.] Will sleep now before Alice comes[.] She insists on coming every day[,] takes a taxi. I'm glad you saw Val. Isn't he a dear boy? He is so fond of her[.] I saw her rush across the garden at his voice[,] throw her arms about him & kiss him. So different to the cold jaw-boney little peck she gives me & always has[.] I am *so glad,* so *glad* she has the Hennell children[.] I despise 'Pa & Ma' for the way they ground her down & took her off from family & friends[,] used her for all they could out of her & came between us. It made an unhealable breach but now I have no trace of bitterness against the *children*[.] They are loyal to her[.] Some of the boys I think will eventually settle in B.C. They love it. (when the war has finished shaking the world.) This is a long ramble[.] Be patient my dear[.] Anyhow it's a step up in notepaper.

Lovingly always[,] Emily & Small
No room for P.S.

March 17, 1944.

Dear Emily:
Just a very short note. Thank you for your two letters which reached me

here yesterday and today: they were forwarded from Toronto to which you had addressed them. They brought me a breath of fresh air from my beloved West Coast and you can hardly know how much that means. We have had most hectic meetings, morning, noon and night. The East seems more and more of a mystery to me. I feel an alien, an outsider here and I have to get back to the West to have a sense of belonging.

I am sorry you are still feeling miserable. I hope soon a change will come for you and that you will find yourself much better. Perhaps the spring will help. Here I think spring will never come. I think the trees may have forgotten about it.

Yes, the thought of my house has been tantalizing but it has been helpful too. I have gone over and over my plans. I can see my trees and my flowers growing far more clearly in my imagination than in my real eye. You are quite right – unreal or imagined things have a reality which surpasses the real in its power and vitality.

I hope to be home by the middle of next week and shall try to go over to see you soon – but I cannot promise *how* soon.

Meanwhile oodles of love to Small. Ever yours
Eye.

Tuesday 9th May / 44

Dear Eye
It's Small! and here's a secret for your ear. Emily [is] better! She's trying to get her head into something like work shape[.] You'll have to make heaps of excuses for her & if you knew what a comfort it is to have you say *you are going to help her* go over H. of A.S. We want to go over things such millions of times and even then are not sure we *forget* so. I would rather never write a word more than bungle it. Eye dear[,] *don't* be afraid of hurting me, do *not be afraid of hurting* and slip the failures away – *please*[,] *Eye*[,] *burn* them & tell me plainly *I am to stop!*

The winds have been bitter[.] One of my new friends came Saturday and took me into the Park. I just had a gown on and it was the first time I'd been farther than one block[.] The flowers were a joy[.] Mrs. 'Kriegel' (the Austrian musician's wife) took me[.] Alice came too. I slept clean round the clock after it[,] just waking to eat[.] Then today the lady who I met at hospital (bird lover and authoress) came to see me (elderly & nice & interesting)[.] Alice was angry at first at some new friends coming but I was glad to have them come[.] All the old ones seemed turned from me or gone away & shut up[.] With Shanks she's not congenial, but I *think* it is good for Alice too[,] only she won't come in and mix[.] She says the number talking all at once is bad for me, but the truth is she *hates meeting strangers.*

How's the garden? I hope somebody snaps it soon. I am most curious to see if it corresponds to my mind pictures[.] They feel as definite as if they were so. I've been trying to do *little bits* of Hundreds & Thousands[.] Some of them are dull[.] I'm afraid they are all little snaps of memory that tickled some fancy or smacked impertinence into my life[,] that appeared of no importance at the time but afterwards you found they'd left a scar or a singing in your life.

I'm mad with that C.B.R. Just as I had a nice stand fixed for my bedside and places for the stamp[ed] C.B.C. envelopes that I use for so many purposes[,] up goes C.B.C. and changes those envelope[s] to a silly little white one [–] no good at all!!! Well if they'll only spend a day letting you help H. of A.S. get into shape[,] I'll never grumble at them again[.] Good night. Tuesday – Peter has been helping me[.] You don't know what a treat it is to do an hour's help with a bright young human[.] Shanks seems just to *get impossible* sometimes[.] I defy a saint to manipulate her. I went out in [a] wheelchair for 40 minutes but the wind was bitter[.] Never were such winds zigzag[ging] back & forth between the poles & equator. I feel stronger the last few days[.] You'll be missing Lawren. I suppose there is always an ache in him when he goes back to Toronto & a wondering if he'll run into her. I wonder if she sold their great mansion. Bess told me he gave it to her (the 1st Mrs.)[.] He was very fond of his 2 older children which are married. The youngest boy was left to her, but Lawren had him for a long visit down in Mexico[.] He is a diabetic[.]

Shanks is a fool when it comes to chair-push tips & jolts, chases all over the road to endeavour to tip the wheel on *every* bump & says she's afraid of the chair getting away on her[.] You'd think she was pushing a wild beast[,] not a meek old woman[.] Every old vacant lot is beautiful just now & the duck's lakes are velvet with mud. How far are you from the Stanley Park,[3] Eye? Be sure to watch for the iris in [the] Park and University[.] Those exquisite gossamer things[;] really going round in

3 Stanley Park, the large, ocean-side park in Vancouver, officially opened on 27 October 1888, by Mayor David Oppenheimer, was dedicated to Lord Stanley, the governor general of Canada, on 29 October 1889.

spring even in a wheelchair does things to your moulding stale invalidism. I am so happy over the crumbs. Happier than I thought I could be over the whole earth. I am going to be off hunting those 'yalla violets' one day soon[.] Dr. [is] going away for 2 weeks. He didn't say 'Don't stay put[,]' so I'm not[.] Yesterday was first day uppish[.] I want to be workish when the H of A.S. descends on me. I wrote a really nice [letter] to Irene. Bill has never written to me[,] perhaps once since he went home from here & maybe even not that he has never mentioned any of the scripts[.] Well I know he's busy.

Those gurgledy birds are singing into the night as tho' they had too *or* burst.

10 days last Monday ought to be tomorrow[.] Well we'll see[.] All kinds of loves[.]

As ever your loving
Emily & Small

---

218 St Andrews Sunday May 22[, 1944]

Dear Old Eye
Well I waited but you did not come[.] Was it *you*, or did 'Clarke' not send the script? Well I've done a lot of work on it, but there is not as much work as I thought there was (script)[.] There are duplicates of all or *almost* all the sections (the ones I had to re-work)[.] I did quite a lot of altering[.] I *hope* your majesty will approve!! I know if he does not he will tell me so & crush me brutally! And I shall take it meekly because, Oh Eye[,] my head is not good for much[.] Big mistakes run in and out of my work now. I *think* tomorrow will see that batch cleared up as far as I can go alone. You may find many things to be changed.

I have been so *happy* working again. In fact I've been happy in lots of ways and hoping hard that you are happy too with problems & decisions clearing. You ought to be settled and homed for many, many years to come. I know you'll be missing Lawren[.] Well, you'll appreciate each other even more when you have each other again. Well I have had a very pleasant afternoon[.] Mr. & Mrs. George C. Clutesi from Alberni[,][4] Dr.

4 George Charles Clutesi (1905–88) was a Nuu-chah-nulth artist, actor, and author to whom Carr bequeathed her paints and brushes. In 1967 he published *Son of Raven, Son of Deer: Fables of the Tse-Shaht People*, and in 1969 *Potlatch*.

Carl from the Museum[,] and a Dr. something from Montreal (soldier) all to visit me today[.] George Clutesi brought me your letter.[5] I do not wonder you were charmed with him[.] I found him delightful[.] At the end of the visit which was 2 hours long when the others were moving away[,] he took my hand with such sincerity and said quietly 'I feel so deep I want to cry, thank you for writing "Klee Wyck." Every Indian will love you for writing that book. It shows you loved the Indians.' Dr. Carl is very nice[.] The Army Dr.[6] was quite a nice person too[.] Margaret Clay asked if he could come [–] he already knew Clutesi & had heard from him he was coming.[7] Oh it was very nice. I so enjoyed it. It meant much more to me than a swell party of stuck ups and did not tire me, because we were all *living* people[.] I wish you'd been there. I felt all of them [–] except perhaps Clutesi [–] rather [felt?] shy of the sketches & *recent* canvases. So I got out that box of field watercolors that Clarke liked and they went all through them[.] You have never seen them. I can't help that. I've never had your eye long enough.

Another cause for happiness is that I feel better & stronger and the wheelchair getting out in the Park freshens me up. I am getting braver over Shanks pushing[.] She is *very* stupid and clumsy[.] Mrs. Kriegel (my Austrian friend) has taken me 3 times[.] She is busy at St Joseph's Hospital & takes me Saturday[.] She gives me so much more confidence than Shanks. I never contemplate a spill. You'd think the same paths had boiled themselves smooth. Shanks makes such a *fuss* over everything. There is one thing however that makes me so glad. Alice comes with us and *enjoys* it. I keep up a running comment to help Alice to see things as clear as I can as we go & now she will ask questions & seem[s] to see it. It used to make her so annoyed & Shanks says *she* (Shanks herself) sees much more for my being along. The park is very beautiful this year[.] I wish you could see it. Don't forget to look at the iris in Stanley

5 Carl brought Mr and Mrs Clutesi to visit Carr (see BCARS, B.C. Provincial Museum Correspondence [1897–1970], letter from Dr Carl to Carr, 25 May 1944, box 1, file 15).

6 Probably the 'Army Dr.' is the Captain Rosen mentioned in Anthony Walsh's note to Margaret Clay, dated 22 May 1944, in which he suggests that Rosen appreciated his visit to Victoria (see BCARS, Edythe Hembroff-Schleicher Collection, MS 2792, box 2, file 12).

7 A letter from Anthony Walsh to Margaret Clay, dated 22 May 1944, and preserved at BCARS in the Edythe Hembroff-Schleicher Collection, MS 2792, suggests that Clay was responsible for 'arranging the meeting between Emily Carr and the Clutesi's [*sic*]' (box 2, file 12).

Park and at the University[.] They are in my mind now all cobwebby with spirit. Poor Alice has had a hard knock. This week Val has been sent overseas. His lump of soldiers (whatever they call it) is being stuck together in Montreal. She will miss him dreadfully[.] He has been so thoughtful for her blindness these last few years. She loves him almost as a son. The kind of love I have for you. You are both nice right through[,] both lovable. So you see[,] all round my dear[,] I've almost been serene for turbulent me.

It's wanted to rain all day but hasn't[.] It ought to or there will be drought[,] they say[,] and the forest fires are bad. Has the Post gone rotten again? I never get any letters but I won't let myself get peeved. I tell myself *everyone* is busy. Dr. Baillie is *away* on holiday[.] He left me in charge of one of those 'baby Doctors' again[.] But indeed one is lucky to get any Doctor *at all* these days[.] One hears of people who *can't* and I hope I won't have to.

Ira, people love me for K.W. and Small and I'm kind of afraid they'll hate me for H. of A.S. because it has not the *love* in it that the others have. Do you feel that? It was a tougher part of life. A woman who typed it called it 'sordid.' Is it? R.S.V.P. I did not mean it to be that. That was before I put in those little bits. 'Old Attic' an[d] odd corners that I felt deep. I spose there is still some galley to come? I miss[ed] several sections[.] Some I know you *did* like[,] so I don't think they've been cut out (the big red Bachelor for one)[.] It makes it a little harder writing now[.] I can't retain things in my mind in such big lumps.

Love to the garden[.] A hug to yourself[.] No word from the Clarke or Clarkess. I guess she is about due [for] another attack of flu. Poor soul. I hope that Hangman Hussey is not playing the devil with M.S. while Mrs. C. is off duty. Have you showed Dr. Trapp your house yet? Had a good brag each to each about your own? Have you named any birds yet? Did you get the yellow violet roots I sent?

Always your loving
Old Emily & your Small

P.S. It is something to have E. better in health & spirits. Small.
P.S.S. Comes this week.

June 27 / 44

Dear Eye,
How can one judge these days when to post a letter so that it will reach to date? But whether this come[s] to you to date or too soon or too late[,] you will know on the right date – the 4th [–] that I shall be thinking of you. It seems only yesterday and yet long, long ago that your mother went. Oh, I know what great lumps of leaden heart you have staggered under. Time does help to heal but the sore place[,] the wanting, never goes away entirely. It is 60 years since my mother died and I go back to the morning as keenly and painfully as the very day. I wrote the other day for Hundreds & Thousands a little bit called 'Happy Happy Children.' It tells how I woke in early, early morning. The candle was lighted beside our bed and an old neighbour (Mrs. Cridge) was sitting very negligently dressed on the foot of our bed[.] Alice was blinking at her half awake. I sat up dazed at Mrs. Cridge's extraordinary statement, 'Happy, happy children[,] you have a mother in heaven[,]' and all the time she was crying anything but happily.

I said 'what does she mean Alice?' and straightaway climbed over the bed's foot & went to see for myself[;] what a crazy way to break to children the news of their mother's death. I have never forgotten the words or the meaning dawning. Dear Eye[,] and you've gone on bravely doing your job which is the only thing to do. I think the earth touching, digging, it breathing the quiet of the woods & possessing a bit for your own, as much as anything can be your own, has helped and healed. God bless you[.] Mothers are such irreparable things to lose. How frightful[,] almost unimaginative to have a *bad* mother[.] And nobody on earth can take a *good* mother's place, even [a] living creature turns to its mother when it becomes self-providing[.] Nature sets it on its own feet. But human beings always turn back[,] even *bad* ones[,] to her who gave them birth[.] All other relationships seem little beside that, just a knocking up against one another. Maybe dear, maybe not dear. I think women always love their sons a *wee* bit better than their daughters.

How's your book coming? Doesn't it need a terrible lot of reading up, research, into different writers' ways & manners, as well as the laws[.] I'm too old & too forgetful to learn now. But have never in my life felt as sorry as I do *now in my old age* that I did not study literature more, and most especially poetry. The first poem I ever read was the 'Lady of the

Lake' by Scott.[8] Father gave it to me for my birthday. Why, I can't think[,] for father was the most anti-poetic one you could imagine. I learnt it almost entirely by heart. – I hope we have some sort of second chance[,] Eye. I'd like to do better[,] wouldn't you? One flops so dreadfully[.] I'm so ashamed of my attitude towards Shanks[.] Perhaps the creature can't *help* being such a fool & I get so out of patience at her stupidity & she flies back *really hateful* & I believe like a fish wife. She is more forgiving than me and oh so rude now. She says 'I don't have to take *anything*[.] Not these days[.]'

Mrs. Jonathan Rodgers came to call on me on Sunday afternoon and stayed 2 ½ hours[.] I was a *wreck*[.] She wanted to wring some early Vancouver Art Club dates out of me. I did not know them and could not be wrung except approximately. She wavered hours about buying a picture[,] a *small* one. But like your wretched Hamber woman ended in talk[.] They are nothing but wind bags, said 'could she come *again* & perhaps my woman (Shanks) could haul out[?]' I said I would not let Shanks touch a picture even to clean behind it. It is bad enough to sit and watch her smash dishes, and to hear her say in [a] most surprised voice 'Did you know that was going to happen[?] It fell apart in my hands!'

Mrs. Rodgers wants to read 'Canadian Art' by F.B. Housser and it is not on my shelves[.] Did I by any chance lend it to you? You are the only person I can think of who I *might* have lent it to. Mrs. Rodgers was over in Victoria trying to get a practical nurse for her husband. He hates the one he has[.] She says he does not *need* one[.] In fact he has 2[:] one day & one night & has for years.

It is a lovely morning. Still keeps cool winds[.] The lily buds are swelling. Am not certain if they will be 'swole' in time to mail and *possibly* you might come over & then they'd lie in [a] box and die.

I'm nearly sleep. Shame on me. 10.15 A.M. I often do, breakfast about 8 & after it fall into sound sleep *but* it is not good for getting work done, and I want to work this week[,] should see 'Indefinitely' done. Then I'm clear again for Hundreds and T. Mrs. Kriegel is having a few days holiday and going to take me out & come & have supper. It will be a treat[.] I have got to positively *hate* having Shanks about me[.] She is so horribly rude. And the next thing she is maudlin & she *won't* do what I tell her. You'd think she owned the house[,] it's *my* this and that[.] I'd be thank-

8 'The Lady of the Lake' was written by Sir Walter Scott (1771–1832).

ful enough if she *could* or *would* take hold. But no! I *can't* leave the simplest routine to her, she forgets & then is rude[,] even calls me fool. Oh if I could kick her out. But I dare not because there's nobody. She's a lying hypocrite. I just keep as far as I can from her. And she pokes in joining in all my conversations with *anybody* who comes prying & poking. Now! I did not mean to mention her or health in this letter and look at it! And I spose everyone has some blights in life especially these days. Bays full of love to you and the book.

As always loving
Emily and Small.

Thursday July 6 / 44

Dear Ira
I am glad you did not come to see me *today*[.] I should have hated you to see me. I've been horrid and you would have loathed me. I loathed myself. Things *were* trying but I'm not *going* to bore you. I'll be aggravating[,] like you – 'all sorts of things have happened but not all of them of interest to you.' But I *am interested* in all things that concern people I love. The middle of the day was best. It was the day Mrs. Royal comes & Shanks goes and first Mrs. Royal & I crated Dr. Best's pictures. I found I had a crate to fit with a little adjusting. Then we took a picnic supper (she & I just) into the park. We ate among those delicious little willow trees opposite the Kents. I wish I could tell how *delightful* it was, the trees are young but quite big and so mysterious and fairy-like. There was a great wildrose bush near a perfect *glory*. Then we went over to the Rose bed[.] Oh Eye[,] such wonders! I do wish you could see them – well if there are any rose gardens in Stanley Park or the University grounds[,] *go and drown yourself in the glory of it*[,] the colors & forms[.] But they've bred the smell out of them. The grand old-fashioned cabbage rose has them all beat for scent. Then a veritable fowl yard of ducks came round my wheelchair & finished the tail of our picnic up. There was just one little disappointment & it concerned Hundreds & Thousands & my heart[,] but there! That brings me to some questions I want to ask you. No 1. Do you think it necessary in a job lot of incidents happening all ways, in all places to all kinds of people, & some not people but creatures[,] do you think they should all be in the same person 1st or 3rd

etc. or *can* they be mixed[?] As now I have some calling us Bigger, Middle & Small[,][9] and some no names at all. You see the incidents are not in any way connected one with another. Some are only one page[,] some 4 or 5. Perhaps to make things plain I'd better send you one or two different ones as samples to see for yourself & judge: there may be some you think should be left out better. But life is not all fun. I feel the bad should be in a collection like that as well as the good[,] don't you think so? To be true to life? To ring true? Or do you think this way that they will just be a hodge-podge? & I should try to discover a common thread on which all the incidents could be hung? Hundreds & Thousands *all* had a *common sweetness*[,] didn't they? Here are the titles to date – subject to change.

1 Introduction explaining Hundreds & Thousands
2 flannel petticoat[,] a felt hat and a bear
3 Corsets
4 Killing the baby
5 I'm glad I can never be the oldest
6 The lisp
7 The spotted dog
8 Happy, happy children
9 Confirmation
10 The family plot
11 Dawn
12 Merry picnic
13 [Indecipherable] of Beast
14 As regards kissing
15 The littlest bridesmaid
16 Maude
17 Snob children
18 Metchosin petunias
19 The healthy oak
20 Red Rose
21 Hermitage and Hurt
22 The sharpening stone
23 December birthday
24 Chivalry

Of course I may twist and cut & abolish and I shall peel & peel & cut out every word I can and still leave them something to tell. I want to get them rough-typed (my own which is awful) so that my thoughts are there and I could work on them if – don't scold or blame the 'If!' I want to make *hay* while the sun shines, it's shining pretty good just now too. I'm laying in my winter's wood & hoping I shall be home to use it.

Now there's things in your letter to answer. I thought you *did* use a type-writer! Well I certainly do not use one for *quickness*. I can scribble twice as quick but only half as legibly and I have to do so much correcting it takes longer than long hand[,] only it doesn't take so long to puz-

9 'Bigger,' 'Middle,' and 'Small' refer to Lizzie, Alice, and Emily (see 'Foundation,' *HS* 3–5).

zle out. I don't think your fist is difficult[,] only a word here & there & it has got flesh & blood behind it instead of ink and mechanism.

2. Yes I think the Bests and Miss Mahon were delightful[.] They were awfully nice to me[.] They said the morning in my studio was the *high spot* in their Western visit & some other things that grew my neck an inch & bust my hat-band.

3. I am glad you drink out of the Breton cups.[10] I am glad they are beyond Shank's smashing paws. Walter Gage did *not* write to me[.] I wish he did. Lawren did *not* come to Vic[.] I wish he had. I have the idea it is not Lawren but Bess that prevents, tho' I think Lawren is allowing himself to be snowed over with obligations to not entirely worthwhile people.

[4]. I feel that knowing George Clutesi will make you & Lawren understand entirely the feelings I had for Sophie the Indian. Sophie was not English taught & had no education or fine expression like George, but she had the Indian mind like George[.] She was all woman, maternal from the soles of her feet to her black Indian hair.

Don't expect to make your garden in one year!!!! It will take hundreds of years & every year you'll love it more. Please R.S.V.P. questions re: 1, 2, 3. Myfanwy is out at Spencerwood[.] I had a note yesterday[.] She is making a terrible fuss about being lazy[.] I *know* it is hard[,] but I think she is headstrong & foolish & does not give herself a chance[,] poor girl. But her notes aggravate me[.] She is always hinting, instead of saying outright & it's confusing. How can people expect you to *understand* if they are not honest & *lucid*[?]

I was so mad[.] When the Bests came and I rose to meet them my voice shut off. I had the greatest effort to whisper & was shamed. All I could say was: 'It will come back presently' (in a whisper). Dr. Best's title is 'Surgeon Captain.['] I guess he understood. He said he thought it wonderful what I'd come through & had accomplished. I said 'thank you, you know I look well & I know lots of people think I'm lazy and put it on. Or else am "nervy"' My voice popped on again after an hour. My radio is on the blink too[.] Not a peep will he give[,] aggravating old brute[,] and goodness knows *when* anyone can fix it. The old world is certainly having a lesson in patience[,] every soul in it. Goodbye my dear[.] I appreciated your taking time to 'phone when you had so little time. I am not sending your lilies *this* week[.] It is too late to risk them

10 Carr had made a present of her 'Breton cups' to Dilworth.

for delivery before the weekend. I'll send them next week. It's 12 o'clock & I'm sleepy[.]

Goodnight
Emily & Small

P.S. Space for tomorrow. Perhaps there is nothing to Maude. It seemed to me there was when I lay there helpless waiting to have my brains knocked out. E.

Aug. 3 / 44 morn

Dear Eye
Your letter comforted me[.] I had a big disappointment. Life is full of ironies. I've wanted my Siamese kitten for years & here he[,] as it were[,] dropped in my mouth. The most delicious part of a kitten or a pup is cuddling it. I knew people with asthma had to keep away from cats. I never thought of cardiac asthma being the same[.] Even the other I thought was stupid & nonsense but cardiac is just the same. I played with 'Siam' for two days & had *bad* asthma. Sunday morning he lay across my breast for two hours[.] We were both fast asleep. My breathing has been *very bad* ever since[.] Now I know, he is the darlingest chap full of play & love[.] Shanks adores him[.] So does Alice. So I've got to drive him away when I want him so, but as long as Shanks is good to him and Alice gets comfort out of him that's a lot. Did I tell you *how* I got him? A Mrs. Berkett breeds them (her husband took on Sohmers old art shop)[.] She knew he had long wanted one of my pictures[,] so she decided on one for his birthday (a cat)[.] I said nothing 'til I'd asked A. who said NO. I offered to give it for her (A) honour[.] After a few days she said provided I kept it in my own flat I could have it. I was so tickled & went off & scoured the land to get her a *singing* canary which I knew she wanted[.] So each got her heart's desire & Mrs. Berkett got hers, was delighted to have $20.00 knocked off her sketch[.] Well these things *do* happen. They say these cats don't bother birds but are good ratters – we have rats – & the beast can be leashed[.] So Alice can hold it safe and get a great deal of hugging & she got her bird this A.M. and is delighted.

We are having it *terribly* hot today & I find it *very very* trying. I am so glad your knee is better & hope you won't have to lose any more teeth. Partial plates or bridges are not so bad if you have some of your own to hold them steady. But *all* teeth are a bit cursey – Night. Dr. Baillie came and found me under my tree on the ramp & paid a long friendly call. He does not altogether blame the cat. He says I had a bad bout about this time last year. He admired the cat and said 'we'll wait and see.' He says Bruce Hutchison[11] has a new book out[,] an enormous thousands of copies & makes him a rich man. I said 'I was glad' & added 'K.W. & Small had not left me rolling in wealth.' He said 'My dear your books will live long long after those of B.H.' I have not heard from Bill[.] I spose they are going to flunk 'H. of-All-Sorts' again. I have not hear[d] from nor written to them for months[.] It has always been my principle to stop corresponding with a party who *does not respond.* I've asked for my scripts 'til I'm sick[.] What's more[,] Eye[,] I don't see they have any right to withhold them from me. I [am] still alive aren't I? The M.S. I should be allowed to hold in my keeping for purposes of working on them as long as I live[.] I could not do anything else with them anyhow[.] I'm all bound up[.] I think Bill should have waited for me to be dead before seizing them & I know he never gets anymore from me (nor from you please) until I am good & dead[.] Biog: of course is your own. I *have* no say there but I *have* over the others & it's fiddle sticks & rot[.] I'd rather they were lost in [the] mail than left alive in an unsatisfactory state. I *have* another very old & fragmentary copy of 'Woo' but as you & I know it's no good making several copies that differ. I bet old Hangman has lost Woo & I'm mad. Thanks dear for permission to write reams & let off steam. And it's a solemn swear you'll send back *any unread* me's.

Thank you for those 'unwrote notes com' – as you drive along they help some. I wonder where they go to? Those and thoughts they say [–] every thought comes from something[.] Thoughts are things[.] If they go to build something what an unholy mess that something must be. I don't think I ask so many questions but I would *appreciate* comments.

I don't think my writing means a thing to you now. You never comment nor ask how it's coming on & like a great fool I go on telling you about it, to ease myself, feeling it means nothing to you anymore. I can quite understand you not having the letter by you but you used to be enough interested to comment from memory[.] That's why I suspected

11 Bruce Hutchison (1901–92), a journalist and writer of fiction, won the Governor General's Award for *The Unknown Country: Canada and Her People* (1942).

garbage pail or furnace of [dancing?] on them or else you put me off with 'I will comment on "Maude," "the night was dark etc" *later on*['] but the promise does not materialize & I'll admit you *have hurt there.* Now don't confuse that word as you often do with 'being *offended*[.]' It does not *mean that* to me (it means straight pain inflicted by indifference)[.] My writing means more to me than anything in life. I spose that's why it *won't* kill but bubbles up again and I go on the same old way & get hurt the same old way, instead of nosing the air, shutting up and not caring. – Been too sick to write at all for several days. A dealer came today and bought 2 sketches. One for himself and one he was commissioned to get for someone else. Keep shrinking on the shelf. Sometimes I see lovely things[,] sk[ies] or trees when I'm out & long to be painting. I think I could do so if it were [not] for the paraphernalia involved. I still see – no Bess is – not at heart – she poses[,] having swallowed the dictionary for the correct terms. Rude creature! Re: your garden[.] I'm glad Phylis gave her back. Oh I wish you and Walt Whitman, Small & I could stroll through your wild garden feeling & loving it together. Small often goes & tells me[.] I often wonder if I have pictured it right. I had your drawing[,] only that to go by. I think some people let their relatives *enslave* them but perhaps it's because I have not any and don't understand[.] Everyone is my relations and nobody. I refer to Dr. Trapp.

Have I made you angry in this letter? Sorry, perhaps I'm mean today[,] but I'm off sleep & off food. Doesn't go for making one nice. Don't think I am not appreciative of all you've done for me. I often picture you sitting there walled in by work[,] some pleasant[,] some *not.* & I marvel at your being bothered to answer or read me *at all.* Don't be hurt & more still *don't* be *offended* with me. I'll write a P.S. that'll knock you off your feet but goodbye *old* dear[.]

As always
Emily and Small

P.S. Shanks is an heiress! Shanks has come into money! Shanks is grown high-nosed[,] doesn't *have* to work! I've a strong notion she will look around quick and gulp a 'man' (before he has got to know her). There are heaps of lazy men who'd like a free housekeeper with a purse[.] Not yourself, Eye. Look out Ira! Don't for your own good be snared by Shanks. E

I like to see you married to a dear woman but she'd have to be that, no Shanks, one with a brain and companionship. Otherwise you'd get more from nature & from books. Your mother spoke of it once to me. She understood you and yet no, there was one part a riddle[.] Isn't everyone a riddle?

Wednesday night & Thursday morn [ca. 9–10 August 1944]

Dear Eye
Your broadcast was beautiful[.] Tears just poured down my face[.] I could not help it. Your selections were beautiful touching and right[.] I pictured the dear old man listening and breathing across space[.] 'Thank you son[,]' for I think there are relationships other than blood and sex[.] They may be between relatives or they may not. They may be between man and wife or they may not. They may be between two men or two women, or between a man and a woman or between races. Sophie & I had it. I think Dr. D.C. Scott & you had it. Lawren & you have it. You and I have it. Once in a letter you discussed something[.] I *think* it was in reference to poetry and you described it as something a 'little beyond the circumference' & I think that describes this love too. It is not legally binding but binding by being dear and deep. You *may* not know the other person very intimately. It extended between Nellie McCormick & I[.] There is usually some connecting tie. Nellie's & mine was the lilies. I think *you* have it with most of *your own people*[,] with Pearl[,] your beloved sister & with your mother & probably Phylis, but I don't know that side of Phylis. She has never shown herself to me. Lawren has it with you & with me.

A few moments before your broadcast Mr. Max Stern rang up.[12] I was so thankful he did not ring up in the middle[.] I'd have hated to miss a word of the broadcast[.] He is coming at 5 o' clock.

Later[.] Mr. Stern came bringing your introduction. I suppose I know *why* he came. He was *very* nice and he stayed from 5 - 8 & I am exhausted but it was best he should go through *all* the pictures[,] better than come and do [the] rest tomorrow. He sorted & made [a] selection[.] Tomor-

12 Dr Max Stern of the Dominion Gallery in Montreal visited Carr in August to arrange an exhibition in Montreal, which opened 19 October 1944 and ran for approximately two weeks.

row he comes again[.] He took Klee Wyck away to read[.] First I told him I *hated Montreal & wanted nothing* to do with the outfit[.] He said he knew they had treated me badly but he had nothing to do with the Gallery himself. A. Lismer & Jackson[13] work with him[.] I spose he is O.K. and of course it is advisable to rid myself of as much as I can[,] not leave the junk on Alice. Crating will be a curse. He liked the work[.] He said he had so much bad stuff to see but this was *good*[.] He picked out some queer things[,] some good[,] some bad & queer[.] He did not want very big things (only 3 big pictures)[.] I suppose it is really an honor[.] They seem to deal with good people. He was going to cable his partner last night. When it came to business I told him[,] 'I was no good[,] to talk to you[.]' (Forgive me for being such a pest[.]) I know you are overburdened. The commission *if* there are any sales is 1/3[.] Lawren told me to sell *if* I could before war ended & people's pay-checks stopped. The ex. would consist of pictures quite outside the Trust pictures.

Well my dear[,] I am very *very* tired[.] Goodnight[.] God be with you.

As always the woman who loves you in oodles
Emily & Small

Thursday evening [ca. 21 September 1944]

Dear Eye
I wrote you a beastly letter yesterday & you must have retaliated by writing me a beast today[,] shading all I *wanted* to know[,] just enclosing Irene's stupid one[.] You casually mention you are *going* East[.] I don't know when or where[,] Toronto or tomorrow, Japan or two years hence. Do you think these things are of no count to me[?] I told Doctor I'd written a hateful blue letter to you[.] I was disgustingly blue & dismal[.] He said 'Good[.] It is splendid to get things off your chest[,] even to talk things over with a dog[.]' He said yes, he talked his cases over with his pup. When do you start? How long gone? Ottawa? or Toronto? Blessings on you all the trip. I'm a little less *low & down* than yesterday[.] Shanks has been troublesome[.] I told you Carol was coming. You did

13 A.Y. Jackson (1882–1974) and Arthur Lismer (1885–1969) were members of the Group of Seven.

not even begin your letter[.] It was sort of hitched onto Irene's & so had no meaning[.]

Yours always
Emily & Small
goodbye

Oh Eye[,] I am so thankful my lip did not go on hanging down & my arm lying dead[.] It's so ugly! I hate ugliness. Be good [and] come back soon[.] Love to the Clarkes & do you think you could bring Woo's life home? Oh drat[,] you have no room except for your toothbrush and pajam[a]. Bring yourself back. The rest don't matter. I'll try and be well when you come back but I *am* tired and such a nuisance.

Friday morning
Sept. 22, 1944

Dear Emily:
Your letter has just arrived. Thanks very much for it and for the good wishes it brought from you and Small.

I am sorry you misunderstood my letter which I wrote on Wednesday and to which this morning's letter from you is a reply. My letter was written before yours (with news of Carol etc.) arrived. Your letter did not reach me until yesterday. I do not know when you wrote it – it was not dated. I am sorry you thought my letter 'a beast' and 'casual.' I assure you it was neither the one nor the other. It was intended merely as a note to give you news of my defiance for the East. In it I told you I would be away for about two weeks and that I was going to Toronto. I also said I would be spending some time with Bill Clarke. I shall be in Ottawa also. I am leaving by train tonight.

I am very glad Carol is coming West. She will be a comfort to you. I hope she and her husband succeed in finding a place which suits them. I suppose they will be looking for a farm.

I was sorry you were feeling so blue when you wrote yesterday's letter and am glad you say in today's note that you are feeling somewhat less blue. I know you find Mrs. Shanks irritating and I have no doubt she gives you cause for irritation but she does many things for you that Alice couldn't do and that you couldn't manage yourself. If she should leave you I am sure you would find it very difficult to secure anyone to take her place. So even though it's hard[,] sometimes the only thing to do is be as patient as possible. It's stupid for me to give such advice when I have almost no patience atall. Never did have very much.

I shall try to get to 'Woo's Life' and bring it back with me.

Again thank you for your good wishes. I must say goodbye for now. Love in oodles to you & Small.

Yours as ever,
Ira

Saturday afternoon [ca. 23 September 1944]

Dearest Eye
Your note just came[.] What can I have said[?] Surely you must have read wrong[.] I couldn't have said your 'letter was beastly[.]' Your letter was part missing & never turned up[.] But oh my dear[,] I could not have said it was a 'beast[.]' Not one of your kind kind letters often written when you always were so hurried. They may have seemed a little casual. All I can say is I *have not* been myself lately[.] Sometimes I'm horrid and it worries me[.] I do things that are not me[.] Forgive me. But after all your goodness to seem thankless & unworthy[,] then your coming over and all. Oh I *was not* ungrateful[.] I do try to bear Shanks & be thankful to have her but I remember ho[w] dreadfully the housekeeper tried you[,] the tiresome one with a family that you had[.] I will try to be patient[.] You are all so good putting pretty fed up with me. Carol comes tomorrow[;] it will be a grief to her too to find me so changed[.] That is why I wanted so to die. I felt this coming & I hated so to feel my friend's turn[.] Oh forgive all the wrong things I don't know about & those *that* I do. I'll ask Dr. Baillie when next he comes if it is medicine [–] maybe the medicine has this effect. I am so unhappy because I *know* I'm horrid.

Thank you for writing[.] You won't write me from the sky[,] you're too disgusted[.] But keep Small close[.] She needs you.

Perhaps what you read was that 'I told Dr. Baillie that I wrote you a beastly letter['] (you see perhaps my conscience was wrong)[.] I don't know how to do my hair yet but I've wound a scarf round my head like old crazy Indian Martha used to – Shanks worried dreadfully about it[.]

Alice can't see. I'll be glad when the dear earth takes *me for her own*[.] Dr. Baillie just says better, better, he doesn't *know* & listens to my fool heart[.] Don't bother to bring Woo home[.] It really doesn't matter a bit[.] I doubt I *can* work her over again.

Mrs. Kriegel has come[.] I must go.

Goodby love, and God bless you
Emily and Small

P.S. I did not call your letter 'beastly' [–] not intentionally anyhow.
P.S. Love to Bill & Irene

Wed. night – Thursday morn [ca. 11–12 October 1944]

Dear Ira
I hope you had as happy [a] thanksgiving as we did[.] Everything was just fine from the weather up with the exception of one trouble which has set Small and I unhappy & which is very mysterious[.] Your ring has lost itself from my finger[.] The time it was lost and the space it was lost in were both so small[,] everyone says it can't help but be found sooner or later[.] Meantime Bill, Carol, Small, Emily & Shanks are on their knees searching[.] We have done all the logical likely places and are now on the impossible unlikely ones[.] [On] Thanksgiving day[,] Carol & I were showing each other[,] she a queer new ring & me yours with its swivel. We had to soap our fingers. I was wearing mine on my biggest finger & it was snug but I *think* when I returned it to my finger I put it on its old place[,] on my left. I was in bed & it was 5 o' clock [in] the afternoon. Well then I got up and put a gown on & came to supper in studio & after supper we all sat round the fire *chatting*[.] I went into my bedroom and put on a cool apron as my gown was too hot. This is the only time I left the room[.] Carol sat on my bed chatting before she went to bed & says she is almost sure my ring was on my hand then[,] but five minutes after she had gone I looked at both hands & discovered I had *no* ring. I got up & looked in several obvious places[.] We'd move & swept everything in those two rooms and no ring[.] It was only lost about 3 hours after it was missed and only in two rooms[.] It is most perplexing. I was going to ask you to relieve me of its care next time you came[.] My hands have got thin & it has lost itself so often[,] but never

so thoroughly[.] Having that heavy stone[,] I do not think it would have rolled far. It must have lodged in some tiny nook.

The man with the enormous name and wife and sister came (a friend of Delisles)[.] He bought the sketch you wavered between – (Mount Douglas dark woods)[.] And I was amused to find Mr. Ira has hoisted the price to 175.00[.] I remember you saying you thought a few should be hoisted[.] All the same[,] I'm glad you got the one you did.

> 'Feel Thee near when my feet are hovering over the brink
> For it maybe I'm nearer death nearer today than I think
> Though I did not know it till afterwards'[14]

I was very near death just then, and there was something very akin to the other world very near me[.] Small's tiny cedars stood just to one side too in the particular spot[.] I can't quite explain it. We are getting on very nicely[.] Alice & my guests are very happy and congenial. Shanks is behaving fairly human[.] That Bill Clarke has not yet written. Men *are* things[.] I have been for some lovely drives right on the bank paths over the sea[.] It is fine to have someone strong & reliable at the handle bar *and* no grumbling. I went to bed dead beat last night & did not sleep one wink.

Bill & Carol are looking at farms[.] Bill loves the West & wants to come out. Carol is Western to the marrow, but seems to me it's going to take time to get moved.

Winter again[.] How disgusting [–] raw cold[,] fog [–] except Carol will be here 'til about Monday next. That will be [in] 10 days[.]

My canary sings beautifully[,] gave me 2 songs last night when I was lying awake & disgusted for want of sleep & I need extra with the extra excitement just now.

Oodles and oodles & I hope the desk pile is reducing nicely.

As always yours
Emily & Small

Tuesday Evening [ca. 24 October 1944]

Dear Eye
Just as I say to myself 'Now I shall rest Ira[,]' not write for a whole week

14 An unidentified citation.

or month or somewhat, along comes something I *must* write about[,] you being my Trustor.

Probably by same mail as Bill's letter came the page proof of House of A.S. came to you. I hope you aren't disappointed in it[.] And another thing[.] Bill writes to let him or you know how I wish the dedications worded. Tell me how to answer[,] Eye? For Alice[,] she says she wants very simple & plain like yours was[.] For the Clarkes[:] what will please their publisher fancy[?][15] I fancy Irene might want something fancier & more sploosh?

Max Stern sent me a catalogue invitation[.] I'll send it on to you.

I'm working a little[.] The rain has come but when the children were here they tidied out my racks & I found a whole pile of culls from former sketching trips & my racks are looking scrawny anyway[.] So many sketches gone. The man with the prodigious name [that] ended in St John of Jerusalem said he could get me some 3 ply[,] so if I work up some of these culls I will be able to a little to replenish[.] There are one or two people whom I don't in least believe in[,] say they want to buy[,] sort of Mrs. Jonathan Rodgers type. It is nice to be at work but I have to *push* rather hard. Dr. B. is away for a week[.] Looked in Saturday to tell me to behave better than I did last time & to tell me to long distance if I was in trouble & to see that all my medicine re-fills were taken care of[.] 3 of the drugs have to have Doctor's fresh prescription before renewal. The b.[16] – no, no, no [–] bitters especially 'stop when it comes to the weeps[,]' he said[,] and I said I came to them long ago but I spose this heavy wet weather is harder on breathing and maybe fills up the cry cisterns. Lady Bess wrote me a postcard today[.] Says Myfanwy has gone to N.Y. for 6 months art work. I am very disappointed in her as a friend. I wonder if she is with me. She professed such affection & trueness. But I think the stamp of her class is as indelibly on her as all the rest. Her last letter was all about how she was coming specially to see me & go with me into the Park. I wrote her 2 or 3 weeks ago just hoping she felt better but never a word back[.] I *will not* write *one-sided*[.] Why should one? It's like talking to yourself in a cupboard. I think [I'll lose] all patience with Myfanwy and we are so very ill & then off we go on a rampage of work again.

Seems to me All Sorts will have to scuttle to be on sale for Xmas?

15 Carr ultimately decides to dedicate part 1 of *The House of All Sorts* 'To My Friends Bill and Irene Clarke' and the second part, 'Bobtails,' 'To My Sister Alice.'

16 Carr is about to write 'beastly.' See letter of 9 September 1944.

Seems to me as you were all over it with Clarke and[,] as you told me of the attention[,] I thought them fine & then Clarke could have gone ahead. Help me out on that dedication and when at it tell me what you'd like me to put in Hundreds and Thousands. I know you like the dedication to yourself in 'Pause' but I don't remember what it was[,] do you? & Now for Dr. Baillie[,] it would [be a] different dedication[.] Seems to me a personal thing[,] something between them and me. I would never want to give a dedication to a big important person for show off, but to someone I loved[.] I'm working, pulling up some old culls from former sketch trip. I can go right smack back in spirit if once I have really felt the place[.] That is a gift I thank God for[,] Eye[,] that ableness to relive & rejoin myself to former environment[.]

I hate Shank[s'] b – nose snooping round while I work. I try to rise above it because I know it is little in me[.] She *is very* tactless & her nose is *not* a nice one[.] Ruth came on Sunday[.] She said she did not hear your University Woman's talk and was so sorry[.] She was told it was very fine & I *did* wish I could have & I was eligible too, being a sham member[.][17] Ruth did not because she is very busy this term[.] She said she also would have liked to see *you*[.] Would these do for dedications? House of A.S. To – what do I say?? Bill and Irene or William & Irene Clarke or Mr. & Mrs.? 2nd To my sister Alice (Bobtails) and To Ira Dilworth[,] my dear friend (I'll be dead then[,] remember?) Hundreds and Thousands[.] *Please* take time off just to answer that for

Emily & Small

Dec 12[, 1944] day before birthday

To make a long story short[,] Alice flared up suddenly against Small & The House[.] Said 'I had exploited the weaknesses of our family dead to build up my writing reputation['] that she said it was *disgusting* & I ought to be ashamed. I said 'I thought you liked Small' but she said underneath was making fun out of Edith & Lizzie's smug hypocrisy. I felt dreadful. I said 'Well I would not write what was *not true* & pretend we were a smooth-running holy-minded like every family and then up &

17 In 1937, Carr had been made an honorary member of the Victoria branch of the University Women's Club (see Walker 80 and *HT*, 2 April 1937).

downs.['] Perhaps this may be hard for *you* to understand[,] Eye[,] too[.] I doubt if a Dilworth could see a fault in a Dilworth. You had the benefit of a mother with you years & years.

I felt awful wondering if I'd been disloyal[,] but how could I write of us unless I write as we were? Down in Beckley I so often gave up because of the things she said & then again I thought she seemed to enjoy the stuff & it was absolutely necessary to show us as we were[.] I am sure I made Small herself no saint. But Alice may give you trouble over Hundreds & Thousands & Biog:[, particularly] certain parts[,] but I *had* to write of those parts to show what drove me to woods & animals[.] She is so narrow and so *family* righteous[,] yet if I leave her out[,] don't read her the comments[,] she's going to be fearfully hurt[.] What must I do?? Now she can't read[,] it seems mean to leave her out[.] If she gets them from other sources than me [–] whew! Dr. Baillie says just go ahead pay no attention (he found me worrying) & he knows Alice is difficult at times.

P.S. She was lovely for my birthday & we just forgot the books. She had Billie framed for me[.] He looks lovely[.] Advise me! Probably I shant take it.

Emily

Wednesday evening [ca. 20 December 1944]

Dear Ira,

Talk about cow tails [–] I'm the last hair of the cow's tail. Can't help it – my movements are all so slow[,] such recuperations between each piffly thing. I am up practically 1st day since birthday[.][18] I always show things after rather than at the time. Well Merry Xmas to you and yours[.] I suppose you are paying up now for your time from the office. I hope 'Aunt' is complete and that means she is good[,] I know.[19]

I told you Shanks was going and an Amazon coming & I'm hoping. Shanks told Alice she wasn't looking [–] 'there was many a ship etc' [–] & I think hopes there will be. But oh, I do *need* help in a thousand ways &

18 Carr was born 13 December 1871.

19 Carr's term for Dilworth's *Anthology of Twentieth-Century Verse.* See note 29, page 44.

if I get that woman out I feel I shall be much better mentally & physically[.] She *can* but she *won't*. She is always behind so there is no time for common decencies[:] window-cleaning[,] curtain washing[.] My house is *dirty* & it makes me unhappy & my soul is dirty with bitterness when she is so rotten to me & then hypocritically dotes on me. It's such a farce.

Ira[,] my gift to you is not quite read[y.] Some sections need re-writing[,] others you will probably burn up as worthless. Do not feel you must read the thing in any given time[.] If it amuses you[,] do so. I don't think it amusing but just read as you would any newspaper or ad[,] *not worrying to criticize from the root*[.] You are too tired[.] After a month or so[,] I'd like it back to add to & re-write parts that are too long drawn on & need crisping. Nobody has seen it but yourself[,] nor I hope will in this state[.] The idea has not worked out as I meant it too. I think[,] Eye[,] it is time for me to bow and scramble behind the curtain[.] I'm tired & *not* what they give me credit for being (courageous). I think I should devote myself more to Alice now[.] It must be gall and bitterness when the mail comes & the parcel[,] to have to wait for them to be waited and explained & described. But she never grumbles. And Christmas comes huddling down over us willy-nilly[.] I hear you have fog[.] We have cold[.] Looks as if it might sharpen[.] Well hang up your sock & smile[.] Ferne will be missing her boy & Phylis her sweetheart. Go out into your *own* lovely woods and look up. Forget the mud of the earth & remember the space & glory of the sky. By the way I was thinking you have none of my seas or skies[,] have you? Yours are all trees galore[.] I hesitate to offer you one when you have your house more than full that you can't accommodate no more unless in the bathroom? If you *want* a sky *ask* me[.] I shall be delighted. They have been going lately more than woods & are getting down. I reserved one from a sale the other day[,] maybe for you[.] I did not tell myself so at [the] time but you can have it[.] I just saw I did not sell that[.] It is a favourite of mine. As a matter of fact I thought it had gone in the trust & was a little sorry and then I found it at the back of others. I have written to Grigsby & Lawren to see if & when I have a show. I've mounted some 20 more & suggest I have a small show in watercolor room. 20 to 7 and I'm ready for bed[.] Get up sure at 4 P.M.

Bobbie sent me such a beautiful card by that Chinese Artist?[20] I'd like to have seen his exhibition.

20 Possibly Lee Nam, the artist to whom Carr refers in *Hundreds and Thousands* (41–64).

Happy Xmas[.] Heaps of hugs from Small. Ira & Ethlyn still look happy & lovely.[21] One is so masculine, one so feminine.

Send back that clipping for my scrap-book? The reviews are *poor* paper [–] that's the best yet[.] I'm inclined to think – but – people who have read her say – but I *do* think 'Bobs' are loved[,] so that's O.K. You can't expect to go through life without some flops. Did Lawren go East? Bess wrote to me *quite* a *nice* letter. Now I'll drag off & mount my daily 3 sketches an[d] that way they get done. Hope cold & Aunt are on the up & up, tho' I do thank the cold (and my birthday) for a long lovely letter which will probably have to do me for next year. As always was & always will be

Emily

P.S. We were told to post even for local by 19 [December]. Have no idea when this reaches [you]. Hundreds & Thousands will come soon. E.

21 Carr is referring to two plants she received as Christmas gifts from Dilworth and Dr Trapp.

Letters: 1945

Sunday Jan. 13 [1945]

Dear *old* Eye

What a horrible day yesterday was! I thought of you in that bouncing bag[1] all day[.] I did not know if you left the plane for a stop-over or were going straight through & of course the storm began early in the morning with a great thunder bang & burst of lightening[.] May have been local only[.] Today is calm & I hope you are too. These trips I know are terribly trying to you. How do you manage even about *clothes*[?] You have such restricted luggage & the degrees of temperature are so terrific and the plane likely heated like an oven. So you can't put on extra & then getting to Winnipeg etc with no more protection tha[n] the equivalent of a paper bag all must be very trying. I wondered if I got a line before you hopped off? But I know every second has to be stretched to the limit to fit things in [and] arrange while you are absent & for Phylis and the work to take with you.

I woke up not too bad last two mornings & thought to do some decent work but alas the work capacity seemed only to last 'til my clothes were on[,] then pouf! I was all in, fell asleep on my typewriter, and in front of my easel & on my supper tray, sleep seizes me [and] someone is saying 'Wake up [–] you are in your soup!'

I did some to that sketch on my [screen?] Made it stronger & pulled it together. Lawren wrote me distressed[.] I'd sent so many to Max. He should have told me sooner he wanted watercolors for the Trust. I can't help feeling very doubtful about the permanent room added to [the]

1 Dilworth had made another trip out east.

Gallery for [the] Trust. Lawren's very helpful always [–] too much so at times. I like to know *really* what Lawren thinks about present & future. All hunky-dory apparently[.] Bess bleats away but does she live up to the bleats? Do you? Do I? Does anybody? We have so little to go on, and every separate outfit picks out what they want & discards the rest. Families brought up in a rigid belief, all believing totally different.

Bobbie seems very pleased with his house or flat, & delighted that his adored Mr. D. went to see it. He loves you[,] that boy[,] & he was dancing on his head about having seen 'Othello.' I'm in a quandary about selecting him a picture. I must but – do you think – but, what's the good, I ask you questions, and they go right out to vacuum space. You used to be a *correspondent* & if there's no response[,] well – why write[?] – just empty nothings are nothing. There's got to be two sides to a conversation. Silence just drives one back and back & back into oneself. You are all the same[:] Bill[,] you[,] Irene. Praps one shut up like me feels non-response *more.* I'm not grunting[,] it's only the cold unresponsiveness of life that smacks your face. Month after month[,] Shanks & Alice. Shanks[,] no wit. Alice, no sympathy[,] no responsiveness[,] though else is such a wonderful being all the while. The cold gold-plate & jewels that are offered as ultimate reward when it's warmth & cuddling up to the heart of things that human nature craves. Our race as beings are cold & dead.

Sunday. Here comes a nice fat special airmail & up swings my heart[.] It is only from Bill[.] He will be annoyed at me going my own way like Lawren is & letting the watercolors go. Well *I've got to live[,] haven't I*[?] If you are all too busy to give me a little help & advice[,] I got to take my own & I'm just too sick to struggle things out[.] Constant sickness cost me a lot. Why should I hand out the whole works to Trust & to B.C.? Haven't I got to live 'til I die & I'm *such* a slow dyer! I've been extremely lucky[.] I don't spose there is [another] Bill book for me. I may *have* to sell before time comes to publish[.] He doubts if 'til after war. Meantime, I'll have doctor nurses hospitals & hearses to meet. I've been very lucky & should not grumble. I started to give *50.* That stretched to 80 & now it swallows the watercolors too & I don't ever see that Trust room *built.* It's Lawren's rose coloured specks. I hope he comes to see me when he is over & I can have a talk. Hope you are sat-comfortably in East by now[.] You can sniff as hard as you like at Irene for her *promised letters next day*[.] It won't hurt me any[.]

Love in old-fashioned ooodles

Yours as ever
Emily

This is one of the days I annoy you & you don't like me like you own[ed] up to last Tuesday[.] I'm about tempted to say 'Don't care[.]' Don't care if nobody in the world does. They needn't!

Clarke says he expects to talk to you[,] surprised you had not told me Dr. Humphrey Milford had asked for an introduction & Clarke had asked you to do it. Sorry you have to have that bother but it won't be hard & references like Aunty anyhow. I hear from Bill [that] he expects to have a long chat with you over various affairs. As I told you[,] he has *at last* written & is distressed. I sent the W.C.[2] to Max[.] Well if you people *won't* answer questions[,] how *can* you expect people to know your wishes. It looked such a nice fat letter & 'air & special[.]' I thought [']Wow! Ira has done himself in['] & it was Clarke's. Now I must write Mr. Claygate Harry's secretary about a lot of business. Income tax. I feel all sixes & sevens & need a new head.

P.S. This piece was overlooked [referring to the part of letter after she signs her name]

P.D. Shanks still here and ultra-revolting. Small's dead (I think) E.

HEADLINE: SIAM CAUGHT A MOUSE [ca. February 1945]

Siam now has a playmate[.] Yesterday our family circle was extended to embrace a 3-month kitten (common or ordinary)[.] They are already galloping in frolic together & Siam proved himself 'big man' by killing a fat mouse[.] Great rejoicing among all but mouse tribe.

Dear Eye

Hope you read and congratulated Siam on the headline. It's great fun to watch the two cats romp together[.] They are good friends & I hope will demolish our overrun of mice[.] They are nibbling their way through all the walls & [are] a perfect nuisance. I turn up holes & they make others in every room in the house[.] Underhouse must be full of them. I got poison but it seems little use.

Well the visit is over[.] Lawren & Bess came yesterday & were very nice[,] only I wished you were there too at the conference. Lady B. did not spend the whole time[.] We got right busy & looked through the new sketches right away while she was there[.] She said she had things to attend to & was not staying & she knew we had a lot of business things

2 'W.C.' is Carr's short form for watercolour.

to discuss[.] She did her puny crits & Lawren did not always agree. He calls her 'sweet' now or 'sweetheart' [–] did you notice? I guess he is *really* fond of her[.] I used to wonder sometimes & I guess she serves him well as a team-mate. At first or in the early days[,] she may have bothered him with her poses but now he is used to them & she is a willing worker & helps him federate. Yes Eye[,] he is a Prince but he's not up to you. He's not so much a man as you. I love you both[,] my Trustors[,] but I love you best[.] I'd go to you for strength. L. often changes or swerves *about* work & he will ask 'what do you feel about it[,] "Sweet"'? He was very kind, he liked the work[,] but I feel that *on* the whole he likes the Mt. Douglas outfit best[.] He thinks they should be two separate shows. I feel myself thes[e] are what you might call 'in lighter vein[.]' Mt. Douglas were very serious. I wish I'd died then [–] not out there, it would have made a nuisance[,] but during thrombosis[.] Don't quite understand *why* I had that comeback. Jane for chief pallbearer (I loved Jane) & that place[,] the one among the thistledown. That *you* have[,] well[,] that's a Hundred & Thousand that has no reason or answer[.] Perhaps it's all right[.] Dr. Herstein wrote me such a nice letter from Camp Borden other day[.] He was the one who pulled me back[.] Dr. Baillie had been on his [']better better better[.'] He said he heard everything was getting along *fine* & was very well. Would he feel robust if he was like I?

Yesterday I went out on the ramp door & gathered a snow drop & a crocus[.] *Do tell me*[:] *Has* Emily done anything yet or did she die or fail or anything?[3] Because she *ought* to have bloomed by now[.] She is the earliest of things and Bess told me a few weeks back she had prunes in blossom in her house, spring prunes [– and] the boulevard trees[.] I'd heard of them on the boulevards here[.] Ruth alway[s] gets it.

But back to yesterday's work[.] Lawren changed several of the prices from 50–60 & to 70 & all this outfit are to be sent over[.] They will not all hang, no room but, should any sell, they will fill in from surplus & pack & send direct to Max Stern *if* he wants them. Lawren looked into my bank acc. & said I was all right for present. I knew that but I put my both feet down at presenting the Trust with the watercolors[.] I said 'All my best canvases have been taken for the Trust[.] I've got to think of Alice & myself & old age and doctors & drugs & even my ordinary living is very high with that worthless Shanks paid as a good cook-housekeeper & general & refusing to do this & all *my* cooking for Alice for last 2

3 Carr is referring to a tree, which she had bought, named 'Emily' in Dilworth's garden.

months.['] I was getting so down[,] no sleep & no food, so Alice took hold & got me some eatable food & cooked it & I paid her $20 extra per month. I won't live on her allowance & besides Shanks $30.00 & the food I buy but *refuse to cook* for Shanks & my rent I have to draw from bank every month. Bill told Lawren (he met the Clarkes somewhere when he was East) my book[s] would take care of me, but I can't see how they would with sickness[.] You see I *had* nearly all coming to me in advance & I spose I'll have to wait 20 years before anything comes of this fool monster they plan *after* the war and after re-habilitation & who's going to buy the thing[?] I shant for one[.] I turned to Bess & said 'What do you think[,] Bess[,] that I should give these watercolors to the Trust?' She replied 'Certainly *not*' 'That's what Ira says too' I said. I thought L. looked a bit disgusted with us all [but] he doesn't know money[.] Look at the expenditure when his mother was ill[.] It must have been enormous[.] He ought to [–]

Well. He looked the watercolors through & made me promise not to sell & do anything with them 'til 3 months anywhere were past. 'If you *need* money you can give one to Max to sell[.'] Well that's silly[.] *Max can't* nor anyone else sell at a moment's notice. Lawren has never had to plan & his propositions are not practical. Only Bess knows pinch. She can hold onto the purse strings. They both loved Picture of Woo and the apple tree & said 'Don't sell that[.]' 'I *don't intend to*' I said[.] L. did not mention the Sedgewick picture you spoke of. If I *need* Lawren before he comes again[,] I am to write & he'll come. Do you see Bess letting him? & Lawren is weak[,] I tell you, lovely[,] gentle but weak. I'm (me) better[,] Eye[,] & longing for spring & the Park. Hope L's lecture last night went well & the one tonight. Victoria is so breedisical. I'd hate him to have just ½ dozen[.] My Cadboro Bay fund is going[.] She says she won't understand it, but can tell me the Federation means all kinds of work. Poor Lawren, he means so well. But Victoria is just *hopeless*[,] *I know*[,] in art.

This is a wretched letter[.] Forgive it. Thanks for your special & the next day your note. They told me lots I wanted to know[.] I like to hear about your & Phylis' home life. That is a nice arrangement with the Benjamins[.] I had thought Bess *might* be helpful with her big house when you were away but then Benjamin is nearer & the old lady, tho' ugly & such head-dresses! I tell you this, hair for old women is a *difficult* problem[.] Men just go straight bald[.] A woman can't without looking disgusting & when your addition won't stay on like mine since the stroke[,] it's hopeless. I often think of adopting a hood[,] only I could not bear the heat. I only have about 3 roots to work on & look at Lawren's white nip and your plenteous waves. Taint me fair.

I ought to write Bill[,] have not for weeks[,] giving him a taste of his own pie. Sky & sea has gone to the framers, with special instructions to keep [wood] & glass *clean.* Cough is better[.] Still hacks but choking paroxysms have persist[ed]. Now for V.O.N. & their old needle.

Funny Jack Nicholles' daughter (the one my will is very protected from) came yesterday. She told me she'd worried over Pa's Xmas Present 'til she saw 'House of A.S.' in a store window. She did not say if Pa liked it. None of my family as far as I *know have read House of A.S.* [–] even Alice. You see[,] I was reading it to her 'til she stopped me by saying I had exploited my family's shortcomings for my own benefit. It hurt & she swung out of the room & I never offered to read it [to] her again[.] But of course there is Lollie who reads selections to her on Tuesdays[.] Perhaps she read it to her[.] We've never mentioned the work since. H of A.S. has given me some heartaches. The Clarkes have sent me very trivial cuttings this time, but I have heard over & over that the reviews in East were *good.* A woman from New York wrote the other day (one I know)[.] She wished Bobtails could be published in a little gift book for animal lovers. I spose people who did not want to spend $3.00[.] I shall love to have Aunty when she is assembled. Why is Sedgewick such a big guy that he can order a book dismembered for his special eye? Eye[,] several times you have grieved & called yourself *not creative* in writing. I think you are quite wrong. I tell you from my heart. They call mine creative writing but most of my writing you have inspired or created through me. If you had not come into my life I doubt my books would have existed[.] I had no one to help[,] no sympathy[,] no love to share in the work or life. 'God moves in a mysterious way[.]' You know in a *few* of the new pictures I have gone a little beyond the circumference[.] Lawren spotted them at once & you know[,] occasionally[,] like in Nellie & the lilies & in old attic Eagles.[4] I know when I am doing it but can't control it [–] it comes[.] I [was] very near the brink & afraid to fall over & drown but I love doing them all the same. I did it a good deal in Mount Douglas. The first time I did it was when I stood on top of Beacon Hill with the Bobbies & felt the world so round & knew the Bobbies' limitations & loved them better for them. It was talking with you that had created the thought & it is not only me you've helped that way[:] your students[,] your public when you speak. You *are* cre-

4 'Nellie and the Lily Field' (*GP* Pt 1, 37–8) and 'Attic Eagles' (*HS*, 200–1).

ative, sometimes through yourself & sometimes through other people. You are a grand man. Put that in your pipe & smoke it!! Not *perfect*, who is? But *grand*[.] I am not the only who says it. From your mother *down* to the big [indecipherable,] I know what is said of Ira. Go look in the bath-room mirror & see your face is pink. You did not have one in your room when you lent it to me. I'm not vain[,] I think[,] but I missed it seeing if I was straight or crooked.

I think I'll say goodbye now – I [am] better I'm sure & it's getting on four now. I'm not dreaming. Oodles.

Yours affectionately
Emily

P.S. Lady Boultbee is paying us a visit next Sunday[.] I believe I hear the poor *poor* aunt Alice already & the dagger looks cast at me. Well the deep harm passed [when] I bawled my head off at what she or any of them have to say. I wonder if it will occur to their perfect selves *why* I chose an heir away from the family? Clarke told Lawren those books would carry me. I hope he is not over favorable. They are not best-sellers[,] you know. It's no good [to] send Sunday Special to Van[.] They deliver with Monday. I wanted you to know why the M.S. did not arrive.

St Mary's Priory[,] Government St. [ca. February 1945][5]

Dearest Ira,
How lovely of you to send me that special and set me purring like Siam. The first letter to be received at the priory[.] Alice brought it after church. I'm prouder than I thought I'd be.[6] In fact I'm swelled[.] Thank you for [the] congrats & general kindness[.] It is nice of you to be glad even if I do know it's your doing[ ] I don't mean conferring the honor as much as making me *worthy*[:] a little school-hater & ignoramus like Small. She is tickled to bits & says isn't it like our beloved Guardian?

5 St Mary's Priory nursing home, into which Carr settled in February 1945.
6 Carr is pleased that the University of British Columbia was considering conferring an honorary doctorate upon her. Hembroff-Schleicher notes that 'the Senate of the University of British Columbia had completed arrangements to confer upon her at the 1945 Spring Convocation the Degree of Doctor of Laws' (1978, 41).

& don't you forget 'I'm Dr. Small' if you are! I shall enjoy telling Dr. Baillie[.] I think he'll fall over backwards & require Brandy & I can hear the clash of Cann's pearl teeth[.] If Lizzie was not dead already she['d] die right off – and Father & Mother? I wonder how they'd have taken it? I think the ugly duckling would have given them a *tremendous* surprise[.] I imagine the next generations will scoff at such things & me are all trash, together to them. Lady Boultbee never came after all. I can see Alice is pleased & surprised. Here's an enormous hug for you from Small & me for you & education.

Well I'm here very much an old lady now, very cold. My room is perfectly [bled?] of sunshine. In fact it opens into a well & the [toilet windows?] as far as my eye can reach is depressing[,] but it is all there was and they say so hopefully there may be a better one *room.* I feel some old bird is pre[paring] her wings for flight. They are very kind & such a welcome[:] 2 sisters & Mother Superior came forward & kind & welcomed me on arrival & the [next] day I have a private bath. There is hot water[,] heat[,] but still it seems *very* cold[.] Perhaps it's the day *and* there are no bells in the rooms[,] a great drawback as I can't *sleep* from 1 – 6 & the room is cold. Alice creeping round at 5 to make the fire up and Shanks at 6 making porridge made me long this A.M[.] The insult got my porridge at 6.30 & I had to wait 'til 1/4 to 9[.] It was rather a disappointment to my stomach and grumbles herself. But oh Eye[,] *not to have Shanks'* domination and cheek!!! Alice is so brave & dear[.] She admitted it was lonesome last night & has just gone home to cuddle the cats[.] She & Mrs. Kriegel settled me in yesterday & I am very comfortable[.] She is having a visitor tonight. She told me the book she liked best was Bobtails[.] I am so glad that dedication was hers & next that she'd only heard parts [of] was 'Pause[.]' She doesn't like the more personal.

Bill wrote me yesterday[.] I think I'll send the letter to you[.] I don't understand why he sends it to me rather than to you. If they've fixed it all up their way[:] d - - m or is it – honestly true that you *cannot further edit for me*? Been so very busy[.] Maybe I should hate anyone's editing after yours[.] It's just evil when you all knock me. Even your little swats of derision I feel *justly deserved* and they made me see so clearly what not to do next time.

I had an awful time getting Shanks out[.] She would *not pack*[.] Said 'she had not time. I could not drive her to it' – Oh to be rid of her!! Joy! I feel like the geese when they came out after morning through a black cloud. Poor Shanks[.] I guess she had her points but they were barbed. I wonder[,] Eye[,] why we were rubbed up against each for 2 *years of misery.* I felt she was making of me a bad creature, souring & hurting my nature. I wonder if I affected her for evil too? I think there is a reason for us coming in contact with *every soul* we meet[,] don't you? It's just meant to be for good or ill. I wonder why I am penned in another of these crock places? Oh I've found the missing M.S. 'Indefinitely.' I think I should rest[,] work for a few days & then I shall write again. Your few words on Hundreds & Thousands heartened me again. I was so relieved you did not think it all piffle, but I am very very tired now & need rest. Too tired to read[,] too tired to think[.] The move has exhausted me. Thinking & seeing for *everyone* before I left & shut the house.

I am glad you like Sea and Sky. I hope it will be an always joy to you & Small when I have grunted my way out, but I'm not going to grunt here. I'm going to be *happy*[.] I was so glad you came this week. Tuesday passed. Wed. passed. & I almost gave hope up[.] I wanted to see Sky & Sea before I left the flat[.] *Don't* go & expect another 10.00 present on the 25th of March now.[7] It is not my habit to elaborately give or receive big presents from young men but I always liked that particular picture done as I came singing home to my creatures & the van[.] I passed a stone's throw from my van sitting on a rise in the field, unpacked all my gear again & painted what I looked into. It never sold though perhaps I never did anything but pull back when it went out on a show & when it came home[,] I was always glad. Then I thought for a long time the Trust had it but it hid in a corner & when it turned up I said 'Eye has the sea & sky of mine[.] We will share that[,'] so we have[.] Alice won't know[.] She felt round the edge of the frame & asked its color & has not thought of it since[.] You ought to have that little Indian school glassed if you want to preserve it[.] Funny[,] I came on that in just the same way[.] A Band man wanted it in Vancouver but he tried to jew me & I No'd him sharp & came across another watercolor & said without a thought 'That's "Ira's[.]"'

Shall I send you 'Pause' soon as it comes? & show Clarke or what does he want me to do with it[:] re-write & alter it? Cause I won't for him[,] so there! & down goes Dr. Carr's foot. I hear you say 'Small[,] Small[,] Bill Clarke has been [as] good was itself to you[.]' Well tell me what to do & also[,] when the day of acknowledgment comes for my Doctorship[,] tell me what to say for I know I must be very formal especially now I'm a doctor. Have you heard of the singing ladies? *None* of the Vancouver Ladies writes to me now. They at least sent Xmas greetings but

7 The date of Dilworth's birthday.

not clear [as] to their whereabouts. A draggle of sun has come in my well & is directing itself in the looking glass. Bless you dear & thanks for all you've done on my behalf. I'm happy and intend to be[.]

Lovingly Emily & Small

Tuesday [in Dilworth's handwriting] Emily's last letter to me
[ca. 27 February 1945]

Dear Eye,
A day of struggled breathing much harder to stand than angina pain[.] I almost look forward to that as a treat now and – they treat me like a semi-lunatic which makes me furious[.] Oh Eye[,] I should *not have stuck with Shanks* so long but you all said to as there was nothing else to be got[.] She has made me mean & no one knows never when [–] it showed when we were alone. But Dr. Baillie[,] Harry[,] You[,] Lawren[,] Alice all said[,] go on[,] so [when] I went through strokes & things I fought[.] She threw taunts at me 'til she put me thinking I was like her. I told her not [to] come to see me in the new place 'but I shall want to know[.]' She said 'Oh well I'll phone your sister[.]' The two parted chummy[.] That was always the way with anyone I disliked[.] Well I'll turn her on like a dirty blotted up page[.] She's gone to Y.W.C.A. Half the nuns & nurses have half[,] the understaffed Prior[y] halved again by flu colds. I'm way off down a corridor where nobody can come or nothing ever happens. There's no bells[.] If anything goes wrong[,] you go wrong by yourself[.] But oh when they treat me like a half-wit & (I know I *am* forgetful) [,] then I want to shout 'I'm *nearly a Doctor*[.] The University are making me one so there! ['] I wish it had not been quite so late[,] Eye. No word from them yet[,] perhaps not 'til 2 days before *the day*. It's very raw & cold[.] My room is like an iceberg[.] The radiator seems ornamental only & I have to have [the] door wide open to breath[.] Been in bed so far[.] Appetite all gone again. Clarke's 'Pause' not come yet[.] Probably the first page only was typed when he wrote[.] Says he has no idea when he'll be West.

I [hoped] I'd had long to look into the anthology when you were here but there was that miserable sky & sea to be backed & so much to say. I don't suppose you & I will ever get time *anyway* in this world to talk out 'til really dry.

This was not intended for a letter only a note[.] May God bless your going through the sky[,] make your business successful[,] bring you safe home. I think you'd better tell Bill[,] don't you? Ouch [–] spose it doesn't come off? (about Dr!) In spite of everything[,] it is more cheerful than Mrs. Clark's[,] each [sealed] in their own tomb for such years[.] There was a hopelessness of waiters in that place. This place[,] they seem to skip of[f] in merrier mood & make room for the next. Mrs. Kriegel has just been in. What a dear kind[,] cheery soul. I love all Austria through her[.] She's away now to see if my sister is O.K. knowing I was worrying a little[.] Alice went up over Menzies ship from here & was to be home & meet Mrs. K. at 5[.] There was no sign of her & I got worried for her[,] being alone.

I've scrambled through a reluctant tea. *I loathe food again.* Lawren knows I'm here from me & *you* must have told him about the Doctor[.] Well, I hope it is no mistake & I'm plain Milly to [the] end of days. Come back soon. Love to Irene & Bill[.] We *all* want you back. What will Small's title be? A Doctorette?

Yours as ever,
Emily & Small

P.S. Tell Bill not to laugh at the Dr. & I'll promise not to do it again.

[1 March 1945][8]

Dear Emily:
Thank you for two letters which arrived this week – one on Tuesday, the other today.

I am glad you have got settled in the Priory. Hope it proves satisfactory. And that you will find yourself increasingly comfortable. It will help, when you can secure a more interesting room. I can see there will be many things in the routine of such an institution to which you will have to adjust yourself and I don't suppose it will always be easy doing so.

As for Shanks, now that she's not with you why not dismiss her from your mind entirely and so get rid of that source of irritation. Just try to

8 As Carr passed away on 2 March 1945, it is unlikely she received this letter

forget that she ever existed. I am sure that, despite the annoyance you felt while she muddled around, Shanks did not really influence you atall – at least, not permanently.

Another thing – don't worry too much about being treated as if you were a 'semi-lunatic.' You know you're not and so do I. You'll be able to demonstrate to the nuns and nurses that you definitely aren't. You know you may be misjudging them. Such people have strange ways of showing their kindness and solicitude for others. I am sure you will find some of the nurses who will be congenial – anyway I hope so.

I was interested to know about 'Pause.' No, I am sure Clarke doesn't intend to suggest that they wish to do your editing, ignoring me. I am sure he won't do that unless you wish him to. When you get 'Pause' back[,] I'll be interested to see it. I haven't laid eyes on it for months. If you like to send the ms. to me when I get back from Toronto I shall do my best to help you with it. I shall talk to Clarke about it – when I am in Toronto. I shall also discuss the 'Pie' with him and my idea of publishing Bobtails and some of the other animal and the bird stories in a separate volume. What do you think of that?

Now about the doctorate. I am sure there can't be any mistake about it. Mr. Sedgewick told me it had been definitely decided upon. Of course the university will have to write to you officially about the matter. You will likely hear from the Registrar. When his letter reaches you all you need to do is to write a simple note accepting their offer. It need not be very formal. I am sure you will do the right thing and do it properly. There is always a certain amount of 'Red Tape' about such official transactions but that does not mean that you as an individual need to become official or formal.

By the way I told Dr. Trapp & Nan Cheney about it. I told them the whole thing was fairly confidential until the official correspondence had been completed. I also wrote to Bill Clarke. Lawren knew about it from Sedgewick. I didn't think any of them would feel free to write to you about it unless it is officially announced and that may be some time. I do hope they don't keep you waiting too long. You & Small will have to try to be patient.

I am leaving for Toronto on Saturday afternoon's plane at 2.45. I have to leave this lovely spring weather and go back to the beastly cold drabness of the East. The birds have been wonderful around my house for the past ten days. Last week the robins arrived with a bounce. One of them set up an humanistic sort of scolding in a tree at our front door. He possibly thought we would have had a better reception prepared for him than he found. This morning one of my big alders was *absolutely full* of little birds, obviously a flock feeding on something. I couldn't get close enough to see what they were – small finches or siskins of some kind – but they kept up a wonderful chirpy and twittering which was lovely to hear. They sounded like a whole orchestra of violins playing with *mutes* on. Perhaps they are just passing through, paying us a brief visit only. I hope they liked our place and will stay for a few days. They gave a more joyous opening to the day.

'Sea & Sky' is a joy to us. Phylis admires it more than any other of yours that I have.

Take care now. Heaps of love.

Yours as ever,
Ira.

Last Will and Testament

My dear Eye
What a blessing you have been in my old age with all my decrepitude. I have loved and trusted you well.

You know what you have meant to my work and to me. Love is the only coin one can pay back with and I have given that abundantly.

I enclose a little letter for Alice[.] Please read it to her. I ask you to do these familiar things because you are nearer to me than my own nieces. My work was the biggest thing in my life[.] The nieces never entered into it, you did, & I'd rather you cleared away the inevitable personal trash and leaves where one has odds & ends half-finished that they want to use for notes as long as life lasts. Don't hesitate to burn[.] It is a clean satisfactory way of disposal. Alice knows what I want done with my things but she can't see to do it & she knows nothing of my material either. I know you & Lawren will help her clean up after me – my Trustees – I should hate my failures looked upon with curious smiles & wondered at. You will recognize them as the inevitable stepping-stones and try-outs.

I'd like you to have any of my books you want. Pick them off my shelves (they will only go to the auction-rooms)[.] I'd like you to take the Whitman, Gitanjali, & your anthology that you gave me and any more you want. The M.S. are yours and the ring from my finger[.] I would like you to wear it. Small will like to see it there.

Should there ever be an 'Etcetera' and she asks 'Who is Small?' say 'Just a fun girl belonging to a woman named Emily – her *little* self – I offered her sanctuary in my waistcoat pocket & Emily & I shared her. Now she is all mine and Emily is away. Small is quite harmless.' Don't grudge her sanctuary.

Keep the sanctuaries[.] They have been joy and comfort[.] They are in one of the pink silk M.S. folders and will be somewhere near me. They have given me such hours of comfort.

The little Indian basket Sophie gave me and you know so well I'd like you to have that & use for your pencils & I'd like you to have Sophie's portrait[,] the original little watercolour used for Klee Wyck.

Forgive me dear for all the times I have been unreasonable or petulant or weepy. I have loved you truly & shall as long as I can[.] Thank you for the love you have given to me. God bless you – goodbye

Your always loving
Emily

Appendix A
List of Altered Vocabulary

abscesses – abcesses
actually – actualy
aerial – aireal
ago – agoe
aggravating – aggrevating
agreeable – agreable
already – allredy
alright – allright
angina – engina
answer/ed/ing/s – answear/ed/ing/s, answard
apart – appart
apartment – appartment
apologize – appoligize
aren't – arent
ashamed – ashaimed
austere – austeer
attendents – attendance
awful – aweful, awfull

balance – ballance
balloon – baloon
barrelful – barrelfull
bachelor – batchelor
belief – beleif
bicycle – bicicle
blasé – blazà
bomb – bom

boisterous – boistrous
booth – boothe
bored – board
borne – bourn
both – bothe
bough – bow
bowl – bole
brag – bragg
brail – braile
brief – breif
browse – brouse
brutally – brutaly
bumpy – bumpey
busy – buisy
business – buisiness, buisness
butchered – buchered
bye – by

cache – cash
caricaturing – caracturing
carcass – carcas
carrion – carion
carry – cary
cataracts – catracts
cavorting – cavourting
cemetery – cemetry
cheapens – cheepens
chiefs – cheifs
chipmunk – chipmonk
choir – chior
choosing – chusing
chords – cords
cleanly – cleanley
cleanliness – clenliness
club – clubb
cockatoo – cucatoe
cocky – cockey
codicils – codicles
college – colledge

complete – compleet
compliment – compliant, compliament
comrade – comrad
control – controll
copies – coppies
correspondence – corespondence
corporation – corporition
courageous – corageous
couldn't – couldnt
crowded – croud(ed)
coupons – cupons
cuckoo – cuccoo
curly – curley

daffodil – dafodil
decent – decint
decency – desency
disposal – desposal
decrepitude – decrepatude
desultory – disultory
diabetic – dibetic
didn't – diddnt, diddn't
died – dide
dilapidation – delapidation, delapitation, dilapitation
disappear – disapear
disappoint – disapoint(ed), dissipointed, disappointents, dissapoin
disapprove – disaprove
dissertation – desertation
doesn't – doesnt
don't – dont
dreadful – dredful
drug – drugg
duty – dooty

editions – edditions
en route – en rout
enthuse(d) – entheuse(d)
epochs – epocs
especially – especialy

eventually – eventualy
exist – exhist
exonerate – exhonerate

fields – feilds
fierce – feirce
flabby – flaby
flu – flue, flueing
forgotten – forgotton
foresee – forsee
freesias – frezias
fulfil – fullfil
fuchsia – fuschia

gaped – gapped
genie – jenii
giggling – gigling
gossamer – gossimer, gossamir
greater / greatest – grater/gratest
greenness – greeness
grief – greif
grievance – greivance

hadn't – haddnt, haddn't
halves – halfs
hasn't – hasnt
hauling – haling
heaps – heeps
hearse – hurse
hence – hense
here – hear
hilariously – hillariously
hiccups – hiccopes
hodge podge – hotch potch
hug, hugger, hugging – hugg, huger, huging
hullabaloo – hullybaloo
hunky dory – hunkey dorey
hussy – hussey
hypodermic/hypo – hipo, hippo, hyppo
hypocrite, hypocrisy – hippocrite, hypocracy, hyppocrite, hypocritcaly

inspirit – enspirit
I'm – Im
I'll – Ill
illegible – illigeble
imagine – imagain, immagain, immaginem immigain
incidence – insidence
indelibly – indellibly
inevitable – enevtable
innate – inate
intolerant – intollerant
irreparable – irrepairable
isn't – isnt
it's – its

kowtowed – cowtowed

lasso – lasoo/lasooing
lenient – leinent
Lieutenant Governor – Leutenant Govoner
lily, lilies – lilly, lillies
literature – litrature
liquor – licquor
lucky – luckey
lose/loser – loose/looser
losing – loosing
luscious – lucious

made – mad
magic – majic
maybe – maybbe, mabey
mementos – momentoes
menagerie – managery
mentally – mentaly
missile – misal
muscles – mussels

nauseates – nauciates
needn't – needent
neuritis – neurites
niece – neice

nosy – nosey
occasionally – occasionaly
offends – offendes
opposite – opposit
ourselves – ourselfs
overcrowded – overcroaded

pallette – pallet
paraphernalia – parenphernalia
paroxysm – peroxsyms
piece – peice(s)
piecing – peicing
pelicans – pellicans
pert – peart
personally – personaly
petticoat – peticote
physically – physicaly
pigeon, pigeonhole – pidgeon, pidgonhole
please – pleese
plum pudding – plumb pudding
plumbing – pluming
possess – posess
precision – precesion
preface – prefface
pretentious – pretensious
prickly – prickley
principle – principell
privilege – priviledge
promissory – promisorry
publicly – publickly

quandary – quandry

racket – rachet
really – realy
rebel – rebell
relief – releif
reproof – reprove
ripened – riped
rotten – rotton

safe – save
sauerkraut – saurkraut
schedule – scedule
scholars – schollars
scolded – scholded
seemly – seemley
selecting – silecting
sense – sence
sensitive – sensative
shadow – shaddow
shame – shaime
shoddy – shoddey
skedaddling – skedadling
smooth – smoothe
smudged – smugged
smug – smugg
snarly – snarley
soliloquy-ing – sololoquing
sorry – sory
soured – sowered
specially – specialy
spiel – speel
spiky – spikey
spiralling – spiraling
spittoon – spitoon
spread – spred
squalid – squallid
still – stil
stomach – stomack, stomache
studied – studdied
superfluous – surpllous
supper – super
sure – shure
surreptitiously – serruptitiously

tailless – tailess
tenants – tennants
terribly – terribaly
terrific, terrifically – territtic, teritticaly
Tuesday – Teusday

that's – thats
their – there
though – tho
tied – tide
topsy-turvy – topsey-turvey
touchy – touchey
transition – transcision
tricky – trickey
triple – tripple
trickster – trixter
trivial – trivyal
twopenny – tuppenny

unimaginative – unimagineative
until, 'til – untill, till, 'till

vice versa – vice verca
vitally – vitaly
wags – waggs
wallflower– wallflour
walnut – wallnut
wasn't – wasnt, was'nt
what, what's – wat, whats
weren't – werent
whopper– wopper
widows, widowers – widdows, widdowers
willy-nilly – willie nilly
wizard – wizzard
won't – wont
worrying – wory(ing)
worrys – worries
wouldn't – wouldnt

Proper Nouns

(Una) Boultbee – Boultby
Brooklyn – Brooklin
Dr. David Baillie – Dr. David Bailie/Bailey/Baily
Irene Clarke – Isleen/Ireen Clarke
Lawren Harris – Lauren Harris

V. Hennell – V. Hennel
Kitsilano – Kitsalano
Melampus – Malanipus, Melanpus
Mrs. Malcombe – Mrs. Malcomb
G. McInnes – G. McInnis
Myfanwy – Myphawny, Miffawny
McCurry – McCurrie, McCurrey
Philharmonic – Philharmonica
Roosevelt – Roosfelt
Saskatchewan – Saschachewan
Terry's – Terries
Dr. Trapp – Dr. Trap
Mrs. Tucket – Mrs. Tuckett
Walt Whitman – Walt Witman

Appendix B
'Small's Gold'

Ira, it's Small – with Emily in the nursing home[.] A nurse just stuck her head in the door and[,] nodding her bonnet at Emily's bed[,] said 'Thank God for one laugh in this house this morning!'

She didn't, how could she know it was me[?] I pushed and pushed but I couldn't get through Emily's 'glum' all week. It was grim – blinds drawn, wet cloth over head, deep quiet – she's two days better now. Emily is always like an invalid cat when she is sick – dark – quiet –

The glow of your bronze-gold chrysanthemums did their best in the nearly-dark room now, with blinds half up they burn in the quiet light – six normal sturdy roly-poly flowers in a green glass vase. Cultivated, full developed but *unforced.* Every petal has a russet face but its back is gold and chrysanthemum curls them over and in towards her heart so that her middle is all pure gold: not metal gilt but *living gold.*

On one side of the gold chrysanthemums stands a vase holding six scrawny ones[,] pale yellows and pinks with grey dried leaves that rattle if touched. Each bloom is twice as big as your bronze-gold ones, lanky[,] crimped bigness, all the robustness and strength forced out of them.

On the other side of yours is a vase of anaemic, yellow, flop-necked, button-chrysanthemums.

Emily opened her eyes at that laugh of mine that the nurse heard.

'Is there a joke[,] Small?'

'It's the flowers[,] Emily, they are so comically like their bringers: fancy lady – floppy lady – my Guardian!' I chuckled. You see[,] Ira[,] having nobody[,] all I *can* do is to chuckle and love or poke and nip 'til I *make* Emily's hands and heart do things for me.

[']Well,['] I said, 'Let's play a game with the six gold flowers, Emily.

The "pinks" and the buttons are too floppy.' So we began. And because you were in it[,] I'll tell the game to you.

* * * * *

I said, Emily[,] we have gone to visit my Guardian's mother in Vancouver[.] We are in his house politely sitting on our favourite seat backing the window. Don't you forget[,] Emily, my Guardian (he wasn't my *legal* Guardian then) specially asked you to bring me along on the visit.

His mother and his adopted daughter are there too, knitting.

My Guardian's car purrs up the drive. Then light steps for so big a man, open & shutting of doors, and he is there rounding the piano. I just know its ivory keys are dumbly begging 'Come let our music out' but his fingers are too full of flowers for the moment.

'Hello folks!'

His women look up but knit on.

He has so carefully pushed the office worries of his heavy day, pushed them off his face. His hair is a little tousled from being un-hatted in the wind, fairish sunshiny hair. He is a wide-ish man[,] no more angles and corners than the chrysanthemums. Oh Emily[,] I wanted so to jump up and give 'Ira Dilworth' a tiny polite hug. How could I with no arms? And *you* sat tight as a barnacle on your cushion[;] so did his mother[;] so his 'daughter-niece.'

'Lie down[,] Small,' you said crossly. 'Dilworths don't! You'd shock the ladies and embarrass him.' So I shrunk. – 'I only meant a tiny one[,] Emily, just to show I was glad he'd come.'

That's the first flower, the littlest, not quite as unfolded as the others. Shall we play on? Hang memories on each of the other blooms?

'Go on[,] Small.'

* * * * *

Flower 2:
The next is a not-quite-out flower too, its goldy heart is still a little tight and hard.

We've been in Vancouver 10 days. It is early morning[.] Sunshine is tapping deliciously on the green linen curtains asking to come in. My Guardian was careful of his old ladies[.] He made his mother & you breakfast in your beds and he came to your rooms to bid you good-morning before he went off to his busy day.

'How is Small?'

There he stands in the middle of the room, clean-shaved and fresh as the morning. In his hand is a sheaf of manuscript. It is the unpublished 'Book of Small' – my book.

Ira said 'While you rest[,] do some cleaning on this Emily,' and laid the manuscript beside you, drew back the curtains to let in the light. He called back 'Goodbye' to his mother and to us and the front door closed. Gurgle, gurgle went his engine and buzz, buzz, all Canada's Western Radio came turmoiling into his brain.

That's only half the memory for this second blossom[,] Emily – about nine in the evening he would say, 'Time old ladies were in bed! Your hot bottles are ready, your lights turned on.['] Then he would arm his eighty year[-old] mother and his seventy year[-old] friend to their rooms. We were getting a mite homesick, you and I.

'Goodnight.'

'Jiggers[,] Emily! I kicked under your chin my hardest. Your face simply *had* to shoot up.'

'Ira, may Small kiss you goodnight[?]'

'Of course.'

He stooped to get the kiss and gave one back. He had only imagined a typed-on-paper Small before: had never realized there was a '*little of Emily*' who had nobody at all but lived on in Emily's heart.

* * * * *

Flower Three:

Real gold, not hot yellow money! – cool translucent yellow, bathed in shimmering light – oh Emily[,] remember! You, my Guardian, me, looking up into that glory which was between us & the sky. Having no tongue[,] *I* could say nothing, neither of you *did.* We dare not look too long[:] the glory would have stolen us. Ira purred his motor down the golden way – full-blown laburnums on either side of us, exquisite brightness, cooly gold.

* * * * *

Bloom Four:

My Guardian took us safely home to Victoria. You remember[,] Emily[,] that you sat with him at a little table on the boat and worked over 'my manuscript.' You were both aware that I was there too. You fixed wrong words and wrong spellings and were very serious over it[.] Sometimes I chuckled – the boat jigged and waves splashed her sides[.] We had nearly reached Victoria when you said in a half-scared squeak –

'Ira' ... Then, after a big full stop your words spluttered out quick. 'May I dedicate the Book of Small to you?'

'I should like that, but, Alice?'

'Small is yours. It was you [who] made her come alive. She was only half real and half forgotten when you found us. You found a publisher for her too. Don't you want her dedication?'

'Oh Emily, you know I do.'

So my book was his and I was glad.

* * * * *

Two flowers left – the biggest two.

Flower Five:
We are sitting at the end of the studio table. Ira neatly sheafed the manuscript & put it in his case. 'Ready for the publisher,' he said and sat back. The hand near us [was] gripping the table's edge.

I knew you wanted to say something[,] Emily[:] your hands were cold, and your insides shaky.

'Ira, the lawyer is coming to fix the law-stuff for the "Picture Trust." You and Lawren are Trustees for the pictures.'

'Yes.'

'He is going to draw up my will too. Ought I ... The manuscripts ... should they be ... provided for?'

Of course[,] he was a professor of English and you had never even wiggled through 'High[.]'[1] Besides[,] you did not know if the public were going to like 'Klee Wyck' and the 'Book of Small.' You felt foolish, as if you were rating your work too high by legalizing it.

My Guardian (who hadn't really been my legal Guardian up to that time) said, 'Certainly you should arrange for the manuscripts[,] Emily.'

'How?'

'By appoint[ing] a Guardian for them.'

'Who? I have only my sister – she's blind.'

'There's me.'

1 High school.

'Do you mean you would?'

'I would not only do it gladly[,] but I would feel honored at the trust.'

You gasped and I made you put your cold shaking hand over his big[,] calm, warm one that gripped the table's edge. I wanted it dreadfully to turn over and take ours into its warmness but it kept its grip on the table and was quite still and we slipped ours away. – I was singing glad that I was going to have a legal guardian. It had scared me a little to think that *anyone* could buy me at a bookstore or borrow me from a library when I was published – because my Guardian had found a publisher and I was coming out pretty soon.

The lawyer came and the will was all fixed up and, Emily, you told him in a letter that I was willed now to him and you sent Ira a picture of 'Small.'

He wrote, and then he came. Then we knew *really* and for '*honest*' that he was *glad* as anything to be legal Guardian of me. He said, 'I could hop into the pocket of his waistcoat right over his heart whenever I liked. I could use it as a permanent address as long as he lived![']

Wasn't number five a proud lovely gold flower to hang that splendid memory on[,] Emily?

* * * * *

'What memory for the sixth bloom[,] Small?'

'It's the goldenest of all' I said.

'Let the memory be shimmery and so clear that it will not dim the flower's gold, Small.'

'It shall be a "feel memory[,]" Emily – for you the joy-feel of his deep true friendship. For me the feel of a fathering love I lost when I was a little girl.'

Did you like our game Ira? The chrysanthemums are still alive[.] Blue Joseph's cage is under them at night. Do they give Joseph golden dreams? I wonder!

[To] Ira from Small – November 7, 1942.

References

Archival Collections

Elise Aylen Fonds, LMS-0204, National Library, Ottawa.
Flora Burns Fonds, MS 2786, British Columbia Archives and Records Service (BCARS), Victoria.
Canadian Authors Association Fonds, MG 38 I 2, National Archives of Canada, Ottawa.
Clarke, Irwin & Company Limited Fonds. McMaster University Archives, William Ready Division, Hamilton.
Edythe Hembroff-Schleicher papers (1915–88), MS 2792, MS 0876, and MS 1067, BCARS, Victoria.
Inglis Collection, MS 2181, BCARS, Victoria.
Newcombe Family Papers, MS 1077, BCARS, Victoria.
Parnall Collection, MS 2763, BCARS, Victoria.
Myfanwy Pavelic Papers, Accession No. 94-5907, BCARS, Victoria.

Works by Emily Carr

Carr, Emily. *An Address By Emily Carr.* Introduced by Ira Dilworth. Toronto: Oxford UP, 1955.
– *The Book of Small.* Toronto: Oxford UP, 1942.
– *Fresh Seeing: Two Addresses by Emily Carr.* Toronto: Clarke, Irwin, 1972.
– *Growing Pains: The Autobiography of Emily Carr.* Toronto: Oxford UP, 1946.
– *The Heart of a Peacock.* Toronto: Oxford UP, 1953.
– *The House of All Sorts.* Toronto: Oxford UP, 1944.
– *Hundreds and Thousands: The Journals of Emily Carr.* Toronto: Clarke, Irwin, 1966.

– *Klee Wyck.* Toronto: Oxford UP, 1941.
– *Pause, a Sketch Book.* Toronto: Clarke, Irwin, 1953.

Reviews of Works by Emily Carr

Rev. of *The Book of Small. Canadian Forum* 22 (Dec. 1942): 284.
Rev. of *The Book of Small. Spectator* 172 (1944): 42.
Bower, B.E. Rev. of *The House of All Sorts. Punch* 210 (1946): 319.
Clarke, G.H. Rev. of *The House of All Sorts. Queen's Quarterly* 52 (1945): 127.
Clay, Charles. Rev. of *Klee Wyck. Canadian Historical Review* 23.1 (1942): 90–1.
Coburn, Kathleen. Rev. of *Growing Pains. Canadian Forum* 26 (April 1947): 234–5.
– Rev. of *The House of All Sorts. Canadian Forum* 25 (April 1945): 24.
Eden, H.P. Rev. of *Growing Pains. Punch* 212 (1947): 48.
Garfield, Viola. Rev. of *Klee Wyck. Pacific Northwest Quarterly* 34 (1943): 101–2.
Harris, Lawren. 'Emily Carr and Her Work.' Rev. of *Klee Wyck. Canadian Forum* 21 (Dec. 1941): 277–8.
Rev. of *House of All Sorts. Spectator* 176 (1946): 412.
Martin, Burns. Rev. of *The Book of Small. Dalhousie Review* 13 (1933): 127.
McKague, Yvonne. Rev. of *The Heart of a Peacock. Canadian Forum* 33 (February 1954): 260.
– Rev. of *Pause: An Emily Carr Sketch Book. Canadian Forum* 33 (February 1954): 260.
Smith, M.L. Rev. of *Growing Pains. Dalhousie Review* 26 (1946): 513.
Watmough, D. Rev. of *Hundreds and Thousands. Canadian Literature* 33 (1967): 72.

Books, Articles, Dissertations

'An Artist Loves the Indians.' *Globe and Mail*, 8 Nov. 1941: B1.
'Artists and Their Doings: A Local Woman Artist.' *Western Woman's Weekly*, 5 Oct. 1918: 7.
Blanchard, Paula. *The Life of Emily Carr.* Vancouver: Douglas and McIntyre, 1987.
Bridge, Kathryn. Introduction. *Klee Wyck* [1941]. Vancouver: Douglas & McIntyre, 2003. 1–15.
Burns, Flora Hamilton. 'Emily Carr.' *The Clear Spirit: Twenty Canadian Women and Their Times.* Ed. Mary Quayle Innis. Toronto: U of Toronto P, 1966. 221–41.
– 'Emily Carr and the Newcombe Collection.' *The Beaver* 293 (Summer 1962): 27–35. Reproduced for Catalogue of Hudson's Bay Company's Exhibition. *The World of Emily Carr* (Victoria and Vancouver, July–August 1962).

Clarke, William Henry. *William Henry Clarke: A Memorial Volume.* Toronto: Clarke, Irwin, ca. 1956.

Clay, Margaret. 'Emily Carr as I Knew Her.' *Business and Professional Woman* 26.9 (1959): 1, 9.

Coburn, Kathleen. 'Emily Carr: In Memoriam.' *Canadian Forum* 25 (April 1945): 24.

Crean, Susan, ed. *Opposite Contraries: The Unpublished Manuscripts of Emily Carr.* Vancouver: Douglas & McIntyre, 2003.

Crosby, Marcia. 'Construction of the Imaginary Indian.' *Vancouver Anthology: The Institutional Politics of Art.* Ed. Stan Douglas. Vancouver: Talonbooks, 1991. 267–91.

Daly, Thomas C. 'To Emily Carr Art and Writing Were Twins.' *Saturday Night,* 15 Dec. 1945: 28.

Davies, Robertson. 'The Revelation of Emily Carr.' *Saturday Night,* 8 Nov. 1941: 18.

– 'An Artist Loves the Indians.' *Globe and Mail,* 8 Nov. 1941: B1.

Dilworth, Ira. 'Emily Carr: Canadian Artist-Author.' *Saturday Night,* 3 Nov. 1941: 26.

– 'Emily Carr: Canadian Painter and Poet in Prose.' *Saturday Night,* 8 Nov. 1941: 26.

– 'Emily Carr, Biographical Sketch.' *Emily Carr: Her Paintings and Drawings.* Toronto: Oxford UP, 1945. 9–19.

– 'M. Emily Carr.' *Canadian Library Association Bulletin* 3.4 (1947): 112–13.

– Preface to *The Heart of the Peacock.* Toronto: Oxford UP, 1953. xi–xv.

Djwa, Sandra. *Professing English: A Life of Roy Daniells.* Toronto: U of Toronto P, 2002.

Dragland, Stan. *Floating Voice: Duncan Campbell Scott and the Literature of Treaty 9.* Concord, ON: Anansi, 1994.

Edmonds, Rebe. 'Wanted ... More Emily Carr Stories.' *Victoria Daily Times,* 27 Dec. 1941: 5.

'Emily Carr, Artist, Writes First Book.' *Victoria Times,* 8 Nov. 1941: 15.

Harris, Lawren. 'The Paintings and Drawings of Emily Carr.' *Emily Carr: Her Paintings and Drawings.* Toronto: Oxford UP, 1945. 20–8.

Hembroff-Schleicher, Edythe. *M.E.: A Portrayal of Emily Carr.* Toronto: Clarke and Irwin, 1969.

– *Emily Carr: The Untold Story.* Saanichton, BC: Hancock House, 1978.

H.F. 'Emily Carr: Her Paintings and Sketches.' *Canadian Forum* 25–6 (Dec. 1945): 218.

Housser, Fred. *A Canadian Art Movement: The Story of the Group of Seven.* Toronto: Macmillan, 1926.

– *The Whitmanic Attitude and the Creative Life.* Toronto: The Disk, 1923.
– 'Walt Whitman and North American Idealism.' *Canadian Theosophist* 11.5 (1930): 136–40.
Humphrey, Ruth. 'Emily Carr: An Appreciation.' *Queen's Quarterly* 65 (1958): 270–6.
– 'Maria Tippett, "A Past Solitaire in a Steel-Claw Setting: Emily Carr and Her Public" (*BC Studies*, No. 20) – A Reply.' *BC Studies* 23 (1974): 47–9.
Humphrey, Ruth, and W.F. Blissett. 'Letters from Emily Carr.' *University of Toronto Quarterly* 41.2 (1972): 93–150.
Lamb, Mortimer J. 'A British Columbia Painter.' *Saturday Night*, 14 Jan. 1933: 3.
Lambert, R.S. 'Artistic Motives: Hidden and Revealed.' *Saturday Night*, 27 Feb. 1942: 20.
'Letters to John Davis Hatch, 1939–43.' *Collapse* 2 (1996): 71–8.
Linsley, Robert. 'Landscapes in Motion: Lawren Harris, Emily Carr and the Heterogenous Modern Nation.' *Oxford Art Journal* 19.1 (1996): 80–95.
Livesay, Dorothy. 'Carr and Livesay.' *Canadian Literature* 84 (1980): 144–7.
– 'Rhythm of Nature Expressed by Emily Carr.' *Vancouver Daily Province: Saturday Magazine* 6 Jan. 1940: 2.
Lugrin, N. de Bertrand. 'Emily Carr as I Knew Her.' *Sunday Times Magazine* (Victoria), 22 Sept. 1951: 3.
McDonald, J.A. 'Emily Carr: Painter and Writer.' *British Columbia Library Quarterly* 22.4 (1959): 17–23.
McGeer, Ada. 'The Emily Carr I Knew.' *Oh Call Back Yesterday, Bid Time Return.* Vancouver: Versatile Publishing Company, 1981. 50–1.
McInnes, Campbell G. 'World of Art.' *Saturday Night* 51.5 (7 Dec. 1935): 27.
McInnes, Graham, C. *A Short History of Canadian Art.* Toronto: Macmillan, 1939.
– *Canadian Art.* Toronto: Macmillan, 1950.
M.E. 'The Problems of the Canadian Painter.' *Canadian Bookman* 5 (1923): 33.
Moray, Gerta. 'Emily Carr and the Traffic in Native Images.' *Antimodernism and Artistic Experience: Policing the Boundaries of Modernism.* Ed. Lynda Jessup and Matthew Teitelbaum. Toronto: U of Toronto P, 2001. 70–93.
– 'Northwest Coast Culture and the Early Indian Paintings of Emily Carr, 1899–1913.' Diss. U of Toronto, 1993.
– '"T'Other Emily": Emily Carr, the Modern Woman Artist and Dilemmas of Gender.' *RACAR: Revue d'art canadienne / Canadian Art Review* 26.1–2 (2002): 73–90.
– 'Wilderness, Modernity and Aboriginality in the Paintings of Emily Carr.' *Journal of Canadian Studies* 33.2 (1998): 43–65.
Newton, Eric. 'Canadian Art through English Eyes.' *Canadian Forum* 18 (February 1939): 344–5.

– 'A Century of Canadian Art.' *Manchester Guardian Weekly*, 14 Oct. 1938: 337.
– 'Greatness and Emily Carr.' *Vancouver News-Herald*, 6 March 1945.
Pearson, Carol. *Emily Carr as I Knew Her.* Foreword by Kathleen Coburn. Toronto: Clarke and Irwin, 1954.
R.F. 'Something of Her Own.' *Canadian Forum* 22 (December 1942): 284–6.
Salinger, Jehanne Bietry. 'Comment on Art.' *Canadian Forum* 10 (March 1930): 209–11.
Shadbolt, Doris. *The Art of Emily Carr.* Vancouver: Douglas and McIntyre, 1987.
– Introduction. *The Complete Writings of Emily Carr.* Ed. Doris Shadbolt. Vancouver: Douglas & McIntyre; Seattle: U of Washington P, 1997. 3–14.
– *The Sketchbooks of Emily Carr: Seven Journeys.* Vancouver: Douglas & McIntyre, 2002.
Shier, Ried. 'Native Son.' Interview with Lawrence Paul Yuxweluptun. *Mix* 24.1 (1998): 48–55.
Smith, Peter L. 'Ira Dilworth: Kindness, Zeal, and Sensitivity.' *Come Give a Cheer! One Hundred Years of Victoria High School, 1876–1976.* Victoria, BC: Victoria High School Centennial Celebrations Committee, 1976. 78–85.
T.C. 'Emily Carr among Indians with Facile Pen and Brush.' *Vancouver Daily Province: Saturday Magazine*, 29 Nov. 1941: 6.
Thorton, Mildred Valley. 'New Carr Show at Gallery.' *Vancouver Sun*, 16 June 1943: 12.
Tippett, Maria. *Emily Carr: A Biography.* 1979. Markham, ON: Penguin, 1982.
Titley, Brian. *A Narrow Vision: Duncan Campbell Scott and the Administration of Indian Affairs in Canada.* Vancouver: UBC P, 1986.
Tobey, Mark. 'Reminiscence and Reverie.' *Magazine of Art* 44.6 (1951): 228–32.
Udall, Sharyn Rohlfsen. *Carr, O'Keefe, Kahlo: Places of Their Own.* New Haven, CT: Yale UP, 2000.
Unger, Merrill F. *Unger's Bible Dictionary.* Chicago: Moodie Bible Institute, 1957 (rev. 1996), 990.
'Victoria Artist Honoured at Reception Today.' *Victoria Daily Times*, 13 Dec. 1941: 6.
Walker, Doreen, ed. *Dear Nan: Letters of Emily Carr, Nan Cheney, and Humphrey Toms.* Vancouver: UBC P, 1990.
Watson, Scott. *Jack Shadbolt.* Vancouver: Douglas & McIntyre, 1990.
Whitman, Walt. *Leaves of Grass.* Ed. Jerome Loring. Oxford: Oxford UP, 1990.

Illustration Credits

Emily Carr reading a letter, 1930. Rare Books & Special Collections, University of British Columbia, BC 1849, Nan Cheney Photo Collection

Emily Carr, *Cedar*, 1942, oil on canvas, 112.0 × 69.0 cm. Vancouver Art Gallery, Emily Carr Trust, VAG 42.3.28 (Photo: Trevor Mills)

Emily Carr, *The Red Cedar*, 1931–1933, oil on canvas, 111.0 × 68.5 cm. Vancouver Art Gallery, Gift Mrs. J.P. Fell, VAG 54.7 (Photo: Trevor Mills)

Window display in book section of department store, Toronto, for Emily Carr's *Klee Wyck*, 1941. F-07884, British Columbia Archives, Victoria

Emily Carr, *Clearing*, 1942, oil on canvas, 68.6 × 111.8 cm, National Gallery of Canada, Ottawa, no. 6354

'Lady Jane, the dog, and Emily Carr wish Ira Dilworth a Merry Christmas.' 1942. I-51568, British Columbia Archives, Victoria

'Lady Jane, the dog, with Ira Dilworth' (attached to a copy of Walt Whitman's *Leaves of Grass*, dedicated to Carr by Dilworth), no date. I-67798, British Columbia Archives, Victoria

Copy of Carr's letter to Ira Dilworth, dated Tuesday, ca. August 4, 1942. Inglis Collection, MS 2181, British Columbia Archives, Victoria

Copy of Dilworth's letter to Emily Carr, ca. September, 1943. Parnall Collection, MS 2763, British Columbia Archives, Victoria

Index

www.ingramcontent.com/pod-product-compliance
Lightning Source LLC
LaVergne TN
LVHW090803070826
844660LV00022B/1067